The Year 2000
Software Crisis

ISBN 0-13-960154-6

ANDREWS AND LEVENTHAL Fusion: Integrating IE, CASE, and JAD
ANDREWS AND STALICK Business Reengineering: The Survival Guide
AUGUST Joint Application Design
BODDIE The Information Asset: Rational DP Funding and Other Radical Notions
BOULDIN Agents of Change: Managing the Introduction of Automated Tools
BRILL Building Controls into Structured Systems
COAD AND NICOLA Object-Oriented Programming
COAD AND YOURDON Object-Oriented Analysis, 2/E
COAD AND YOURDON Object-Oriented Design
COAD AND MAYFIED Java Design: Building Better Apps and Applets
COAD WITH NORTH AND MAYFIELD Object Models: Strategies, Patterns, and Applications, 2/E
CONNELL AND SHAFER Object-Oriented Rapid Prototyping
CONNELL AND SHAFER Structured Rapid Prototyping
CONSTANTINE Constantine on Peopleware
CONSTANTINE AND YOURDON Structured Design
DEGRACE AND STAHL Wicked Problems, Righteous Solutions
DeMARCO Controlling Software Projects
DeMARCO Structured Analysis and System Specification
EMBLEY, KURTZ, AND WOODFIELD Object-Oriented Systems Analysis
GARMUS AND HERRON Measuring the Software Process: A Practical Guide to Functional
    Measurements
GLASS Software Conflict: Essays on the Art and Science of Software Engineering
GROCHOW Information Overload: Creating Value with the New Information Systems Technology
HAYES AND ULRICH The Year 2000 Software Crisis: The Continuing Challenge
JONES Assessment and Control of Software Risks
KING Project Management Made Simple
McMENAMIN AND PALMER Essential System Design
MOSLEY The Handbook of MIS Application Software Testing
PAGE-JONES Practical Guide to Structured Systems Design, 2/E
PINSON Designing Screen Interfaces in C
PUTMAN AND MYERS Measures for Excellence: Reliable Software on Time within Budget
RODGERS ORACLE®: A Database Developer's Guide
SHLAER AND MELLOR Object Lifecycles: Modeling the World in States
SHLAER AND MELLOR Object-Oriented Systems Analysis: Modeling the World in Data
STARR How to Build Shlaer-Mellor Object Models
THOMSETT Third Wave Project Management
ULRICH AND HAYES The Year 2000 Software Crisis: Challenge of the Century
WARD System Development without Pain
YOURDON Decline and Fall of the American Programmer
YOURDON Managing the Structured Techniques, 4/E
YOURDON Managing the System Life-Cycle, 2/E
YOURDON Modern Structured Analysis
YOURDON Object-Oriented Systems Design
YOURDON Techniques of Program Structure and Design
YOURDON AND ARGILA Case Studies in Object-Oriented Analysis and Design
YOURDON, WHITEHEAD, THOMANN, OPPEL, AND NEVERMANN Mainstream Objects: An
    Analysis and Design Approach for Business
YOURDON INC. YOURDON Systems Method: Model-Driven Systems Development

The Year 2000 Software Crisis:

The Continuing Challenge

Ian S. Hayes
and
William M. Ulrich

YOURDN PRESS
Prentice Hall PTR
Upper Saddle River, New Jersey 07458
http://www.phptr.com

Editorial/production supervision: *Nicholas Radhuber*
Manufacturing manager: *Alexis R. Heydt*
Acquisitions editor: *Stephen Solomon*
Editorial assistant: *Bart Blanken*
Marketing Manager: *Dan Rush*
Page layout: *Bear Type & Graphics*
Cover design: *Design Source*
Cover design director: *Jerry Votta*

© 1998 Ian S. Hayes and William M. Ulrich
Published by Prentice Hall PTR
Prentice Hall, Inc.
A Simon & Schuster Company
Upper Saddle River, New Jersey 07458

Prentice Hall books are widely used by corporations and government agencies for training, marketing, and resale.
The publisher offers discounts on this book when ordered in bulk quantities.
For more information, contact:
    Phone: 800-382-3419, Fax: 201-236-7141
    E-mail: corpsales@prenhall.com
    or write:
    Corporate Sales Department
    Prentice Hall PTR
    1 Lake Street
    Upper Saddle River, NJ 07458

Printed in the United States of America
10 9 8 7 6 5 4 3 2 1

ISBN 0-13-960154-6

Prentice-Hall International (UK) Limited, *London*
Prentice-Hall of Australia Pty. Limited, *Sydney*
Prentice-Hall Canada Inc., *Toronto*
Prentice-Hall Hispanoamericana, S.A., *Mexico*
Prentice-Hall of India Private Limited, *New Delhi*
Prentice-Hall of Japan, Inc., *Tokyo*
Simon & Schuster Asia Pte. Ltd., *Singapore*
Editora Prentice-Hall do Brasil, Ltda., *Rio de Janeiro*

Dedication

To my parents, Edith and John Hayes

—Ian Hayes

*To my son, Maximillian Jerome Ulrich, and my parents,
John and Katherine Ulrich*

—William Ulrich

Acknowledgments

The authors wish to acknowledge the readers of our first book, *The Year 2000 Software Crisis: Challenge of the Century*. This book was directly inspired by the questions, ideas, and suggestions received from you through e-mails, letters, telephone calls, and meetings at conferences and other events. You convinced us to tackle writing another book before we fully recovered from writing the first one. Your support kept us going as we attempted to balance writing with increasingly busy consulting schedules and hectic family lives. We especially wish to acknowledge the hard work and dedication that all of you are putting into solving the Year 2000 crisis at your respective companies and government agencies. Without your efforts, the crisis would truly become the catastrophe predicted by the doomsayers.

We also wish to acknowledge the contributions of our clients. As we have worked together on projects over the past several years, our clients have continually presented us with new challenges to solve and have forced us to reconcile theoretical answers with the pragmatic needs of the real world. We hope that this book serves as a small payback for their continuing loyalty and support.

This book could not have been written without the ideas, work, and contributions of many dedicated individuals. It is impossible to acknowledge everyone by name, and the authors apologize in advance for any omissions. Our errors of omission in no way reflect a lack of gratitude on our part.

The authors wish to express their gratitude to the following people: Senator Bob Bennett, Neil Cooper, Ken Czajka, Allen Deary, Irene Dec, Dionysius Exiguus (Little Dennis), Gartner Group, Lorraine Gornick, Stephen Jay Gould, Steven Hock, The Honorable Stephen Horn, Jaffer Hussain, Michelle Johnson, Brian Keane, Michael Lips, Ken Owen, Joan Paul, John Saunders, Major Ron Spear, Michael Sperling, Michael Tiernan, Dale Vecchio, Stephan Weil, Joseph Weizenbaum, Edward Yardeni, and Ed Yourdon.

The production of a book requires many long and hard hours of work researching, formatting, and proofreading. Special thanks to Anne Hayes and Elizabeth Ward for their assistance in putting together the initial drafts of the book. Without their help, this project could not have been completed.

Finally, we would not have an opportunity to write a second book without the success of the first book. For this opportunity, we wish to thank all the individuals and companies that purchased our first book. We especially wish to thank Gregory and Michael Hales of Advanced Information Technology, Inc. for their ceaseless support and attendance at numerous book signing tables. We look forward to working together on this book!

Ian S. Hayes
Clarity Consulting, Inc.
South Hamilton, MA

William M. Ulrich
Tactical Strategy Group, Inc.
Soquel, CA

January 1998

Contents

Chapter 2
Strategy Update: Shift to Risk Mitigation,   43

Preface

 This is our second book about the Year 2000 software crisis. It begins where our first book, *The Year 2000 Software Crisis: Challenge of the Century*, left off. Building awareness about the Year 2000 problem—the inability of computer software and hardware to correctly process dates in the next century—is no longer an issue. The issue has leapt from the realm of obscure technologists to the world of international politics. It is a regular topic in the media, gracing the cover of *Newsweek* and appearing frequently in newspapers and radio and television shows. Within corporations, the issue has moved from the computer room to the boardroom, no doubt aided by predictions of over $1 trillion in legal costs from Year 2000-related lawsuits. Respected economists are warning about the possibility of a Year 2000-triggered recession. Finally, the crisis has become a business issue rather than a technical issue.

When our first book was launched, we never expected it to become by far the best-selling book on the Year 2000 crisis. We were taken by surprise by the demand and the media attention that we received. In addition to our ongoing consulting projects, we frequently appeared as guests on radio talk shows and local TV news programs and William Ulrich represented us on the "Today Show." We spoke at conferences and industry events for the IT, investment, and legal communities. Tiring as this schedule has been, it gave us the opportunity to speak to thousands of our readers around the world. We heard about the challenges and frustrations facing Year 2000 projects in virtually every industry segment. This interaction was immensely rewarding, and we are grateful to all who shared their knowledge and opinions with us. We heard what worked, what didn't, and where help was needed. In no uncertain terms, we were told what our readers wanted in a new book. This book is written to meet those needs.

In the course of the past two years, the needs of our readers have changed. The topics in the first book, such as how to start and run a Year 2000 project, remain relevant and important, but new and thornier issues have arrived. It is now clear that achieving Year 2000 compliance within a given company is not enough. If the company's suppliers cannot deliver raw materials or its customers cannot buy product or services, the company is as affected as if its own systems failed. The date problem appears in new and increasingly insidious locations. Computer chips relying on dates are embedded everywhere in our highly automated society, running everything from our telephone systems to manufacturing assembly lines and medical equipment. Testing the compliance of hardware and software is turning out to be more costly and difficult than imagined.

On the positive side, software tools have undergone an amazing evolution. The variety of tools on the market is truly stunning. Sifting through these tools is a challenge, as many of the claims seem either exactly the same or strain credibility. At least the ever-present desire for a magic "silver bullet" solution has finally subsided to manageable levels. Consulting services have also blossomed. The Year 2000 problem has been a windfall to many consulting companies. Although the market was slow to take off, predictions of staffing and consultant shortages have finally come true. The high rates provided by Year 2000 projects have enabled consulting companies to retool their offerings, adding tools, training, and methodologies to the mix.

Perhaps the scariest change has been the realization that most companies will not achieve full century-date compliance in time. Contingency planning and risk management are two of the hottest subjects in the market today as companies attempt to prepare for the inevitable. The rallying cry has become "if you can't do everything, at least do the right things!" as companies seek to direct scarce resources to those projects that provide the greatest overall risk reduction. Given this realization, protecting the company from the failures of others becomes increasingly important. The complexity of physical and electronic supply chains is such that the failure of a single link in the chain can compromise the entire operation.

This book is written to address these new topics. It seeks to supplement and extend the discussion started in our first book. Our intent is to provide our readers with the latest information and best industry thinking possible. We hope that armed with this information, our readers and their organizations will be better prepared to handle the challenges that face them as the new century approaches.

Audience for this Book

This book is written for corporate executives, IT managers, business managers, software vendors, consultants, and other individuals who require an in-depth understanding of Year 2000 issues. It is written in ten chapters and designed to meet two goals. The first goal is to update readers on changes and advances that have occurred in the Year 2000 field since the authors' first book was published. The second goal is to expand, where merited, upon topics already discussed in the first book.

Those individuals charged with implementing a century-date compliance effort will want to read all chapters in detail and use this book as an ongoing reference on the Year 2000 topic. This book is intended to supplement the first book and assumes a basic understanding of Year 2000 topics. Readers unfamiliar with these fundamentals should seek our first book or another reputable introductory text.

Summary of Contents

This book is divided into ten chapters. Each chapter covers a particular topic or topics. Where appropriate, related topics were grouped together to provide a more complete picture of what is happening in the Year 2000 area.

The first chapter, "Year 2000 Progress Update," is a general progress report on the global effort to achieve century-date compliance. It includes an industry-by-industry analysis of potential Year 2000 impacts and current progress toward resolving the problem. It looks at the worldwide economic impact and examines U.S. and international government efforts toward compliance. Finally, this chapter takes a critical look at current media coverage of the Year 2000 topic.

Chapter 2, "Strategy Update: Shift to Risk Mitigation," explores the various strategies and steps that should be undertaken by those organizations that find themselves running out of time to fully complete their Year 2000 conversions. The foundation of these efforts lies in preparing, evaluating, interpreting, and acting on proper business risk assessments. Chapter 2 discusses how best to approach the risk assessment process.

Continuing with this "risk" theme, Chapter 3, "Legal Issues and Protections," deals in general terms with the legal risks and ramifications of the Year 2000 facing companies. While particular companies may be more at risk than others, all companies will have to deal with potential legal liability arising from Year 2000-related failures. Chapter 3 suggests some actions that companies can take to minimize their legal exposure.

Chapter 4, "Non-IT Issues and Answers," looks at those areas other than IT that are particularly susceptible to Year 2000 problems. It begins by examining the ramifications of Year 2000 failures in specific industries and continues with a discussion of the oft-neglected supply chain, external partner, and embedded technology areas.

Chapter 5, "Getting Help: Factories, Outsourcing, and Services," describes some of the methods in which companies can deal, and are dealing, with the resource issue. It is no secret that Year 2000 projects are imposing a heavy burden on IT staff and that additional resources are becoming scarce. Chapter 5 deals with the approaches that an IT organization can take to ameliorate the problem, ranging from setting up an internal factory to supplemental staffing to contracting with external factories.

Chapter 6, "Standards, Tools, and Techniques Update," talks about the current state of Year 2000 remediation. It focuses on the presence or lack of date formatting standards, how to maximize remediation productivity and current techniques available and/or in use in the remediation process.

Chapters 7 and 8 offer an in-depth look at the nuances of century-date certification testing. Year 2000 testing techniques differ in a number of critical ways from standard testing approaches. Chapter 7, "Year 2000 Testing Basics," discusses some fundamental rules about Year 2000 testing that each organization should be familiar with before it launches its testing program. The chapter explores the differences between Year 2000 and regular testing, the scope of Year 2000 testing, the types and levels of tests that will have to be conducted in any Year 2000 test program, and how to adapt and reduce the testing process using risk-based methods.

Chapter 8, "Implementing a Year 2000 Test Program," explains how to set up an organizational Year 2000 testing program. It discusses the activities and tasks that must be performed at the enterprise and application levels to establish a solid testing program. These steps include building the infrastructure necessary to conduct testing and creating the test plans, schedules, test data, test scripts and myriad other pieces that must be in place to manage and execute the testing process.

Following these chapters is Chapter 9, "Contingency Planning: When Time Runs Out," which deals with a sensitive but critical topic. Chapter 9 takes our hidden fear—not finishing in time—and exposes it to daylight. The chapter explains the concept of contingency planning, discusses ways in which systems or technology could go wrong or fail, and follows with some concrete ways in which companies can develop, and invoke, contingency plans for the various risks faced.

Chapter 10, "Managing the Transition: Surviving the Inevitable," takes us forward in time to the century transition and looks at what we can and should do to prepare ourselves for any problems, and to mitigate any ensuing damages. It concludes with an introspective look at the Year 2000 issue and explores what we've learned, the lingering problems that remain, the positive side effects, and the opportunities to prevent similar problems in the future.

An appendix containing a noninclusive list of tool vendors, consulting firms, and conversion companies is provided as an aid to our readers.

Final note: As Year 2000 activities accelerate, new issues and solutions will appear at an ever-increasing rate. Government attention, both in the United States and abroad, is creating an influx of new legislation and regulations that impact Year 2000 projects, vendors, and investors. Given the speed of these changes, the authors have launched a newsletter service through Triaxsys Research LLC to provide up-to-the-minute information on the topics covered in this book. Readers interested in further information about this newsletter are invited to read the Triaxsys company description in the appendix where it is listed with the authors' firms.

Chapter 1

Year 2000 Progress Update

In the Year 2000 industry, news briefs are emerging on an increasingly regular basis. Some of the news provides useful information, but much of it is merely "noise" that has been regurgitated over and over again by the mainstream media. The Year 2000 landscape is riddled with hyperbole, overused quotations, and misinformation. As the popular press spends more time covering the topic, much of this misinformation has grown into urban folklore. Fortunately for us, the truisms and patterns noted in our last book[1] continue to cut a clear path of reason through a forest of confusion. Note, for example, that there is still no "silver bullet" solution, the Year 2000 is still a management problem, government agencies are still behind schedule, and no (this was not in our last book, but we had to mention it), your microwave oven will not explode.

The goal of this chapter is to provide an evenhanded look at how the world is dealing with the Year 2000 problem. This coverage includes a general industry progress report, a discussion of how hype and extremism have compounded the problem, a look at the projected economic impacts, and a reiteration of why now, more than ever, executives must treat the Year 2000 as a business problem. We also present an industry-by-industry impact analysis, including a look at the public sector's role in addressing the problem, and a discussion of progress on the international front. While Chapter 10 takes a look into what the future holds, this chapter sets the stage for that discussion and for the remainder of this book. It is important that executives, IT professionals, and the public in general take an honest look at the progress and the mistakes made to date, so we can all work more effectively to mitigate risks associated with the Year 2000 problem.

1.1 Year 2000 Update

1998 is the year that most senior executives claimed that their computer systems will have been modified to achieve Year 2000 compliance— well in time to spend 1999 on integration and cross-industry testing. If anyone actually believes this to be true outside of a relatively small number of companies that got an early start on their projects, they probably have not spent much time tracking industry progress. Companies are just now waking up to the fact that time is running out.

1.1.1 Studies Paint Disconcerting Picture

A recent survey[2] sheds light on the progress being made to resolve the Year 2000 problem. A December 1997 study, performed by Rubin Systems, Inc. and sponsored by Cap Gemini of New York, surveyed the preparedness of major employers for the Year 2000. The tracking poll of 108 IT directors and managers in 14 sectors, including 100 Fortune 500 companies, began in March 1995 and was one of the longest-running surveys to systematically monitor corporate America's Year 2000 readiness. It is important to note that respondents to this poll comprise about one-seventh of the United States' gross domestic product. The following findings paint a pessimistic picture.

1. *One in five employers surveyed—20 percent—has begun implementing a full-fledged strategy to achieve Year 2000 compliance.*

2. *One in three companies—33 percent—has a detailed Year 2000 compliance plan in place.*

3. *Four out of five employers—82 percent—report having underestimated their Year 2000 costs.*

4. *More than 77 percent have changed their approach to the problem since they started.*

5. *The number of companies perceiving a need to increase staff grew by 60 percent since April 1997—an increase from 45 percent to 72 percent.*

6. *Ninety-five percent report that finding new staff will be either difficult or impossible.*

7. *Seven percent of the surveyed firms have already experienced a Year 2000-related failure.*

With only one in five companies having launched a full-fledged strategy and only one in three having a detailed plan to address the Year 2000, it seems that progress to date is clearly not moving at the rate that many people may have perceived. This lack of progress is even more disconcerting given that 82 percent have underestimated project costs, more than 77 percent have modified resolution strategies, and more than half underestimated staffing requirements. This slowness means that the percentage of companies that are just getting going (80 percent based on point 1 above), are dealing with staffing shortages, budget problems, and the fact that they are likely to change their approach. These findings highlight the fact that the Year 2000 problem is not under control at many large companies.

The following points, also found in the Rubin Systems survey, shed light on management's perception of the progress being made on the Year 2000 problem.

1. *Top management involvement in solving the Year 2000 problem has increased during 1997 from 70 percent to 100 percent.*

2. *Respondents "strongly agree" that Year 2000 is a high priority and that "conversions must begin now."*

3. *Nearly nine out of ten employers—87 percent—expect more than half of their systems to be Year 2000-compliant by the end of next year.*

4. *Sixty percent intend to perform complete, "end-to-end" testing (a protocol that tests the integrity of upgraded systems through both pre-2000 and post-2000 date scenarios).*

5. *Three-fifths of those planning end-to-end testing intend to perform it on no more than a quarter of all their systems.*

6. *Twelve percent are preparing to discuss the Year 2000 in annual reports or shareholder statements and 8 percent expect to discuss it in filings with the Securities and Exchange Commission (SEC).*

The fact that management is on board, as stated in points 1 and 2, is great. The level of confidence in management's ability to meet the Year

2000 deadline, however, defies earlier survey findings. Most respondents stated that half of their systems will be compliant by year end 1998. Remember, however, that as of year-end 1997, only one company in five had begun implementing a full-fledged Year 2000 compliance strategy. This slow start means that while most surveyed companies had not launched a full-fledged strategy by year-end 1997, they still believe they can fix at least half of their systems in the first full year of deployment. If you spend any time with project office teams that have been into the implementation and testing process for a year or more, you will find that this optimism can be attributed to naive managers who are unaware of what awaits them. In other words, this is a much more complicated and far-reaching problem than they have envisioned.

Gartner Group findings also support the premise that management is being unrealistically optimistic. Speaking at their Symposium in Orlando, Florida, in October 1997 (Figure 1.1), Bill McNee, vice-president of Gartner Group, said that by the end of 1999, 30 percent of externally focused, mission-critical systems and one-half of all systems will fail to achieve compliance.[3] If, according to Gartner Group, only half of all systems will be fixed by the end of the century, how can executives claim that half of all systems will be fixed one year earlier—by the end of 1998? Somewhere there is a discrepancy and our personal experiences thus far suggest that Gartner is much closer to being right than being wrong.

> *"By the end of 1999, 30% of externally focused mission critical systems, and 50% of all systems will fail to achieve full Year 2000 compliance."*
>
> *- Gartner Group*

Figure 1.1 Bill McNee, Gartner Group, Inc., vice-president speaking at Gartner Symposium in Orlando, Florida, October 1997.[3]

Another concern is the level of testing that companies plan to do based on the Rubin Systems study. Sixty percent intend to perform complete, "end-to-end" testing. Three-fifths of those planning end-to-end

testing intend to perform it on no more than a quarter of all of their systems. This approach, which can be described as selective or "risk-based"
testing, is a strategy that we discuss in Chapters 7 and 8. The bottom line
is that there will not be enough time to test all the systems to the level
that they require. Most systems (60–65 percent if we calculate three-
fifths of 60 percent) will undergo a level of testing that will not determine if they can function properly in post-1999 transition time frames.
While we are not claiming that companies have an alternative at this
point (see testing chapters for detailed recommendations on risk-based
testing), we would like to point out that even those "completed" systems will likely encounter numerous date-related problems in the early
days of the next century.

One last point is that the outward optimism of many executives certainly does not seem to be reflected in their willingness to share Year 2000
project status with shareholders. Only 12 percent are preparing to discuss
the Year 2000 in annual reports and only 8 percent expect to discuss it in
filings with the SEC. Either they do not think it an important enough matter (this would signal a total lack of understanding of the gravity of the situation) or they have something to hide (which would be an even bigger
problem). We would like to believe all of the positive hype that we hear
from the cheery optimists, but the evidence, both physical and anecdotal,
tells us otherwise.

1.1.2 The Real Story

Procrastination has driven the Year 2000 problem to crisis proportions. Complicating matters is the fact that the exact status of the problem
remains unclear to most people outside of a given company. According to
U.S. Senator Robert Bennett (R-Utah), "What troubles me most about the
Year 2000 problem is the lack of accessible information about the readiness
of specific banks and other businesses."[4] In other words, details are hard to
come by. We do know, however, that many companies have still not
launched full-scale remediation efforts and that, in the ones that have,
shortcuts are commonplace. This state of affairs will guarantee that, in
addition to correcting century-date problems, companies will spend the
early part of the next century repairing quick and dirty fixes that have
been applied to mission-critical systems in haste.

Many companies are already admitting failure. Contingency planning and triage, which we discuss at length in Chapter 9, are the hottest
topics among Year 2000 project teams. Failure of embedded systems and
supply chains (see Chapter 4) is a rapidly growing concern. The latest

trend is compliance retraction letters from vendors who claimed compliance in early vendor surveys. Yet amazingly, there are still people who believe the problem is a fraud perpetuated by consultants or are betting that their systems are compliant without even testing them.

The scope of the problem is much larger than expected. The Year 2000 problem has turned out to be like peeling an onion (see Figure 1.2). As we learn more about the problem, we keep finding new layers of issues. The much maligned COBOL mainframe systems may account for the greatest volume of code, but given the tools and consulting support, they are the easiest to correct. We discovered that client/server systems are not completely compliant (and much harder to fix). Desktop and client/server systems are fraught with problems. Just because Excel and Access are compliant, for example, does not mean that the applications using them will function properly. To date, we have not personally found a "new" system, built to handle a four-digit year field, that has tested compliant on the first time around.

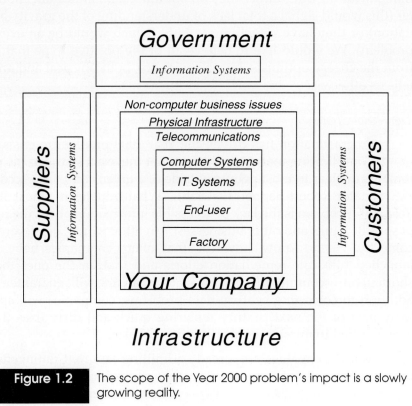

Figure 1.2   The scope of the Year 2000 problem's impact is a slowly growing reality.

Complicating what IT already knew to be a huge challenge are date problems that appear in a wide variety of non-IT systems and devices which include security systems, telecommunications equipment, networks, factory equipment, consumer products, and a wide range of embedded chips. Are all of these components affected by dates? No, but one factory test found that over 50 percent of its process control equipment encountered date-related problems. This result means that we must identify and test these systems or risk the consequences of an unexpected failure. Unfortunately, the later we discover a new layer, the less time we have to correct problems.

1.1.3 Where Is the Sense of Urgency?

Why are organizations waiting so long to ramp up Year 2000 projects? Perhaps it is because management considers the solution to be so simple—until they learn the true nature of the problem. Many attribute it to the fact that the problem seems so nonstrategic. One psychologist even attributed it to basic numerology, stating that because 2000 seems so far removed from 1995, 1996, or even 1997, people have refused to pay attention to the problem. Other reasons behind this delay include analysis paralysis, politics, the fear of making a mistake, confusion, lack of budget appropriation, or just ignorance of the effects of the problem. Whatever the reason, delay is no longer acceptable or justifiable to stockholders, constituents, or business partners.

Two messages ring loud and clear. The first is that organizations must start fixing mission-critical systems now! This admonition, of course, assumes that the systems in question are not compliant. Sophisticated project prioritization efforts, while important over the life of the project to ensure the viability of critical business functions, are not required to start conversion work. In other words, management must quickly identify the five most important systems based on business criticality and fix these systems first. The second message is that if you think a system is compliant today, begin testing it as soon as possible. Testing systems already deemed to be Year 2000 compliant leaves time to remediate those systems should they fail, facilitates the stabilization of test environments, and decreases project scheduling conflicts later. We constantly hear about systems that organizations assumed were compliant and found out that they were not—but only after the systems failed.

1.1.4 Coming to Grips with Reality: Look at the Details

Who is and who is not in control of their Year 2000 project? We work with many companies and have found that projects where executives lack detailed status information are not managed as well as those projects where management tracks the status carefully. Here is a quick test. Based on the two statements made by the CIOs below, select the CIO whom you believe has the Year 2000 problem under control in their organization.

CIO 1: Progress is grinding along on mission-critical systems. We should have the majority of these systems, which reflect 45 percent of our total portfolio, into testing by early 1999. Our testing team is setting up compliant test environments for high-impact functional areas and we hope to be ready to begin certification testing by mid-1998. Business analysts are researching partner and supplier risks, but we have not been able to gain a good sense of secondary supplier status. We have begun preliminary testing of our client/server systems and discovered compliance problems in the application code and the operating system. We have status meetings every two weeks and I spend more than one-half of my time tracking Year 2000 project status. I must say that I have problems sleeping at night.

CIO 2: We will have all systems upgraded by the end of 1998, which will allow us 1999 for testing. The Year 2000's impact on our organization is not as problematic as it might be on some others because we are in the midst of replacing core systems with an SAP package. This should be finished by second quarter 1999. In addition to this, we feel that our client/server environments are in good shape. Our biggest concern is with small companies that we do business with because our situation is under control. My people meet with me every month or so to provide me with a project status. They tell me that things are moving along nicely.

Does anyone want to stake their reputation on the fact that CIO 2 has things under control? CIO 2 is reading a typical script that has been prepared by a project team that is either deluding itself about the current status of the problem or does not have the guts to tell the CIO the truth. If any supplier, regulator, or business partner reads you this scripted nonsense, it is a clear signal that you need to dig more deeply into their situation—or find a new partner.

CIO 1, on the other hand, is deeply engaged in the problem and the solution. These comments reflect the sincere and realistic comments of an organization that is working hard on the problem and is providing a realistic assessment of progress to the top levels of the company. No one is deluding themselves here. If you are looking for an organization to do business with, the company represented by CIO 1 is the one you want.

Unfortunately, the comments we hear from senior executives more often than not reflect the tone of CIO 2 than the statements made by CIO 1.

1.2 Media Update

The media, money hungry entrepreneurs, investment analysts, and others looking to make quick money on the Year 2000 problem are hurting, not helping, the situation. One marketing firm actually trademarked "Y2K" and other commonly used terms in the hopes of making money from the use of these terms. This diversionary activity, launched by a company that delivers no value to companies struggling with this problem, is hopefully being ignored by mainstream players. Investors have also jumped into the Year 2000 fray by putting money into any company that faintly appears to be in the Year 2000 market. Investors would be better served by examining the impacts of this problem in mainstream industries.

One of the biggest concerns to those of us in the field is how the media is covering the Year 2000 issue. Reusing lame quotes about microwave ovens, 100-year phone calls, elevators, and other trite issues over and over again has trivialized the problem in the minds of executives and the public. Mainstream newspapers, as a rule, continue to quote the same people over and over again with little new information being given each time. In other cases, isolated circumstances are reported without providing a context for the information being delivered. Some of these publications have demonstrated stunning levels of incompetence by challenging the validity of the problem itself. If the media covers other topics as poorly as the Year 2000 issue is being covered, its overall credibility is certainly in question. Some examples of the media treating the Year 2000 as a myth on one hand, and overhyping it on the other, help explain some of the perception problems that people may now have.

1.2.1 The Year 2000 Myth?

The *Los Angeles Times* published an article on November 3, 1997, called "Debunking Year 2000's Computer Disaster." The article said that the Year 2000 problem is overhyped. This article was likely in response to the prophets of doom claiming that worldwide disaster is looming due to Year 2000 bugs. This article was a ludicrous attempt to debunk the issue. For example, the article said that the Year 2000 market is "vendor created." This tired myth is absurd, particularly to vendors that would have chosen a less risky topic if they could have created a demand for their services— which they cannot. In fact, one large consulting firm, specializing in embedded systems, backed out of the market due to the inherent risks of working on Year 2000 projects.

The article also quoted questionable sources, including David Starr, CIO of Reader's Digest and poster child of the "no problem" movement. While the article refers to "others in similar positions," this anonymous group refused to go out on a limb with Starr. Additionally, in quoting sources at the Federal Aviation Administration (FAA), Bank of America, and the Defense Department as being on target with their projects, the article hurt its own credibility. It was the FAA that spent billions trying to replace aging systems and failed and Bank of America that lost two project office leaders while trying to launch their initiative. The Defense Department, discussed later in this chapter, has more types of computers than anyone can imagine. No sane person would want to bet that these organizations will achieve 100 percent Year 2000 compliance by the end of 1999.

The article also quotes Tom Mock of the Consumer Electronics Manufacturers Association as saying that VCRs have "no internal calendar." Mock may want to explain how the Magnavox VCR model CRN130AT01 that we tested knows that 01/01/00 is a Saturday without having an embedded date function. Mr. Mock is one of the "electronics experts" quoted as saying that less than 5 percent of embedded chips have date functions. These counterpoints were first detailed in a December 8, 1997, *Computerworld* article.[5] The bottom line is that when the media publishes irresponsible articles, it plants doubt in the minds of executives and directors who still think the Year 2000 problem is a joke.

1.2.2 Silver Bullets Abound

Another problem with the mainstream press is their inability to tell reality from false hope and total hype.[6] The mainstream press leads us to believe that the only people offering Year 2000 solutions are a 77-year-old man from Texas and a 14-year-old boy from New Zealand. In the summer of 1997, the *Wall Street Journal* reported that Bob Bemer had come up with a silver bullet solution to the Year 2000 problem.[7] This "solution" involved the dangerous practice of patching object code to correct field size limitations. The approach is difficult to maintain and reflects an idealistic view of the problem. Those familiar with the impact that patching Autocoder at the object code level realize that this approach would introduce chaos into the software management process. As of this writing, Bemer has not yet delivered a solution.

A similar stir was created in New Zealand when 14-year-old Nicholas Johnson created a PC BIOS scanner. There are a numerous tools on the market that perform this function. CNN, however, reported in September 1997 that "a 14-year-old New Zealand boy claims he has designed a program to topple the world's biggest computer glitch."[8] CNN's headlining trivialized work being done by millions of professionals around the world, while fueling the notion that the Year 2000 is no big deal. Nicholas, to his credit, was quoted in a *ComputerWorld* article (September 22, 1997) as "worried about the way it's portrayed in the media."

The writers of these articles give one a feeling of closure when they say that the problem has been solved. The naive reader believes that the "millennium bug" must no longer be an issue. When we read these reports, we can only shake our heads in disgust and disbelief. Where is the media when real companies announce real solutions? There are dozens of software tools available to help find and fix the date problem on different hardware and software platforms. These companies are not being covered by CNN or the *Wall Street Journal* because they do not offer a news angle that seems exciting. The media does not need to sensationalize this issue because we do not have to look far to find topics worth covering. Perhaps when the enormity of the problem finally hits home over the next two years, the media will figure this out.

1.2.3 Extremists Hurt the Cause

Extremists, in the Year 2000 market, come in all flavors and sizes. Those quoted in the *LA Times* story discussed earlier are clearly taking an extremist view: The Year 2000 problem is not a problem. On the other side of the issue, we find those claiming everything from a worldwide banking disaster to the termination of power and water resources. These folks, while basing certain assertions on real-life problems, have nevertheless forced counterreactionary forces to claim that the problem cannot possibly be that bad. In reality, prophetic claims of an impending disaster do not really do anyone any good and have, in some cases, caused people to ignore the problem further.

Somewhere between "panic and disaster" and the belief that "everything is under control" lies the reality of the situation. Black and white, shortsighted reporting by the media has fed these extremist views because this seemingly simple concept is apparently difficult for nontechnical people to understand. Extremist views on both sides of the problem have ultimately stalled planning, funding, and implementation efforts. If organizations truly wish to mitigate Year 2000 risks, they must strike a balanced and realistic view of the problem. And that reality is where people must begin to find a solution.

1.3 Business Problem Requires Business Solution

A well-thought-out, balanced attack on the Year 2000 is the only option left for large, computer-reliant organizations. That is why it has become a business problem—pure and simple. Although the root of the problem is technical, procrastination has pushed the Year 2000 into the board room and executive suites. Many of the most critical issues, such as customer and supplier compliance, are outside the control of IT. Legal and audit concerns, resource and budget requirements, and the effects on merger and acquisition strategies force the Year 2000 issue into the domain of senior management. As awareness grows, overall responsibility for corporate Year 2000 projects is shifting from IT to the business community.

Viewing solutions from this angle helps Year 2000 project office and application management teams maintain a balance between technical and business options, while not pinning their hopes on a single tool or vendor. Success, and a sustained focus, require that senior business executives take responsibility for Year 2000 compliance within their individual business unit or division. Business unit executives must, for example, work with IT and senior management to ensure continuity of operations through the process of internal and external risk mitigation. The business unit executive sponsors the project, sets strategy, procures budget, drives risk analysis, plans for contingencies, and prioritizes remediation projects within the business unit. The business unit executive must balance business and Year 2000 needs on a continuous basis, appoint business area coordinators, handle high priority customers and suppliers, determine triage strategies, and represent the business unit on the Year 2000 advisory board.

While the buck starts and stops with the business unit executives in charge of the Year 2000 solution, they cannot solve the problem alone. Business area coordinators have the responsibility of identifying PC and end-user applications, educating other users on compliance requirements, and checking out the technical infrastructure within their business unit. These coordinators must also review non-IT impacts, such as forms, work with customers to ensure that their concerns are addressed and that purchase orders continue, work with purchasing to verify that suppliers continue to deliver products and services, and assist IT with strategies and awareness. Business personnel did not create the problem. Unfortunately, at this late date, they are going to have to pitch in to help solve the problem.

1.4 Industry by Industry Status

While the Year 2000 problem itself is not partial to a particular market or industry, the severity of the problem, the type of preparation one must perform, and the timing of those preparations does vary by industry. For example, companies in the financial and insurance industries tend to encounter dates in the next century at an earlier stage than do other industries. Manufacturing companies, on the other hand, could feel the ripple effect of supply chain failures for several years after 2000 has come and gone. Different industries have also reacted with varying urgency in dealing with the Year 2000 threat (see Figure 1.3). In the following sections we have outlined how various private industry sectors are addressing the Year 2000 problem along with some predictions as to how these industries will weather the storm over the next two to four years. Government and international activity are addressed separately in a later section of this chapter.

Industry Progress Report—12/1997

INDUSTRY	% COMPLETED
Financial/Banks/Insurance	6%
Medical/Health Care	11%
Government	8%
IT Suppliers/Consultants	7%
Transportation/Utilities	7%
Wholesale/Retail	17%
Manufacturing	9%
Communications	20%

Figure 1.3 *Source: The Sentry Group—taken from a study published in Software Magazine, December 1997.*

1.4.1 Banking

If government regulators feel that a bank is not meeting its obligations to correct the Year 2000 problem they can issue a "cease and desist order." In these circumstances, the bank is given a certain amount of time to fix the problem. If the bank rectifies the problem, the cease and desist order will be lifted, but if the bank does not comply with the requirements of the order, the bank could be closed. In 1997, a Cease and Desist Order was imposed on Putnam-Greene Financial Corp. of Georgia when regulators audited the bank and determined that they did not have an adequate plan in place to address the Year 2000 problem.[9] The regulators keeping watch over U.S. financial institutions include the Officer of the Comptroller of the Currency, the Federal Deposit Insurance Corp., the Office of Thrift Supervision, and the National Credit Union Administration. State regulatory agencies are also looking into the issue.

The banking industry has been seeing more than its share of merger and acquisition activity over the past few years and this ultimately has a big impact on the systems at the acquiring bank. Ending up with two of each type of system creates a special challenge to Year 2000 planning teams and could force decisions to be made that would have been delayed for a period of time had there not been a Year 2000 problem. In addition to this issue, many banks are in the midst of consolidating systems, business partners, services, and customers at this time. Seventy-two percent of U.S. banks have had their computing systems impacted by a merger or an acquisition in the last 24 months.[10] This level of systems and organizational upheaval complicates the Year 2000 management process, drains personnel resources, and increases the risk of introducing a problem during the systems conversion process.

When one speaks of the banking industry, many times we envision the top banks with billions in assets (see Figure 1.4 to see what some of the nation's largest banks are doing to address the problem). Many of the banks in the United States fall into the small to medium category. These institutions do not have the same control over their destiny as do larger banks because they outsource numerous functions. Seventy-three percent of banking institutions are using outside service providers to supplement resources or are totally outsourcing tasks such as check sorting and deposit posting.[10] This situation creates a dependency on business partners that must be investigated during the Year 2000 project. This dependency has turned the Year 2000 project at many small to mid-size banks into one giant sleuthing exercise.

Banking Activity To Address Year 2000

Chase Manhattan Corp.	*Spending $250 million**
Citibank	*Dedicating 50-70% of technology staff to problem**
BankAmerica Corp.	*Spending $250 million**
First Chicago NBD Corp.	*Spending $100 million***
LaSalle National Bank	*Spending $30 million***

Figure 1.4   **Source:* Chicago Tribune, *November 20, 1997.*[10]
**Source: Crain's Chicago Business, *October 13, 1997.*[11]

The banking industry, because of the amount of money that it manages and the fiduciary responsibility assigned to it, will face tremendous pressure from many factions as the Year 2000 nears. Bank executives should consider the following Year 2000-related issues as the century comes to a close.

1. *An increase in regulatory inspections by state and federal regulators.*

2. *Pressure from business partners to demonstrate that the bank has a detailed understanding of Year 2000 risks, a plan to correct them, and contingency plans in case there are problems.*

3. *A reduction in merger and acquisition activity as senior executives are increasingly consumed with Year 2000 compliance issues.*

4. *Increased pressure from securities firms to comply with "street testing" requirements for data exchanged with other financial institutions.*

5. *Reviews from credit card companies trying to verify that credit card clearing software is compliant.*

6. *Public scrutiny regarding the willingness of people to open new accounts or to leave money in banks that regulators have branded with a Cease and Desist Order.*

7. *Invocation of contingency plans to correct mission-critical failures that impact customers and revenue capabilities.*

8. *Buyout bargains for banks that have waited too long to fix their Year 2000 problem and have no choice but to be taken over by larger banks.*

9. *Worse case scenario: A bank is not compliant, word gets out, and people withdraw money from that institution.*

According to a September 1997 American Bankers Association study, only 20 percent of banks had begun the implementation stage of their Year 2000 project with another 17 percent still in the awareness raising stage.[12] This data is not a good sign. Banks should get moving or they could get shut down. If a bank wishes to assess its compliance status prior to a regulatory agency showing up at their door, they can sign on to "www.bog.frb.fed.us/y2k/frbQuest.htm" and pull down the Federal Reserve Board's compliance questionnaire.

1.4.2 Securities Firms

The securities industry has been credited with being well out in front of every other industry in addressing the Year 2000 problem. The Securities Industry Association (SIA) maintains a Year 2000 committee to share information, track compliance status, and ensure the integrity of data being shared among financial institutions. This effort is being done for exchanges, depositories, utilities, clearing houses, and other entities that participate in the ongoing trade of monetary instruments. One SIA-sponsored initiative, street testing, has gotten significant attention from other industries because it exemplifies the cohesiveness with which an industry can undertake a very complex task.

The goal of street testing is to verify that the trading of securities remains uninterrupted as we head into the next millennium. According to Michael Tiernan, chairman of the SIA Year 2000 Committee, "street-wide testing is a global effort. The industry needs to coordinate across international boundaries to include members in the United States, Europe and the Pacific Rim. We may even declare a holiday on December 31, 1999, which is why we require this to be a global initiative." Dawn Lowell, chair of the Participant Street-wide Testing Subcommittee, added that "all major firms are represented on the subcommittee. Our charter is testing requirements from a participant's point of view. This exercise includes identifying participants, procedures, data and test conditions. We play the role of overall coordinator. In 1998, we will run a dress rehearsal, or beta test, that includes eight firms and in 1999, we will execute the full test. The bottom line is that each firm is responsible for defining test scripts and validating the results to their own satisfaction."

The fact that the securities industry is focusing intently on the street-wide test should give some relief to traders around the world. The amount of money flowing through these organizations is staggering and the level of effort being put forth is clearly warranted. The downside of a problem arising in this industry is that a single data error could send shock waves through the financial community (refer to the discussion on the financial supply chain in Chapter 4). Consider some of the following issues that could occur over the next two to three years.

1. *A proposal to cancel trading on December 30, 1999, January 3, 2000, and/or January 3–7, 2000 (numerous ideas are being considered) to account for and correct Year 2000 glitches.*

2. *Call by Arthur Levitt, Jr., SEC chairman, to delay a planned switch by stock exchanges to decimal prices from fractions because "there are issues to consider, such as the Year 2000."*[13]

3. *A reduction in merger and acquisition activity due to executives who want to focus on a stable business model until Year 2000 changes are completed.*

4. *Customers switching to firms that disclose information about how they are dealing with the Year 2000.*

5. *Data errors, initiated at one firm, ripple through exchanges and clearing houses—causing a massive joint cleanup effort.*

1.4.3 Manufacturing

The manufacturing industry, first thought to have minimal Year 2000 exposure, is actually at the mercy of a triple threat: embedded systems, the supply chain, and internal systems which are typically third-party packages. In manufacturing environments, embedded systems control automated factories, assembly lines, environmental control units, robotics, quality analysis and control, design processes, ergonomics, statistical and trend analysis, simulation devices, and a host of other specialty categories. Some of the equipment is date sensitive and some of it is not. The problem is that most of these devices are highly customized, contain difficult to decipher microcode, are not registered in a centralized inventory, and have not been tested and certified to be Year 2000 compliant.

Embedded systems are utilized by large and small companies alike, and this is where the real problem lies. The manufacturing industry is trailing much of the industry in Year 2000 progress (see Figure 1.3) and many small firms tend to be even further behind. This result is due to the fact that the management at small manufacturing companies tends to view computer technology as a necessary evil that can be readily outsourced. They may figure that their software vendor will handle the Year 2000 problem for them and that this is the ultimate extent of their exposure. What they have not considered is that the machines that they have been running since the 1970s contain chips that may be exposed to the problem. The lack of an inventory on these systems and any clear sense as to the level of their exposure to the Year 2000 problem are common in many of smaller companies and this introduces yet another problem: the supply chain.

The supply chain, which is discussed at length in Chapter 4 along with embedded systems, is a wall of dominos waiting for the first one to drop. A supplier is defined as a third party that provides a company with parts, raw materials, finished products, energy, water, services, software, or information. In the case of the manufacturing supply chain, a series of companies depend on a series of other companies to produce the parts that ultimately end up in a product. For example, a thousand or more companies are required to produce parts to assemble a car. If one supplier falters, because of an embedded system, supply chain, or IT system failure, the entire supply chain may come to a halt and vehicle assembly lines could shut down. The ripple effect on local and national economies, which has not been carefully modeled at this point, will likely be quite devastating.

Finally, manufacturers are also prone to IT and related application system Year 2000 failures. One case in point is the high degree of dependency on inventory systems. In some manufacturing sectors, companies have jointly implemented Just In Time (JIT) inventory management systems. Using the JIT inventory management approach has reduced the amount of inventory a company must keep on hand for the manufacturing process. JIT has reduced the risk of stocking large quantities of parts should demand for a product slow, warehouse space requirements, and the associated overhead of managing high inventories. In other words, few companies using JIT maintain a large, on-hand backlog of parts and this makes manufacturing firms susceptible to inventory system, supply chain, and embedded system failures. Manufacturing firms should consider the following factors over the next two years.

1. *Exposure to a supply chain failure could shut down large- and small-scale manufacturing companies.*

2. *Embedded systems should not be assumed compliant until checked out (note that custom changes to these systems make it difficult to get compliance information from vendors).*

3. *Work with associations to the degree possible to ascertain the compliance status of companies that play a key role in the supply chain.*

4. *Do not assume that because you are a manufacturing company that you have no Year 2000 problems or related costs (GTE is spending $150 million to address the problem[14]).*

5. *Build contingency plans to accommodate supply chain failures.*

6. *Consider that supply chain problems may not reach your company until mid-year 2000 based on supplier inventory levels and the time it takes for the problem to ripple up the chain.*

1.4.4 Retail

Hardware stores, clothiers, supermarkets, and a host of other retail categories are exposed to the Year 2000 problem through point of sale systems, financial services that could malfunction, and suppliers that may not notify a retailer of problems until too late. According to Figure 1.3, the retail field is making progress on the Year 2000 problem. Another study by the National Retail Federation (NRF) indicates, however, that 87 percent of mid-size retailers ($300 million to $2 billion in revenues) are still running noncompliant retail management systems.[15]

While larger companies, such as Sears, have been working on the Year 2000 problem for some time, smaller companies are not taking action to research and correct it. Supply chain problem awareness and assessment efforts, which lag in the manufacturing area, are almost nonexistent in the small to mid-size retail environment. Retailers will have to consider the following strategies over the next two years.

1. *Work with NRF to jump-start awareness, vendor research, and supply chain strategies.*

2. *Work with vendors to ensure that point of sale, inventory, and related systems are compliant.*

3. *Improve awareness in order to ensure that the proper resources are allocated to the Year 2000 project.*

4. *Consider phone and Internet systems that automatically take and fill orders to be high-risk systems that, should they fail, could quickly alienate a customer base.*

5. *Ensure that Electronic Data Interchange (EDI) functions work properly by contacting key information suppliers in order to street test interfaces well before 2000.*

6. *Develop contingency plans (fortunately the Year 2000 problem falls immediately after the biggest shopping period of the year) for supplier, point of sale, and EDI failures.*

1.4.5 Transportation

The transportation industry will likely experience scheduling, routing, tracking, reservation, onboard control, radar, collection, billing, and other system problems that can impact customer satisfaction and safety. Most of the press has centered around projected problems with airlines and the air traffic control systems. Safety-related exposures in the airline industry are very high. According to the Dutch airline KLM, there are as many as 160 date-dependent systems on a commercial aircraft and many of these systems require supplier input to determine compliance.[16] KLM plans to sponsor an industrywide forum for airlines in mid-1998 to share strategies for dealing with this and other airline-related issues.

Another fear is that air traffic control systems will not function properly after the end of 1999 and this has caused KLM to consider halting flights into certain countries until the situation appears stable.[18] Airlines depend on these air traffic control systems, along with Global Positioning Systems (GPSs), to a tremendous degree but have little influence over the how or when these systems achieve Year 2000 compliance. This lack of leverage is one reason that the airlines should band together to address many of these safety-related concerns. The good news is that airlines are taking the problem seriously. KLM is spending over $100 million,[16] American Airlines will spend $100 million, and TWA plans to spend $20 million[17] to correct the Year 2000 problem.

There are numerous other means of transportation that will be impacted by the century rollover. Public transportation commissions must consider routing, fare collection, and scheduling systems in the scope of their analysis. Railroads rely on extremely complex routing and scheduling systems to track where a particular car is at any point in time. Ships, cars, trucks, buses, tractors, cable cars, subway systems, and other means of transport contain embedded chips that may not be Year 2000 compliant. The transportation industry should consider some of the following strategies as we head into the next century.

1. *Companies should ensure that safety-related devices on vehicles are checked out carefully with vendors to ensure safe operating capability into 2000.*

2. *Public transport systems should take precautions to ensure that noncompliant, safety-related systems running between December 31, 1999, and March 1, 2000, be fixed or shut down for a period of time.*

3. *Routing, scheduling, collection, reservations, and other supporting systems should be brought into compliance.*

4. *Data interchange among transport companies and government agencies requires special analysis to ensure that critical data is not lost or corrupted.*

5. *The airline industry should cooperatively work to ensure that communication, air traffic control, GPS, and onboard computer systems are certified compliant or not in use during critical transition periods.*

6. *Industries may want to establish a moratorium on travel as we head into 2000 (this will crimp many a New Year celebration).*

1.4.6 Telecommunications

Mergers, deregulation, opening of new markets, joint ventures, and new technologies come together to create a telecommunications industry in flux. The Year 2000 problem's impact in this extremely high-tech industry is significant according to the International Telecommunication Union (ITU), an agency of the United Nations. The ITU, which represents hundreds of companies in almost 200 countries, has determined that the Year 2000 problem impacts message handling systems, directory services using two-digit year fields, call charging, billing, and other record keeping systems.[19] Other problems have been reported in various types of switching equipment.

The impact of widespread telecommunications problems in a world that is so highly reliant on this industry could impact safety (emergency calls), commerce, and the general quality of life. According to banking giant Citicorp, telecommunications providers are not doing enough to stave off problems. Citicorp has been so vocal about this problem that the U.S. General Accounting Office (GAO) has launched an investigation into telecommunications companies and their lack of effort on the Year 2000 problem. Problems cited by Citicorp include [20]

1. *No consistent compliance definition and no consistent way of achieving compliance;*

2. *Getting a very late start on their Year 2000 projects;*

3. *Providing customers with nebulous, misleading, and incorrect information;*

4. *Incorporating Year 2000 work into new development work that has been subject to delays and additional costs; and*

5. *Being unaware of the date problem in acquired components.*

In addition to the standard telecommunication companies, little has been said about the archaic systems being used in the radio and television community. Our visits to these sites lead us to believe that this industry is inundated with ancient hardware and software systems that will have no way of understanding the century date rollover. Telecommunications companies should consider the following issues going forward.

1. *Mission-critical, embedded communications technology should be a high priority.*

2. *Companies should band together (with the ITU) to identify the highest-risk, highest-priority areas on which to focus.*

3. *Billing and other support systems should take a high priority (and not be subject to yet another failed systems replacement project at this late date).*

4. *Data interchange problems, particularly where customers are concerned, should be fixed (using street testing concept) or customers will flock to competitors.*

5. *Contingency plans should be worked out with the Federal Communications Commission (FCC) and ITU to prevent a breakdown in international communications capability.*

1.4.7 Utilities and Energy

This industry includes nuclear power plants, fossil fuel plants, water processing plants, and a variety of energy-related operations in the oil and natural gas field. One of the biggest infrastructure risks faced by the world stems from potential problems that could arise if utilities experience a Year 2000 failure that interrupts power supplies or impacts people's safety. A 1997 study by Digital Equipment Corporation (DEC) claimed that one-third of all utility companies had not begun Year 2000 projects and another third were seriously behind schedule on their projects.[21] This situation is very disturbing in light of the fact that we all depend on these companies for basic day-to-day survival.

In the nuclear industry, the Year 2000 problem falls into a category called an "Unreviewed Safety Question" or USQ. This categorization means that any existing circumstance that could potentially place the plant in a condition adverse to safety must be reviewed for adverse impact as soon as the condition is discovered.[22] This requirement puts the onus on utilities to resolve this problem as a high priority. In other words, it is not good enough to take a vendor's statement that a device is fine; these systems must be checked out for compliance.

Assuming for a moment that the embedded systems that directly control the reactors are not date-sensitive (this assumption is still being verified and not valid until each system is carefully analyzed), there are numerous support and administrative systems that could cause problems. These include security systems and their impact on plant access, systems used in federally mandated drug testing, data interchange with other entities, inventory control systems, scheduling, and event logging systems.

For example, if a plant experiences a SCRAM (this is, we are told, a routine event), logging systems are the main vehicle used to track what is happening during the SCRAM and used to reconstruct the event after it ends. If this system does not function, the plant is left in an Unanalyzed Condition[22]—this is a bad thing according to most sources. If one of the embedded systems fails, the problem is likely to worsen. The Nuclear Regulatory Commission (NRC) may decide to shut down every plant that does not prove conclusively that it is Year 2000 compliant. Nuclear power accounts for nearly 20 percent of total U.S. domestic power electrical generation capacity and nearly 40 percent of the Eastern seaboard's capacity.[22] We believe that the severity of the problem speaks for itself.

In the energy field, early findings suggest that problems can be expected on offshore oil platforms and at refineries. Out of 1,200 systems inspected at a North Sea oil platform, a 12 percent failure rate was found. In addition to this, research at a refinery found three faulty systems out of ninety-four, two of which would shut down when they reach the Year 2000.[23] Failures at these types of installations could systematically shut down selected oil processing plants and result in at least a temporary shortage of fuel.

Utilities must consider indirect impacts that could shut them down as well. For example, a transportation problem could stall coal or other fossil fuel deliveries and cause power plants to shut down due to a lack of raw materials. Another indirect impact could stem from supply chain problems causing a shortage of parts needed to maintain a power plant. The energy industry faces huge challenges over the next two years and should consider the following strategies.

1. *Perform extensive risk analysis (Chapter 2) and contingency planning (Chapter 9) for all mission-critical functions that have a direct or indirect relationship to a computer system.*

2. *Work jointly with existing or ad hoc industry groups to identify at-risk embedded devices and high-impact supply chain dependencies.*

3. *Check vendor Web sites and other sources as a means of supplementing (not replacing) the painstaking effort required to research embedded system compliance status.*

4. *Document each step of the inventory, analysis, testing, and remediation process for legal reasons and as a means of helping other utility companies and suppliers.*

5. *Lobby for government support where legislative changes or other public sector initiatives can expedite the risk management and contingency planning process.*

6. *Continue checking systems into and beyond 2000 because failures may occur at various stages in the next century.*

Refer to Chapter 4 for more information on embedded systems in the utility and energy field.

1.4.8 Health Care, Insurance, and Pharmaceutical

The health care, insurance, and pharmaceutical industries form a group of highly interrelated companies that manage the health of the nation. Companies within these industries share massive amounts of critical information via EDI and, in one way or another, have a major impact on people's health and safety. These industries must work cooperatively to mitigate Year 2000 risks or people will have a very difficult time getting adequate health care and related services in the Year 2000 and beyond.

The health care industry includes hospitals, hospices, retirement homes, special care units, and a wealth of other categories that are being continuously redefined in today's world. A 1997 Gartner Group study ranked health care providers as being the least prepared for the Year 2000. The survey showed that 50 percent of respondents had no Year 2000 budget, and that 25 percent had no project teams in place. A second study by Gordon & Glickson, P.C. indicated that 47 percent had not inventoried their systems and that 18 percent had taken no steps to achieve compliance.[24] These numbers reflect an industry that has gotten, but can ill afford, a late start on Year 2000 projects.

Hospitals and other care facilities rely on numerous diagnostic, monitoring, and other types of medical devices that contain computer chips. The level of reported date sensitivity found within these devices has varied from company to company. One of our clients reported that close to half of their medical devices contained date-sensitive technology and required replacement. Other estimates have been lower. One company discovered the possibility of patients receiving a radiation overdose from a noncompliant device. Embedded chips can be found in intravenous drip, kidney dialysis, defibrillator, and other devices that could fail because they think they may have exceeded maintenance intervals.

The overriding issue in the health care field is not the percentage of devices that can malfunction, but the possibility of even a single device failing that could result in harm to a patient. This fact, coupled with inconclusive research into product risks, means that the health care community must expedite supply chain risk management. Suppliers in the health care field deliver a wide variety of critical products that may or may not contain computer technology. The risks of inventory outages are not isolated to embedded technology. If, for example, a hospital cannot obtain latex-free gloves or certain anesthetics, patients may have to delay critical procedures.

All of these risks are compounded by the fact that many health care providers manage razor thin profit margins and lack Year 2000 project funding. This lack of funding could serve to increase merger and acquisition activity in the health care field over the next couple of years. This prediction may seem to run counter to the prediction that mergers in other fields may decline heading into 2000. This result is attributed to the fact that health care functions, such as scheduling, patient admitting, and other administrative processes, tend to be generic enough that a compliant hospital could cut a noncompliant hospital over to their systems more quickly than could happen in other industries. Look for merger and acquisition activity in this area to increase in 1998 and early 1999.

Pharmaceutical companies utilize embedded systems in the process of drug production and ongoing research and complex IT systems in all aspects of their business. These companies also supply critical drugs to the health care community. In addition to this problem, the retail end of the pharmaceutical industry exchanges critical patient data between doctors and insurance companies that could be at risk due to a Year 2000 failure. Pharmaceutical company compliance efforts are likely to be better than the level of preparedness depicted in Figure 1.3 for the medical field in general. However, there is little room for error here since these companies play a pivotal role in patient care and well-being.

Not all insurance companies deal in life and death matters, but the role of many insurance companies in health care management is significant because a funding holdup could delay timely medical care. For this reason, EDI in the insurance industry is just as important as data exchange in any other industry, although there has been little emphasis on industry-wide data interchange analysis. In general, the insurance industry took an early lead in correcting Year 2000 problems in their IT systems. Some companies will make it and some will experience large-scale, multimillion dollar problems in certain business areas. Every insurer is a supplier in one sense or another and every company that procures insurance services should take a close look at the level of preparedness of their provider.

Strategies in the health care field over the next two years should include the following considerations.

1. *Hospitals should research and mitigate risks related to suppliers of embedded devices, drugs, medical supplies, and information exchanged across the industry.*

2. *The industry should coordinate efforts to assess the status of medical devices that contain embedded computer technology.*

3. *Health care providers should look into or expedite merger and acquisition activity if it turns into their last contingency option to stave off closure.*

4. *Pharmaceutical companies should verify that any systems linked to drug safety are at the top of their mission-critical list.*

5. *The health care community should consider contingency plans for pharmaceutical company failures that could result in shortages of certain types of drugs.*

6. *Insurance companies should publicly disclose their Year 2000 compliance status for the good of the companies and the general public that uses their services.*

1.4.9 Service Industries

The services industry, which includes hotels, travel agents, doctors, law offices, dentists, not-for-profit agencies, golf courses, and a host of other small and large providers, could be blindsided by the Year 2000 issue. For smaller service firms, still unaware of what the Year 2000 means to them, it may be just a matter of replacing old hardware and vendor software packages with new ones. A chiropractor did just that recently. When this particular chiropractor queried the five vendors that he was considering about Year 2000 compliance, only two of the five claimed to have the situation under control. Had this practitioner not checked the compliance status of these systems, he could very well have spent a great deal of time and money leasing, installing, and training his staff on a non-compliant system.

Large national or international service providers are more likely to be ahead of the awareness curve than are the smaller "mom and pop" businesses. Exceptions are popping up, however. In one case reported from Myrtle Beach, South Carolina, local businesses seem to have overcome the awareness problem as a community.[25] Hotels, golf courses, and local businesses are busily ensuring that computer systems are either compliant or upgraded to be compliant in time for the Year 2000. Since this problem is one that will have to be dealt with at the community level, we strongly recommend that community networking groups include not-for-profit organizations as well. Service providers should consider the following strategies heading into the Year 2000.

1. *Examine all point of sale, accounting, scheduling, or other systems for compliance.*

2. *Contact your hardware and application vendor or vendors to obtain a statement of compliance and upgrade information.*

3. *If you are considering replacement of older or obsolete equipment (this is common in small retailers using 286- or 386-based hardware), verify that replacement systems are compliant.*

4. *Large national service providers should assign a large enough team of personnel to research systems at branches and franchises to ensure continuity of revenue into and beyond 2000.*

5. *Consider forming a community-based Year 2000 group that could be organized by the local chamber of commerce to educate and network local service providers.*

1.4.10 Small to Mid-Size Companies

Small companies are not immune to the Year 2000 problem and are more likely to be unaware of its impact on their bottom line. One Gartner Group study, performed in late 1997, found that of all the small companies (most had under 2,000 employees) queried in one survey, one-third had not yet started to deal with Year 2000 problem.[26] In the United States, there are more than 10.5 million companies (by sic code) and more than 35 million home businesses. These companies make up the backbone of the U.S. economy. The reasons for not dealing with the issue stem from two factors. The first is lack of awareness for organizations that do not have an in-house IT department. Conquering this is primarily an education problem that will eventually disappear as more people understand that they are at risk.

The second factor is thinking that your company is immune to the problem because you use only PC, client/server, or mid-range systems believed to be Year 2000 compliant. This idea is the greatest fallacy in the Year 2000 market. As of mid-year 1997, 47 percent of the PCs being shipped failed the compliance test. One study found up to 80 percent of existing PCs to be noncompliant.[27] Client/server and mid-range systems also contain noncompliant operating systems, routing software, applications, and development tools. The sooner a company realizes this, the more quickly they can correct their problems.

Another issue is that many small companies have the same supply chain and embedded systems problems that large corporations will experience. A number of small to mid-size companies are in the manufacturing, health care, and retail fields—all of which have embedded system and supply chain vulnerabilities. These companies, in many cases, will be blindsided by failures in noncompliant embedded systems and at suppliers. Research into these areas should mirror efforts at larger companies but should utilize industry associations and community organizations to whatever degree possible.

Small companies also are under the impression that the vendor that supplied their accounting, billing, and other IT systems will handhold them into the next century. Many of these vendors may go out of business if profit margins are too small to fund the upgrading of their software systems. Other vendors are likely to force a company to buy the latest upgrade—which a company may not need. One final problem for smaller companies is that once they realize that they have a problem, many consulting companies are unwilling to help them. Profit margins are such that large companies cannot make money by placing one person part time into 1,000 or more different companies.

With these factors in mind, Year 2000 strategies for small to mid-size companies should include the following considerations.

1. *Do not call conversion factories, tool vendors, or service providers that cannot scale down to your requirements (many vendors will waste your time and theirs during a sales cycle).*

2. *Check references to ensure that a vendor has experience with small to mid-size companies.*

3. *If you cannot afford consulting help, lease the tools and do the job yourself.*

4. *Utilize the Internet as a networking tool into other similar companies.*

5. *Network with other small companies in your industry to see if pressure can be put on an application vendor to supply a compliant replacement or upgrade*

6. *Work with your local community to come up with creative solutions where possible.*

1.5 Government Update

Governments, whether they are U.S., foreign, state, or local, tend to do things less efficiently than do companies in the private sector. They start later, depend on a greater degree of bureaucratic wrangling, place vendors through more contractual hassles, and entail greater project over-runs. Most government agencies, whether at the international, national, state, or local level, are staying true to form when it comes to Year 2000 projects. In this section, we have provided an update on how the U.S. federal, state, and local government agencies are doing with their Year 2000 projects. We also review progress for schools and universities.

1.5.1 U.S. Federal Government

The power of positive thinking, in the case of the U.S. federal government, is not enough to get Year 2000 projects moving in a timely fashion. In February 1997, Sally Katzen, the federal government's former virtual CIO, said that she "is confident that the (Year 2000) problem will be solved without disruption of programs."[28] In November 1997, Congressman James Leach, (R-Iowa), chairman of the House Banking Committee, told Reuters Financial Television that as far as the Year 2000 problem was concerned "the Federal Reserve board and the U.S. Treasury will be thoroughly prepared."[29] Unfortunately, the news as of year-end 1997 was not so good.

In December 1997, Congressman Stephen Horn (R-California), chairman of the House Subcommittee on Government Management, Information, and Technology, stated that "we have accepted misleading reports, sloppy and incoherent data, and overly optimistic schedules. Another year has passed and the latest data show that the current work on the Year 2000 in federal computers is unacceptable and potentially disastrous."[30] Horn's statements were included in an update on how well federal agencies are doing with their Year 2000 projects. Among all of the bad news was the fact that, based on current progress, the Treasury Department (see Figure 1.5) will finish its project in the year 2004.

Wayward Agency Year 2000 Status—12/1997	
U.S. Federal Department	**Projected Date Of Compliance**
Labor and Energy	2019
Defense	2012
Transportation Office of Personnel Management	2010
Agriculture	2005
Treasury	2004
General Services Administration	2002
Justice & Health and Human Resources	2001
Education, AID, FEMA	Mid-2000
NASA	Early 2000

Figure 1.5   Source: Cox News Service, "Government May Be Late In Fixing Millennium Bug," December 15, 1997.

The federal government is addressing the Year 2000 in typically ponderous fashion. The House of Representatives began hearings on the problem in 1996 and will likely continue these hearings into the Year 2000. The Senate is looking into a bill that would require companies to fully disclose their Year 2000 status. A look at current progress includes the following updates.

1. *Fourteen federal departments (see Figure 1.5), including Treasury, Health and Human Services, Defense, and Transportation, are projected to finish their projects after 1999.*

2. *Estimates shown in Figure 1.5 only account for mission-critical systems being repaired and not for mission-critical systems being replaced, secondary systems, and embedded systems.*

3. *The State Department, for example, omitted 30 mission-critical systems from this report because they are being replaced (project overruns would leave the agency exposed).[30]*

4. *The Transportation Department omitted FAA systems entirely when these systems are likely to be the most critical of the lot.[30]*

5. *Defense Department findings did not report on critical command and control systems. This is unthinkable given the importance of these systems to the national defense.[30]*

6. *Federal Emergency Management Agency (FEMA)—which is one agency we may really need when the Year 2000 problem hits in full force—is slated to finish in mid-2000.*

7. *Horn called for a change to the reporting process,[30] which is fortunate because Year 2000 risks cannot be assessed or managed until the status of all impacted systems is considered.*

8. *Social Security Administration (SSA), the supposed Year 2000 leader at the federal level, omitted 33 million lines of state disability determination services code from their analysis.[31]*

9. *Office of Management and Budget (OMB) is calling for a shift of hundreds of millions of dollars from non-Year 2000 projects to Year 2000 budgets.[32]*

These problems may shock some people, but not if one looked carefully at earlier government Year 2000 completion projections. The government's original target dates, delivered in a May 1997 report from the OMB[33], were definitely suspect. First, Year 2000 remediation and testing tasks must be interwoven because project teams always run a regression test before returning a system to production. The government plan reflected no such understanding. Second, testing of allegedly compliant systems should begin as soon as possible to stabilize test environments and this is also not reflected in the report. Third, any plan that claims to finish conversion work by late 1998 and testing in 1999 is paying lip service to analysts who have suggested setting aside time in 1999 for system testing. Finally, establishing implementation dates that leave no room for project overruns, as this report indicates, are hopelessly optimistic. These plans in no way reflect the reality of the situation. On top of all of this, we now discover that thousands of mission-critical replacement projects, embedded systems, and secondary systems were left out of the report.

The OMB move, referred to in point 9, is certainly a welcome one. It is likely, however, to be a case of too little, too late. Shifting funds, stopping projects, and launching new Year 2000 initiatives in a large bureaucracy at this late date are unlikely to translate into real progress. Congressman Horn's efforts, and those of Senator Bennett, are clearly positive ones. Horn will have to get even more vocal as time moves on and Bennett may have to revise his bill which is currently on hold. Time will tell. One thing the government must do quickly is reduce legislative demands on over-burdened IT environments pressured by tax, welfare reform, or securities changes. Not doing this is sending a mixed signal to Year 2000 project teams and mid-level management.

The one fact that seems likely is that a number of federal agencies will not meet their Year 2000 deadline and that no agency will achieve 100 percent compliance. In addition to this failure, when the status of replacement projects, embedded systems, and nonmission-critical systems becomes apparent, the picture will definitely darken further. Some agencies will experience Year 2000 failures that are likely to ripple through private markets and into state and local agencies. Individuals, corporations, and local government agencies should track progress for various federal agencies, assess the impact that these failures could have on them, and prepare themselves accordingly. The U.S. federal government casts a long shadow and failure scenarios will have a huge ripple effect on society as a whole—and the international scene.

1.5.2 U.S. Department of Defense (DOD)

Defense has more types of systems, languages, databases, and computer platforms, running specialized and traditional IT systems and embedded technology, in more locations than any other organization on earth. According to a letter sent to various high-ranking personnel, Major Ron Spear states that "we must deal with the Year 2000 now so that our soldiers can continue to place a well-founded confidence in their weaponry and automation tools through the change in the millennium. To this end, each Army organization responsible for system development and maintenance should ensure that the Year 2000 is a high systems resource priority." Spear added that "as part of this process, each system will be seriously considered for elimination. Only those automation systems which truly assist in mission accomplished should remain in your inventory." [34]

One concern with the DOD situation is the fact that mission-critical replacement projects and embedded systems have not been included in the government Year 2000 status reporting process. There are likely a number of replacement projects slated to consolidate mission-critical systems that have not been reported to the OMB and are covering up the fact that existing mission-critical systems will fail—should these replacement projects miss the mark. The Standish Group International study stating that more than 90 percent of IT projects are late, canceled, or downsized applies even more so to government environments. DOD and other agencies are out on a limb on this one.

Embedded systems, which in this case include weapons, satellite, command and control, onboard navigation, radar tracking, and a whole host of highly classified technologies, are not included in this list. This seems unconscionable given the importance of these systems to our national defense and to that of our allies. The fact that DOD is earnestly working on these systems is not enough—the government groups auditing these efforts, Congress, and the public need to know how they are doing.

1.5.3 U.S. State Governments

At the state and local level, awareness is poor, action is slow, and funding is hard to come by. Some states have claimed compliance on basic financial packages in isolated agencies. Press reports would have us believe that these states have achieved Year 2000 compliance, but this is a myth. A state by state report came out at the end of 1997 stating that total estimated costs to repair systems at the state level exceed $2 billion.[35] Concerns abound. For example:

1. *Ten states had not completed their assessment;*

2. *Twelve states listed "not applicable" under estimated cost;*

3. *Fifteen states listed "not applicable" under estimate of work done;*

4. *Arizona and Maryland will spend $100 million, New York $250 million, but California (the world's seventh largest economy) will spend only $200 million (can this be correct?);*

5. *Alabama is spending $92 million, but neighboring Georgia has no estimate to date;*

6. *Ohio has not completed its assessment but claims to be 20 to 25 percent completed;*

7. *New Jersey and Wisconsin have both completed their assessments, yet have no stated estimate of costs or the percentage of work completed; and*

8. *Delaware is spending only $600,000 (how can this be?).*

Reading this report gives one the feeling that only a handful of states have their act together for the Year 2000 problem. This fact has not prevented them from taking action in the legislative arena, however. For example, New York eliminated the warranty period for vendor software, allows damages beyond those required to repair or replace the noncompliant product, and puts the onus on vendors to ensure that date handling capabilities of new packages integrate with the existing environment.[36] California has introduced a bill that would limit damages that one can claim against companies. Only physical injury could be taken to court. The goal is to get companies to move to California prior to the end of the century.[37] Nevada is seeking immunity for itself from Year 2000 damages. [38]

Many states will put a positive spin on their progress. While some states will not even be close to being Year 2000 compliant in time, a handful will face limited problems because they will be very well prepared. Most states will probably fall in the middle range, however, and encounter a steady stream of complaints for years to come with (hopefully) few major disasters awaiting them.

1.5.4 U.S. Local Governments

Prison release, rabies vaccinations, water usage trend analysis, juvenile tracking, property tax, public health, civil accounting, pretrial management, mental patient tracking, payroll, and countless other functions are controlled by local city, county, and municipal government computer systems. Many municipalities are not funding remediation projects at all, while others have work underway. King County, Washington is spending $4 million and McHenry County, Illinois is spending $4.5 million on their projects.

The city of Chicago decided to reduce its $50 million project estimate by buying a totally new computer system[39]—a recipe for disaster in highly inefficient government work environments. Chicago's decision landed it on the Year 2000 Doghouse Web site for foolishly believing that a replacement decision at this point in time could actually eliminate the need to fix their existing systems. The city of San Francisco has set aside a half million dollars and plans to utilize systems from local county governments to help solve the problem. Fort Worth appears to have the situation well in hand, while the city of New York seems to have gotten a late start. Washington, D.C. recently set aside $44.5 million for its project.

Smaller and more remote municipalities will likely not hear about the Year 2000 problem until too late. We believe that one way to help is to work with community leaders at the local level to ensure continuity of public functions. We have spent some time doing this in the municipalities in which we reside and have found it rewarding so far. Year 2000 analysts and technical leaders around the country should seek out local officials to donate time.

1.5.5 Schools and Universities

Left behind in the Year 2000 rush are schools and universities that do not have the funds to assess or correct the Year 2000 problem. Administrative functions, student history and grades, identification cards, and research computer systems are all at risk from the century date problem.

Some universities are fixing the problem, many are upgrading to newer systems, and some are doing nothing. Purdue University is considered a model for other institutions of higher learning because they started earlier and have used automated technologies to help find and fix the problem.[40]

While some universities, such as the University of Akron, are spending millions of dollars to fix the Year 2000 problem, tens of thousands of high schools and grade schools are likely to be unaware of the problem or have little funding to address it. The main consideration at these schools involve PC- or client/server-based administrative systems and the millions of personal computers being used by students for class work. School administrators should proactively determine if PC and Macintosh computers are compliant using PC date checking tools or manual techniques, upgrade any BIOS found to be noncompliant, and issue guidelines to users to accommodate incompatibilities in various types of PC software. Some systems may have to be replaced or, in some cases, students may need to just set the date back to a pre-2000 time frame.

Again, the biggest problem at small schools is awareness and funding. Computer professionals should check with local schools to see how they are doing and offer advice to school administrators to ensure that the academic world is prepared for the Year 2000.

1.6 International Update

Because this problem affects virtually every computer system, the Year 2000 is truly a global issue. Yet, the rest of the world lags the United States in awareness and action by six months to a year or more. Skepticism about the reality of the problem is common in England. European concern over European Monetary Union (EMU), which means that countries will begin using a common currency called the Euro, is slowing their response to the problem. Asia and Latin America are even further behind. The bad news is that Year 2000 failures in the rest of the world will impact U.S.-based corporations. The ray of good news is that other countries can learn from our mistakes, which should accelerate awareness. We have provided a brief update on worldwide Year 2000 status by geographic region.

1.6.1 Canada

Canada is working on the problem, but they have resource and funding shortages just like those found in the United States. Canada actually has a National Year 2000 Program Office headed by an ex-banking executive. The central government is much less proactive than the United

States or the United Kingdom in trying to convince or legislate the private sector to take corrective action. While good statistics on how well Canada is doing with their Year 2000 efforts are not kept as readily as they are in the United States, most analysts consider Canada to be about six months to a year behind U.S. Year 2000 efforts, but the fact that most comparable companies and government agencies have less code may even things out.

1.6.2 Europe

In Europe, the status of Year 2000 awareness and remediation effort varies dramatically from country to country. The reasons for this include the following:

1. *Europe has undergone radical geographic (there are several new countries that did not exist a decade ago) and political changes that have distracted them from the Year 2000 issue;*

2. *General economic and business restructuring has overloaded IT organizations already concerned with EMU planning;*

3. *Ill-defined specifications for the EMU, including rate structures, 1999 and 2002 transition management issues, and timing factors, have delayed work on the Euro conversion;*

4. *The U.K. began work on the Year 2000 problem prior to seriously considering entry into the EMU;*

5. *Germany and France have been all but consumed by their efforts to move to a common currency;*

6. *Italy is busy preparing for celebrations and pilgrimages in the Year 2000; and*

7. *Historical skepticism and less well funded IT organizations tend to delay many new initiatives.*

This being the case, time has continued to march forward toward the end of the century with Europe now waking up and realizing that the century deadline cannot be changed (unlike the EMU dates which are man-made). A late 1997 study indicated that Europe's confidence in making the Year 2000 deadline is lower than confidence in making the Euro deadline.[41] While this may seem illogical, it shows where Europe's thinking currently is on these two issues.

In the U.K., there is good news and bad news. British Telecom is spending between $320 and $480 million to fix its Year 2000 problem and has taken a proactive message to business partners, which includes helping smaller suppliers gain compliance.[42] In addition to this good news, the current government is taking a bigger lead than the previous one in building awareness and support for government departments and private industry. However, in one U.K. study,[43] where Year 2000 awareness is supposedly much better than it is in mainland Europe, the statistics were much less encouraging.

1. *Forty-five percent of respondents have not performed a Year 2000 audit;*

2. *Over 74 percent of respondents' customers are not insisting on their being compliant;*

3. *Over 53 percent are not insisting on supplier compliance; and*

4. *Fifty-seven percent are not planning to allocate budget in the 1997/1998 time frame to fix the problem.*

One final U.K. study indicates that one in ten companies (representing 29 percent of gross domestic product [GDP]) will fail to achieve compliance by 2000. If schedules slip by as little as three months, the noncompliance rate jumps to one company in four, representing 37 percent of the GDP.[44] This news is a frightening economic statistic and represents the very best case Year 2000 scenario in Europe.

As far as Europe as a whole is concerned, they are so far behind that radical action is warranted. Getting from initial awareness to the point where organizations take radical action is usually a path that takes executives and government leaders one or two years to achieve. This adjustment time is gone; so too are the chances of integrating the Year 2000 upgrade with the Euro conversion. A couple of years ago, this was an option for a few, mature organizations. At this point, government leaders must face facts and delay the requirement for EMU until sometime after the Year 2000 mess has been cleaned up. This mandate may seem unthinkable to politicians in Germany, France, and other countries, but if the Euro conversion is not delayed so that IT can fix the Year 2000 problem, Europe will be in total chaos for years to come.

1.6.3 Pacific Rim/Japan

Japan is way behind the curve in dealing with the Year 2000 problem. One late 1997 study[45] found the following concerns in Japan.

1. *Companies studying the problem: 71.7 percent.*

2. *Public sector organizations studying the problem: 86.8 percent.*

3. *Companies with work underway: 28.4 percent.*

4. *Public sector organizations with work underway: 13.2 percent.*

This lack of progress means that, while companies and government organizations are studying the problem, little work has been done to date. Japan is one of the most computerized countries in the world and had assumed, at one point, that because they use the emperor's birth date, they did not have a Year 2000 problem. In reality, the birth date is used on screens and reports, but a Western date is still taken from the compiler and used in computation and comparison logic. A late start, coupled with major ripples rocking the financial markets of Asia, do not bode well for Japan's compliance efforts.

The impact of the Year 2000 problem on the rest of Asia varies depending on the country. Some banks are working on the problem in Hong Kong, but they are also behind due to a high degree of computerization. Singapore is taking a very proactive role in building awareness and fighting the problem. Vietnam, Burma, and other countries with little computer technology are unlikely to experience much of a problem. Australia will likely spend $8.2 billion to fix their Year 2000 problem and is probably somewhere between the United States and the United Kingdom in awareness and completion levels.

1.6.4 Other Regions of the World

South Africa appears to be working on the Year 2000 problem, as are many Middle Eastern countries. The use of special dates reduces some of the impact of the problem, but, as with Japan, the Western date is received from most computer operating systems and used in calculation and comparison logic. South America is, according to some reports, severely behind in its Year 2000 remediation efforts. Governments representing these countries should take a proactive role in making sure that private industry and government agencies heed the Year 2000 warning.

Other regions of the world have either gotten a terribly late start on fixing the Year 2000 problem or are trying to take advantage of the issue. India, which has mostly newer computer technology, has mobilized thousands of professionals to work in conversion factories fixing Year 2000 problems in systems from all over the world. The same is true to a degree in the Philippines, Russia, the Czech Republic, Hungary, Ireland, and other locations.

1.7 Worldwide Economic Impacts

Edward Yardeni, chief economist at investment banking firm Deutsche Morgan Grenfell, predicted in 1997 that the chance of the Year 2000 problem causing a moderate global recession was around 35 percent. In

March 1998, Yardeni increased his prediction to 60 percent. One way or another, there will be major economic impacts on a global scale. The world is a global economy that is more intertwined than ever. A financial institution in New York could receive bad data from a firm in Germany. The ripple effect could be significant, but the information supply chain challenge is only one issue. The domino principal enters in where major problems are encountered in manufacturing, health care, insurance, retail, telecommunications, and other industries.

Europe, South America, the Far East, and other countries around the world are way behind schedule—and the United States is not doing that well either. Resources are tough to come by, but that may not be the only problem. The mythical man-month is in effect here on a global basis. It is unlikely that if unlimited human resources were available to every organization today that management could mobilize the teams to incorporate massive changes in such a short period of time. Time has run out on us all—at least globally. How can we deal with this reality? The remaining chapters of this book address that question. Good luck—we will all need it!

Endnotes

1. *The Year 2000 Software Crisis: Challenge of the Century,* by William M. Ulrich and Ian S. Hayes, Prentice Hall, 1996

2. "Only One in Five Major Employers Has Launched Full-Fledged Strategy to Fix 'Millennium Bug,'" *Y2K Wire*, December 1997.

3. "Year 2000: Not a Pretty Picture," by Allan E. Alter, on-line news story, October 10, 1997.

4. Lawmaker Pushes For More Year 2000 Information," Yahoo Finance, November 4, 1997, http://biz.yahoo.com/finance/97/11/04/z0000_38.html.

5. "Is the Year 2000 Problem Overhyped? Impossible!" by William Ulrich, *Computer-World*, December 8, 1997.

6. "To the Mainstream Press: Get a Clue!" by William Ulrich, *Year/2000 Journal*, November/December 1997, p. 16.

7. "Cobol Pioneer Pitches Year 2000 Fix," by Tim Ouelette and Bob Scheier, *Computer-World*, August 11, 1997, p. 4.

8. "Teen Claims He Has Solved Millennium Bug," CNN interactive, September 14, 1997, http://cnn.com/TECH/9709/14/nzealand.millenium.

9. "Year 2000 Credit Check," by Tim Huber, *Minneapolis-St. Paul City Business*, December 15, 1997, www.amcity.com/twincities/stories/121597/story3.html.

10. "Industry's Major Worry: Wear Links," by William Gruber, *Chicago Tribune*, November 20, 1997.

11. "My Year 2000 Problem Is Bigger Than Yours," *Crain's Chicago Business,* October 13, 1997.

12. "Banks Lag in Preparing for Year 2000," by Bruce Caldwell, *Information Week*, September 15, 1997, p. 134.

13. "Delays for Quotes in Dollars, Cents," Infoseek News Channel (originally published in the *St. Louis Post*), http://guide-p.infoseek.com/Content?arn=ix.SLMO1997102109530006X&col=IX, October 21, 1997.

14. "Failure Overseas 'very Serious Threat' to U.S.," by Pat Widder, *Chicago Tribune*, November 20, 1997.

15. "Retailers Slow to Check Out Year 2000," by Thomas Hoffman, *Computerworld*, October 13, 1997, p.4.

16. "KLM to Fly in Rivals to Thrash Out Date Bug," *ComputerWeekly*, November 20, 1997, www.computerweekly.co.uk/news/20_11_97/08598503239/C5.html.

17. "2000: The Clock Is Ticking," Margie Manning, *St. Louis Business Journal*, December 1, 1997, www.amcity.com/stlouis/stories/120197/story3.html.

18. "Year 2000 Glitch May Ground KLM Flights," by Andy Patrizio, *TechWeb News*, November 11, 1997, www.techweb.com/wire/news/1997/11/1111klm.html.

19. "ITU Work to Resolve Y2K Problems Moves Up a Gear," Newsbytes News Network, November 17, 1997.

20. "Citicorp Attacks Telecoms Firms for Millennium Mess," *ComputerWeekly*, October 16, 1997, www.computerweekly.co.uk/news/16_10_97/08598503239/B3.html.

21. "Utilities Pose Terrible Disaster Potential Worldwide," published in *Year/2000 Journal* (original story source "*Daily Oklahoman*"), November/December 1997, p. 8.

22. "Partying Like It's 1999 or Dancing in the Dark??," by Rick Cowles, Utilities and the Year 2000, www.accsyst.com/writers/nuclear.htm.

23. "Energy Industry Must Act Fast to fix millennium bug," *ComputerWeekly*, December 11, 1997, www.computerweekly.co.uk/news/11_12_97/08598503239/C19.html.

24. "Health Care Industry Ranks Last in Y2K Readiness," Cosgrove, Eisenberg & Kiley, P.C, *Year 2000 Update*, Vol. 1, Issue 1, October 1997, p. 2.

25. "Local Concerns Get Ready for 2000," by Colin Burch, *Sun News*, September 29, 1997.

26. "Year 2000: No Small Job," by Bronwyn Fryer, *Information Week*, November 10, 1997.

27. "Jan. 1, 2000: Is Your PC Ready?" by Michael Cohn, published for the *Atlanta Journal-Constitution*, October 12, 1997.

28. "Getting Down to the Wire," by Bob Violino, *Information Week,* February 10, 1997, p. 126.

29. "2000 Bug No Problem for Large Firms—Congressman," by Neil Winton, *':Netly News*, November 26, 1997.

30. "Agency Delays Could Stretch Conversion Schedules," ITAA's *Year 2000 Outlook*, Vol. 2, No. 46, December 12, 1997.

31. "Double-check Your Bridge to the Year 2000," by Gary H. Anthes, *Computerworld*, November 17, 1997, p. 37.

32. "Clinton to Order Millions Redirected to Fix Year 2000 Problem," taken from Associated Press, *Augusta Chronicle*, December 12, 1997.

33. "Getting Federal Computers Ready for 2000," U.S. Office of Management and Budget, May 15, 1997, http://www.cio.fed.gov/yr2krev.htm.

34. "Year 2000 Fixes—Top Priority," letter from Maj. Ron Spear, November 18, 1997, http://www.army-y2k/army-y2k/.htm.

35. "Year 2000, State by State," *USA Today*, December 17, 1997.

36. "Empire State Imposes Towering Y2K Warranty," ITAA's *Year 2000 Outlook*, Vol. 2, No. 47, December 19, 1997.

37. "California Bill Would Limit Y2K Liability," by Patrick Thibodeau, *Computerworld*, December 10, 1997.

38. "State to Seek Immunity Against Year 2000 Glitch," by Phil Kabler, *Gazette*, November 19, 1997.

39. "City Prescribes Cure for Millennium the Bug from Computers," by Gary Washburn, *Chicago Tribune*, October 15, 1997.

40. "Universities Struggle to Eradicate Millennium Bug," by Jeffrey Selingo, *Chronicle of Higher Education*, November 21, 1997.

41. "Computer Preparations for Euro Trail behind Year 2000," by VIASOFT, Inc., Press Release, November 24, 1997.

42. "Big Telcos Subsidize Smaller Rivals in Y2K Problem," by Andrew Craig, *TechWeb News*, December 11, 1997, www.techweb.com/wire/story/TWB19971211S0004.

43. "Government Stirs on Millennium Problem," by Giles Turnbull, PA NewsCentre, October 24, 1997, http://www.pa.press.net/tech/year241097.htm.

44. "Survey Finds 1 in 10 Will Miss Date Deadline," ITAA's Year 2000 Outlook, Vol. 2, No. 43, November 14, 1997.

45. "Survey for Year 2000 Issue," Japan Information Service Industry Association, November 13, 1997.

Chapter 2

Strategy Update: Shift to Risk Mitigation

With less than two years remaining on the Year 2000 countdown clock, most companies must focus on selective prioritization and risk mitigation. This chapter discusses risk mitigation issues by outlining a process for prioritizing remediation projects based on business impacts. It also looks at strategies for those companies that got a late start on their projects and for those that have fallen behind on their implementation efforts. Survival is the name of the game and companies may have to adjust plans midstream to survive.

Topics covered in this chapter include a snapshot of where companies should be right now, business risk analysis and mitigation, evolving software package options, strategies for the far behind, and how to beat the clock. The package options discussion is an area of exposure that many companies are having difficulty addressing and we want to give this topic a high profile in the risk mitigation discussion. Anyone wishing to manage and mitigate Year 2000 risk factors, regardless of where they are in the completion spectrum, should review Chapter 2.

2.1 It's Late in the Game, Now What?

The September 8, 1997, issue of *ComputerWorld* stated that 60 percent of companies are still assessing the Year 2000 problem, while only 25 percent are actually working on it. Even worse, fewer than 10 percent have actually begun testing systems to determine Year 2000 compliance. These figures were provided by Allen Deary, CFO at Peritus Software Services, Inc. in Billerica, Massachusetts, and are further supported by comments from Neil Cooper, an analyst at the Irvine, California-based investment house Cruttenden Roth. According to Cooper, "the big dollars will not be spent until 1998." Even at this late date, many senior executives are still in denial about the breadth and complexity of the problem.

Another startling fact, courtesy of Montgomery Securities, is that 62 percent of companies have not started their conversion work and 61 percent believe the Year 2000 problem to be "no big deal." These statistics are alarming when coupled with Montgomery Securities impact studies stating that 90 percent of applications are impacted by the Year 2000 problem, but only 10 percent of all applications are typically updated during the course of a given year. This background means that application teams working on this problem are, for the first time ever, required to update four to five times the number of applications over the next two years than they have ever updated in any given prior year. The fact that maintenance changes typically touch a small percentage of applications and Year 2000 upgrades typically affect upwards of 90 percent of the programs in a system means that conversion teams face a huge challenge.

Two years ago, when we wrote our first book on the Year 2000 problem, we would never have believed that the industry would be so far behind at this point in the process. Enough has been said about this by analysts and the press. The question remains, can we convince the executive holdouts that they are truly in a dangerous position and must take action to mitigate the internal and external risks to their organizations? It is too late for many companies to continue to try and beat this problem to death with a stick. Even the overly optimistic IT community is, in many cases, beginning to admit that there is not enough time to fix everything. Be realistic in assessing your situation and take action accordingly.

2.1.1 Achieving Full Scale Deployment

As of January 1, 1998, the industry will have roughly 400 work days, 100 weekends, 730 actual days, and eight quarters left to get ready for the Year 2000. Given that many of our clients have production systems that fail every month due to a Year 2000 bug and that systems will fail at an increasing rate during 1999, the perceived two-year lead time does not really exist. The most telling statistic here is the number of quarters left until 2000. This figure is a good countdown measure because it is easy for executives, driven by quarterly profits and earnings statements, to picture project delivery requirements within this time frame.

The one factor that remains a problem for most IT teams is scaling up to the point where they are delivering the minimum number of projects required per quarter to ensure that mission-critical functions remain viable. In many cases, project teams have gotten themselves into a situation where they have not been able to muster the resources to launch more than one or two projects at a time. This situation may be related to budgetary constraints, conservatism, a lack of centralized project control, or a host of other factors. The fact is that each quarter that passes without achieving critical project mass increases the number of projects that must be completed in an increasingly short span of time. A chart depicting projects per quarter is shown in Figure 2.1.

Project Completion Window

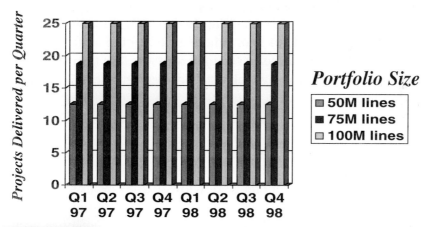

Figure 2.1 Minimum number of projects to be delivered each quarter given a minimum of one project per 1/2 million lines of code. (Project line count is typically 250,000—which would double the number of projects needing to be completed.)

Let us take, for example, a company that must fix 50 million lines of code between January 1997 and January 1999. If each remediation project addresses 500,000 lines of code, which by the way is too large in most cases, project teams must deliver 12.5 fully converted, fully tested projects per quarter over eight consecutive quarters. Because functional and technical boundaries, distributed environments, and management considerations move most projects into a 250,000-line range, most companies of this size are looking at delivering close to 25 projects per quarter. If you have a portfolio of around 100 million lines of code, you could be looking at delivering 50 projects per quarter for eight consecutive quarters. This criteria shows how companies should define full-scale deployment. By the time companies reach this stage, it may be too late to stabilize mission-critical systems.

This state is certainly not a good one given Standish Group International studies stating that IT projects are late or never delivered at all more than 90 percent of the time. If your project team is just beginning to ramp up and faces this type of volume in early 1998, the challenge is immense and translates into a number of painful realities. The first is that most companies are behind before they even get started. The second reality is that your 1999 integration testing window is gone. If you do not think that this is a big deal, refer to the testing chapters found later in this book. The third problem is that dozens of project teams will be attempting to gain access to limited hardware and personnel resources in a severely compressed space of time. Again, testing suffers the most when resource constraints appear. The final reality is that the number of options that management has available to address the Year 2000 problem are dwindling quickly.

2.1.2 The Declining Options Picture

Five years ago, when we first began working on Year 2000 projects with our clients, the options were wide open as far as strategies to avoid system failures. This situation is depicted in the bottom-left-hand portion of Figure 2.2. In 1993 or 1994, for example, a replacement project was still an achievable goal. Most companies did not meet this goal for reasons that we communicate in Chapters 18 and 19 of our last book and the last chapter of this book. It is interesting that some individuals just learning about the Year 2000 problem believe that a full replacement of existing systems is the best way out of the dilemma. If that has not happened in the last ten years, it is certainly not going to happen in the next two.

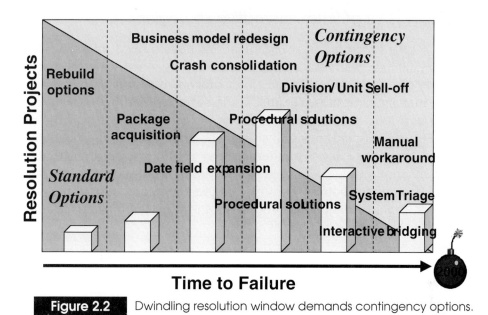

Figure 2.2   Dwindling resolution window demands contingency options.

As we moved into 1995, a complete package replacement option still appeared feasible. The strategy to tackle a major cross-functional package implementation project, as many companies did during this time frame, was still an option. Those projects, in many cases, have demanded two to four times the resources originally envisioned and are nowhere near completion. The time for starting new replacement projects has passed. In some cases, contingency planning is required for package implementation projects that have gotten out of hand. Only single-function packages, a point-of-sale package for example, or very limited scale implementation projects at small to mid-size companies should be undertaken at this juncture.

In 1996, the vast majority of IT executives stated that date field expansion was their remediation solution of choice. In 1997, the vast majority of companies shifted their strategy to the procedural solution where a windowing option was employed. This shift is judiciously being maintained today, with the caveat that field expansion may be applied to selected systems, files, or databases depending on business or technical requirements. As the gap narrows, however, several new solutions are being touted. Timeboxing, where a date is reset to -28 years during the execution phase of a system, has recently been introduced as the latest silver bullet. We address various bogus solutions and related risks in Chapter 6. The point here is that IT is being backed into a corner as far as conventional solutions to the Year 2000 problem are concerned.

2.1.3 Running Out of Time: Alternative Strategies

Like it or not, most organizations have moved into a phase of the Year 2000 problem where they can no longer extricate themselves by applying all-night working sessions, draconian mandates, or even Dilbert-like management fads. IT must get the attention of the business community and look for alternative options to the problem or systems will fail and business operations will suffer. The upper-right-hand portion of Figure 2.2 outlines a series of alternative or contingency options that organizations may pursue. Contingency planning and invocation are based on business impact, bottom-line criticality to a company's survival, the potential of a mainstream solution failing, and how the business would view various alternative courses of action.

For example, business executives are the only source for developing an alternative strategy to fixing a leasing system such as selling the leasing business to another company. Organizations buy and sell business units every day. Most of the time these decisions are based on the fact that a business unit has been a marginal performer or that a company wants to refocus on its core business. Now another factor is coming into play: The fact that a Year 2000 problem is either too time-consuming or too costly to resolve in a marginally performing business unit. On the other side of the equation is the company, a bank for example, that wishes to expand its leasing operation by buying the customer base of its competitor. In this example, both companies win.

This type of strategic interchange is not in play yet at most companies. Maybe this is due to the fact that business managers are not involved in the Year 2000 planning loop. It could also be attributed to the irrational optimism that prevails within most IT areas. A recent visit to a county government determined that the IT department had its Year 2000 project well underway. Upon further questioning, the county administrator admitted, however, that no research had been performed in other non-IT departments with their own computing systems, PCs, traffic lights, water control systems, and a wealth of other potential problem areas. This lack of research occurs because these Year 2000 failure points are all out of the reach of IT and IT has been the sole driver of Year 2000 solutions. If this situation does not change, a lot of business managers are going to be in for a big shock when 2000 rolls around. The first critical phase of involvement for business users is in the initial business risk assessment phase of the project.

2.1.4 Launching Parallel Activities

Figure 2.3 depicts a plan for launching concurrent Year 2000 assessment, infrastructure setup, and remediation projects. This plan may seem impossible or may be counterculture to many companies or government agencies, but it is a prerequisite to surviving the Year 2000 problem if work has not yet begun. The main requirement for launching these tasks concurrently is top-level sponsorship from senior business and IT executives. Without this level of support, it is unlikely that the resources and cooperation required from a wide array of resources can be mustered in a short space of time.

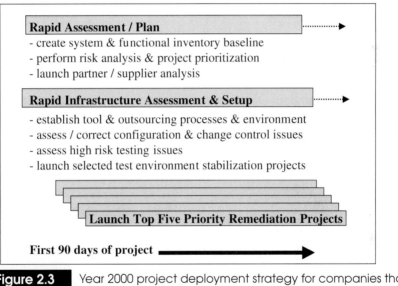

| **Figure 2.3** | Year 2000 project deployment strategy for companies that are getting a late start. |

The enterprise assessment must focus on an inventory and a risk analysis to determine which systems should not be remediated while other systems are fixed. The infrastructure setup ensures that tools, processes, personnel, and hardware environments are established properly. Infrastructure projects also verify that test environments are prepared in time to certify systems Year 2000 compliant. While not ideal, this situation is what companies that are seriously behind schedule must face to ensure the continuity of mission-critical functions. The business risk assessment described in the next section is a key part of the survival equation.

2.2 Year 2000 Business Risk Assessment

In our last Year 2000 book, we addressed the fact that executives should drive a business risk assessment to mitigate bottom-line exposure to the business. To update this concept, we have broadened the risk mitigation discussion to position the risk assessment as the first piece of the risk management process—with the second component being contingency planning as discussed in Chapter 9. This section provides industry examples of how business risks should be managed throughout the life of a Year 2000 project, discusses the development of risk models, and outlines strategies based on recent industry progress.

The Year 2000 poses major business risks to most every organization, even if an organization is not highly dependent on information technology. There is a real potential for business operations to be interrupted by a Year 2000 computer failure or by a failure at a supplier, business partner, or other external entity. Executive refusal to believe that the Year 2000 is a business problem that poses bottom-line risks will be the downfall of more than a few companies. Maintaining this position, after all that has been said about the Year 2000's impact, could fuel litigation claims from consumers, stockholders, and business partners. It will be interesting to see how long executives continue to gamble with the future of their companies given the mounting evidence that they must take action now.

A second, yet less obvious, risk is posed by managers who acknowledge having a Year 2000 problem, but who do not know how to neutralize risks in critical product and service areas due to time and resource constraints. Neutralizing Year 2000-related risks requires focusing resolution efforts on critical systems and external entities where exposure is greatest. The business risk accomplishes this while solidifying sponsorship from business executives, facilitating project prioritization, and providing input to contingency plans. Gaining business executive sponsorship is required to commit business unit funding and to ensure that user personnel are actively engaged in the solution. Project prioritization, which dictates project execution sequence, and contingency planning, which establishes a fallback position in cases where failure is likely, are essential to ensure the continued viability of mission-critical functions.

In support of these goals, the business risk assessment identifies each business area, related products and services, systems or external entities that support these products and services, projected failure dates, and exposure in terms of lost revenue or other risks. Identifying product and service interruptions that could result from a Year 2000 failure positions the discussion in terms that management readily understands. Communicating potential failures in, for example, customer tracking, order entry, revenue procurement, insurance claims, monetary fund transfers or other critical business functions is a powerful way to focus a business executive's attention on the Year 2000 issue. Areas of exposure include financial losses or litigation that can result from harm to shareholders, customers, business partners and constituents, and regulatory violations at the local, state, and federal levels.

Analysts must consider all mission-critical business areas, related systems, and impact of external entities in a business risk assessment. The risk assessment should be treated as a subproject within a Year 2000 enterprise assessment that then continues throughout the life of the Year 2000 project. The risk assessment, which results in the prioritization of resolution projects designed to neutralize negative Year 2000 impacts stemming from in-house systems, also identifies risks posed by the introduction of errant data from external sources and from supply chain or business partner interruptions resulting from Year 2000 problems at external entities.

The business risk assessment requires identification of all systems used within the enterprise, external points of data interchange, and suppliers, agents, and other business partners. This information should be stored in an integrated tracking facility or repository that can reflect Year 2000 compliance status for a system or external entity upon request. Various status reports may be generated from the tracking facility. The following guidelines represent a set of best practices in the risk assessment area.

2.2.1 Begin Fixing Five Most Critical Systems Now!

If you have not begun any conversion projects to date, start fixing the top five most critical systems immediately. The reason behind this strategy is that time is running out and companies are having a hard time launching the first few projects. While first projects generally take longer due to learning curves and other environmental factors, early successes and key learning can be used as a way to streamline future projects. This approach is especially true in cases where third parties, such as conversion factories, outsourcing teams, or systems integrators, are involved.

Organizations can typically pick out their top five systems in terms of business criticality. Management should review each line of business, select the top revenue producing areas, and begin remediation work on these systems. If the systems have been marked compliant already and just require certification testing, proceed with establishing a test environment, develop future test data to test key transition dates in 1999 and 2000, and begin testing that system. If an important system is known to have a near-term failure date, it would be a good candidate to move to the top of the priority list. If a conversion factory or other external process is to be used, use these systems to establish required off-site configuration and change control procedures.

One thing to note is that priority conversion projects can be performed concurrently with other activities. As previously depicted in Figure 2.3, conversion work can begin in parallel with other planning activities including the systems inventory, infrastructure setup, and other assessment activities.

2.2.2 Solidify Systems Inventory

The systems inventory, an enterprise assessment byproduct, includes all applications, packages, end-user systems, embedded systems, hardware, and system software. Because distributed and end-user systems are particularly hard to find, the evolution of the systems inventory continues until 2000 arrives. Undoubtedly several end-user or distributed environments, missed during earlier inventory efforts, will encounter problems in the early part of the next century. Tracking this information in an easily cross-referenced, updated, and accessible format is essential to managing the project and related risks. Readers should reference the Legacy Transition Meta-model discussed in our first book and refined in Appendix C of that book for additional information on the role of a Year 2000 repository.

Management should consider several important factors when integrating the systems inventory into the business risk assessment. Because the target audience for the risk assessment is the business community, system software and hardware status should be reported on separately. If certain hardware, such as automated teller machines, is directly linked to a critical business function's viability, the hardware should be included in the risk assessment. End-user systems should be included in the assessment but may not fall into a mission-critical category based on the functions they support.

Embedded systems, particularly if they support the development of a key product or the delivery of a core service, must be included in this analysis. These systems, for a variety of reasons, have been particularly hard to inventory. This challenge does not mean that they should not be included. Infrastructure systems, including telecommunications, environmental controls, security, and other facility-based systems, provide direct support to business continuity and must be inventoried as well. Finally, computer technology that is embedded in the products delivered to customers must be inventoried by engineering and production teams as priority items.

2.2.3 Identify Data Interchange Points

In addition to identifying risks that could be linked to in-house systems, business areas must assess risks involving third-party data interchange. Errant data may enter a compliant system and cause that system to malfunction. In a worst case scenario, data may filter through numerous databases that are linked to mission-critical systems. In other cases, data may originate at your company and be sent to external entities and cause them harm. Infecting another company's data could result in serious litigation risks. For these reasons, a jointly staffed team of IT and end-user personnel should be assigned to external data interchange analysis.

Data interchange points should be assessed as follows.

1. *Survey each business area (this is part of the functional area analysis described later in this section) requesting points of data interchange with external organizations.*

2. *Survey each IT area (this is part of the standard inventory) for points of external data interchange.*

3. *Cross-reference this information to build a comprehensive view of data interchange across system areas.*

4. *Verify that all Electronic Data Interchange (EDI) points are documented.*

5. *Summarize incoming and outgoing data interchange, by functional area, as follows:*

   - responsible owner and area
   - receiving or sending entity name and type (i.e., business partner, government agency, etc.)
   - type of data and business function
   - file and/or database name (include format where available)
   - lifespan of interchange (include plans for new interchange points prior to 2000 and planned termination dates where applicable)

6. *Review data interchange points with business owners and determine if any can be eliminated prior to remediation planning.*

7. *Starting with the most mission-critical data (based on business end-user input), begin contacting external entities to*

   - determine if the entity is planning to be Year 2000 compliant
   - assess plans for data format changes
   - come to a conclusion on data change dates and integration testing plans

8. *If any data is related to an industry category, such as the securities industry, work cooperatively with industry organizations to establish a coordinated strategy.*

Remediation activity surrounding external data interchange focuses initially on getting the problem corrected at the point of origin and secondarily on building a firewall to determine that errant data stays out of your computing environment. In some cases, the completion of a firewall may be futile because the dates that the errant data is based on may not have been included in the interchange itself. The firewall, which is typically part of a data interchange contingency plan, is a fallback position.

The main thing to remember is that a given company may have hundreds, and in many cases, thousands of data interchange points that require research and correction. Because not all of these interchange points can be examined, integrating data interchange analysis into the risk assessment effort is key to prioritization and contingency planning.

2.2.4 Identify and Document External Entities

Business analysts should identify and meet with business partners, brokers, agents, suppliers, customers and any other type of external entity that is critical to the continuity of business operations. High-level and detail-oriented meetings may be required to verify that these companies are pursuing a Year 2000 solution and will be solvent when the time arrives. Manufacturing companies must further verify that systems sold or distributed to third parties (the customer) continue to function. External entity analysis is one of the most important, yet most overlooked, areas of the risk assessment process.

Work should commence quickly on research into external dependencies. Because no company's fate is entirely in its own hands when it comes to relying on third parties, assuring continuity of mission-critical functions in this area may be the most difficult task within a Year 2000 project. It also happens to be the area where organizations have spent the least amount of time although this is somewhat industry related. The securities industry, for example, is well aware of the interdependent nature of its business and is aggressively pursuing research work in this area. On the other hand, small to mid-size manufacturing companies have done little to ensure that continuity of suppliers is maintained.

With these issues in mind, business personnel must systematically document each and every external relationship and the criticality of each relationship from a business impact perspective. The process recommended for completing this analysis includes the following steps.

1. *Verify that a business executive is sponsoring the Year 2000 project for each business unit or division where this analysis is to be performed.*

2. *Verify that a purchasing executive is committed to this process.*

3. *From a central purchasing perspective, document the following and equip research analysts with this information to support individual business unit external dependency analysis:*

   - external corporate services including legal, accounting, security, or other centrally contracted service offerings
   - centrally contracted product agreements such as paper, supplies, or other products
   - utility resources including water, electric power, and so on
   - insurance, health care, banking, and other financial agreements
   - contracts for any services that may have been procured for a given business unit or division

4. *From an individual business unit perspective, work with business personnel in each area to identify*

   - component supply companies required to manufacture end products
   - product companies needed to maintain business operations
   - service companies needed to maintain business operations
   - agents, brokers, business partners, or other entities critical to the sales, distribution, billing, or collection of your products or services

5. *Document external entity attributes as follows:*

   - list company name, category, location, and contact name
   - identify the type and name of products or services being supplied
   - for business partners, brokers, agents, and so forth, list the amount of revenue that the entity accounts for over the course of a given year
   - assess whether an external entity can be replaced by an alternative option

6. *If you work for a manufacturing company with supply chain dependencies, perform the following tasks:*

   - contact first-tier supply chain senior executives to determine the supplier's awareness of Year 2000 issue
   - communicate to first-tier executives that you expect them to be ready to face the Year 2000 without operational computer interruptions
   - emphasize the risk of problems in Programmable Logic Controllers (PLCs), robotics, environmental control systems, and other shop floor systems

- communicate need to make second-tier suppliers aware of Year 2000 risks

- work with industry groups (where applicable) or take other action to ensure that the entire supply chain understands Year 2000 risks

7. *Review external entity analysis and consolidate redundancies across multiple business units or divisions.*

8. *Place third-party data into a readily accessible and easily updated repository.*

Once external entity analysis has been documented, business analysts will need to integrate this information into the overall risk assessment. This integration process is dependent on which functional areas are impacted by a given external entity.

2.2.5 Document Business Functions

It is impossible to assess the scope of an organization's Year 2000 problem, or to determine where to focus project resources, without modeling the interdependencies among business functions, applications and external entities. Business analysts, along with support from IT teams, should list major business functions for each functional area. Figure 2.4 depicts a sample list of functions that apply to a banking environment. Analysts may be able to derive business functions from business process reengineering or similar projects that have already performed much of the functional analysis. Once identification of business functions has been completed, analysts should review redundancies across business units and reconcile them accordingly.

Upon documenting functions for each business area, business teams will need to work with IT teams to determine the dependence that each function has on one or more application systems and/or external entities. Occasionally, the process of identifying functions within a company is simplified by using application systems as a springboard for this analysis. For example, a payroll system can readily be linked to a payroll function.

Identifying a business function's relationship to an external entity may also be inferred from the existence of that entity. A supplier to a manufacturing firm would, by default, mean that the company performs some function related to this supplier. Another approach to documenting functions is to work backward from the list of products and services that an organization offers. This approach works well for private industry and government agencies. Each product and service should be accounted for in the development of the functional inventory. The bottom line is that knowledgeable business analysts are required to perform this work and that leveraging prior research efforts can the streamline functional discovery process.

Banking Function Table

BUSINESS_FUNCTION_0107	Community Bank	BUSINESS_FUNCTION_0129	Fund-Raising & Marketing Div.
BUSINESS_FUNCTION_0108	Account Verification	BUSINESS_FUNCTION_0130	Home Improvement Loans
BUSINESS_FUNCTION_0109	ATM Operations	BUSINESS_FUNCTION_0131	Human Resources
BUSINESS_FUNCTION_0110	Bond-Coupon Collection	BUSINESS_FUNCTION_0132	Installment Loans
BUSINESS_FUNCTION_0111	Branch Banking	BUSINESS_FUNCTION_0133	Lending Division
BUSINESS_FUNCTION_0112	Cash Management	BUSINESS_FUNCTION_0134	Marketing
BUSINESS_FUNCTION_0113	Check Clearing and Posting	BUSINESS_FUNCTION_0135	Merchant Acquisition
BUSINESS_FUNCTION_0114	Commercial Lending	BUSINESS_FUNCTION_0136	MIS
BUSINESS_FUNCTION_0115	Commercial Real Estate Lending	BUSINESS_FUNCTION_0137	Mortgage Lending
BUSINESS_FUNCTION_0116	Consumer Lending	BUSINESS_FUNCTION_0138	Operations
BUSINESS_FUNCTION_0117	Consumer Real Estate Lending	BUSINESS_FUNCTION_0139	Overdraft/Pre-Authorization Credit
BUSINESS_FUNCTION_0118	Corporate Trust	BUSINESS_FUNCTION_0140	Payroll
BUSINESS_FUNCTION_0119	Credit Card Issuance	BUSINESS_FUNCTION_0141	Personal Trusts
BUSINESS_FUNCTION_0120	Credit/Debit Card Operations	BUSINESS_FUNCTION_0142	Regulatory Compliance
BUSINESS_FUNCTION_0121	Customer Credit Card Billing	BUSINESS_FUNCTION_0143	Stock Management
BUSINESS_FUNCTION_0122	Customer Service	BUSINESS_FUNCTION_0144	Strategic Planning
BUSINESS_FUNCTION_0123	Data Network Operations	BUSINESS_FUNCTION_0145	Telecommunications
BUSINESS_FUNCTION_0124	Debt & Debentures	BUSINESS_FUNCTION_0146	Teller Operations
BUSINESS_FUNCTION_0125	Deposit Accounts	BUSINESS_FUNCTION_0147	Transaction Accounts
BUSINESS_FUNCTION_0126	Employee Benefits Trust	BUSINESS_FUNCTION_0148	Trust Division
BUSINESS_FUNCTION_0127	F&A and Operations Division	BUSINESS_FUNCTION_0149	Trust Securities Trading
BUSINESS_FUNCTION_0128	Facilities Management		

Source Thinking Tools, Inc.

Figure 2.4 Banking functions—defined by users as baseline for business risk assessment.

Documenting this information in a repository or risk assessment tool (see Appendix for more information on specific products) facilitates the next stage of analysis: linking the definition of business functions to supporting systems and external entities. Year 2000 teams should note that management may initially reject this level of functional analysis as extraneous to the core Year 2000 project, regardless of how well a case is made for proactive risk management. Executives should note, however, that many of the delays associated with managing large-scale transition projects, such as a replacement or package implementation effort, are a direct result of not knowing which systems support a given business function. This information, once collected, should be institutionalized for use on an organizationwide basis. At a minimum, management needs to know which functions are at risk.

2.2.6 Relate Systems to Business Functions

Linking applications, embedded systems, computerized products, and end-user systems to the functions that they support establishes a baseline for project prioritization strategies. One result of this involves finding systems that can either be triaged or consolidated based on the discovery of a functionally comparable system in another area. One of our clients has, for example, scores of order entry systems. One goal for this company would be to eliminate some of these systems in favor of an order entry system in another business unit. Figure 2.5 highlights the relationships between business functions and applications within a manufacturing environment. The process for performing this analysis involves the following steps.

1. *Review the list of business functions collected for each business area.*

2. *Obtain the inventory results completed on all systems to date as follows:*

   - break up application systems by major function
   - include real-time and embedded systems
   - consider excluding end-user systems that only provide reporting or querying capabilities
   - include products (bought or sold) that contain embedded chip technology

3. *Work with IT and business analysts to assign applications to related business functions as follows:*

   - research situations where a function is not related to an application system
   - research situations where an application is not related to a function
   - document unrelated functions and systems for later resolution

4. *Where a function depends on another function, be sure to reflect this relationship.*

5. *Be sure to include embedded systems in this analysis as required for*

   - manufacturing environments
   - health care product requirements
   - other industry situations as required

6. *Review each application to determine if that application depends on another application as follows:*

   - If a system receives required data from another system, it depends on that system.
   - If a system receives a transaction from a system, it depends on that system.

- If a system utilizes a database updated by one or more other systems, that system depends on each of these other systems.

7. *Record this information in a risk assessment tool or repository.*

The key to recording relationships between business functions and application systems is to fully trace the dependencies between each function and other functions, between functions and between applications, and between application and other applications.

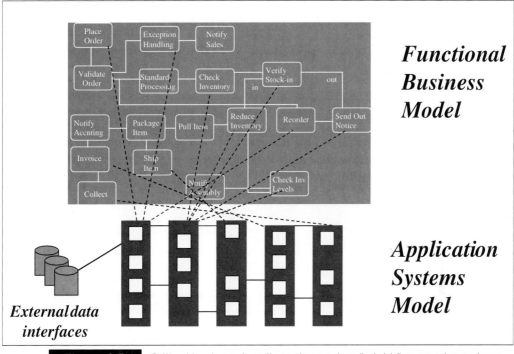

Figure 2.5 Critical business functions depend on "at risk" computer systems.

2.2.7 Relate External Data Interfaces to Business Functions

The process of linking external data interfaces to business functions is an extension of the process of linking applications to functions. The relationship between external data interfaces and business functions is driven by the relationship between the receiving or sending system and the functions that these systems support. For example, an external data interface, shown in Figure 2.5, feeds orders into an order entry system from an out-side wholesaler. The order entry system, in turn, directly supports the order taking function within the enterprise.

Understanding these relationships provides management with a way to estimate the importance of external data interfaces and the entities that create this data. While the wholesaler creating this data would likely be identified during external entity analysis, discussed in Section 2.2.8, key data interfaces could just as easily be missed. The process required to document external data interfaces is discussed in the following steps.

1. *Assign at least one full time analyst to research data interfaces for each major business unit.*

2. *Obtain all previously documented lists of external data interfaces that may be available.*

3. *Obtain a list of applications and a list of external data interfaces by business unit.*

4. *Work with business users and IT personnel to assess which systems are sending and receiving data outside of the organization.*

5. *Review list of external entities, as determined in Section 2.2.4, as a potential source of data interfaces.*

6. *Review end-user systems as a source for data interchange.*

7. *Continue this process across business units and look for opportunities to eliminate redundant data streams.*

8. *Document each external entity along priority lines based on the business functions that the related systems support.*

9. *Work with appropriate business analysts to determine the following:*

   - the level of compliance that the entity sending or receiving this data plans to achieve

   - how entities sending data plan to test the system creating that data

   - format changes that the sending entity plans to make, such as date field expansion

   - what types of format changes any receiving entity expects

   - timing requirements for format changes and interface compliance testing

10. *Assess street-wide testing requirements for situations where data flows through a defined network of companies within a given industry (such as the securities industry).*

Documenting external data interfaces is one of the most underestimated tasks in a Year 2000 project. One company believed that they had only 300 external data interfaces. Initial research, however, uncovered well over 1,000 data feeds to and from outside organizations. The message here is to move quickly to assess the level of compliance that each entity will achieve prior to the Year 2000.

2.2.8 Relate External Entities to Business Functions

The process of relating external entities to the functions they support rests squarely on the shoulders of business analysts because IT has little or no knowledge of these relationships in most cases. This portion of the assessment process has been grossly understated in many organizations. The lack of end-user involvement and corresponding work plans provides evidence of this fact. The analysis must be performed, however, because providers of goods and services are the lifeline of most companies. External entity analysis is an essential component of every Year 2000 project.

This analysis requires that business analysts obtain the list of business functions and external entities created in prior steps. Figure 2.6 depicts relationships between internal business functions and the external organizations that these functions rely on to support a business unit of a manufacturing company. When one examines this model, it quickly becomes apparent that survival of certain functions relies on the continuation of many external products and services. Risk management, in this case, is extremely difficult because one must depend on forces outside a company's immediate control. External entity analysis includes the following steps.

1. *Focus on one business unit or division at a time, including IT and corporate functions, when performing this analysis.*

2. *Start the process with a complete list of functions and external entities for each area to ensure that the inventory is built quickly.*

3. *Review the nature of each external entity and link each company with one or more functions as depicted in Figure 2.6.*

4. *Have multiple analysts participate in the development or review of these relationships to avoid missing key service or product providers.*

5. *Rank suppliers and partners by their relative priority and related impact to the business.*

6. *Send a letter from a senior executive, typically from purchasing, to each sup-plier, business partner, broker, agent, and other external entity that includes the following items:*

   - a statement summarizing the Year 2000 problem and its importance

   - notification that the supplier or partner must be Year 2000 compliant or they will be eliminated and replaced

   - a contact point, typically the regular point of interface between the third party and your organization, for questions

   - for mission-critical suppliers, tell them that you plan to contact them directly and want to review their plans and results

7. *If you have thousands of suppliers and cannot contact them all, identify the most important ones to be contacted directly.*

8. *If you are heavily dependent on a third party for major revenue flow, such as an offshore bank or an exclusive distributor, make sure that you perform a site visit to review progress.*

9. *For supply chain partners, consider the following options:*

   - Meet with all first-tier suppliers to communicate the importance of being compliant.

   - Provide first-tier suppliers with a sample letter and strategy for them to take to their suppliers.

   - Encourage each supplier in the supply chain to promote compliance from their suppliers.

   - If an industry organization is available to help leverage this process, work with other companies in your industry to ensure continuity of supply.

   - Develop contingency plans as required where weaknesses in the supply chain become apparent.

10. *Verify that you have included health care, banking, financial services, and other administrative services that executives may take for granted.*

11. *Continue to work with external entities for the life of the Year 2000 initiative to mitigate risks to the highest degree possible.*

12. *Build contingency plans for each area where third parties have a significant impact on your business.*

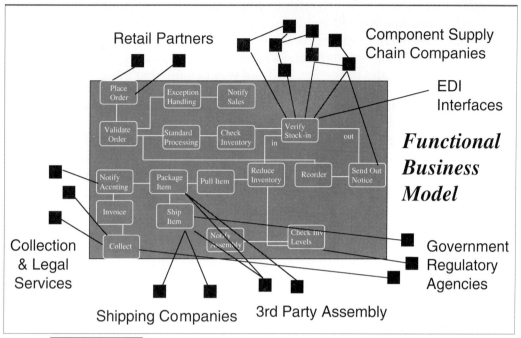

Retail Partners

Component Supply
Chain Companies

EDI
Interfaces

*Functional
Business
Model*

Collection
& Legal
Services

Government
Regulatory
Agencies

Shipping Companies   3rd Party Assembly

Figure 2.6   External entities pose equal risks to key business functions.

2.2.9 Identify Event Horizons

Event horizons, as discussed in our last book, dictate the time that remains to correct and test a given system or correct problems with external data interfaces before they encounter a post-1999 date. A risk assessment must, by definition, include an analysis of the time to failure. Event horizon data becomes more critical as 1999 approaches because systems are likely to begin failing at a much faster pace within one year of the century mark. To date, major financial institutions have been experiencing one or more Year 2000 failures per month in their systems. Maintenance teams have been able to patch many of these systems or instruct users to work around problems. Patches correct an isolated problem but do not constitute a compliant system. As the pace of failure quickens, and more resources are consumed with remediation and testing, maintenance teams will no longer be able to keep up with problem correction.

Analysts should continue to strive to capture event horizon data for all functions, systems and external entities because they have a direct bearing on remediation and certification testing project schedules and priorities. Industry experience to date has shown that application teams are not supplying this information to the central Project Office on a consistent or reliable basis.

This problem appears to stem from the fact that IT personnel do not know when systems will fail and do not want to invest in the research to find out. One alternative to surveying application teams is to ask users what the time horizons are for various business functions (a five-year lease, three-year credit card, 90-day sales projection, etc.) as a way of gathering this information.

Vendor-supplied packages can be similarly researched, although vendors should supply this information during the survey process. Systems that typically will not fail before January 1, 2000, include embedded technologies (programmable logic controllers, MRI equipment, etc.), facility systems (elevators, security, etc.), system software, hardware, and selected applications with no forward looking logic. Assuming that you wish to continue using these systems, remediation projects must be scheduled to test, repair, or replace them prior to the Year 2000. Lead times for this process include the remediation work itself, testing, implementation, and related dependencies. The goal of identifying dependencies among related applications, defined in Section 2.2.6, is to allow one system to inherit an event horizon from one or more supporting systems. This effort can only be managed on a large-scale basis through Project Office coordination, ongoing research, and some type of repository or risk assessment management tool. Figure 2.7 depicts an example of one such tool. Event horizon analysis must, therefore, remain a top priority going forward.

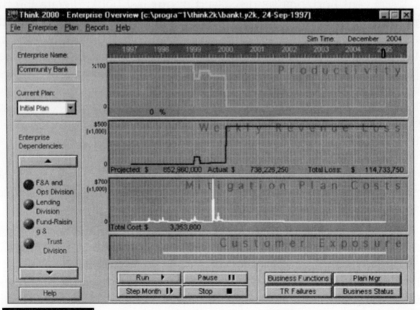

Figure 2.7   Banking simulation model facilitates executive visualization of Year 2000 risks.

2.2.10 Identify Revenue- or Customer-Related Risks

Financial risks are typically unique to a given business market's sensitivity to a system failure. A trading system failure could, for example, have disastrous effects on a firm. Patient admitting system failures could have a similarly catastrophic effect on a hospital. Each business unit must, therefore, make its own determination as to the exposure that could result from a systems failure in their area. Risk analysis involves the identification of the function, system or entity, related risk, event horizon, and potential downside of failure.

In the case of revenue- or customer-related risks, it is essential for assessment teams to provide management with clear risk definitions and projected losses to highlight the immediate need for project prioritization and contingency planning. We have listed some examples of revenue- or customer-related risks for several different industries below.

1. *Manufacturing market*

    - Crash of programmable logic controller, robotics, environmental, or other assembly systems.

    - Inability to produce products due to a breakdown in the supply chain.

    - Retail partners' computer problems that reduce customer income stream and goodwill.

    - Failure of embedded technology in products used in the manufacturing process.

2. *Health care market*

    - Patient admitting system failure limits ability to process new accounts.

    - Failed diagnostic equipment prevents hospital from providing services.

    - Failure of billing and collection systems retards income processing abilities.

3. *Insurance market*

    - Field-based agent systems failure slows influx of new customers.

    - Actuarial system underestimates policy rates based on age-related errors.

    - Billing system failure inhibits ability to invoice customers.

4. *Banking industry*

   - Failure of demand deposit system at an institutional lending partner causes customers to withdraw money.
   - Leasing miscalculations undercharge leasing customers.
   - International trading partner failure shuts down international revenue stream.

5. *Securities industry*

   - Trading system crash costs millions in lost revenue.
   - Clearing system overpays commission amounts.
   - Date-related spreadsheet miscalculations misappropriate money.

6. *Airline and aerospace industry*

   - Reservations system fails to hold seats—resulting in loss of customer revenue.
   - Inventory system fails to secure parts which grounds planes and in turn forces refunds.
   - Inability of a brake parts provider to deliver shuts down assembly line and income stream.

7. *Telecommunication and utility companies*

   - Billing system fails to notify accounting of delinquent accounts.
   - PBX system failure forces company to issue refunds due to service shutdown.
   - Billing data exchange error between two service providers miscalculates amounts due.

8. *Government institutions*

   - Revenue collections system fails to notify government of delinquent tax payments.
   - Ineligible welfare recipients are paid due to age-related miscalculations.
   - Overpayment of social security benefits are caused by age miscalculations.

These examples must be expanded dramatically to incorporate a broad range of revenue-related risks unique to your organization. When analysts are developing this list, they must systematically focus on each of the business functions, products and services, systems, embedded technology, and external impacts that pose financial threats. The financial downside, when viewed in aggregate, should motivate executives who are still in denial, unwilling to fully fund the project, or unwilling to engage business managers in contingency planning efforts.

2.2.11 Identify Legal and/or Regulatory Risk

The potential of a legal challenge resulting from a Year 2000 problem is something that business executives would hopefully view as an imminent danger that must be addressed. The analysis of legal risks is required for service and product contracts, merger and acquisition activity, computer products that are bought or sold, data interchange errors, customer and shareholder impact, and employee relations. When linking these legal risk factors to a given business area, business analysts should examine the impact of a given product or service being interrupted for an extended period of time and how various parties would be harmed by these disruptions. Regulatory violations present similar threats to the business. Legal and regulatory risk examples are shown below.

1. *Manufacturing market*

    - Quality control system fails to detect flaw in a brake part that is later installed in a car that fails.

    - Failure of embedded technology in products sold to customers results in litigation against manufacturer.

    - Environmental control system failure forces waste into a river resulting in a shutdown by a regulatory agency.

2. *Health care market*

    - Failure of chips in pacemaker or defibrillator causes loss of human life.

    - Computer diagnostic equipment, such as an MRI or X-ray machine, causes a doctor to misdiagnose a patient.

    - Patient monitoring system shuts down in critical care ward.

3. *Insurance market*

    - Data interchange errors result in regulatory reporting violations.

    - Failure of a policy management system accidentally cancels a policy causing customers to not receive due compensation.

    - Massive revenue decline causes stockholders to file class action suit against company.

4. *Banking industry*

- Vendor software contract dispute results in large-scale litigation.
- Misappropriation of interest amount results in class action lawsuits.
- Bank regulators discover irregularities in bank reporting system due to date-related errors.

5. *Securities industry*

- Data interchange errors corrupt commissions system and cause firms to challenge each other in court.
- Trade processing system errors result in regulatory reporting violations.
- Tax payment errors force government to levy fines against offenders.

6. *Airline and aerospace industry*

- Failure of air traffic control system results in lost lives and civil litigation.
- Maintenance system problems causes the wrong part to end up in a plane.
- Nonpayment of benefits results in employee walkout and court challenge by unions.

7. *Telecommunication and utility companies*

- Power grid shutdown forces millions of customers to be without power and results in class action suit filed by customers.
- Overcharging customers results in regulatory fines.
- Event recorder (computer) crashes during a routine SCRAM at nuclear facility making event logging inoperable.

8. *Government institutions*

- Automated lighthouse system shuts down, causes a ship to crash, and results in loss of life and major property damage.
- Failure of air traffic control system results in lost lives.
- Defense system failure results in loss of life.

While regulatory and legal risks may not be as easy to identify as revenue-related risks, they clearly exist. The process of identifying legal risks typically requires support from in-house legal counsel. Similarly, the process of identifying regulatory risks requires help from internal and external audit teams. These support functions, if not already involved in the planning process, must get involved in the business risk assessment at this juncture.

2.2.12 Prioritize Remediation and Testing Projects

Once the risk assessment has been completed and event horizons are clearly defined, analysts must assign priorities to remediation and testing projects. We should note that, at this point, an organization's five most critical projects should already be underway. Other systems must be ranked by business impact, event horizon, and related systems impact for each division and/or business unit. There is certainly no reason to start from scratch when prioritizing Year 2000 projects. Disaster recovery plans, for example, may already contain basic risk rankings that can be used to establish project priorities.

Figure 2.8 depicts two-way ranking that may help analysts depict priorities more clearly for senior executives. Ranking revenue/customer risks separately from legal/regulatory/safety risks ensures that a low revenue impact/high safety impact system is listed as a top priority. A rating of 5 means immediate and substantial problems will result if a system fails. A ranking of 4 indicates slightly less immediate problems. Analysts should use their judgment when ranking systems as a 3 (moderate impact), a 2 (low impact), and a 1 (no impact-triage candidate).

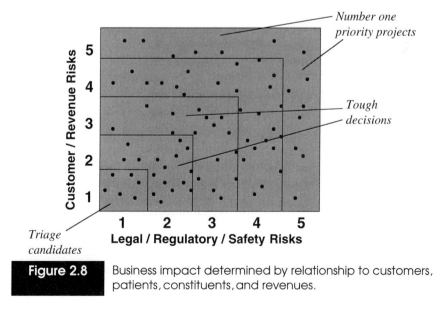

Figure 2.8   Business impact determined by relationship to customers, patients, constituents, and revenues.

Analysts should work with business executives to prioritize IT-driven projects as follows.

1. *Rank system projects by business impact*

   - review revenue, regulatory and legal risks associated with each business function as previously identified in Sections 2.2.11 and 2.2.12

   - establish a remediation and/or testing project ranking for each system linked to a given business function

   - consider upgrade unit segmentation strategies when assigning project priorities

   - define and rank related projects required to correct external interfaces as previously defined in Section 2.2.3

   - ensure that allegedly compliant systems are assigned a testing project priority

   - continue this process for each business unit and or division

2. *Rank systems by event horizon*

   - obtain project rankings based on business impacts defined in step 1 above

   - based on failure dates and project size, establish a project start date for each system

   - perform a reality check to ensure that enough time is set aside to ensure that a project is completed prior to the system failure date

   - expand this analysis to include projects required to deal with external data stores

   - verify that event horizons provide enough lead time to correct a system prior to its corresponding failure date

3. *Refine rankings based on related systems impact*

   - review all systems that are linked directly to other systems, but not to a given business function (a pension system, for example)

   - consider the impact of this system's failure on related systems and indirectly related functions as previously defined in Section 2.2.6

   - refine system rankings based on these dependencies

4. *Review and adjust rankings based on cross-functional dependencies*

    -   review cross-functional impacts between business areas (for example, failure of a life system that shares customer data with a health system in another division)

    -   refine and adjust rankings based on relative business impact of a failure in one area on another area

5. *Create initial system triage strategy*

    -   work with central project office and senior executives for each business unit to assess overall capacity to deliver systems

    -   review low-priority (no impact/low impact) system rankings (see Figure 2.8) to determine if these systems can be scheduled for triage (left as is or deactivated)

    -   continue this process for other low priority systems to ensure that sufficient resources are available to correct high priority systems

    -   work with business analysts to determine alternative options including elimination of redundant systems, shutting down business units, or working around issue manually

    -   continue triage analysis across business units by taking into account overall business strategies

One discrepancy typically found in many Year 2000 strategies is that aggregate remediation plans require the delivery of an unrealistic number of projects in a constrained space of time. For example, management may plan to fix 60 million lines of code over the next 18 months. This plan could require delivering as many as 240 projects during that time span. This requirement equates to delivering an average of 40 projects per quarter for six consecutive quarters. This conclusion is overly optimistic in the best of circumstances but made even more unrealistic by the fact that you may only have ten remediation projects currently underway. The project office is responsible for performing periodic reality checks throughout the life of the project. When you realize that you cannot achieve total compliance by the Year 2000, the importance of project prioritization will become even more apparent.

2.2.13 Prioritize Business End-User-Driven Projects

Special consideration should be given to project requirements that originate in business areas. Awareness of the roles of the business user in a Year 2000 project has grown slowly. This low awareness level is primarily due to the reluctance of executive management to recognize the Year 2000 as a business problem. Hopefully, this discussion can help highlight business user responsibilities and alleviate this reluctance. User-driven projects involve tasks that IT analysts either should not or cannot manage or perform directly. These projects require assessing business partner compliance, developing supply chain strategies, correcting end-user systems, and investigating contingency options. Business users must perform the tasks below, in addition to helping IT develop system remediation priorities.

1. *Review external relationships, inventoried in Section 2.2.4, with suppliers, brokers, agents, resellers, and other business partners.*

2. *Rank external entities that must be investigated to ensure business unit survival as follows:*

   - Top priority includes entities where no substitute exists or where a business relies heavily on that entity (i.e., power company, key supplier, key agents, etc.).

   - Rank secondary entities as those where a replacement is readily available or where failure of that entity would not cause an immediate business disruption.

   - Rank low priority entities where an entity supports a noncritical business function or where backup suppliers already exist.

3. *Send letters from purchasing executives to all third-party CEOs on this list requesting*

   - Current compliance status for key functions and business units relating to your needs.

   - Plans for compliance including risk assessment results.

   - The date they plan to achieve compliance in the business area that relates to your requirements.

4. *For top priority business partners and suppliers, schedule a site visit to assess Year 2000 compliance status and progress.*

5. *For supply chain partners, meet with each priority supplier to set strategy as follows:*

   - Assess first-tier supplier's ongoing ability to deliver product to your organization.

   - Where automated production technologies are involved, review compliance upgrade progress for those systems.

- Work with supplier to develop letter to be sent to their suppliers requesting compliance status.

- Work with industry associations and competitors to create newsletters, Web sites, seminars, or other communication media to support ongoing awareness program.

6. *Review and remediate, replace, or triage end-user systems as follows:*

   - Ensure that executive commitment is in place to drive an end-user Year 2000 strategy.

   - Review end-user systems inventory and procedures to keep this inventory up to date.

   - Assess the criticality of each system using risk assessment model applied to IT systems.

   - Triage end-user systems wherever possible to reduce the scope of the effort.

   - Create and communicate a strategy for spreadsheets that includes windowing options, data exchange, and data format changes.

   - Consider options for either replacing end-user systems with an IT system or other end-user system.

   - Maintain end-user focus into the Year 2000 to ensure stability in end-user areas.

7. *Work with IT teams to develop contingency plans for the following areas:*

   - IT systems that support functions in each business area.

   - Business partners critical to the continuity of revenue and customer satisfaction.

   - Supply chain-related issues including backup suppliers for critical areas.

   - Correction and coordination of external interfaces.

   - Critical end-user systems.

   Note that Chapter 9 contains a detailed discussion of contingency planning and invocation options for various situations and industries. Each business area should have its own Year 2000 plan identifying projects, tasks, personnel assignments, start dates, completion dates, and IT support requirements. A full-time business coordinator must be responsible for this plan. If business areas choose to ignore these requirements, they could find themselves in a precarious position when the Year 2000 arrives.

Performing a business risk assessment should not be a long, drawn out process. Analysts must move quickly to establish a barometer by which to gauge organizational exposure to the Year 2000 problem and to verify that the resolution phase of a Year 2000 initiative focuses the proper level of resources on mission-critical systems. Ongoing monitoring of these risks may eventually lead to the invocation of contingency plans when time runs out on project teams attempting to meet very tight Year 2000 resolution deadlines.

2.3 Evolving Application Package Options

Recognizing the need to inventory, analyze, and upgrade vendor-supplied software packages, whether they are system software or application packages, is critical to the success of virtually every Year 2000 initiative. Management should not be caught off-guard by assuming that vendor packages are Year 2000 compliant or that the situation is well under control at the vendor site. In many cases, the complexities of achieving Year 2000 compliance in a vendor package environment are as great as those found in a custom-built software environment. The following scenarios outline how management might pursue certain package upgrade options based on various levels of vendor compliance. Unfortunately, several of these scenarios are based on real-life situations currently being played out in the industry.

2.3.1 Vendor Has Delivered Compliant System

This situation is the best case scenario. Once a compliant system has been delivered from a package vendor to the application team, management has regained control of the destiny of the business area that this package supports. Implementation and testing must proceed immediately. Prior to obtaining the package, the vendor should have provided answers to the questions outlined in Figure 2.9. Under this scenario, questions 6 through 9 are of particular interest. These issues are discussed below.

1. *Address unrelated functional updates to compliant release as follows:*

   - If vendor integrated functional changes into compliant release (which complicates testing and is ill-advised), work with vendor to develop appropriate test plan.

   - If you have modified vendor source code, consider moving back to vendor baseline and foregoing customized changes to achieve compliance.

- If custom modifications must be added into new vendor release, utilize change control tools to automate identification and reinsertion of custom changes.

- If vendor package was surrounded with custom programs, synchronize update changes for these programs with the compliance approach employed by vendor.

2. *Propagate data interface and related compliance modifications*

   - If vendor employed date field expansion, either mimic approach in interface systems or build bridges and/or interface routines to accommodate new data formats.

   - If vendor expanded selected key and/or sort fields, be sure to expand these fields in all programs sharing data with vendor package.

   - If procedural workaround (windowing) was employed by vendor, ensure that same windowing technique is used in all interface systems.

   - If vendor used a base date calculation, consider impact of this approach on interface systems and employ similar approaches judiciously (these routines may be tricky).

3. *Obtain and/or develop date certification tests plans and results*

   - Request vendor test plans, test data, and test results prior to building your test plan.

   - If vendor refuses to provide these, ask them how you can be sure the system was certified compliant.

   - If vendor continues to refuse to provide test plans and results, work with user groups to pressure vendor into providing this information.

   - Incorporate test plans, test data, and test results into your testing process.

4. *Determine impact of new release on installation lead times as follows:*

   - Develop realistic plan to install new release that accommodates earliest system failure date.

   - Consider interface and bridge development, custom code changes, propagation of vendor compliance approach and testing in calculating lead times.

   - Be sure to assign adequate personnel and hardware resources in project plan.

- Accommodate multirelease upgrade requirement with distribution plan.

- Review project plan and progress with project office early and often.

Remember that when a vendor delivers the compliant version of a package to your door, the real work is just beginning. It could take up to six to nine months until comprehensive implementation and distribution (in the case of mid-range or distributed systems) is completed. Plan accordingly.

Year 2000 Package Software Questionnaire

1. Is product Year 2000 compliant (will it process time dependent events, regardless of century value)?

2. Which releases are compliant / not compliant?

3. What strategy is vendor recommending to help customers deal with the Year 2000 issue?

4. What approach was used to ensure compliance (expanded dates, workaround strategy, a mix)?

5. What is time frame for making current release compliant?

6. How much lead time do customers have to install new release prior to encountering century date problems?

7. How will data interfaces impact customers in compliant versions (i.e. force them to expand all, selected or no date fields)?

8. What kind of date certification tests were / are being performed?

9. Were / are other updates applied to compliant version of product?

Figure 2.9   Detailed information is required to develop a comprehensive vendor package strategy.

2.3.2 Vendor Fixed the System, But It Is Still Not Compliant

Occasionally a vendor will deliver a new release that is said to be compliant but in reality is not. This situation should be discovered either during a walk-through of the changes that have been applied, or during testing. Some guidelines for uncovering this situation and determining what to do when it occurs are discussed below.

1. *Pursue the following steps to facilitate early discovery of noncompliant packages*

   - Request audit trail reports depicting compliance changes applied to source code from the vendor (these are output from remediation and/or change control tool).

   - If vendor cannot produce these reports, contact a vendor executive and reevaluate the process used to achieve compliance.

- In absence of above, run your own source code comparison tool between last baseline version of product and compliant version.

- Alternatively run an impact analysis tool to see what was done to dates and date logic.

- Review changes to see if vendor applied their alleged solution and if solution will work.

- Use these audit trails and impact results as input to the testing process.

- When you are comfortable with the fact that the system underwent an appropriate compliance upgrade, proceed with testing.

2. *When testing for compliance*

- Ensure that you have an adequate test plan and test data in place (refer to testing chapters later in this book).

- Establish a feedback loop with the vendor so that problems can be turned into fixes quickly and efficiently.

- If minor noncompliant discrepancies are found, report these for correction.

- If extensive noncompliant discrepancies are found, halt testing run or rerun analysis in step 1 above and meet with vendor to obtain a new release.

3. *Upon discovering noncompliant package code, consider the following steps*

- Work with vendor to obtain a new release.

- Work with in-house counsel to alert them to problems (they may need to act later).

- Alert users to the fact that discrepancies have occurred.

- Monitor and manage lead times appropriately.

4. *For systems where source is not delivered with the package, consider the following issues*

- Omit the source code analysis process discussed in step 1 above, but continue to request vendor audit trail results (these become even more important now).

- Move into the certification testing stage quickly, using vendor test plans and data where available.

- Work closely with vendor to determine data format modifications and compliance approach in order to synchronize updates with in-house developed code.

5. *For distributed system packages where multiple copies of the system are deployed, consider the following points*

   - Centralize compliance testing so as to minimize replication of testing process at remote sites.

   - Determine if custom changes have been applied at distributed processing sites and adjust lead times.

   - Determine if standard deployment time (which in some companies can be up to 12 months) is adequate based on vendor lead times and adjust as required.

Management should note that vendors attempting to deliver a compliant version of a package will likely run into compliance problems. These issues should be planned for and worked into the schedule. Team up with the vendor to ensure that the process goes smoothly.

2.3.3 Vendor Is Fixing System, But Delivery Times Misses the Compliance Deadline

Even the most honorable vendor can miscalculate lead times when targeting a compliance deadline. Many vendor packages, after all, are legacy systems with complicated data and date formats that can easily delay a remediation project. This explanation is not an excuse for a software vendor that should have known better, just the reality of the situation. Consider the following when you run into this problem.

1. *Run an impact analyzer on system source code to determine impact of hitting a failure date prior to 2000*

   - Review references to hard-coded dates that project forward in time.

   - Review references to expiration dates, due dates, maturity dates, or other dates that project into the future.

   - Look for screen inputs that request future date values.

2. *Determine if a code patch can keep system working past failure point (for example, the credit card industry patched systems to hard code "99" into expiration date year field).*

3. *If a patch is not acceptable, investigate manual workaround options (for example, calculate sales forecast manually until system is made compliant).*

4. *If failure point is 1/1/2000 (or just beyond this date) and you cannot get the system fixed in time, invoke contingency options that may include*

    •   Replacing the package with another package (this option would need to be invoked with at least a one to two year lead time).

    •   Employing manual workarounds (issuing invoices manually, taking reservations by hand, etc.) until the system is fixed.

    •   Letting the system work in a failed state for a period of time (this option is rarely feasible, but some systems are currently malfunctioning and nobody has noticed).

    •   Pursuing other options jointly determined by the business and IT team.

This situation is not a good one and can be minimized by maintaining close contact with the vendor at a technical and management level. The worst thing that can happen to one in this case is to be blindsided by a failed package.

2.3.4 *Vendor Refuses to Provide Compliance Status*

Comprehensive information regarding a package vendor's status is required to make certain implementation decisions. Figure 2.9 outlines key questions that an application package vendor must provide in order for IT teams to implement and test a compliant release. Support teams may need to be extremely persistent in order to gain access to this information. A vendor who refuses to provide accurate information regarding compliance status creates a frustrating situation for IT teams and business users. In cases where a vendor refuses to cooperate, the following options should be considered as quickly as possible.

1. *Review contract language to assess options for performing an internal audit at the vendor site.*

2. *Work with other users of the product, through a user group if possible, to assess how multiple companies using the product might bring pressure on the vendor to disclose status.*

3. *Meet with legal counsel in order to put pressure on the vendor to disclose Year 2000 status.*

4. *Have in-house teams determine exact event horizons so that code can be patched to keep it functioning for at least an interim period of time (see Section 2.3.3).*

5. *If the vendor goes out of business or states that they are refusing to upgrade the product, review options in Section 2.3.5.*

6. *Bring legal proceedings to collect whatever you can from the vendor in mone-tary damages.*

2.3.5 Vendor is Not Going to Fix the System

When a vendor states that they are not going to fix the system, one may feel a sense of both panic and relief. While you should be thankful that the vendor is being honest, your organization is now on its own to address the Year 2000 problem with the system. The following options should be considered.

1. *Determine if the source code is available for possible modification*

    - Review vendor contract to assess options for obtaining code from escrow account.

    - Use backup version of source code if contract permits.

    - If selected modules are missing, consider using source recovery options (see vendor tools references in Appendix).

2. *If source is available and legal team authorizes you to proceed, begin remedia-tion work on system to meet compliance deadline.*

3. *If deadline is pre-2000, consider patching the system to keep it functioning until full remediation effort is completed (see notes in Section 2.3.3).*

4. *Consider teaming with other companies in the same situation as follows:*

    - Identify other users of the system (user groups are a good source).

    - Consider forming a consortium to maintain the system centrally.

    - See if this consortium of users (possibly working with a consulting company) could tackle the compliance upgrade project as an inte-grated team.

    - Consider developing an integrated certification testing team to streamline this process and reduce the work required by any one company.

5. *Where source code is completely unavailable, consider the following business-based contingency options:*

- Review replacement options for small systems with enough lead times using another package or comparable in-house system.

- Determine if users can perform tasks manually until system is replaced.

- Consider shutting down or selling the business unit that depends on this system.

- Let the system fail and adjust business processes accordingly.

6. *Continue legal proceedings to collect whatever monetary damages you can from the vendor.*

This last situation may seem like a worst case scenario, but it is uncertainty of a vendor's position that seems to cause the most ulcers in this industry. Nobody likes to be strung along and vendors should strive to resolve these issues directly with their client and customer base. This cooperation will, hopefully, minimize litigation—where no one wins.

2.4 Strategies for the Far Behind

If you are reading this now and are still in the midst of a Year 2000 enterprise assessment and/or inventory project, you must streamline assessment deliverables to an absolute minimum. This minimization initiative means managing risk by assessing project priorities based on business impact and, secondarily, on event horizons. This effort may translate into letting a low priority reporting system fail, while remediation teams fix a high-impact trading, clearing, order entry, assembly, or maintenance system. Management must also begin to initiate painful triage discussions. For example, do we let one system die and save another system or should executives shut down the entire business unit?

In order to help with these decisions, we have outlined some guidelines to ultimately reduce risk, while following a path to safe corner cutting. We have summarized essential mobilization, enterprise assessment, infrastructure upgrade, remediation and testing tasks that streamline certain recommendations identified in our last book. We reiterate where certain tasks should continue to be performed, even though time lines are tight. Finally, we offer guidance on selecting those top five "must fix" systems that you will begin fixing as soon as you finish reading this chapter.

2.4.1 Targeting to Reduce Risk

As of right now, a Year 2000 "to do" list has two major items that require attention: keep mission-critical systems working as failure dates arrive and ensure that third parties do not bring you down. These requirements mean delivering remediation projects on mission-critical systems, monitoring compliance work with key business partners or other external entities, and performing certification tests on systems already believed to be compliant. This effort is a risk mitigation strategy that, frankly, many IT professionals may have a hard time swallowing. There will always be the desire to fix a "pet" system or fix an ancillary reporting system because a user does not believe that data can be presented in any other format. Battles will be waged, but when all is said and done, the systems that keep you in business must be the ones that you fix.

The risk-based prioritization plan presented in the previous risk assessment section is key to winning this battle. Communicating this concept to business units and executives that may still not fully grasp the enormity of the problem is likely to be the overriding challenge—along with minor disruptions caused by triaging noncritical systems. We want to reiterate our emphasis for building an internal and external communication strategy, particularly when senior executives turn their attention to the Year 2000 problem for the first time. They will want quick answers and the risk mitigation will, in the end, provide them with what they need to know to make and communicate difficult decisions.

2.4.2 "Safe" Corner Cutting

Organizations are now reaching a point where they are going to cut corners and take shortcuts. This situation is fine if they cut corners in noncritical areas and continue to pursue solutions where corner cutting is not an option. The problem is that many organizations do not see the difference. We have developed some suggestions as to where one can cut time out of a Year 2000 project and where one generally should not. If you disagree with a premise in one case or another and have a good reason for disagreeing, then by all means proceed with your original intentions. The point here is that many organizations are not following common-sense guidelines when the clock is ticking down.

The following list suggests areas where corner cutting is acceptable for various Year 2000 project phases.

1. *Mobilization*

    - Raising awareness—minimize your social calls and limit them to essential sponsorship building.
    - Meetings to discuss progress—limit them and communicate via e-mail and status reports.
    - Building a process or methodology—you can buy or lease one.
    - Tool analysis—skip this process entirely in this phase.
    - Third-party consulting selection—do not dally, be quick about it, and try to select a company that can serve as an integrator of other third-party solutions.
    - Advisory board—attempt to utilize existing standing committees where possible.
    - Quick inventory—refer to the enterprise assessment section below.
    - Preliminary risk assessment—boils down to selecting those top five, high priority systems.
    - Building an enterprise assessment plan—just do it.

2. *Enterprise assessment*

    - RFP (Request For Proposal) creation—no one will reply or if they do, they are likely to be unqualified.
    - Tool analysis—you do not have the time at this stage, so pick an inventory tool that meets minimum requirements.
    - Inventory—you will need one sooner or later, so create a first-cut inventory for core systems, begin work on these and refine the list as you proceed.
    - Identifying internal data interchanges—if you are using the procedural approach (windowing), this item is not overly critical.
    - Building detailed upgrade unit remediation plans—skip it, they can be created just prior to beginning work on an upgrade unit.
    - Detailed budget finalization—with time being the enemy, just take a broad stroke at a budget (detailed budgets are usually wrong anyway) and refine it as you go.

3. *Infrastructure setup and stabilization*

- Standards and guidelines—get what you can from the Internet and build the rest as you go.
- Configuration and change control—avoid drastic changes while focusing on the management of change control for remediation projects.
- Production turnover processes—stabilize to the point required for this project.
- Remediation work environment—conversion factories alleviate much of this work and be sure to utilize readily available hardware and software environments.
- Testing environment analysis—spend your time on high-risk applications.
- Tracking repository—keep it to a simple Access database if at all possible.
- Special infrastructure upgrade projects—focus efforts on stabilizing test environments for mission-critical business areas.

4. *Remediation*

- Building an RFP—no one will reply or if they do, you do not want them working on your project.
- Tool analysis—use whatever your consultants recommend or get recommendations from other companies that have remediation work underway.
- Date field expansion—apply this solution judiciously and selectively.
- If you use date field expansion, delay screen and report field redesign (it complicates testing) until post-1999.
- Be sure to shut off unused reports in systems before fixing or testing a system (they waste valuable analysis time).
- Do not fix programs or systems that are no longer in use (this advice may seem obvious, but one company fixed 400 programs that are not in production).
- Sort utility special date handling features (no expansion required)—can be used as long as you plan to correct the unexpanded dates later (post-1999).
- Avoid fixing obsolete languages and one-of-a-kind technologies—consider triage or replacement, particularly for end-user systems.
- Remember to fix mission-critical systems as a top priority.

5. *Testing*

- Apply risk-based testing guidelines (see chapters on testing for more detail) to avoid overtesting low-risk/low-date impact systems.

- Do not spend inordinate amounts of time driving up test data coverage on low-risk/low-date impact systems.

- Limit special case and boundary testing to high-impact/highly date-dependent systems.

6. *External entity management*

- Organize external entities into high-, medium-, and low-impact categories.

- Limit communications with low- and medium-impact third parties to letters and phone calls.

- Follow similar screening procedures when examining external data interchange.

2.4.3 Unacceptable Corner Cutting

The following list suggests areas where corner cutting is *not* an option. Again, use common sense because no single set of guidelines applies to every situation or company.

1. *Mobilization*

- Establish a project office quickly to cover project planning and tracking, user interface, vendor contracting, communications, and general oversight functions.

- Develop at least a ballpark budget (the line of code model serves this purpose).

- Begin project planning and tracking immediately.

2. *Enterprise assessment*

- Triage—begin tossing systems out of the plan at the inventory level.

- External data exchange analysis should not delay remediation work but pursue this analysis throughout the life of the project—watch for event horizons.

- System software inventory—you still need to get a list, test questionable releases, and coordinate lead times with test environments.

- Packages—get to the vendors quickly to assess compliance status and strategy.

- Ballpark a plan based on immediately apparent high priority systems and get moving.

3. *Infrastructure setup and stabilization*

- If you are using a conversion factory or off-site facility, be sure to establish procedures for packaging, shipping, and returning upgrade units.

- If you are fixing systems in-house, utilize automated remediation tools—they are getting much more sophisticated.

- Assess testing weaknesses in high-risk business areas and take appropriate action (see testing point 5).

4. *Remediation*

- Make sure that managers develop project plans prior to starting remediation projects and manage those plans.

- Monitor overruns, particularly in development or replacement projects where contingency plans may need to be invoked.

- Do not utilize bogus solutions—like time-boxing a system into running in a -28-year time frame.

- If procedural workaround techniques are employed, verify that interfacing systems select the same windowing strategy.

- Check audit trails closely—whether they come from conversion factories or in-house teams.

- Track library utilization carefully—it is easy to mix up the original and the upgraded versions of a system.

- Do not get fancy with your solutions—keep them simple and you will reduce the error introduction rate.

5. *Testing*

- Increase test data coverage for high-risk/high-date impact applications.

- Work with subject matter experts and/or users to create special case test data for high-risk/high-date impact systems.

- Document testing procedures for mission-critical systems.

- Ensure that plans are in place to test high-impact data interfaces with external partners.

6. *External entity management*

- Develop inventory of business partners, suppliers, agents, brokers, and so on and sort them into high-, medium-, and low-impact categories.

- Review compliance plans and status for high-impact partners closely.

- If supply chain continuity is an issue, manage first-tier supplier compliance status closely.

2.4.4 Launch Top Five Priority Remediation Projects

Launching initial remediation projects today is very different from launching pilot projects a couple of years ago. There is no time for extraneous pilot tests where noncritical systems are upgraded, but not returned to production. Each project launched from this point forward must have meaning—particularly the first projects out the door. The first Year 2000 remediation and testing projects should adhere to the following general guidelines.

1. *Identify your most critical business areas and the systems that support those business areas.*

2. *Identify five systems that require Year 2000 remediation and/or testing.*

3. *If you plan to utilize an off-site conversion center, launch at least some of the projects with that vendor.*

4. *If work is being performed in-house, set up the tools and processes and launch one or more in-house remediation projects.*

5. *Try to find one critical system that is allegedly compliant and schedule a certification test for that system as a means of shaking down the testing process and test environment.*

6. *Be sure to manage off-site work carefully and refine the processes and guidelines required for future projects in these initial projects.*

7. *If one or more of these projects applies to embedded systems, system software, hardware upgrades, or other infrastructure-related activities, pursue these projects quickly.*

There is no magic to launching high priority projects and five is not a number that has any special meaning to it. The bottom line is that if organizations do not start upgrading systems to achieve compliance soon, full-scale deployment will be out of reach. In addition, until you actually convert a system and go through the testing process, you will not know what it takes to perform this work in your environment. The same is true for testing a relationship with a newly signed on vendor. As Nike says, "just do it!"

2.5 Beating the Clock in 1998 and 1999

It is not always the swiftest runners who ultimately win the race. We learned this when we were young and first read the story of the tortoise and the hare. Comments from Irene Dec, vice-president at Prudential Insurance in New Jersey, support this premise. If anyone has reason to consider the Year 2000 problem to be an overwhelming challenge, it is the program manager for an insurance company with more than 100 million lines of code. Dec states that companies must "strategically determine business risks and establish schedules based on what is most important to customers and the business. Trying to correct every application is a sure path to failure. Running a year 2000 program means driving a smart, strategic approach. Implementation of a status tracking program is critical or you get stuck in awareness."

Dec also adds that "if you are just starting out, be smart and be strategic." The race against time in 1998 and 1999 will not be won by Year 2000 teams with the fastest coders or with the best tools. It will be won by those organizations that manage risk, work smart, and remain calm when others panic. This challenge will be the true test for many organizations.

Legal Issues and Protections

As if the technological challenges posed by the Year 2000 crisis were not enough, companies also have to worry about the legal aspects of the problem, or more specifically, being sued. Why should companies dwell on, or even plan for, litigation? Unlike other IT-centric problems, the Year 2000 issue affects virtually every aspect of a corporation, and virtually every corporation. Like other large-scale, widespread social disasters, such as the savings and loan crisis, environmental contamination, and asbestos poisoning, the Year 2000 crisis will spawn copious finger pointing and litigation. All of the factors conducive to litigation are present—large amounts of money are at stake, the problem itself is quite complex, and some degree of failure is inevitable. In total, Year 2000 failures have far-reaching, significant economic consequences. Even compliant corporations may suffer financial and other damages if they interact with other organizations that are not themselves compliant.

Whenever there are significant risks of exposure—financial and otherwise—organizations will seek to shift those risks to others. Similarly, when risks do materialize, and an organization suffers the consequences, it will seek to be made whole for any damages by pursuing claims against responsible parties. Dealing with these risks affects many aspects of a corporation's business, from how it drafts contracts, conducts tax planning, staffs its departments, and discloses material public information. Planning for and reacting to these risks and damages is a necessary part of any Year 2000 effort.

The legal landscape affecting companies' planning and conduct in the face of the Year 2000 crisis is constantly changing. During the latter half of 1997, and carrying into 1998, a series of unrelated events charged the Year 2000 atmosphere. Government hearings skyrocketed, Congressional bills were introduced, federal agencies were put more and more on the hot seat, the SEC and IRS came out with public statements concerning Year 2000, federal and state officials held a compliance summit, and there were even rumors that President Clinton would ask the European community to postpone the Euro implementation to devote resources to Year 2000 compliance. By the time this book is published, the authors expect that even more significant changes will have unfolded. As the non-IT community of legislators, regulators, lawyers, economists, and analysts more fully grasp the breadth of the Year 2000 problem, there will be a plethora of public reaction in the form of legislation, regulations, hearings, committees, guidelines, lawsuits, market adjustments, and on and on. Our strong advice to readers is to keep up-to-date on the legal landscape by consulting reputable publications, your lawyers, tax advisors, and others to determine what the best stance is, legally, for your company.

The authors call your attention to the fact that they are not lawyers and have no legal training. Therefore, the contents of this chapter should not be construed as legal advice. Individuals and companies should consult their own lawyers and advisors for advice in their particular situations. The authors wish to thank the San Francisco-based law firm of Thelen, Marrin, Johnson & Bridges, pioneers in providing Year 2000 legal insight and services, for their instrumental help and guidance in formulating this chapter. Thelen, Marrin, Johnson & Bridges maintains a Web site at www.tmjb.com containing many informative articles on the Year 2000 issues. Many of the lawyers at Thelen, Marrin, Johnson & Bridges lecture at Year 2000 conferences worldwide. In addition, the authors wish to acknowledge the Washington, D.C. law firm of Dickstein, Shapiro, Morin & Oshinsky for their practical insight on Year 2000 insurance issues.

This chapter is divided into seven sections. The first section explains why the reader should be concerned about the legal aspects of the Year 2000 problem. The second section describes ways in which a company can minimize its Year 2000 costs and risks. The third section discusses certain vendor issues, followed by a section on how to create a paper trail for future litigation. The fifth and sixth sections contain a brief update on insurance and government issues. The final section touches on other legal aspects of the Year 2000 problem including employment, offshore conversion, and copyright issues.

3.1 Why You Should Care About This Legal Stuff

There are many stakeholders in the Year 2000 crisis and each will be affected in some way as we progress toward the year 2000. Stakeholders include companies, directors, officers, managers, employees, vendors, shareholders, lawyers, accountants, government employees, suppliers, and on and on. Every time a corporation makes a decision to draft a contract in a particular way, to take a tax deduction, to publicly disclose financial information, there is an effect on some stakeholder. A tax deduction may result in more expendable income enabling a company to hire more employees. A contract may be drafted such that the vendor, and its employees' jobs, are completely at risk if a Year 2000 project fails. Disclosing negative financial information can lower stock prices and severely impact the profitability of a corporation.

In some cases, the individual directors and officers of a corporation may be personally liable to the shareholders of the corporation for damages resulting from Year 2000 problems. This liability arises from the fact that, legally, these persons have a fiduciary duty to act in the best interests of the corporation. A director or officer must meet an applicable standard of care, defined by state law, in order to avoid personal liability. These "standards of care" may be defined under state law but may also be developed by the courts. Figure 3.1 contains a sample statutory provision defining the duty of care that a director must bring to his or her job.

Duty of Care –
California Corporation Code

A director shall perform the duties of a director, including duties as a member of any committee of the board upon which the director may serve, in good faith, in a manner such director believes to be in the best interests of the corporation and its shareholders and with such care, including reasonable inquiry, as an ordinarily prudent person in a like position would use under similar circumstances.

Figure 3.1 Duty of Care—California Corporation Code.

A director or officer is generally permitted to use his or her own "business judgment" when arriving at decisions. Courts are usually reluctant to examine whether or not a particular business decision was sound or to substitute their judgment for that of the corporate officers and directors. However, in order to take advantage of the "business judgment" defense and to strengthen similar due diligence defenses, directors and officers should document their efforts in dealing with the Year 2000 problem. In the event of future litigation, key factors in establishing a defense might include how long it took the directors to reach a decision, how well-informed each person was, whether any inquiry was made into the matter, whether reliance on outside information was reasonable, and whether alternative courses of action were considered. The remainder of this chapter discusses some of the things that directors and officers can do, and can have the company do, to show that they diligently investigated and addressed their Year 2000 problem.

Besides personal liability for the directors and officers of a company, the company itself is at risk of shareholder lawsuits and enforcement actions by federal or state securities authorities. These lawsuits are typically based on a public company's failure to sufficiently disclose its Year 2000 problem in its public filings with the Securities and Exchange Commission (SEC) or with state securities regulators.

3.2 Minimizing Costs and Exposure

A company can take several measures to minimize Year 2000 costs and expenses. First, steps can be taken to proactively minimize the Year 2000 remediation costs that the company must bear. Second, steps can be taken to proactively minimize and shift the risks, and economic consequences, of Year 2000 noncompliance to other organizations. These steps are memorialized in documents, contracts, and agreements entered into by a company. These agreements are often drafted to avoid future disputes and litigation, but, if future litigation is inevitable, they hopefully serve to ensure a predictable outcome.

3.2.1 Contract Issues

In an effort to minimize the cost of and exposure to Year 2000 risks, all companies, including users and vendors of IT products and services, should review existing contracts to determine their current rights and obligations. Going forward, companies should carefully structure new contracts, licenses, and agreements to obtain assurances that products and services will accommodate the century change. In each case, companies should consult their tax advisors to ensure that agreements are properly crafted to produce the desired tax consequences.

To minimize or shift the costs of century compliance, companies should conduct a legal analysis of all current contracts, including representations, warranties, limitations on liability, indemnification, and other significant provisions. This analysis should focus on identifying the party that may be legally responsible for solving the problem, contributing to fixing it or paying for any damages resulting from Year 2000 failures. Warranties typically serve as the basis for holding a party responsible for remediation costs. For example, a party may warrant that "the software will perform in accordance with its documentation" while the documentation may state that the software is Year 2000 compliant. Liability provisions indicate what types of claims or damages a party is liable for (actual or consequential damages), and the extent to which a party may be held liable (usually expressed in dollars). Following this contract review, a company should consider sending appropriate written notices to each responsible party, notifying them of their obligations under the contract. See Section 3.3 for a discussion of certification letters.

In most cases, companies will find that existing contracts do not specifically address the Year 2000 issue. Rather than expressly addressing Year

2000 compliance, general contractual language dealing with "failure to perform" or "substantial nonperformance" will be the operative warranty terms. See Figure 3.2 for sample warranty language that could be triggered if a Year 2000 problem surfaces. In simple terms, this warranty states that if the software doesn't perform according to its documentation, within the 90-day window after it is delivered to the customer, then the vendor's only obligation is to make reasonable efforts to correct the problem. Defects encountered after the 90-day window are not covered by the warranty. If the vendor cannot correct a problem covered by the warranty, then it will refund the money paid for the software but the customer has to return the software. The vendor does not have any obligations under the warranty if the customer changes the software.

Non-Year 2000 Specific Warranty

Licensor warrants that the Software, for a period of ninety (90) days after delivery to Licensee, shall perform substantially in accordance with the Documentation. Licensee's exclusive remedy and Licensor's sole liability under this warranty shall be for Licensor to attempt through reasonable efforts to correct any material failure of the Software to perform as warranted, if such failure is reported to Licensor within the warranty period and Licensee, at Licensor's request, provides Licensor with sufficient information (which may include access to Licensee's computer system for use of Licensee's copy(ies) of the Software by Licensor) to reproduce the defect in question. Licensor shall have no liability with respect to any failure of the Software to perform as warranted under this section if such failure results from any changes or modifications made to the Software by Licensee. In the event that Licensor cannot, after repeated efforts, remedy such failure, Licensor shall refund any license payments actually received by Licensor from Licensee hereunder and terminate this Agreement, provided that Licensee has returned all copies of the Software and Documentation. This warranty is made solely to Licensee and Licensee shall be solely responsible for any warranty to, or claims by, end-users or other third parties.

Figure 3.2   Non-Year 2000 Specific Warranty.

Hopefully, the responsible party under the contract will be induced to undertake the remediation itself either to avoid Year 2000 problems or to avoid potential liability. Companies may find that they are responsible for performing all remediation work and cannot look to another party to defray the cost. Even if a third party is legally responsible for performing the remediation, it may not have sufficient economic or other incentives to do so. For example, a vendor may choose to declare bankruptcy rather than incur the cost of upgrading thousands of versions of packaged software that it has sold over the past 20 years. Or some hardware and software vendors may decide either to abandon their products or to force customers to upgrade to the latest versions in lieu of spending money to fix Year 2000 problems. In these situations, suing a vendor provides little benefit because the vendor will either not have the money to fix Year 2000 problems or will be facing so many lawsuits that the chances of a significant monetary recovery are slight.

Even when the wording of a particular contract appears to be unambiguous, in the American legal system there is always room for a difference of opinion. Therefore, despite the most careful contract analysis, and regardless of whether the contract obviously appears to address an issue in a particular way, there is apt to be litigation concerning who is responsible for performing Year 2000 upgrades and paying for them. Lawyers will sue software vendors on behalf of buyers, making claims that seem implausible to the vendors. Vendors will sue other vendors based upon claims that may or may not be appear to be justified. If there is money to be made by lawyers and their clients, lawsuits will be launched no matter what a contract obviously appears to say.

Sometimes mission-critical and other key licensed software is accompanied by an escrow agreement. The purpose of the escrow agreement is to ensure that the licensee can continue using the software in the event of some typically disastrous event such as the bankruptcy of the licensor, the failure to ship additional software, and so on. The source code to the software is held by an escrow agent, a neutral third party, that can be petitioned to hand over the source code to the licensee when one of the release conditions is triggered. Upon a release, the escrow agreement normally spells out the terms of the license to the source code that will be granted to the licensee. Companies should carefully review all escrow agreements to see if the release conditions encompass the refusal of the licensor to remedy an inevitable failure of the software. If a licensor refuses to remedy a potential Year 2000 failure, or refuses to respond to company inquiries, then the company must be prepared to act quickly to petition the escrow agent for access to the source code. If the software is truly key to company operations, then the sooner the company can obtain the source code, the sooner it can start addressing Year 2000 issues. When modifying licensed software, beware of the copyright issues discussed in Section 3.7 and the terms of the original software warranty. Most warranties are automatically voided if third parties perform software modification work without the authorization of the licensor.

In future contracts and agreements, most companies purchasing hardware, software, and services will insist on express Year 2000 representations and warranties. If they have sufficient leverage, they will probably succeed in having some language addressing the issue in the contract. Figure 3.3 contains a sample Year 2000 warranty. Warranties and representations that only vaguely address Year 2000 compliance will be worthless; they will either provide no protection to the buyer or will expose the seller to unlimited risk of litigation for breach of the representation or warranty.

Year 2000 Specific Warranty

Licensor warrants to Licensee that the Software accommodates same-century and multi-century date values and same-century and multi-century data processing capabilities, and that the Software will neither fail due to, nor produce incorrect results in, date-related processing, including in connection with dates later than 1999.

Figure 3.3   Year 2000 Specific Warranty.

Companies may also need to enter into other types of ancillary agreements during the course of their Year 2000 projects. Because the problem is so pervasive and impacts relations with vendors, suppliers, partners, employees, and others, there will be a greater need for sharing information, some of which may be valuable trade secrets or intellectual property. For instance, in order to determine whether packaged software is truly compliant, a company may wish to review the changes that were made to the source code. Appropriate nondisclosure, escrow, and access agreements will need to be crafted to enable all parties to share information while protecting company intellectual property assets. In the employment arena, creative compensation packages and specialized noncompete agreements may be required.

Any company that is engaged in or planning a merger or acquisition should conduct business due diligence to determine what, if anything, has been done or planned for the Year 2000. The results of this diligence should be reflected in the various provisions of the transactional documents. Given the cost of the typical Year 2000 project, a buyer will want to adjust the purchase price based upon the Year 2000 work remaining to be done. Appropriate warranties, representations, indemnification, and purchase price adjustment provisions should also be negotiated based upon the results of the diligence. In some cases, a buyer may want the right to rescind the transaction if Year 2000 problems are much larger than anticipated. If diligence discloses that Year 2000 issues are wildly out of control at the seller, the buyer may decide to forgo the transaction rather than assume an unknown, potentially huge, liability. For ongoing Year 2000 projects, a buyer may need to provide "golden handcuffs" to the project team members to ensure that they remain committed employees throughout the course of the project. Overlaying all of these concerns is the fact that, in some industries, regulatory bodies must approve the merger or acquisition. As part of the approval process, these bodies may review the parties' Year 2000 plans and condition their approval on the adequacy of those plans.

3.2.2 Disclosure Obligations

A public or private company confronting the Year 2000 problem, whether as a user or supplier of IT products and services, must generally disclose the problem to some extent to the investing public. Every company is legally required to inform its investors of all "material" facts known to the company at the time when each investor makes an investment decision. These disclosure requirements are embodied in a legal regime overseen by the SEC. The statutes, rules, and regulations enforced by the SEC are grounded in antifraud concepts. To prevent companies from defrauding investors, these securities laws provide that a company cannot sell or buy its securities unless it has disclosed all material information to its investors. This disclosure obligation extends to trends or uncertainties that are known to management and which can be reasonably expected to have an unfavorable effect on company income or operations. Disclosure occurs at various points in time, most typically in reports filed on a quarterly (10-Q) and annual (10-K) basis with the SEC.

There is no single, simple test to determine if information is material. Rather, information is generally deemed to be material if it would have been important to a reasonable investor in determining whether to buy, sell, or hold a security. As companies prepare their SEC reports, or make public statements concerning company performance, they must apply this "materiality" filter to all information which appears to be eligible for disclosure. Unfortunately, the question of whether information is truly material is most often determined in hindsight, when an investor sues a company for failing to disclose material information that resulted in some harm to the investor.

How do these legal standards apply in the Year 2000 context? Generally, companies face three significant Year 2000 issues: the cost of fixing the problem, the cost of not fixing the problem in time, and the risk of third-party failures. Using the materiality test described above, if Year 2000 remediation costs, the cost of anticipated internal failures, or the failure of a critical vendor to supply goods due to Year 2000 problems are material to the income or operations of the company, then disclosure is not only appropriate, it is also required. For example, if a company with a traditional, annual IT budget of $4 million faces a bill of $15 million in remediation costs, that would likely be a material fact requiring disclosure. On the other hand, two companies facing identical Year 2000 project costs could reach opposite disclosure decisions depending on whether the costs were significant when compared to company cash flow. Further, if Year 2000-related issues constitute a "known trend or uncertainty" reasonably expected to result in unfavorable effects on company income or operations, then they must also be disclosed. Given some of the published costs of implementing a Year 2000 remediation plan, and considering the potentially disastrous results of not achieving timely compliance, either alone or with external providers, it is difficult to imagine how any company could deem its own Year 2000 project, and the potential impact of external failures, as immaterial.

In situations where Year 2000 remediation costs, or the specter of noncompliance, are so unquantifiable that a company feels it cannot provide meaningful disclosure, SEC guidance states that the company should balance the probability of the event occurring against the magnitude of the problem in deciding whether, and what, to disclose. If the cost of a company's internal Year 2000 program is immaterial, but the failure of its external suppliers in achieving Year 2000 compliance could result in an irrecoverable hit to the bottom line, then even with a 30 percent probability of occurring, the risk should be disclosed.

The SEC has not enacted specific regulations or rules requiring disclosure of Year 2000-related issues. Rather, the SEC believes that current laws—requiring disclosure of *material* events—adequately cover the Year 2000 issue. The SEC has issued guidance, in the form of Staff Legal Bulletin No. 5, on Year 2000 disclosures. In October 1997, the SEC issued its first comprehensive bulletin advising companies of their Year 2000 disclosure obligations. After several Congressmen publicly expressed their dissatisfaction with the SEC's "soft" stance, the SEC revised the bulletin in January 1998, so that companies could use the new guidance in preparing their 1997 annual filings. The revision, in strong language, requires companies to address the Year 2000 issue in their filings, even if they are uncertain as to whether their Year 2000 problems are material. Further, companies must discuss Year 2000 issues in their fillings even if they believe that their remediation, contingency or other plans will shield them from problems. The bulletin also specifies certain minimum disclosure requirements which must be "specific and meaningful" and not boilerplate.[1] While SEC staff legal bulletins do not have the force of law of an SEC rule or regulation, but rather are forms of "guidance," any company that ignores the SEC "guidance" is apt to trigger an SEC enforcement action or a class action lawsuit by shareholders. We can expect 1998 to be a watershed year in terms of Year 2000 disclosure in public filings.

Looking at actual disclosure reports filed with the SEC prior to 1998, the number of companies disclosing Year 2000 issues for the first time has increased from one in 1995 to several hundred in 1997. Disclosure has been most common among manufacturing companies than in any other non-IT sector. Although the increase in disclosure is heartening, it is still stunning to realize that the majority of companies have disclosed nothing on the issue. This means that most companies continue to view the issue as immaterial—in terms of remediation costs and the impact of third-party noncompliance—to their business.

To get a better understanding of how these disclosure requirements work in practice, we can look at some of the Year 2000 disclosures found in actual pre-1998 filings. Figure 3.4 is a good representative disclosure—it describes the current status of the Year 2000 project, the total cost of the project and its funding source, and how the company is accounting for the costs. The disclosure found in Figure 3.5 alerts the reader to the fact that third-party noncompliance could have a negative effect on the company, something that this company deemed to be material considering the nature of its internal systems. Finally, Figure 3.6 provides a disclosure example that is deficient in several respects. First, the company cites a specific date by which it will be compliant. What happens if this date isn't hit? Second, the cost of resolving the problem is not quantified, which may be a crucial piece of information for investors. Third, the company is not in a position to represent that all new software, whether developed internally or purchased as packages, will accommodate the Year 2000, since even newly-developed software may contain noncompliant code, or may fail if passed noncompliant data.

Sample Disclosure– Problem Quantified

"In January 1996, the Company began converting its computer systems to be Year 2000 compliant. Approximately 40% of the Company's systems are now compliant, with all systems expected to be compliant by the end of 1998. Total cost of the project is estimated to be $4.3 million and is being funded through operating cash flows. The Company is expensing all costs associated with these system changes. As of December 31, 1996, $1.6 million has been expensed."

© Thelen, Marrin, Johnson & Bridges LLP 1997.

Figure 3.4   Sample Disclosure—Problem Quantified.

Sample Disclosure– Interdependence

"Due to the interdependent nature of computer systems, the Company may be adversely impacted in the year 2000 depending on whether it or other entities not affiliated with the Company address this issue successfully."

© Thelen, Marrin, Johnson & Bridges LLP 1997.

Figure 3.5   Sample Disclosure—Interdependence.

Sample Disclosure-Vague
and Overly Optimistic

"Like most companies in the world, the Company is facing the Year 2000 problem. The Company plans to have its problem resolved by December 31, 1998. The Company has replaced or is in the process of updating or replacing a number of its financial application and other operating programs. The new software will accommodate the millennium change."

© Thelen, Marrin, Johnson & Bridges LLP 1997

Figure 3.6   Sample Disclosure—Vague and Overly Optimistic.

3.2.3 Company Statements

In addition to the formal reporting requirements imposed by the SEC, companies, through their spokespersons, make many more informal, yet public, statements. These public statements should be consistent with what is disclosed in the SEC reports and also should be internally consistent. For instance, if SEC disclosure documents report that Year 2000 remediation costs for a $500 million company are expected to be in the range of $50 to $75 million dollars, then the company CEO should not tell analysts that remediation costs are negligible. Similarly, if those documents disclose that Year 2000 efforts are underway and are expected to continue for two more years, the company CIO should not tell a journalist that the company is currently Year 2000 compliant.

To achieve consistency in its public Year 2000 comments, each company should have one or a few individuals responsible for developing careful, thoughtful statements relating to the issue. The company should disseminate these statements throughout the company to those individuals who make public statements about company issues in the course of their jobs. It is crucial that IT reviews and signs off on the accuracy of these statements since it has the most intimate knowledge about the current status of the Year 2000 project. In addition to these company statements, each company should have some sort of written statement or "fact piece" for its investor relations personnel to use with company investors. Once a consistent company statement is created, it should be reviewed on a periodic basis—quarterly may be sufficient—to ensure that it is current. A company should conduct quarterly reviews of the company statement at the same time that it prepares its quarterly report (10-Q) for SEC filing.

After adopting a controlled Year 2000 disclosure policy, a company has to continually monitor the efficacy of that policy to ensure that it doesn't undercut its efforts. Carefully crafted public statements may be irrelevant if the company's publicly promoted Web site contains outdated, inaccurate information that directly, or indirectly, refers to Year 2000 issues. Public statements touting the company's Year 2000 progress will be damaging in subsequent litigation if internal memos and documents refer to overwhelming Year 2000 implementation problems.

Lastly, the preceding discussion focused solely on disclosure requirements under federal law. There are other federal laws, and a large body of state laws, that may also mandate company disclosure of events or facts beyond, or in conjunction with, the federal disclosure scheme. Companies may need to investigate numerous laws applicable to them to determine whether Year 2000 issues trigger additional disclosure obligations under those laws.

3.2.4 Tax Law Issues

The Year 2000 problem will have a variety of economic consequences including federal income tax consequences relating to the costs to fix the problem. As of this writing, neither Congress, the IRS, nor the courts has explicitly addressed how remediation costs are to be treated for federal tax purposes. Tax advisors have come up with some general treatments for these remediation costs based upon existing tax law. As the magnitude and the cost of the total Year 2000 effort becomes more quantifiable, Congress and the IRS could take action to ensure that remediation costs do not adversely impact the U.S. tax base. In the interim, the following points should be considered.

A distinction should be drawn between how remediation costs are treated for tax purposes and for accounting and financial reporting purposes. First, tax treatment is determined by federal tax law while accounting treatment is determined by various regulatory agencies including the SEC and the Federal Accounting Standards Board (FASB). In many instances, the tax treatment and the accounting treatment of an item will differ and may even be opposite. Second, a company will generally want to treat costs differently on its books than it does on its tax return. For instance, if a cost is treated as a current expense, it will be subtracted from income on the books of the company, thereby immediately reducing the company's earnings. A reduction in earnings is obviously not good news for investors. On the other hand, if a cost is capitalized rather than expensed, a company will subtract only a portion of the cost from its income over a fixed period of time, thereby diminishing the reduction to earnings in any single period. Conversely, for tax purposes, a company will generally want to currently deduct or write off the entire remediation cost, thereby reducing taxable income and the amount of income taxes that it must pay. Without a current tax deduction, a company has to amortize the remediation cost, or take a portion of the deduction over time, thereby decreasing the value of the deduction.

The accounting treatment of Year 2000 remediation costs has been explicitly addressed by FASB. In 1996, FASB took the position that Year 2000 remediation costs should be expensed as incurred rather than capitalized. This requirement means that in all financial reporting, companies must subtract Year 2000 remediation costs from their income, thereby taking an immediate hit to earnings. The hit to earnings will be directly proportionate to the amount of the remediation costs. Because the majority of Year 2000 conversion efforts are multiyear, this rule means that a company's earnings may be negatively impacted over several years.

On the tax front, with limited guidance from Congress or the IRS on the issue, tax advisors have looked to existing law to determine how to interpret and apply it in the Year 2000 context. In most cases, these advisors are looking for some justification in the law for a company to currently deduct 100 percent of the remediation costs incurred during the year. To take advantage of favorable tax law provisions that might permit a current deduction, contracts dealing with the provision of Year 2000 products or services must be carefully structured.

There are two possible avenues under the tax law for currently deducting Year 2000 remediation costs—if the costs qualify as either "repairs" or "research and development" costs for self-developed property. Among other things, repairs must neither "materially add to the value of the property nor appreciably prolong its life." To determine whether remediation costs are deductible repairs, all of the facts surrounding the work must be documented and will be examined by the IRS. Given that the availability of this deduction hinges on the outcome of a very fact-specific inquiry, and that the U.S. tax base could take a big hit if every company availed itself of this deduction, it is unlikely that the IRS would, as a general matter, rule favorably on Year 2000 remediation costs as repairs.

The second way in which remediation costs may be currently deductible is if they qualify as research and development (R&D) costs. Again, any Year 2000-related contracts and agreements must be crafted especially to take advantage of this deduction. Briefly summarized, the tax laws permits a company to elect to currently deduct R&D expenditures. The company must affirmatively elect to deduct the expenses, and the expenses must satisfy certain criteria as to what constitutes "research and development." If an independent contractor incurs the R&D expenses on behalf of the company, the company must assume all of the risk of performance, that is, there can be no guaranties or warranties by the independent contractor as to the success of the results. Fixed-price contracts, where the independent contractor agrees to perform Year 2000 remediation for a set price, put all of the risk on a contractor and therefore may not merit R&D treatment.

If remediation costs do not qualify as currently deductible repairs or R&D, forcing a company to amortize the cost, then most companies prefer to amortize over the shortest period of time possible. Generally, costs attributable to computer software may be amortized over a three year period. In October 1997, the IRS issued a ruling allowing Year 2000 remediation costs to be amortized. Among tax advisors, the sentiment was that although welcomed, the ruling did not break new ground.

For companies having international operations, special tax concerns are raised when a domestic company and a foreign subsidiary engage in organizationwide Year 2000 work. Generally, when affiliates in a controlled group of corporations perform services for the benefit of another affiliate, federal tax law provides that the service provider must be compensated at market rates. If the companies do not, in fact, compensate one another in this way, which is not an unreasonable assumption, the IRS will determine what the "deemed" compensation would be and will shift income and deductions among the affiliates to arrive at the corresponding result. Since tax planning for multinational corporations is very sensitive, companies would do well not to jeopardize their careful planning by having the IRS redistribute and recalculate tax items.

3.2.5 Internal Risk Management

Every company should consider setting up an internal risk management team to ensure that Year 2000-related risks are addressed in a centralized, cohesive way. As discussed in Chapter 2, the collection of risk data is a crucial part of any Year 2000 project. Risk data helps determine the priority of system remediation and testing and is used to develop contingency plans to be invoked when Year 2000 failures loom. Each company should be able to establish that it thoroughly examined the potential risks raised by the Year 2000 issue and that it attempted to minimize those risks.

To empower the internal risk management team, executive management must sponsor and endorse the actions taken by the group. The risk team will have to interact with all parts of the organization and may, in some cases, have to request certain action to be taken by these other areas. Without executive management's stamp of approval, the risk management team would have a difficult time getting other areas to listen to them and to follow through on action items. Setting up a team and then leaving it virtually powerless is evidence that a company did not take Year 2000 issues seriously, a damaging flaw in any litigation.

Having an empowered, centralized group responsible for collecting, tracking, and monitoring risk data will be invaluable to a company in helping to prove that it acted diligently and reasonably in response to the Year 2000 crisis. If a company is unable to show that it evaluated and responded to risks in a thoughtful, reasonable fashion, it, and senior management, are likely to be viewed as having acted negligently or recklessly in the face of a known crisis.

3.3 Vendor Considerations

Many vendors will find themselves in the same situation as the customers they serve. Vendors, after all, are IT users and will often have the same packaged software issues as their customers. Vendors will need to take all of the steps mentioned above, along with every other member of the IT community.

Unlike other companies, vendors face some additional Year 2000 hurdles. Besides getting a handle on their own internal Year 2000 problems, vendors have to address the Year 2000 status of the products and services that they provide to the public, which may include responding to certification letters and providing ongoing status reports. This dual role puts vendors in the unenviable situation of having to manage "internal" and "external" Year 2000 projects, with the concomitant resource demands and scheduling difficulties. Additionally, many vendors are members of supply chains whose Year 2000 compliance is critical to the manufacturing and production of finished consumer products and goods. Supply chains raise additional issues surrounding the timing of remediation efforts and exchange of data.

Software and hardware vendors are also susceptible to class action lawsuits brought on behalf of the purchasers of their products. As discussed in Section 3.2.1, many vendors will be subject to warranty and other contract claims if their software fails to correctly handle century dates, regardless of what the contract actually says. In particular, vendors that do not agree to provide upgrades free of charge are likely to be targeted by disgruntled customers. In December 1997, the first class action lawsuit was filed against Software Business Technologies, the maker of PC-based accounting software packages, alleging that the vendor's failure to remedy Year 2000 noncompliance for free was a breach of its warranty obligations to its customers. A second, similar class action lawsuit was filed against software vendor Symantec in February 1998.

3.3.1 Certification Letters

Following the contract review described above in Section 3.2.1, most companies will send "certification" letters to their vendors. These letters essentially request the vendor to disclose the Year 2000 status of its product and/or services and, if there is any noncompliance, its plans for achieving compliance. Frequently, the letters threaten the nonrenewal of maintenance agreements for unresponsive vendors.

As with most issues, there are two different perspectives on certification letters. These dual perspectives result from the nature of our legal system which often pits companies and their vendors as opposing parties in lawsuits. Rather than emphasizing cooperation, both parties are primarily interested in protecting their own, individual positions in anticipation of potential litigation. Discussed below are company and vendor views of certification letters.

Companies sending certification letters hope to achieve several things. First, they want an answer to the question so they can make their own Year 2000 plans, factoring in the vendor's response. Second, companies want to establish that they were diligent in attempting to address the Year 2000 problem with all external entities with which they interact. Sending out certification letters may establish a due diligence baseline but more activity may be required to prove that companies acted reasonably in light of how other companies within their industry were acting. For instance, a company may need to follow up the letter with an exchange of remediation plans, continual monitoring, mutual testing, exchange of data, and so forth. Knowing what others in your industry are doing is critical to showing that a company acted prudently and with reasonable care.

A vendor that receives a certification letter may react differently depending on the products or services that it supplies and the level of its Year 2000 preparedness. Initially, a vendor's reaction may be to not volunteer information that could hurt it later. However, depending on the relationship with its customers, and the leverage that they may wield, a vendor may have to respond in some manner. Any vendor response must be carefully crafted and consistent from customer to customer. The vendor's goal in making any response is to provide as little information as possible and to not obligate itself to do anything in particular. These goals are designed to reduce the vendor's future exposure in the event of litigation. A vendor that states that it "expects its products to process century dates before the turn of the century" has not agreed to any particular timetable that could establish false hopes and claims by its customers. A vendor may find, however, that its customers will demand more meaningful, detailed information so that they can solidify their own Year 2000 plans. Further, a vendor may find that it reaps more goodwill by agreeing to work alongside its customers to resolve the problem satisfactorily.

Sending out certification letters has more ramifications than merely establishing a due diligence defense. Depending on how it is written, a certification letter could conceivably affect the ability of a company to bring a future lawsuit against the vendor because of Year 2000 noncompliance. For example, a customer may know with certainty that third-party software has a Year 2000 problem after encountering a software malfunction during a simple compliance test. Assuming that the vendor is responsive to fixing the problem, the company may fire off a letter stating that the software doesn't work and demanding that the vendor fix it. This letter serves to establish the earliest date that the company knew it had a warranty claim for nonperformance or a breach of contract claim against the vendor. Depending on the statute of limitations in the applicable state, the company will now have a fixed window of time in which to actually file suit against the vendor. If a company does not bring its claim within this time frame, it will be foreclosed from pursuing the claim against the vendor at a later date. The company alternatively could request that the vendor agree to extend the statute of limitations in exchange for the company's agreement not to bring suit immediately during which time the parties will negotiate to reach a mutually satisfactory resolution to the Year 2000 problem. The advantage of this approach is that the vendor salvages valuable time to spend actually fixing the problem instead of defending a lawsuit. From the company's perspective, it achieves its goals of spurring the vendor to action and preserving its ability to sue if things later turn sour.

3.3.2 Supply Chain/Partner Issues

Many industries and other homogeneous groups are forming committees or action groups to deal with Year 2000 supply chain issues. (See Chapter 4 for a discussion of supply chain issues.) The supply chain problem is especially acute in the manufacturing industry where a single finished product may require supplies and parts from hundreds to thousands of vendors. For example, it is estimated that the production of an automobile requires parts from several thousand discrete suppliers. With so many potential suppliers in the chain, centralized communication about, and standard approaches to, Year 2000 compliance are critical.

From the manufacturer's or consumer's perspective, dealing with suppliers on a case by case basis has its drawbacks. Contacting and monitoring the Year 2000 progress of several thousand suppliers can be a logistical nightmare. Collecting the information by itself is a huge task. Moreover, while a single consumer may have little leverage to induce a supplier to respond to Year 2000 inquiries, to fix product problems, or to adopt a particular standard for data interchange, collectively a group of consumers wields a great deal more power. This collective bargaining power is extremely advantageous for single companies in seeking to influence their suppliers.

From the supplier's point of view, dealing with a single, cohesive group is far preferable to dealing with thousands of consumers, each with its own agenda. Rather than respond to numerous Year 2000 certification letters, suppliers need only communicate with a single body. Further, while the action group will typically have the leverage to set the standard for data interchanges, the supplier is much better off as there will be only a single standard to adopt. The group can also force a recalcitrant member to toe the party line, saving the supplier the time and effort, and potential loss of goodwill, that would arise in battling its customer.

In addition to these larger industry groups, similarly situated entities and entities that share or exchange data, from local to state governments, universities, and others, are banding together to share experiences and other information in an attempt to coordinate and streamline the Year 2000 conversion process. In October 1997, representatives from 42 states and 10 federal agencies met to discuss Year 2000 issues and agreed on a four-digit year standard in all state-to-state and state-to-federal data interchanges. Further, participants agreed to cooperate on a broader scale in creating an inventory of data interfaces, mutual testing, certification, and data bridging standards. It is likely that these state and federal agencies will also require any private sector entities with whom they exchange data to adopt the same date format standard.

From a legal perspective, whether or not there are any written agreements in place, suppliers that take directions from and respond to these industry groups will most likely be entitled to rely on the directions given by the group as a defense in a suit by a member of the group. Savvy suppliers may want to ensure that they are protected from future Year 2000 lawsuits in exchange for their cooperation with industry and other groups. Depending on the nature of the industry and other factors, the business leverage that is applied by an industry group may raise antitrust and other restraint of trade issues. Industry groups in particular must be circumspect in how they communicate Year 2000 issues to their suppliers, and in how they mandate Year 2000 compliance, to ensure that they are not exerting undue, anticompetitive pressures on their suppliers.

3.4 The Paper Trail

As part of any Year 2000 project, a company needs to spend time considering and planning for legal defenses that may be available to it in potential Year 2000 proceedings. By assuming that it will be sued, a company can take proactive steps to minimize the damages. As discussed above, these steps can focus on effective contract drafting, sending vendor certification letters, and so forth. In addition, a company should examine what sort of internal documentation, or paper trail, it is developing for eventual discovery by an adverse party. The company should consider what types of documentation will be favorable to it in litigation and should seek to create and save these types of documentation. Conversely, a company should consider what types of documentation would look unfavorable to it in a courtroom and should take steps to ensure that those items are either never created in the first place or dealt with in a reasonable way.

An accurate, sufficiently detailed, and credible paper trail can benefit a company in many ways. Most importantly, it can be used to establish that a company diligently pursued Year 2000 compliance according to acceptable standards of conduct and that it was not negligent or reckless in what it did, or what it failed to do. Of course, it goes without saying that any written record is only as good as the information or content contained in the record. Copious, detailed documentation that sheds an unfavorable light on company action not only wastes the company's money in terms of collection and maintenance costs, but it may also cost even more in the event of litigation.

Companies should beware of "rogue" memos and e-mails. These memos are often hyperbolic and opinionated diatribes about project management (and often managers themselves) authored by team members who feel underappreciated. Although a company cannot eradicate these types of memos, it should attempt to discourage them by explaining their potential damaging effect to employees. Companies should actively investigate and respond to these memos when they do appear. Keeping a record of management's response to rogue memos and e-mails will be helpful to establish in any eventual litigation that the company reacted reasonably under the circumstances.

Many types of written documentation are likely to be useful in establishing a due diligence defense. Cited below are a few of the significant ones.

- **Minutes of Meetings**

  Whenever company or Year 2000 decision makers meet, accurate records of the meeting should be kept to establish a due diligence defense not only for the individuals involved, but also for the company. Among other things, minutes should disclose who attended the meeting, the level of discussion, and length of time devoted to a topic, should refer to any supporting materials considered by the attendees, and should indicate any resolutions or action items resulting from the meeting.

- **Assessment Outputs**

  Any output from the assessment phase of the Year 2000 project, including the application inventory, risk analysis, interviews, surveys, legal contract review, certification letters, and vendor responses, should be saved. Enterprise- and application-level remediation plans, along with any supporting documentation, should also be retained.

- **Testing Plans and Results**

  Enterprise- and application-level test plans are critical pieces of information because they show that a company took the extra effort to prove that their Year 2000 changes actually worked. In addition to saving the test plans, a company should be able to show that it executed tests according to the plan and, for each test, the results and any ensuing action. For instance, if several applications fail their certification tests, the test plan should indicate that the applications were sent back for remediation, were resubmitted for testing, and passed the same certification tests that they failed earlier. Similarly, if tests must be rerun due to insufficient data, insufficient resources, or other problems, this information should be tracked to show that the test plan was not mere window dressing.

- **Contingency Plans**

  A company should save its Year 2000 contingency plans to show that it evaluated the risks of Year 2000 noncompliance and attempted to minimize the consequences, and costs, of the failures.

- **Vendor/Partner Letters and Responses**

  All certification letters, vendor responses, and other communications with business partners or suppliers concerning Year 2000 issues should be retained to demonstrate that a company understood the risk of noncompliance from external entities. Although no company can force another to become compliant, a company that can establish that it reasonably attempted to quantify the risk and educate itself about the compliance of its partners, particularly the significant ones, will shore up any due diligence defense.

- **Communications**

  A company should maintain a clear record of everything it discloses about its Year 2000 problems, both internally and externally. Significant memos created to educate internal personnel, to convey status information to management and vendors, and any updates to that information should all be retained.

For every written plan created by a company, the plan itself should not be considered as the end-all to establishing due diligence. A company must show that it followed the plan, and, if it diverged from the plan, that the divergence was reasonable under the circumstances. In some cases, it may be unreasonable for a company to continue to pursue a plan that is clearly incorrect, inadequate, or insufficient in light of the circumstances then existing. Similarly, as plans are changed, a company should retain each version of the plan along with a detailed record of why it decided to change the plan as it did. Some tools available on the market today help to automate the storage and retrieval of multiple iterations of plans and other project-level data. An inability to track changes to plans, or to explain why particular changes were made, could be detrimental to a company involved in litigation over its Year 2000 project.

In order to give more credibility to project plans and other documentation and to strengthen a due diligence defense based on the plans, a company should consider obtaining an outside review of its Year 2000 plans. Year 2000 consultants and certification organizations are available to review initial plans and project progress at various milestones. Because these outside reviewers are objective, and typically have years of industry practice and knowledge of best practices in the IT industry, they are able to provide a baseline with which the company can measure its plans and performance. For example, the Information Technology Association of America (ITAA) conducts a certification program that examines the processes and methods used by companies in performing their Year 2000 conversion work. After analyzing these processes and methods, the ITAA determines whether they embody the core capabilities necessary to address the Year 2000 problem and will certify a company accordingly. Companies should carefully consider, however, what action to take if they fail a certification program or if they decide to diverge from the advice given by outside consultants. Again, a careful record of these actions will help the company if they are forced to justify their actions as reasonable in a courtroom setting.

3.5 Insurance

Every company will face costs and possibly losses and other damages resulting from Year 2000 failures. To cover remediation costs, losses, and damages, companies will look to their own insurance coverage and third-party insurance coverage. Of course, at the same time, insurance companies will be looking for ways to limit or deny coverage under existing policies written before Year 2000 consciousness was raised and will certainly try to exclude Year 2000 coverage in newly written policies. The discussion below briefly describes some important aspects of insurance issues. You should consult your own lawyer to determine what your coverage is in any particular case.

First-party insurance policies, or policies held by a company, most likely include comprehensive general liability, property, errors and omissions (or malpractice), business interruption, and, perhaps, directors' and officers' liability. Current policies should be reviewed as part of the general contract review referred to in Section 3.2.1. The language of each policy should be carefully reviewed, particularly as it relates to limitations in coverage, exclusions from coverage, and retroactive premiums.

General liability policies usually contain an agreement by the insurance company to pay money that the insured party legally becomes obligated to pay as damages because of "bodily injury" or "property damage." "Property damage" is often defined as physical injury to tangible property or loss of use of tangible property. A basic issue is whether Year 2000 software problems and the ensuing loss of use of computer systems and other property, are considered "property damage." Courts have reached different conclusions on the question. Further, these general liability policies often contain several exclusions that might apply in the Year 2000 context. The most important exclusion relies on the concept of "fortuity." The fortuity factor basically excludes from coverage any damage that was expected or intended. Insurers can be expected to argue that a company definitely had knowledge of the Year 2000 problem and, therefore, that any ensuing damage was clearly expected. Companies may counter that although the generic Year 2000 problem was expected, that the particular harm that actually occurred was not expected.

At the time of writing, it appears that insurance carriers are now poised to use specific written exclusions for Year 2000 damages in 1998. These exclusions would cover bodily injury and property damage claims related to Year 2000. The Insurance Services Office, Inc., which publishes standard insurance forms, has developed an endorsement for general liability policies which excludes coverage for Year 2000 failures and inadequacies.

Directors' and officers' (D & O) liability insurance comes into play when the company's directors and officers are sued for failure to take action to avoid Year 2000 failures or failure to disclose Year 2000 risks. D & O policies generally will not make payments for losses arising from dishonest or fraudulent behavior, which may be precisely the type of behavior at issue in a securities lawsuit.

Professional liability policies cover negligence or other errors or omissions relating to the discharge of professional responsibilities. In the Year 2000 context, this coverage would typically apply to faulty design of software or hardware. This type of coverage typically will not apply to express warranties, or guarantees, made by the insured. If a Year 2000 claim is based upon a breach of warranty, rather than for negligence, then the insurance company will generally refuse to cover the loss. However, if the breach directly results from professional malpractice, which is the heart of the coverage, some courts have held that insurers cannot exclude coverage.

Even if an existing insurance policy appears to cover Year 2000 losses, it may apply only to claims made during the policy period. This limitation means that if the policy is canceled or not renewed—which can often be done at the option of the insurer—the policyholder is not covered for subsequent Year 2000 losses. Often, a policyholder can extend, or purchase additional coverage if a policy is canceled or not renewed; this feature should be carefully considered for those policies that appear to cover Year 2000 losses.

Some insurers are marketing new insurance policies specifically for Year 2000 risks. From press reports, these policies are designed to cover unforeseen business interruptions after computer systems are converted to accommodate century processing. Depending on the type of coverage, the premiums for this type of insurance may be prohibitive (up to 50 percent of the covered losses). To date, no information has been published as to whether companies are actively purchasing this type of coverage. Even if a company decides to purchase new insurance, getting coverage is not a foregone conclusion. Insurers are likely to carefully scrutinize an applicant's Year 2000 plans before they will insure against the risk of Year 2000 failures. If those plans are inadequate, an applicant will not be insured.

3.6 Government Aspects

Government agencies and legislatures, at the federal and state levels, could potentially impact companies' Year 2000 plans either by mandating Year 2000 compliance or disclosure or by requiring other affirmative actions. These governmental bodies could also offer relief, to themselves and private sector entities, from Year 2000 litigation by establishing safe harbors which would protect those who take certain actions or meet certain standards of conduct. As of this writing, there are no legislative requirements mandating Year 2000 compliance by companies in the private sector. However, this state could quickly change as the Year 2000 landscape is evolving on an almost daily basis. The following discussion could be outdated by the time of publication.

One important piece of advice—don't look to the government to solve your Year 2000 problems. To date, many government agencies have shown an inability to deal with their own internal Year 2000 problems. As with most monolithic bureaucracies, the government will move too slowly to address or resolve Year 2000 problems in a timely manner. In fact, if you consider where the vast majority of government agencies are today—still recommending studies and reports on the Year 2000 issue—you won't take much comfort in its ability to pull off its own Year 2000 project plans.

3.6.1 Regulatory Agencies

In a nutshell, regulatory agencies are pseudolegislative bodies typically created to enforce and oversee some legislative program or agenda. They can provide guidance or standards for companies to follow in particular areas of business such as financial reporting and disclosure, tax planning and reporting, and others. Regulatory agencies also often have enforcement authority entitling them to civilly and criminally prosecute offenders, penalizing them with fines and/or imprisonment. Examples of federal regulatory agencies include the SEC, IRS, Federal Drug Administration (FDA), and Department of Transportation (DOT). State and local agencies oversee securities regulation, environmental protection, zoning, and other areas.

These regulatory agencies are each concerned, to some extent, with the Year 2000 status of the private sector companies that they oversee. As of this writing, it appears that neither the federal government, nor any federal regulatory agency, has enacted any statutes, rules, or regulations legally requiring private sector companies to become Year 2000 compliant. In many instances, agencies may already be adequately empowered and authorized to ensure private sector Year 2000 compliance under existing rules and regulations. Therefore, it is unlikely that most agencies will adopt specific Year 2000 rules and regulations. For example, the FDA enforces regulations which currently require that all medical device manufacturers investigate and correct problems with medical devices and notify the FDA of any problems detected. Under the authority of this regulation, the FDA sent letters to several thousand medical device manufacturers discussing the Year 2000 problem and the need to review all embedded and nonembedded technologies.

Although regulatory agencies may not adopt specific Year 2000 regulations, other than perhaps mandating standards for data interchanges, certain of them can be expected to use their review and enforcement authority to pressure the private sector to respond in a timely and appropriate manner to Year 2000 issues. For example, in October 1997, the Federal Reserve Board in conjunction with other federal agencies, issued a cease and desist order against a Georgia bank, ordering it to stop certain practices, among them failure to develop Year 2000 plans. Federal agencies with oversight authority for the financial services and banking community are anticipated to use their review and enforcement authority most actively to ensure that these two industry groups are prepared to handle the century transition even to the extent of examining the compliance of supply chain partners.

The SEC has considered the Year 2000 problem, as discussed in Section 3.2.2, and has concluded that its existing regulatory regime adequately addresses the issue, and that specific Year 2000 regulations are not required. At a Senate subcommittee hearing held in October 1997, an SEC representative reiterated that specific Year 2000 regulations were not necessary, that companies had to determine themselves whether their Year 2000 issues were material enough to warrant disclosure but that the SEC did intend to monitor Year 2000 disclosure with targeted reviews of specific industries. In January 1998, the SEC published additional guidelines on Year 2000 disclosure requirements in time for 1997 annual report filings due in calendar 1998.

The IRS has not, to date, taken a position on the deductibility of Year 2000 remediation costs. However, given the significant amount of these costs over all private sector companies, and the potential effect on the U.S. tax base, it is likely that the IRS will take a position on these matters in the future.

On the banking front, the Office of the Comptroller of the Currency (OCC) has acknowledged the seriousness of the Year 2000 problem in the banking industry. In June 1996, the OCC sent an advisory letter to the CEOs of all national banks, warning them that they should remediate any Year 2000 problems by the end of 1998, leaving 1999 for testing. The OCC has also examined several hundred banks to ascertain whether they had proper Year 2000 plans in place and is expected to examine hundreds more in 1998.

3.6.2 Congress

Over the past year, Congress has conducted several public hearings about the Year 2000 issue, usually designed to put federal agencies on the spot about their Year 2000 plans and status. Occasionally, in the course of these hearings, a member of Congress has informally suggested adopting legislation to deal with Year 2000 issues. These suggestions have included legislation aimed at creating safe harbors for financial institutions that have fixed their own systems but still encounter problems due to failures in other, external systems and shutting down noncompliant banks rather than risk corruption of the entire banking system.

At the time of this writing, the first few instances of specific Year 2000 legislation have been proposed. To pressure the SEC into issuing additional guidance, Senator Robert Bennett (R-Utah), chairman of the Senate Banking Subcommittee on Financial Services and Technology, proposed a bill that would require companies to disclose their Year 2000 remediation progress and anticipated litigation costs and expenses. Congressman James Leach (R-Iowa) has proposed giving federal banking agencies discretionary authority to eschew civil monetary penalties for "inadvertent" Year 2000-related violations of law. Leach also proposed to modify existing federal copyright law to permit certain persons to copy software solely to correct century-date problems if the software vendor fails to grant timely permission to do so. Aimed at federal agencies, and not the private sector, the Millenium Act, introduced by Senator Robert Kerrey (D-Nebraska), seeks to "assure the integrity of information, transportation and telecommunications upon the arrival of the Year 2000." With little specifics, the bill directs several federal agencies, including the Federal Communications Commission, the National Institute of Standards and Technology, and the DOT, to evaluate potential dangers and threats relating to the century change and to propose solutions, in their respective infrastructure areas. Although all of these proposed pieces of legislation indicate that Congress is taking a serious look at the problem, given that no legislation has been officially enacted at the time of this writing, will they have the desired effect?

3.6.3 State Government

On the state government front, Year 2000 activity has picked up and can be expected to increase in the coming months. As with the federal government, two distinct types of legislation can be expected. One would direct state agencies to become Year 2000 compliant, probably requiring that all newly acquired hardware and software be Year 2000 compliant. Another measure would protect state governments from liability for Year 2000 problems or failures. That said, in the summer of 1997, the Nevada legislature passed a law providing immunity to the state for claims arising from date processing errors. The law states that "no cause of action, including, without limitation, any civil action or action for declaratory or injunctive relief may be brought under [Nevada statutory provisions] on the basis that a computer or other information system produced, calculated or generated an incorrect date, regardless of the cause of the error." This legislation effectively precludes individuals or other entities from suing the state of Nevada for damages or losses relating to Year 2000 problems. Given Nevada's example, it is surely only a matter of time before other states adopt legislation protecting them from Year 2000 suits.

In October 1997, the governor of California, Pete Wilson, issued an executive order directing state agencies and departments to complete their Year 2000 conversion activities by December 31, 1998. The executive order states that Year 2000 solutions are a state priority and directs the state Department of Information Technology (DIT) to coordinate related activities. Further, the order curtails spending on new computer projects to those required by law and mandates that all new systems, hardware, software, and equipment must be Year 2000 compliant. The order also empowers the DIT to define compliance standards for the state, to monitor agency progress, to issue progress reports to the legislature, and to address legal issues which may affect the state. California should be congratulated for officially and publicly addressing the problem in this way. Let's hope that other states follow their lead.

In addition to these legislative measures, the attorney generals of several states are evaluating whether to sue the vendors of noncompliant software and hardware sold to those states. Expect to see more on this topic in the coming months.

3.7 Other Legal Aspects

The Year 2000 problem will have an effect on various other legal aspects of a company's business in addition to those described above. Depending on the organization, and its particular Year 2000 remediation plan, a company may confront some or all of the issues noted below. Careful legal planning is necessary at the outset of most Year 2000 activities to help avoid or minimize problems in the future.

3.7.1 Staffing

Due to their immovable deadline, Year 2000 projects are very labor intensive. Programmer shortages are reported, more and more offshore factories are cropping up, and retired programmers are being pressed back into service. Companies must now recruit, train, and deploy waves of new hires, deal with independent contractors, and hire "leased" employees.

Whenever demand exceeds supply in the labor market, the effect can be seen in compensation and other incentive packages and the "poaching" of employees from one company by another with the promise of better pay or benefits. All of these actions have legal ramifications as compensation and incentive packages must satisfy securities and tax laws, antipoaching and noncompete agreements must satisfy employment laws, and overall hiring practices must satisfy a variety of federal and state laws. In addition, as companies staff their Year 2000 projects with independent contractors, or temporary hires, they need to ensure that these individuals are not treated as employees, thereby making them eligible for employment benefits.

When the demand for Year 2000 resources decreases, as it inevitably should, the excess personnel will be let go, thereby generating a wave of labor and employment-related claims. As employers staff up, they should be wary of laws that may later affect their ability to downsize.

The best advice for companies dealing with the foregoing and other employment issues is to consult a lawyer during the hiring process, and the negotiation and drafting of any employment agreement, to reduce the chances of later litigation. While a very tightly drafted noncompete provision may look advantageous from a company's perspective, many states will not enforce that type of agreement. There may be alternative, legally enforceable ways to achieve the same result, such as entering into mutual antipoaching agreements with competitors.

3.7.2 Offshore Factories

Prior to entering into outsourcing or consulting agreements with offshore entities, companies should ensure that they thoroughly understand the jurisdictional aspects of the transactions, including an understanding of any foreign laws that might apply. In many cases, a U.S. company will need to hire a foreign-based lawyer to ensure that its needs are properly addressed in the negotiation and drafting of the agreement. Key issues to focus on include the law governing the agreement, the proscribed forum, if any, for future litigation or arbitration, other dispute resolution clauses, and methods of payment and currency conversion. Litigation in foreign jurisdictions can be vastly different from U.S.-based litigation and produce unpredictable results. In particular, copyright laws, and their degree of enforcement, vary from nation to nation.

Companies should also ensure, prior to shipping any software overseas, that the software does not contain cryptographic and other sensitive code that is prohibited from being exported. Certain software may contain encryption algorithms (for electronic funds transfer, communications, etc.) in order to securely transmit processed data. Under the Arms Export Control Act, certain encryption software is barred from export. Companies with cryptographic software will either have to keep the code in the United States for remediation and testing or will need to consult a lawyer to determine if the code is eligible for export to an offshore service provider.

3.7.3 Copyright

There are several notable copyright issues related to Year 2000 projects. One issue concerns the use of independent contractors to effect Year 2000 fixes to company-developed software. Under the federal "work made for hire" doctrine, an employer typically owns the copyright in works prepared by its employees within the scope of their employment. Conversely, an independent contractor will own the copyright in works that the contractor prepares unless the parties agree in writing that the work is a "work made for hire" and the work fits within one of nine specified categories under copyright law. In the Year 2000 context, a company could find itself in the untenable situation of owning the copyright in the underlying software while the independent contractor holds the copyright in the Year 2000 modifications. In that case, the company would have to seek the permission of the independent contractor, through a license or otherwise, to further modify the remediated code. To avoid this situation, companies should explicitly address the ownership of copyrights in all agreements entered into with independent contractors, whether individuals or factories.

Another important copyright issue raised by the Year 2000 problem arises when a company seeks to modify software that it has licensed from a third party. As mentioned in the preceding discussion, a company could find itself having to remediate licensed source code if a vendor refuses, or fails, to do so. Under copyright law, the party owning a copyright in a work, including software, has the exclusive right to modify that work to create derivative works. This modification right can be licensed to others but must be done so explicitly in a license agreement. If another person modifies copyrighted software, without having a license to do so, the copyright owner can sue the modifier for infringement.

If a company needs to modify licensed software, it should examine its license agreement, and any related escrow agreements, to determine if it is authorized to do so. If not, the company should seek the licensor's permission to make any modifications. Copyright law does provide some defenses to a claim of infringement that could be available to a company making unlicensed Year 2000 modifications. However, these defenses should be used only as a last resort when a license or permission is unavailable.

If a company determines that it is authorized to modify licensed software, it may choose to have a Year 2000 service provider make the modifications. Before giving the service provider copies of the software to load onto its system, the software license should be reviewed for confidentiality restrictions. These restrictions are commonly found in software licenses and prohibit the licensee from disclosing, or providing a copy of, the software to an unauthorized third party without the consent of the licensor. Again, if such a restriction exists, a company would have to seek the permission of the licensor before making the software available to an outside service provider.

If a company does not have access to the source code for its licensed software and cannot get the vendor to promise that the software will be

Year 2000 compliant, the company may decide to decompile or reverse-engineer the object code version of the software to create the corresponding source code. Most licenses bar a company from taking this action. Even if a defense is available to the company under federal copyright law for modifying software for Year 2000 compliance, if a company contractually agreed not to reverse-engineer licensed software, this promise would take precedence and the company most likely would be prevented from asserting the defense. In some cases, a company may decide to take a calculated risk and reverse-engineer or modify the software even if contractually prohibited from doing so. The costs of Year 2000 failure may be higher, and more certain, than the risk of the vendor instituting a breach of contract or copyright infringement lawsuit.

Endnote

1. SEC Staff Legal Bulletin No. 5 excerpt: "If the Year 2000 issues are determined to be material, without regard to countervailing circumstances, the nature and potential impact of the Year 2000 issues as well as the countervailing circumstances should be disclosed. As part of this disclosure, the staff expects, at the least, the following topics will be addressed: (a) the company's general plan to address Year 2000 issues relating to its business, its operations (including operating systems) and, if material, its relationships with customers, suppliers, and other constituents; and its timetable for carrying out those plans; and (b) the total dollar amount the company estimates will be spent to remediate Year 2000 issues, if such amount is expected to be material to the company's business, operations, or financial condition, and any material impact these expenditures are expected to have on the company's results of operations, liquidity and capital resources."

Chapter 4

Non-IT Issues
and Answers

An inadequate level of attention has been paid to the potential problems that the Year 2000 poses in non-IT environments. The reason for this problem is quite simple. IT management sounded the Year 2000 alarm and began to take action to alleviate application-related problems with, or without, the blessing of the business community that it services. Business executives, due to a lack of information regarding non-IT impacts, believed that IT could correct the Year 2000 problem with little involvement from them. IT management, on the other hand, had little knowledge of the direct or indirect impacts that the Year 2000 would have on an organization outside the IT function.

This miscommunication delayed meaningful discussion of non-IT Year 2000 impacts until early 1997 when several large manufacturing firms realized that their supply chains were at risk. These supply chains, comprised of thousands of small companies, are highly interwoven and could break down if even a handful of key companies failed to deliver certain products to market. These same companies concurrently discovered that much of the embedded technology running the assembly line, quality monitoring, environmental control, and a host of other computerized functions contained noncompliant date functions. Unfortunately, the 1997 time frame was well beyond the point where research into non-IT issues should have begun.

As word of this dilemma spread to other industries, the realization that only part of the Year 2000 problem was being addressed started to sink in. In addition to manufacturing firms, health care, transportation, defense, and a wealth of other critical industries are dependent on embedded technology and complex supply chains. This chapter discusses how to assess and correct supply chain and business partner vulnerabilities, along with how to deal with various types of non-IT systems in a number of industries. We discuss the issues, impacts, analysis processes, and ways to alleviate risks in each of these areas with a focus on industry-specific challenges.

4.1 Defining Non-IT Year 2000 Requirements

Non-IT Year 2000 requirements are dictated by the direct or indirect impact of a failure in a computerized system that was not accounted for during an organization's Year 2000 initiative. This impact could be related to a business partner that failed to correct a situation that resulted in harm to your company. It could also be related to a breakdown in raw materials, products, services, or information supplied to your organization by third parties. Finally, embedded technologies, including facilities, Programmable Logic Controllers (PLCs), environmental control systems, and other non-IT computerized products could put an organization or individuals at risk in countless ways.

How organizations deal with Year 2000 problems that occur outside the IT area is a real challenge because the impacts tend to be indirect, non-apparent, and, in many cases, beyond the control of the impacted organization. It is difficult, for example, to dictate how business partners and suppliers should deal with the Year 2000 problem. It is also a time-consuming and resource-intensive process to research all the embedded technologies hiding inside a company. For these reasons, many companies feel that the non-IT aspects of the Year 2000 may be the most difficult to resolve and opens them up to some of the greatest risks.

4.1.1 Business Partner Impacts

Business partners are defined as two or more organizations that agree to work together, typically under a contract, on a given set of activities to achieve a mutually agreed upon set of goals. This broad description translates into numerous incarnations depending on the business in which a company is currently engaged. A bank may work with credit card companies, brokerage firms, and other banks as business partners. An insurance company may work with agents, reinsurance groups, and other insurance companies to further its business goals. The securities industry relies on all types of business partners that range from stock exchanges to clearing houses. Business partners are a necessity for most businesses and the nature of those relationships tends to be unique to a given company.

Problems in this area stem from unforeseen business partner failures that can negatively impact your revenue stream, customer delivery capability, or other critical business functions. Business analysts must research partner impacts for each business unit within their company. IT may provide input to the nature of this analysis, but the responsibility for ferreting out this information and determining what action to take rests solely on the shoulders of the business unit that would suffer most should a given partner fail to meet its obligations.

4.1.2 Supply Chain Challenge

If you receive raw materials, parts, finished products, energy, water, services, or information from a third party, you rely on suppliers. A Year 2000 problem at a supplier becomes *your* Year 2000 problem if it prevents or delays a supplier from delivering a critical product or service that your business needs to thrive. Figure 4.1 shows how interdependencies in even a small supply chain for a parts manufacturer expose a company to risks that are, to a great extent, beyond their ability to control. This illustration may seem trivial on the surface, but the gravity of the cumulative impact of even a small number of critical suppliers could shut down production lines or revenue streams. Supply chain failures are a real threat because the bulk of the product and service suppliers are small to mid-size companies—the least educated and least prepared in terms of the Year 2000 problem. Section 4.3 provides an in-depth discussion on business partner and supply chain risks and resolution strategies.

4.1.3 Embedded and Other Non-IT Technologies

Embedded systems contain a computer or a device based on computer technology that can be used to control the operation of a manufacturing environment, piece of equipment, or control device. Embedded systems have been applied to many uses over the years. As with IT systems, the designers of embedded systems never imagined that these systems would

Supply Chains and Business Partners

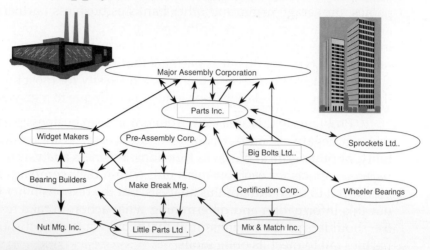

| **Figure 4.1** | Supply chains and business partners: The greatest hidden Year 2000 exposure. |

survive into the next millennium. Embedded systems are commonly found in commercial environments but are increasingly used in office and consumer products. Cars, video cameras, recording devices, photocopiers, and clocks all contain embedded technologies. While failure in many of these devices could result in consumer inconvenience, failures in health care, safety, quality control, or nuclear containment systems would result in more serious consequences.

Some people think that embedded technology problems are unique to manufacturing, aerospace, or military environments. Some examples of the non-IT embedded systems that could impact nonmanufacturing environments include elevators, telecommunications equipment, security systems, end-user desktop solutions, and power supply dependencies. Management in all industries must take a proactive approach to dealing with non-IT system challenges in order to find, diagnose, replace, or upgrade these systems in time to head off Year 2000 problems.

Unfortunately, the majority of these systems were customized on a case-by-case basis many years ago by developers and consultants who have long since disappeared. Further, most of these systems rely on archaic software or hardwired firmware that is difficult to diagnose via traditional analysis techniques. There is no single solution or easy answer that can address all or even most of the problems that a company could run into with these types of environments. That is why we strongly encourage management to research issues and solutions as quickly as possible.

One unwelcome outcome is that non-IT research projects will likely uncover numerous systems that exist outside IT environments. These systems include major applications, departmental PCs, spreadsheets, networks, engineering systems, and other special function systems that were created in-house or procured from outside vendors. IT management may be too busy to include these systems in their assessment plan or may not be aware of them, but business unit managers should include these systems in their risk assessment efforts (see Chapter 2). The guidelines provided in Chapter 2 should help business analysts research non-IT systems and address them accordingly. Additional information on software tools that can support distributed systems analysis and remediation efforts can be found in Chapter 6. We recommend that nontrivial end-user systems be researched jointly with the Year 2000 Project Office so that enterprisewide solutions can be applied to streamline the process.

4.1.4 Non-IT Problems: Consequences and Timing

The potential negative impact of non-IT problems on large corporations can be significant. Boeing, for example, had a supply chain failure that resulted in a $1.6 billion loss.[1] No one is likely to ever find out what went wrong at the Boeing supplier sites, but it caused production of the 747 jumbo and 737 aircraft models to be halted for one month. When similar supply chain failures occur as a result of Year 2000 problems at one or more suppliers, the impact could spread across a much wider spectrum of suppliers and last much longer. Now consider that hundreds or even thousands of these events could occur over a brief period of time. Would you be prepared? How would your company manage?

We live in a highly integrated global economy. Just look at the impact that the 1997 Asian market problems had on Wall Street. The 1997 UPS strike also had a devastating effect on thousands of companies as did the Chrysler plant strike before that. In one situation that occurred a couple of years ago, an automotive service supplier forced a shutdown of a truck plant that cost the manufacturer and the local economy over $20 million. Imagine 50 assembly lines shut down for weeks or even months. The costs could soar into the billions, while local economies are brought to a standstill.

When these problems will strike is also a major consideration. Supply chain and business partner failures will not strike at midnight on December

31, 1999. Rather, these problems will trickle up slowly through supply chains. A company that keeps large inventories on hand and does not actually encounter production problems until late first quarter 2000 might not negatively impact the supply chain until April or May 2000. This situation is likely to occur if, for example, a production control system failed on February 29, 2000, as it did in one test conducted by a manufacturing company. A transportation company problem, resulting in a delivery slowdown for products, parts, and raw materials, would have a similar delayed impact. In other words, optimists may think that they have cleared Year 2000 hurdles and find that the real problems are yet to come.

Other Year 2000 impacts could be delayed even well beyond first quarter 2000—and take longer to correct. For example, an inventory control system at a supplier in the middle of the supply chain might malfunction for a period of time without anyone noticing. At the point where a part that is typically stocked for four to five months runs out, it may be close to mid-Year 2000. Should it take another month or two to procure this part, supply chain impacts may not reach the top tier of the supply chain until third quarter 2000. This problem may seem trivial, unless it impacts hundreds of companies up through the supply chain—hitting the largest company when they thought they had put their Year 2000 problems well behind them.

The most problematic factor is not the time it takes to realize one has a non-IT Year 2000 problem, but rather the window of time it takes to correct the problem once it appears. Indirect impacts take longer to fix because one's ability to dictate the outcome of the situation is limited to one's ownership of the actual problem. In other words, your organization may have little control over a situation that could cost millions and take months to correct. The Boeing example highlights this problem. That is why it is so important to research business partner, supply chain, and embedded systems failure points well in advance of when they will fail.

4.2 Industry-Specific Non-IT Challenges

Each industry has the potential to encounter unique problems outside the IT area. Gaining a general understanding of industry-specific non-IT impacts helps companies that are working independently or collectively to deal more effectively and proactively with these problems. Business unit managers and senior executives should focus on these issues and take corrective action immediately. We have provided a brief update on selected non-IT issues that may erupt in several key industries below.

4.2.1 Telecommunications

Suppliers of information, equipment, parts, and telecommunication services form an extensive web of technology that requires telecommunication companies to thoroughly research critical partnerships and suppliers. Data interchange problems, discussed at length in Chapter 2, pose a significant area of exposure for telecommunication companies. Parts required to keep equipment functioning are also critical to communication business strategies. The biggest area of risk for telecommunication companies, however, comes from embedded technology used to control complex communications networks.

This issue is important enough that the International Telecommunication Union (ITU) has gotten involved and plans to monitor data and voice carriers and equipment vendors worldwide for Year 2000 readiness.[2] The ITU, an agency of the United Nations, posts updated information on the World Wide Web and they plan to develop industrywide contingency plans should problems occur on or after January 1, 2000. This type of industrywide monitoring and cooperation is an outstanding example of how a given industry sector can take proactive action to police Year 2000 status in areas critical to communication and commerce. The ITU represents 188 countries and more than 450 companies worldwide.

4.2.2 Energy and Power

In September 1997, the U.S. Nuclear Regulatory Commission (NRC) stated that they did not see any problems in safety-critical systems.[3] Discussions with vendors of digital protection systems, including Westinghouse, General Electric, Combustion Engineering, Foxboro, and Allen Bradley, confirmed the NRC staff's determination that safety-related initiation and actuation systems (e.g., reactor trip systems, engineered safety feature actuation systems) are not subject to Year 2000 problems. This determination was based on the fact that computer-based safety-related initiation and actuation systems do not rely on date-driven databases in order to perform their required functions.

The NRC does acknowledge that there may be problems in non-safety-related computer-based systems. For example, a database failure could result in a plant shutdown. Important, nonsafety-related computer systems, primarily databases and data collection necessary for plant operations, are date-driven and may need modification to become Year 2000 compliant. The significance of Year 2000 problems at operating nuclear plants will vary from plant to plant, depending on the applications that are affected by the Year 2000 and its consequences.

While the NRC contends that safety-related systems will function as intended, they envision a worst case scenario where a common-mode failure of nonsafety-related computer-based systems, required for plant operation, could significantly challenge plant staff. As a result of these failures, operators could face a plant trip that would result in a power loss, subsequent complications in tracking plant status, and recovery problems linked to a loss of emergency data collection and communications systems. Even under such a scenario, plant operators are trained to use emergency procedures to maintain safe plant conditions. This state of affairs signals good news and bad news for the energy industry. The absence of problems in safety-related systems is good as long as it does not make the industry complacent in researching ancillary risks in supporting equipment.

Research into the impact of the Year 2000 problem on regulated industries, with utilities being the most notable of these, is lagging. A 1997 DEC study cited in Chapter 1 claimed that one-third of all utilities had not begun their Year 2000 projects and another third were seriously behind schedule.[4] Critical infrastructure support industries, including oil production and distribution, natural gas and water suppliers, all depend on embedded technologies and suppliers to ensure operations continuity. Oil companies have claimed that pipeline control units and oil rig equipment utilize date-sensitive computer chips. If you are considering turning to wood for a source of power, even these plans could be thwarted. The forestry industry noted problems with chips found in process control devices at lumber mills.

Non-IT problems are likely to be the biggest problems faced by utilities—and are the source of major risks. If computer-controlled water supply, power girds, or other critical infrastructure systems malfunction due to a Year 2000 failure, life would likely be brought to a standstill. Utility executives in various business units must research these matters quickly because the analysis, testing and replacement process is likely to be quite time consuming.

4.2.3 Health Care

Supply chains, information interchange, and embedded technology are integral to the health care industry. If any of the hundreds of critical supplies, ranging from latex gloves to functioning diagnostic equipment, were somehow cut off for a period of time, lives could be at stake. Information interchange between hospitals, doctors, patients, HMOs, insurance companies, and the government could delay critical services. Hospitals are also users of numerous embedded technologies that include diagnostic, monitoring, and control devices.

One health care provider found that up to one-half of their computerized diagnostic, monitoring, and control devices were date-sensitive, not Year 2000 compliant, and required replacement by the end of 1999. Date sensitivity in these critical systems can be linked to maintenance checkpoints, where a chip continuously monitors last maintained date, or to other time critical functions. Equipment categories that should be examined include chemotherapy, intravenous drip, kidney dialysis, heart monitoring, and numerous other types of equipment. While some may argue that problems in this type of equipment are rare, who really wants to bet a human life on this presumption?

4.2.4 Manufacturing

Manufacturing is probably the most exposed industry in terms of non-IT impacts. The supply chain for some manufacturers can reach tens of thousands of companies where a failure in even a handful of these companies could bring production to a standstill. The Boeing example discussed earlier demonstrated the financial dependence that huge corporations have on suppliers. The auto, consumer goods, electronics, and virtually every other manufacturing industry is at similar risk. Supply chains in many manufacturing industries are multitiered.

The fact that embedded systems within manufacturing firms control production, product quality, environmental factors, facilities, and countless other functions compounds this challenge. A supplier could experience an inventory or production problem based on a failure in an IT system or in an embedded system. That supplier could, in turn, impact hundreds of other companies.

Large-scale problems like this could easily result in the shutdown of entire towns that rely on the success of a given manufacturing industry for their livelihood. For example, if a town's economy depends on an automotive plant for the bulk of the residents' income, a plant shutdown would eventually cause most of the other businesses in that town to close. In other words, the manufacturing industry is not only highly vulnerable to non-IT Year 2000 impacts, but problems in this industry could quickly ripple through the service, retail, wholesale, and financial markets that rely on these companies for their survival.

4.2.5 Wholesale, Retail, and Service Industries

The flip side of the manufacturing problem is reflected in the wholesale and retail industry. Product shortages and product failures could hit wholesalers and retailers in a delayed domino effect. Product shortages are likely to hit wholesalers first, because they fall higher in the distribution channel than retailers. Take the auto industry for example. If production is halted on a certain brand of car, dealers distributing that type of vehicle will have no product to sell. Auto dealerships represent a one-on-one manufacturer/retailer relationship. A dealer could also find itself in the position of selling a defective product, which could be even more troublesome.

A major problem for retailers is that they are at the top of the supply chain and this puts them in a precarious situation. Manufacturing firms are heavily involved with the production of a fixed number of products and may even have documented the intricacies of the supply chains upon which they depend. Retailers, on the other hand, typically have little knowledge of which parts go into their products beyond the name of the company that built the finished product. This dilemma will leave many retailers in the dark when it comes to predicting the availability and quality of products they sell should supply chain problems occur.

A second challenge to retailers is the vast numbers of suppliers that some companies must manage. Sears, for example, has close to 56,000 suppliers. There is little chance that it will determine if all of their suppliers will be compliant. The good news is that, according to a June 1997 conference presentation in Chicago, Sears has adopted a strategy of prioritizing critical suppliers to ensure that supply lines linked to high revenue and high product volume are not interrupted.

Product warranties are another area where retailers could be caught between a manufacturer of a noncompliant product and the consumer. A customer may want a replacement for the video camera they just purchased. The electronics store may subsequently be flooded with returned merchandise that, in the near term, could cause serious cash flow problems for that store. Product warranties, on the other hand, should encourage manufacturers to proactively test products to ensure Year 2000 compliance.

Point-of-sale systems also rely on embedded technology and, at some companies, fall outside the realm of the IT function. The first Year 2000 lawsuit involved a retailer suing a point-of-sale systems vendor in Detroit. Retailers also depend on credit card bank processing systems, utilities, telecommunication companies, transportation providers, and security firms for operational continuity. Retail associations and retail management teams must, therefore, investigate a broad range of non-IT risks well in advance of the Year 2000.

Service industries, in general, rely on other service providers to stay in business. Doctors, lawyers, dentists, and travel agencies all rely on information exchange with suppliers. Many of these service providers also depend on various products, computerized and otherwise, in their day-to-day functions. Airports (computerized baggage handling), car dealers (chips in the cars' dashboards), gas stations (computerized gas pumps), supermarkets (checkout scanners), radio stations (control booths), and countless other retail and service industries routinely employ embedded technology they may or may not know about. Few industries are immune to the Year 2000 problem and, unfortunately, many of the ones on this list are not focused on solving it.

4.2.6 Transportation Sector

The most immediate concern to the transportation industry is handling failures in systems that control navigation, routing, safety, and other critical industry functions. The most commonly discussed example involves concerns over air traffic control systems that direct airplane takeoffs, landings, routing, and ground control. Airlines routinely rely on these systems to keep planes from crashing into one another in the air and on the ground. This service is supplied by federal governments in most cases and, in the United States, by the Federal Aviation Administration (FAA).

On-board computer systems are another source of risk that is not limited to airplanes which, by the way, are said to be fine according to the manufacturers of most newer planes. Ships, trains, military transport vehicles, and spacecraft all contain embedded technology. All these systems should be researched carefully. In addition to on-board systems, ships, railroads, and other transport vehicles utilize satellite-based Global Positioning Systems (GPSs) that are believed to have a similar date problem due to the use of a base date routine that rolls over in August 1999. Weather system failures, another government service, could also put transportation companies at risk or, at a minimum, inconvenience customers.

The transportation industry is also prone to delays in obtaining replacement parts from suppliers. The Boeing supply chain problem cited earlier highlights not just the downside to the manufacturer of a product, but also the impact on the companies that plan to use that product. Airlines are awaiting shipments of planes and if those planes are never delivered, a downturn in an airline's ability to transport customers is a real threat to the profitability of that airline. Similar risks exist in every transportation sector.

4.2.7 Financial

While most of the concerns surrounding supply chains have centered on the manufacturing and health care market, many have not considered the information supply chain found within the financial services industry. Figure 4.2 depicts this information supply chain. Banks, for example, perform credit card information exchange, ATM transfers, and international funds transfer. The securities industry exchanges information on trades among brokerage houses, banks, various exchanges, clearing houses, and other institutions. This conglomeration is the financial supply chain and it is essential to the financial survival of business around the world.

Couple Year 2000 problems with the fact that banks and financial institutions in Europe are in the midst of converting to a common currency. This conversion, in itself, has a major impact on most computer systems in Europe. Combined with the Year 2000, it will increase information supply chain risks during Year 2000 transition windows. The Euro

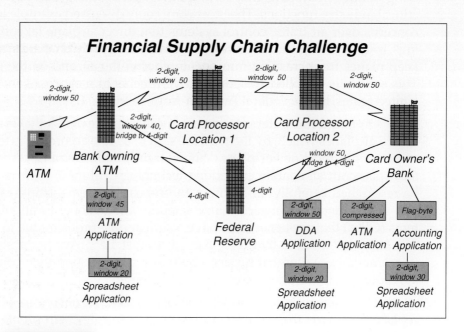

Figure 4.2   Financial institutions rely on an information supply chain that is as strategic and at risk as any physical supply chain.

conversion is preventing many companies from fixing their Year 2000 problem. Because most companies cannot cope with performing both the Euro conversion and the Year 2000 project, it is likely that both will suffer and information exchange errors will explode.

4.2.8 Government and Defense

Non-IT challenges in the public sector are unique because governments regulate infrastructure sources like energy, tend to be the largest buyer of goods and services, supply services to the private sector, and utilize a staggering array of embedded technologies. Governments' exposure to non-IT related Year 2000 risks is significant. If regulated industries, such as communications, utilities, and water supplies, fail, the government will be held accountable for not taking action to head off these problems. If other government services, including air traffic control, water regulation, veterans hospitals, or defense fail, countries could be at a standstill.

Defense is one area where embedded technology, some of which dates back 20 or more years, is used extensively for mission-critical functions. Failures in some technology areas will surface early. Ships at sea, planes in the air, or communication systems that are kept operating on a continuous basis will experience problems from the century rollover first. Certain missile systems, rarely used aircraft, ships that have been mothballed, and other types of equipment may not display problems until they are actually deployed—several years after the turn of the century. We discuss embedded technology, used in both the military and civilian markets, later in this chapter.

4.3 Supplier, Business Partner Challenges

There are three basic types of third-party dependencies: business partners, suppliers, and government entities which tend to be dealt with as a special case. A government tax agency may, for example, deal with your organization on a regular basis but not be considered a business partner or a supplier. A business partner is defined as a company that you rely on to support customers or provide revenues. For example, a bank may process all foreign transactions through another bank that is located in a different country or deal with a unique market sector. A supplier is a company that provides your organization with goods or services.

Suppliers could cease to deliver products or parts because of an inventory, financial, or other IT systems failure. They could also have production, packaging, or delivery problems linked to the failure of one or more embedded systems. A supplier may also have problems if one of their service, raw material, parts, or product suppliers has a problem that impacts a mission-critical business function. Worst case scenarios may even involve suppliers that deliver corrupt data, noncompliant computer technology, or flawed products related to a quality control or production problem that was never noticed by manufacturing teams.

Supplier problems may have the biggest cumulative impact on a given economic sector. This result is due to the ripple effect that a failure at one or two suppliers could have on hundreds or thousands of companies and the people and economies that rely on those companies. For purposes of this discussion, we are combining research and resolution strategies for business partners and suppliers because the process is basically the same. The level of strategic importance is what differentiates one third-party from another. This section discusses different third-party categories, supply chain principals, awareness building strategies, and approaches for dealing with third-party imposed Year 2000 risks.

4.3.1 Supplier Categories

Suppliers and business partners come in many varieties. A supplier of financial services may be a strategic business partner. The same is true for a value-added reseller of your products. Suppliers and business partners can be broken down into the following categories.

1. *Raw materials: This category includes steel, lumber, or other basic materials required to build a product or maintain an environment.*

2. *Component parts: Parts are typically used to produce products and are the basic building blocks of a supply chain. Component parts can include computer hardware or software technology.*

3. *End products: Final products include everything from computers, to machinery used to assemble products, to elevators. The difference between a final product and a component part is that a final product is used directly by a company or a consumer and not embedded in another product. An end product can include computer hardware or software.*

4. *Services: This includes maintenance, banking, insurance, health care, legal, temporary help, and a wide variety of other private or public sector functions needed to stay in business.*

5. *Infrastructure: We recognize this category of supplier as a provider of basic infrastructure needs including electricity, water, gas, heating oil, coal, and communication capabilities.*

6. *Computer hardware and software: Computer hardware and software fall into a separate category because Year 2000 compliance certification requires a special level of research.*

7. *Data or information: Data supplied via Electronic Data Interchange (EDI), tape, or any other means is considered an asset acquired through suppliers.*

4.3.2 Supply Chain and the Domino Principal

The supply chain concept evolved over a long period of time. The idea is simple. It does not make sense for any one company to make all the products that it either uses or incorporates into its own products. For example, an automobile seat assembly is comprised of hundreds of separate parts made by many different specialty manufacturing firms. If a large automotive company had to make each of these parts, economies of scale would dictate that the end-product would cost more and take longer to make. The result is that each manufacturer buys parts and assembles the final product from those parts. This concept can be extended throughout any manufacturing and some service industries.

This supply chain concept has actually evolved into a science. The automotive industry decided to reduce the total number of direct suppliers to eliminate the headache of managing tens of thousands of separate relationships with small to mid-size companies. The industry has also required that key suppliers utilize a computerized Just-In-Time (JIT) inventory program where minimal levels of on-hand supplies are maintained to reduce stock costs and storage requirements. Computer systems track supply levels and facilitate the reordering process so that inventories do not run out. Maintaining minimum inventory levels, however, increases the vulnerability of a supplier or a customer to production or transportation problems —should they arise.

Figure 4.3 depicts the upward and downward dependencies in a small cross section of the automotive supply chain. If we expand this picture to show all suppliers (which would be very difficult due to the size of the automotive supply chain), we could see how the auto industry directly and indirectly impacts the lives of millions of people. There are roughly 6,000 unique tier-one suppliers and about 60,000 unique suppliers overall that provide parts and services to the automotive industry in the United States.

An example of how a product shortfall from a single tier-three supplier can have a major impact on a supply chain helps illustrate the challenges involved in managing Year 2000 supply chain compliance. Let us assume that a second-tier supplier builds brake assemblies, which it manufactures at three

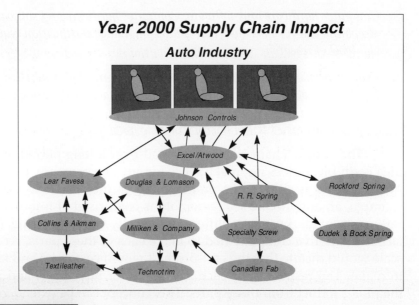

Figure 4.3 Supply chain example depicts high degree of reliance on numerous small manufacturing firms to create a single product.

separate plants. Each of these brake plants must purchase parts from 75 tier-three suppliers in order to build the brake assemblies. One of the 75 suppliers produces springs that are used in 50 percent of the brake systems built by this tier-two supplier. The tier-two brake assembly manufacturer in turn supplies brakes to seven of ten plants owned by the auto industry.

These seven plants, which also buy 10,000 unique parts from 2,000 other suppliers to build a car, employ 50,000 production line workers in total. There are 9,000 other second-, third-, and fourth-tier suppliers providing parts for the manufacturing process performed at these seven plants. These other suppliers employ another 35,000 employees. What happens if the spring supplier has to shut down because of a severe Year 2000 problem in a PLC? They cannot manufacture or ship any springs for five business days.

1. *Spring Supplier: The spring supplier scrambles to fix the problem and ascertain its contractual status and exposure with the tier-two brake assembly supplier.*

2. *Brake Manufacturer: Lack of springs shuts down manufacturing lines at three of its plants. The brake manufacturer notifies the auto manufacturer that it will not ship brake assemblies to seven of their plants. Resumption time of future shipments is unknown.*

3. *Auto Manufacturer Plant Managers: Determine that 50 percent of their pro-duction lines will be shut down in eight hours. The plant manager notifies headquarters and the union of the potential impact—about 25,000 workers will be affected. Managers also notify 1,900 other suppliers that they may have to stop shipping parts if the problem is not fixed.*

4. *Manufacturer's Headquarters: Estimated impact per plant per day is $2 mil-lion or $14 million per day for all seven plants. They call the tier-two brake assembly supplier and remind them of their contractual commitment to sup-ply parts.*

5. *Auto Manufacturing Plants: After eight hours, brake assemblies are no longer available, production lines are shut down, workers are sent home, and other suppliers are told not to ship more parts.*

6. *Other Suppliers: Shut down their production lines and send employees home.*

7. *Industry Impact: About 25,000 auto industry production workers are sent home and about 35,000 supplier employees are impacted. Auto manufacturer begins loosing $14 million dollars per day, which does not include revenue losses at 1,900 other impacted suppliers.*

8. *Broader Economic Impacts: At locations around the country, small businesses are losing revenue due to work stoppages at thousands of plants.*

Many people might say that the automotive example is larger and more threatening than one might find in other industries. While the auto-motive example may represent a larger supply chain than that found in other industries, the auto industry, at least in the United States, has a unique advantage in dealing with suppliers. It is an oligopoly that is capa-ble of working through a single source, the Automotive Industry Action Group (AIAG), to bring suppliers in a multitiered supply chain into com-pliance. Other industries, health care for example, do not have the same luxury because companies that function in supply chains that do not ser-vice a short list of large companies may not be compelled to address their Year 2000 problems in a timely manner. Awareness is step one in the sup-ply chain management process.

4.3.3 *Supplier Strategies: Methodological Approach*

Organizations should attempt to follow a methodological approach to identifying, mobilizing and certifying suppliers and partners to ensure operational continuity pre- and post-2000. Identifying suppliers and build-ing awareness among those suppliers as a way to motivate them to take action on the Year 2000 problem is a major challenge. Staying on top of the situation in order to ensure that these suppliers are certified compliant is more akin to an art than a science. This section defines these concepts.

4.3.3.1 Identifying and Prioritizing Supplier Requirements

Finding out who your suppliers are may not be that simple. We recommend working with central purchasing and other business units that may have direct supplier contact. Business analysts researching this matter should create a master list of suppliers and sort these by the amount of money spent with those suppliers over the course of a year. This exercise establishes the first level of qualification to determine which suppliers are to be contacted and which ones may be skipped. Note that multitiered supply chains are handled somewhat differently and are discussed in a subsequent section.

Analysts should then categorize suppliers into each of the seven categories identified earlier. This effort is important because each supplier category should be researched somewhat differently. For example, management may not research a raw material supplier's financial systems for Year 2000 compliance as long as that supplier demonstrates that they are actively pursuing a general compliance program that seems reasonable. Detailed research into financial systems is applicable, however, if a company is supplying financial services to your organization. Once suppliers are categorized, they should be prioritized so research can proceed to the degree necessary to avoid interruptions in your organization's business operations. The following guidelines apply.

High Impact: Requires customized letter, one or more on-site visits, high-level management contact, close review of certification progress.

1. *Suppliers / partners doing more than a fixed amount of business per year (cutoff point is dependent on what a company considers high volume—$250,000 for example).*

2. *Suppliers / partners that are directly responsible for customer satisfaction.*

3. *Suppliers / partners that account for more than a fixed percentage of revenue (for example, any supplier that accounts for more than 5 percent of revenue).*

4. *A sole source supplier (where no other option exists).*

5. *Suppliers / partners that are considered strategic by the executive team.*

Medium Impact: Requires general letter (customized by category), possibly one on-site visit, mid-level management contact, periodic review of certification progress.

1. *Suppliers / partners doing less business per year than high-impact category cutoff point, but more than low-impact cutoff point (between $100,000 and $250,000 for example).*

2. *Suppliers / partners that are indirectly responsible for customer satisfaction.*

3. *Suppliers / partners that account for more than a fixed percentage of revenue (1 percent to 5 percent, for example).*

4. *Suppliers / partners that are considered important, but nonstrategic by the executive team.*

Low Impact: Requires general letter, no on-site visit, one follow-up phone call.

1. *Suppliers / partners doing less than low-impact cutoff point (under $100,000 for example).*

2. *Suppliers / partners that have no customer satisfaction impact.*

3. *Suppliers / partners that account for under a fixed percentage of revenue (less than 1 percent, for example).*

4. *Suppliers / partners that are considered nonstrategic by the executive team.*

5. *Suppliers / partners that are easily replaced or eliminated without impact to company.*

4.3.3.2 Supplier Awareness

Awareness is still a problem at many of the companies composing corporate supply chains. The companies that form the foundation for these supply chains typically fall into the small to mid-size category. Studies show that management's awareness of the risks posed by the Year 2000 within this group is low. An October 1997 study from Gartner Group revealed that 88 percent of all firms with fewer than 2,000 employees had not begun their Year 2000 projects as of October 1997.[5] A second study by Tate Bramald Consultancy in England found that 57 percent of small firms had not allocated Year 2000 budgets in the 1997–1998 time frame.[5] These companies are the primary supply source for the parts and services required by consumers and other companies.

Approaches for making suppliers aware of the impact of the Year 2000 problem tend to differ based on the amount of clout one has with a given supplier. If you are a large retailer and your supplier does $10 million a year in business with you, your organization has a lot of clout. If, on the other hand, you are a hospital and represent a small percentage of a given supplier's revenue, then you have very little financial leverage over that supplier. Based on this premise, we recommend the following awareness strategy.

1. *If you are a very large company at the top of a multitiered supply chain,*

   - notify first-tier and/or high-impact suppliers via letter that the Year 2000 problem requires correction in order to continue existing or future contracts
   - call all first-tier and/or high-impact suppliers together (mandate attendance) to communicate the problem and your strategy to ensure supplier compliance
   - continue tracking

2. *If you are in an industry where an industry association (AIAG, Securities Industry Association, RX2000, etc.) can assist with supplier research,*

   - use the association to work with other companies as a way to encourage supplier responses and reduce individual company research time
   - send jointly crafted letter to vendors in each category (or applicable category)
   - hold group meetings with vendors to craft a jointly agreed upon strategy to achieve compliance

3. *If you are a large company with no industry association and many suppliers,*

   - prioritize all suppliers carefully as discussed in the previous section
   - perform direct research into strategic and first-tier suppliers required to maintain operational continuity
   - perform minimal levels of research on low- and medium-impact suppliers

4. *If you are a small company with no industry association to work through,*

   - utilize similar prioritization and research techniques for high-, medium-, and low-impact suppliers
   - consider critical financial, health care, product, and service suppliers and partners in the review process

One, somewhat unique, approach to creating supplier awareness was used by Citibank.[6] They spelled out a six-point plan for telecommunication firms to support their customers better. Citibank, speaking at a 1997 telecommunications conference, took an aggressive approach by claiming that suppliers had provided nebulous, misleading, and incorrect information to them. A company this size has unusual latitude in terms of motivating suppliers to work more effectively with them and with other users of various products and services. More large companies may want to consider speaking out to promote industrywide awareness of supplier and business partner problems.

4.3.3.3 Supplier Risk Analysis

Any number of risks can result from supplier and business partner failures—particularly when those problems are unforeseen. If your organization utilizes any or all of the previously identified supplier categories, management should consider the inherent risks associated with each category as shown by some examples listed below. These risks should be incorporated into the risk management review process performed on selected suppliers and discussed in Chapter 2.

1. *Raw materials*

   - Inability of supplier to extract or prepare materials due to embedded chip problems in equipment (some diesel engines contain date-sensitive chips).

   - Inability of transportation suppliers to deliver parts to market.

   - Customer, billing, or inventory system tracking problems inhibit ability to deliver materials to customer.

   - Other in-house system failures cause instability in business operations.

2. *Component parts*

   - Suppliers fail to deliver sub-parts required to build these parts.

   - Embedded chips in parts being assembled fail because they were not checked for compliance.

   - Production problems stem from noncompliant controllers in plant.

   - Transportation suppliers unable to deliver parts to market.

   - Part tracking (bar coding system) failure loses track of component parts in supply chain.

   - Supplier problems inhibit production capabilities.

   - Customer, billing, or inventory system tracking problems inhibit ability to deliver parts to customers.

   - Other in-house system failures cause instability in business operations.

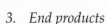

3. *End products*

   - Suppliers fail to deliver sub-parts required to build critical end product or products.

   - Embedded technology in product being assembled fails because it was not checked for compliance.

   - Production problems stem from noncompliant controllers or other devices in production process.

   - Transportation suppliers unable to deliver end product to market.

   - An inferior part was passed along from a supplier and caused problems in an end product (for example, a flawed catalytic converter placed in a car).

   - Parts supplier problems inhibit production capabilities.

   - Customer, billing, or inventory system tracking problems inhibit ability to deliver parts to customers.

   - Facility system failure in security system prevents building entry.

   - ATM system failure prevents customers from accessing cash.

4. *Services*

   - Computer processing problems cause company to lose track of billing, accounting, customer, and other critical information.

   - Transportation problems prevent company from delivering service.

   - Products/tools used to deliver the service are back ordered (supplier problem), flawed, or fail when used.

   - Financial services provider has problems related to various accounts that cause delays in money transfers.

   - Insurance services provider cannot pay claims due to policy system failure.

   - Health care services provider has patient tracking, admitting system, or medical devices fail due to Year 2000 problems.

   - Legal or temporary help service cannot deliver services due to system problems.

5. *Infrastructure*

   - Electric power outage (failure of nonsafety-related system at nuclear plant) shuts down headquarters for three days.

- Gas outage due to distribution technology failure in delivery mechanism.

- Water supply problems in local processing plant turn off water to your company.

- Postal and express air deliveries are halted due to computer problems at post office.

- Communication system shutdown stymies ability to contact people via e-mail and telephone.

6. *Computer hardware and software*

- Third-party-procured computer hardware or system software failure shuts down ability to run applications on those systems.

- Financial, inventory control, human resources, or other application package failures seriously impair operations.

- Unforeseen embedded technology problems arise in various scanning or tracking systems.

- Desktop PC problems arise in systems that were previously considered compliant.

7. *Data or information*

- Electronic Data Interchange (EDI) incompatibilities hinder data transfer with insurance companies, financial institutions, government agencies, and others.

- Errant data from information supplier enters database and corrupts strategic supplier information.

4.3.3.4 Assisting with Compliance

The level of assistance that a company provides to a supplier or a business partner is directly related to the importance that management places on the survival of that company. A supplier of paper goods who could easily be replaced with another supplier deserves little assistance in achieving Year 2000 compliance. A tier-one supplier of seat assemblies that interfaces with 50 critical tier-two suppliers, however, is likely to gain significant attention from the automotive manufacturer that relies on this company. We, therefore, recommend focusing time and energy on a select group of strategic business partners and suppliers that are considered essential to the survival of your company.

Help comes in many forms. The following suggestions outline some ideas on how to help business partners and suppliers remain viable in the face of the Year 2000 threat.

1. *For manufacturing environments, provide supplier with a list of industry-specific embedded systems research material.*

2. *In a multitier supply chain environment,*

   - provide tier-one suppliers with briefing materials and advice on how to help lower-tier suppliers
   - establish Web sites, hot lines, and briefing material to lower-tier suppliers
   - assist, where possible, in sharing third-party supplier compliance data

3. *For strategic business partners or suppliers that are integral to organizational survival,*

   - review partner's risk assessment, compliance plan, and contingency plans
   - assist, where possible, in sharing third-party supplier compliance data
   - take a position on company's Year 2000 steering committee (if appropriate)
   - offer to provide any other assistance as required or practical to ensure compliance

4.3.4 Documenting Multitiered Supply Chains

Without a clear understanding of the relationships among companies within complex supply chains, it is likely that entire industries, and certainly major companies, will experience significant economic problems in 2000 and beyond. This information is critical to contingency planning so that companies can build alternative strategies in areas where they are the most exposed. However, documenting a supply chain is one of the most confounding challenges in the Year 2000 arena. Most corporations have never been concerned with how a supplier obtains component parts, end products, or services, as long as they continue to fulfill their contractual obligations. One of the few exceptions can be found in the automotive industry where major players have proactively cut down the absolute number of tier-one suppliers in order to reduce the volume of companies and contracts they must manage. Most companies and industries lack this leverage.

We believe it is important to apply a process of documenting multi-tiered supply chains that works regardless of the leverage one may have as an individual company. This effort is especially required in industries such as manufacturing and health care that depend heavily on tiers of suppliers to stay viable. The concept is simple; however, the process of completing the analysis is complex. Prior to undergoing such an analysis, companies should determine the strategic importance of this analysis, if they can work cooperatively to streamline the time to complete the analysis, and if any independent associations can take the lead on researching the supply chain structure.

For example, this analysis is important to the automotive industry and other oligopolies like commercial airline manufacturers because a supply chain breakdown would hurt all of them significantly. Other industries, such as health care, have a less clearly defined supply chain infrastructure meaning that the research could take much longer and only marginally benefit a given hospital. If the health care industry decided, however, to focus their analysis through an association, then the task of documenting the health care supply chain becomes more feasible.

A repository is required to keep track of a large supply chain and the relationships in that supply chain. This requirement is due to the size, potential volatility, and recursive nature of the supplier/customer relationship. The last point focuses on the fact that a company could be at tier five and at tier two of the same supply chain because a part they sell is required by one of their suppliers. Figure 4.4 depicts a simplistic repository data model for tracking these relationships. The supply chain example in this figure could be extracted from this repository once loaded and maintained with actual data. The process begins with a given customer and follows the chain of suppliers for that customer and all of their suppliers.

The real challenge in documenting supply chain infrastructures is in performing the research required to capture this information in the first place. The two things that facilitate this process are a unifying agent (like the AIAG) to drive the process and a compelling reason for suppliers to collect and share this information. A unifying agent can be an independent association that already has relationships in place with most or all of the suppliers in a given industry sector or it could be an ad hoc organization formed for just this purpose. The key requirement here is that the agent have a degree of independence and no bias toward any supplier. The use of an agent is a political issue that should be resolved early in the analysis process.

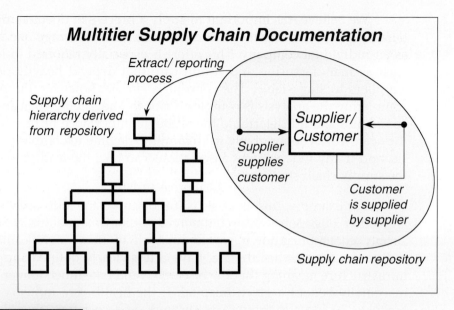

Figure 4.4 Supplier is also typically a customer in the supply chain documentation model.

Establishing a compelling reason for all the suppliers within a supply chain to provide input into this analysis process is the most difficult requirement to fulfill. Each supplier must disclose each of their suppliers by name. This data may be considered proprietary information, or a supplier may have other reasons for not disclosing this data. Who, then, would be able to coax this information out of a supply chain? Major auto industry players, Boeing, or other highly dominant companies or oligopolies within a given industry might be able to do so. Health care companies, if they truly understood the risks to the industry and to the people it serves, should be willing to cooperatively undertake this analysis. The analysis would have to be driven by the top-tier providers of medical devices—working as a team until 2000 arrives. If industries need an example to follow, they should consider what the Securities Industry Association (SIA) has done in terms of testing the information supply chain that flows through the financial industry. It can be done, if the industry leadership exists.

4.3.5 Supplier Responses

We have been discussing the impact of Year 2000 supplier problems from a customer standpoint, but it is important to look at the issue through the eyes of a supplier as well. Every supplier is also a customer and open to the vulnerabilities inherent in a supplier/customer relationship. Suppliers need to be sensitive to inquiries about their products and services, both from direct customers and indirect customers.

Many suppliers have created form letters and boilerplate answers to Year 2000 inquiries from other companies, government agencies, and individual customers. Answers are typically well rehearsed and should reassure a customer that has no critical or high-risk dependency on a given supplier. In some circumstances, however, more information is required. This happens when a supplier finds a rather large or influential customer demanding a supplier's Year 2000 project plan, testing strategy, risk analysis, and contingency plans. It is clearly up to a given customer as to how they reply to these inquiries, assuming it is not a government regulatory agency demanding this information. However, a degree of cooperation could go a long way to securing that customer for long-term, post-2000 business, especially if your competitors fail.

4.3.6 Supplier Contingency Options: Hedging Against Failure

Contingency planning is covered in depth in Chapter 9, but we thought it would be judicious to discuss it here in terms of alternative supplier options. Any company that depends on a given product or service for their livelihood should take all measures to ensure that product or service availability continues in a post-2000 environment. Securing backup suppliers, rerouting products or services through an existing supply chain, or moving the creation of a part, product, or service in-house are all options.

Securing backup suppliers is a common contingency option when a critical resource is in doubt or so important that no interruption can be tolerated. An example of this is the power supply at a hospital. Other examples may not be life threatening but could put a company out of business. Use discretion here and base your backup plans on the risk management guidelines in Chapter 2 and contingency planning guidelines in Chapter 9. Rerouting parts through the supply chain would require close coordination with backup or alternative suppliers and their customers. It is worth considering, however, if alternatives exist and suppliers at multiple tiers are amenable to the concept. Temporarily moving a service or product development capability in-house assumes you have the ability to do so on relatively short notice or have done a good job of contingency planning. Buying a company and correcting the cause of the supplier's problem might fulfill this requirement. Other contingency options should be drafted to ensure supplier continuity as events unfold.

4.4 Year 2000 Embedded Technology Challenge

The Year 2000 industry loosely defines the term "embedded system" for any system that runs outside the IT environment. However, non-IT systems include embedded systems as well as a wide range of applications that have been acquired, built, managed, and maintained by engineers, business analysts, plant managers, and other professionals. These "applications," which run in plants and other decentralized locations, are written in assembler, FORTRAN, Pascal, C, and other more obscure languages that may or may not interface with an embedded system. An example of a non-IT systems hierarchy is shown in Figure 4.5. We recommend using the guidelines described in our last book[7] to assess and correct these higher-level application systems in situations where they may be overlooked because they are not directly connected to an embedded system function.

An embedded system is defined as computer technology that monitors, controls, or in some way facilitates the functioning of a machine, component device, or an environment—such as a factory or office building. The

Plant / Manufacturing Systems Hierarchy

Facility Management Systems	Plant management & administration
	Planning, scheduling, QA/QC & operations
	Process control & data acquisition systems
	Programmable logic controllers & other types of controllers
	Instrumentation, actuators, sensors, microprocessors & subassemblies

Figure 4.5   Manufacturing plants contain a systems hierarchy with embedded technologies being at the lower two tiers.

term "embedded" means that it is essentially an inaccessible black box. Project teams chartered with embedded systems analysis will also encounter many types of application systems that directly or indirectly interface with embedded systems. For example, Ladder Logic is used to program PLCs. While the PLC itself is an embedded device, the code developed to program it is considered low-level application software. This software must be examined and corrected along with the PLC. In many cases, it will be difficult to distinguish the embedded device and the software that was used to program that device.

Embedded systems, and the application code that directly interfaces with these systems, typically play a key role in the operation of the machine, component device, or environment that they support or control. Noncompliant code associated with one of these devices must be fixed or replaced. Embedded technologies are typically concealed, difficult to identify, and hard to understand without extensive analysis by highly specialized experts. Most embedded technology tends to work day in and day out without anyone really knowing that it exists—until a problem occurs. As with IT-based systems, if any portion of the computer hardware or software embedded in a monitoring, control, or facilitation device is date-sensitive and not Year 2000 compliant, it could fail.

4.4.1 Embedded Systems Challenge

Embedded systems range from simple systems running a single circuit to complex, integrated hybrid systems developed for a very specific purpose. These integrated chip environments are called Application Specific Integrated Circuits or ASIC. ASIC inputs come from a detector or sensor while outputs feed a switch or activator that starts and stops a machine, opens and closes a valve unit, controls the flow of oil through a pipeline, or performs a host of related functions.[8] Some embedded systems are more sophisticated and can be programmed using various assembly or computing languages. Early embedded systems had storage and programming constraints similar to many IT systems and these constraints translated into the same Year 2000 problem, but the similarities end there.

For example, lines between the hardware, operating system, and "application" functionality tend to blur. Problems with an embedded system are, therefore, harder to debug and correct. These systems also tend to be customized into a unique format that cannot be readily modified by the owners of the systems or the original vendors—if they can be found. The high degree of customization in embedded systems also increases the difficulty of coming up with a replacement system. The nature of the Year 2000 problem can also vary dramatically within an embedded system.

One variation includes embedded systems that work off fixed base dates and time intervals. For example, a base date may calculate so many days after 1930—which could be miscalculated if the Real Time Clock (RTC) delivers a 00 in the year value. Fixed time intervals tend to signal maintenance dates or other checkpoint dates and trigger some type of event or intervention point—such as replacing a part. Some systems work continuously without ever shutting off (like the Voyager space craft), while other systems are built to start and stop periodically. Many embedded systems have been around for a very long time. Their developers, whoever they may have been, likely did not envision these systems being around at the turn of the century.

In relation to possible actions there are two distinct categories of embedded systems. Some systems have inaccessible software called embedded firmware that cannot be changed. In other cases, the software may be accessed and modified, but is too complicated or obscure to do so successfully. Much of the firmware and software found in embedded systems is unlikely to be the same technology that was originally designed or built by the designers of these systems.

4.4.2 Year 2000 Embedded Systems Impacts

Embedded system research challenges include not knowing how many embedded systems you have, where you can find them, and how best to identify them. A second challenge is not knowing which embedded systems have devices that are date-dependent or how or when these problems will come to light. One example is the leap year calculation problem which may not surface until March 2000. One major obstacle to embedded systems research is the difficulty required to get the information needed to determine which systems are at risk. Research efforts can be tedious and haphazard due to the "embedded nature" of these systems.

Basic technical Year 2000 problems typically found in embedded systems are highlighted in Figure 4.6. We refer to this checklist during the embedded systems analysis discussion in a later section. These problems include platform or hardware compliance problems, not being able to recognize or reflect the proper date after 2000, inability to restart properly, storing only a two-character year field when internal calculations or comparisons require a four-digit year field, and interface problems with higher-level control or IT-based systems. In order to correct these problems, research projects require business knowledge, knowledge of the application in which the systems are used, engineering talent, and IT skills. These skills are becoming increasingly scarce and growing more expensive to utilize.

Individual microprocessors are found in small devices like sensors, smoke and gas detectors, circuit breakers, and so on. It is unlikely, but certainly possible, that these systems will be impacted. If they are, they will require replacement. Small assemblies of microprocessors with no timing function are found in flow controllers, signal amplifiers, position sensors, and valve actuators. It is unlikely that these will be affected, unless they rely on an internal clock that is impacted by the Year 2000 problem. Subassemblies with a timing function include telephone exchanges, traffic light systems, elevators, switching gear, data capture and monitoring systems, diagnostic and real-time controllers. These systems could pass errant data into applications, databases, and networks. Errors in systems with timing functions may become apparent before 2000 (if a system attempts to mark a future event), on 01/01/2000, and

Embedded Systems—Diagnostic Checklist

Problem Type System Type	Platform Non-Compliance	Date Rollover Problems	Restart Failure or Errors	Date Calculation Errors	Date Interface System Errors
Communication					

Energy					

End Products					

Facility					

Financial					

Governmental					

Health Care					

Manufacturing					

Transportation					

Figure 4.6 High-level diagnostic checklist, by category, ensures the comprehensiveness of embedded systems research effort.

after that. More information on embedded systems is available by contacting the Institute of Electrical and Electronics Engineers (IEEE) Millennium Embedded Systems Working Group.[8]

4.4.3 Embedded Systems: Types and Categories

The previous discussion introduced the numerous functions that an embedded system may perform. These systems are in homes (temperature controls, security systems, VCRs, video cameras), in virtually every type of modern vehicle, in factory and headquarters building sites, on oil rigs, buried underground (telecommunications, oil pipeline valve controllers), and in the skies (satellites, space stations, shuttle craft, airplanes). There are few areas in our lives that are not touched by some type of computer or another—and many of these are embedded systems. As a prerequisite to researching, correcting, and testing these systems, we felt that it was important to divide the numerous types of embedded systems into several higher-level categories.

This categorization process should help management streamline the assessment and remediation tasks at hand. These categories include communication, energy, products, facilities, financial and retail, governmental, health care, manufacturing, and transportation. Each subcategory listed below is included as a point of reference for organizations that must research embedded system impacts. Where applicable, we have noted commonly held beliefs on how these systems might be impacted by the Year 2000. Unfortunately, research into many of these system categories is either lacking or privately held by the companies that vend these products.

4.4.3.1 Communications

Communication systems fall into numerous subcategories and are under the control of the telecommunication companies, government agencies, and private companies that have installed their own systems. Some of this equipment is definitely at risk, while other areas are likely immune to the Year 2000 problem.

1. *Telephone switches, PBXs, and communications exchange*

   Older switching equipment has been determined to be noncompliant and requires replacement.[2] Potential exposure includes synchronization, date/time stamping, self-checks, and event logging.

2. *Cable systems*

    Potential exposure includes signal processing, synchronization, and communications protocol issues.

3. *Satellites—Global Positioning System (GPS)*

    Currently set to roll over and encounter date problems in late 1999.[9] Potential exposure includes synchronization, event logging, date/time stamping, error checking, system interface formats, and communications protocol management.

4. *Data switching equipment*

    Heavy focus on protocol management, logic routing, error checking, peer-to-peer communications.

5. *Voice mail*

    Date and time logging errors could find a system that deletes messages based on date problems.[10]

6. *Internal telephone systems*

    In-house telephone system failures could shut down internal billing. A PBX could stop operating if it encounters an "invalid" date.[10]

7. *Fax, copy machines*

    Exposure includes communication protocol, error checking, transmission monitoring, memory management, date/time stamping, function logic, usage tracking, service monitoring, logging and interfaces.

8. *Mobile telephones*

    Exposure includes protocol management, communications management, signal processing, signal protection, function logic, date/time clocks, and system interfaces.

4.4.3.2 Energy

The energy industry is clearly at risk in many areas. The embedded system categories below should be reviewed by energy firms to verify compliance.

1. *Fossil fuel plants*

    Exposures include power management, date/time stamping, event logging, interface management, controls, data acquisition, performance monitoring, and alarm systems. Tests have demonstrated that resetting a date to post-1999 can, in some cases, cause the system to reset itself to 1980. Discrepancies between control units could cause a plant trip.[11]

2. *Power stations and power grids*

   Embedded systems in these facilities contain numerous computer chips—not all of which are compliant. Embedded logic control is in every facet of operation, from load dispatch and remote switchyard breaker control to nuclear power plant safety systems.[10] Entire operational environment should be checked for compliance.

3. *Uninterruptable Power Sources (UPS)*

   Exposures include event logging, time/date stamping, and performance monitoring. Invalid dates in these systems have the ability to shut them down.[10]

4. *Oil pipelines, refineries, storage facilities*

   Exposures include flow monitoring and control, alarms, sensor analysis, date/time stamping, and system interfaces. Valve control units (buried underground) contain flow control chips that should be analyzed. According to engineers at certain North Sea oil companies, an offshore oil platform contains over 10,000 microprocessors, some of which are deep below sea level. Engineers claim that all of these systems must be reviewed.

5. *Gas and related metering devices*

   Hand-held ITRON metering devices utilize two-digit year fields.[11] This becomes a problem when information is downloaded into databases for processing. It is not clear if these have been tested for compliance yet.

6. *Surveying and location equipment*

   Exposures include date/time stamping, event logging, signal processing, and system interfaces.

7. *Construction plant*

   Numerous types of systems (see Figure 4.5) can be found at all levels of a construction plant. All of these systems must be reviewed for compliance to ensure that environmental controls, process controls, quality monitoring, and other types of systems are verified to be compliant.

4.4.3.3 End Products

This category includes consumer products and durable goods that are manufactured and sold to the general public and other companies. The most important concern from the supply side perspective is the stated or implied warranty. If someone bought a device that has been discontinued or replaced with a newer model and the warranty period has expired, a no-cost upgrade or replacement is unlikely. There are clearly gray areas that are best left for consumer affairs groups to decide, but companies that sell end products should consider the implications of noncompliance and establish customer friendly policies sooner versus later. A short list of items is provided below.

1. *Still and video cameras, VCRs, televisions*

   Exposures include function controls, date/time stamps, and error checking. Setting a recording time or having a device reflect the correct day of the week is the biggest concern here.

2. *Microwave ovens*

   Exposures include function controls, date/time stamps, and error checking. Probably nothing to worry about.

3. *Radio equipment (all types)*

   May include date/time stamping, but unlikely to be impacted in a major way.

4. *Personal computers*

   BIOS chips in most older and many newer computers do not handle the century rollover. One manufacturer will make good on any problems encountered for systems purchased after October 1997. Customers are out of luck, however, for systems purchased prior to that time. BIOS devices can be upgraded in newer model computers, but customers should check with their manufacturer. Networked systems introduce more areas where problems can occur.

4.4.3.4 Facilities

Figure 4.7 highlights selected facility categories that a typical office or headquarters installation should research. This research effort requires working with facility coordinators, building management, and landlords.

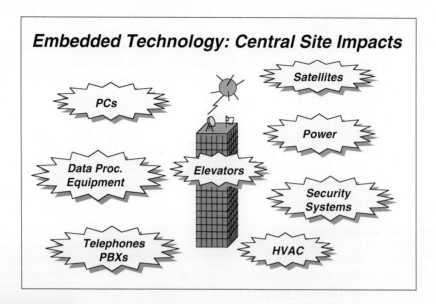

Figure 4.7 Embedded systems control security, communications, heating, ventilation, air conditioning and other facilities.

1. *Elevators and escalators*

   Yes, the elevator problem is real due to embedded functions that include date/time stamping, scheduling, maintenance checking, performance sensors, and condition analysis. Early tests determined that elevators would descend to the ground floor until the system was rebooted. Most people do not care about elevator problems, unless they are on an elevator going up to the operating room of a hospital for an emergency operation. Facilities managers should review these systems, regardless of vendor compliance claims.[10]

2. *Electrical supply, measurement, control, protection*

   Exposures include date/time logging, error (alarm) checking, performance monitoring, flow monitoring, and interfaces to higher-level tracking systems. Complex systems in major facilities could be vulnerable to problems.

3. *Backup lighting and generators*

   These systems could be critical during a Year 2000 failure of main power sources. Exposures include switch-over logic, sensor controls, conditions monitoring, system interfaces, and date/time logging.

4. *Fire control systems*

   Exposures include self-checking and testing, schedule monitoring, test and maintenance date tracking, and event logging.

5. *Heating and ventilating systems (HVAC)*

   Multifunction building climate systems have date dependencies due to holiday and weekends. One multimillion dollar HVAC system does not have date rollover capability, and the chip manufacturer is out of business costing one company more than $150,000 for a full replacement. Exposures include date/time scheduling, performance monitoring, trend analysis (to regulate power consumption over time), and system interfaces.

6. *Sprinklers*

   Exposures include date/time schedule tracking, maintenance testing and checking, logging, and control system. Automated fire sprinkler systems should be checked due to the criticality to human life. Exposures include date/time scheduling, logging, maintenance checking/testing, control systems, and interfaces.

7. *Security systems, security cameras, and locks*

   At an airport, field access is controlled by a security system that uses an expiration date. One month after expiration of a person's security clearance, the system checks renewal dates. If no renewal is set, then the file is deleted. A Year 2000 rollover test could delete all access to the field as no test has yet been attempted and no disaster recovery plan is in place. Complex systems are characterized by lasers, light sensors, ground and motion sensors, heat sensors, and other complex tracking devices. Exposures include monitoring, control systems, interfaces, date/time stamping, logging, and scheduling. Testing may be difficult if the system cannot be brought off-line.

8. *Door locks*

   This situation is similar to that found for a bank vault (refer to next section), although it may not carry the timing implications. Exposures include monitoring, control systems, interfaces, date/time stamping, logging, and scheduling.

4.4.3.5 Financial

These systems include embedded technology used directly by the financial community and financial systems used by retailers to address financial transactions. Consider the safeguards used at American Express vaults, Fort Knox, and similar institutions.

1. *Automated teller systems*

   Some automated teller systems are already undergoing replacement according to sources in the financial community. Exposure includes date/time stamping, scheduling, performance monitoring, data interfaces with higher-level applications, transaction logging, and database utilization.

2. *Credit card systems*

   These systems have already experienced problems. Credit card systems on gas pumps are known to be noncompliant.[13] Other commercial applications have similar problems and credit card companies have not issued cards with a "00" in the expiration date for this reason (as well as the fact that upstream applications are also noncompliant). Exposures include communications issues, protocol management, date/time stamping, performance monitoring, data interfaces with applications, transaction logging, and database utilization.

3. *Point-of-sale systems including scanner/cash systems*

   One lawsuit has already been filed because a credit card reader shut down an entire retail operation for a weekend costing that retailer significant business. Exposures are very similar to credit card processing systems with the added fact that some of these systems contain additional date-sensitive logic that could also fail.

4. *Safes and vaults*

   Some vaults operate on a date-based timer and could conclude that tomorrow has never arrived during the century rollover process.[10] Exposure includes date/time stamping, logging, access controls, alarms, maintenance checking and testing, interfaces, and override functions.

4.4.3.6 Government Systems

Government systems exist at the local, state, and federal level. State and local systems, discussed first below, tend to support basic local services, while federal systems cover a broader set of categories. One major concern at the federal level involves military defense systems.

1. *Ticketing systems/machines*

    Date dependence is still unclear at this point. Magnetic strip processing systems should be checked. Exposures include performance monitoring, error checking, date/time stamping, logging, controls, and interfaces.

2. *Parking and other metering categories*

    Exposures include date/time stamping, usage calculations, sensors, and system interfaces. Many traffic meters contain no computerized technology.

3. *Traffic lights*

    Exposures include date-sensitive microchips that manage rush hour, holiday, and weekend traffic, resynchronization of lights reset by emergency vehicles (via special strobe lights), and pavement sensors that track traffic volume and flow. These systems interface with main computers and the date debugging process has not always succeeded on the first attempt. Exposures include date/time scheduling, maintenance checking and testing, override functions, synchronization, and system interfaces.

4. *Water distribution*

    SCADA (Supervisory Control And Data Acquisition) systems run in real-time and nonreal-time mode. Systems must accommodate different flow and distribution situations. Pressure control functions dictate changes automatically or set off alarms. Data acquisition functions support data downloading and trend analysis to support capacity planning. Problems could arise well beyond 2000 due to errors in trend analysis. Sensor, logging, maintenance, meter monitoring, control, and distribution functions should all be reviewed.

5. *Water and sewage systems*

    ITRON metering devices utilize two-digit year fields and are not currently compliant.[11] Other exposures include date/time stamping, controls, alarms, interfaces, and maintenance tracking.

6. *Environmental monitoring equipment*

   Exposures include problems with instrumentation, date/time logging, communications, regulatory interfaces, protocol management, calculations, and performance monitoring and checking.

7. *Emergency response systems*

   These systems include a major number of system interfaces and automated functions. Exposures include alarms, communication functions, data/time event logging, trend analysis, override capabilities, and automatic functions.

   Defense systems encompass a separate category that includes weapons, satellite, command and control, on-board navigation, radar tracking, and a whole host of other technologies that are highly classified. Considering that, as of December 1997, the U.S. federal government was not reporting Year 2000 compliance status of embedded systems (they only included the status of IT systems undergoing remediation), we have no clear knowledge of what is going on in the U.S. military—let alone the status of overseas friends and foes.

   It is impossible to create a representative list or specific guidelines for the many specialized technologies used in military environments. General problems that analysts should examine in defense-based systems include event logging, time/date stamping, interface management, communication capabilities, monitoring, tracking, control capabilities, alarms, and maintenance tracking. The following short list identifies some of the challenges that defense agencies face between now and 2000.

1. *Surveillance tracking*

2. *Field communications*

3. *Missile and weapons guidance*

4. *On-board navigation, defense, and tracking systems*

5. *Nuclear containment*

6. *Radar, sonar*

7. *Satellite communications*

4.4.3.7 Health Care

   Medical diagnostics, monitoring, and life-support systems are a troubling category. This concern is not due to the fact that a high percentage of equipment is known to be noncompliant, but because the risks of a problem occurring in even a low percentage of sensitive equipment could be life threatening. We do know that some hospitals have discovered that up to 50 percent of their equipment requires replacement or upgrading. There is still much debate on the potential impacts in this category, but there is absolutely no room for error.

The following device categories should be examined for problems in date/time logging, event logging, self-monitoring, error checking, warning functions, calibrations, trend analysis, communication functions, system interfaces, maintenance schedules, functional logic, date- and age-based calculations, usage monitoring, and scheduling. Where applicable, additional notes have been included for each of the following categories.

1. *BIO medical devices*

2. *Defibrillator*

    When crossing the millennium boundary a defibrillator may shut down, thinking it has not been calibrated for 99 years.

3. *Blood and urine analysis equipment*

    Could also have potential calibration issues.

4. *Patient monitoring systems*

    Maintenance checking could force a monitor to malfunction.

5. *IV drug dispensing systems*

    Could go out of calibration or shut down thinking it has been 100 years since last calibrated.[14]

6. *Pacemaker monitors*

    Maintenance checking could be a problem.

7. *Infusion pumps*

8. *X-ray equipment and dosimeters*

    This device could overdose a patient with radiation.

4.4.3.8 Manufacturing and Process Control

Figure 4.8 highlights some of the problematic areas that should be reviewed in a given manufacturing environment. The list below is quite long due to the fact that the manufacturing category covers many industries and subcategories. The following categories should be examined for problems in date/time logging, event logging, self-monitoring, error checking, maintenance schedules, alarm functions, calibrations, trend analysis, communication functions, system interfaces, programmable logic, date-related calculations, monitoring, and scheduling. Where applicable, additional notes have been included for each of the following categories.

1. *Programmable Logic Controllers (PLC)*

   Also called a Step Process Controller (SPC) in Europe. Device itself could have noncompliant chips as well as logic problems in the ladder logic software used to program the device. Look for information coprocessors during the inventory process.

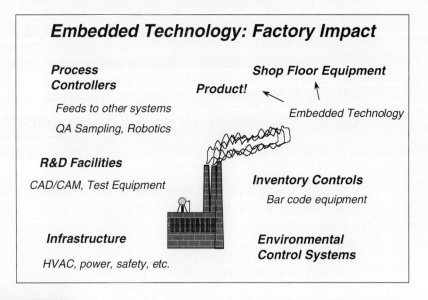

Figure 4.8 Shop floor, quality control, environmental control, R&D, safety, and power all rely on embedded technology.

2. *Automated factories—robotics*

   Includes complex motion controller that can translate data into the required motion. Robots may include a PC which is used to interface with a user or network.

3. *Alignment, balancing, and scales*

   These special categories are used in the automotive industry and typically have date/stamping functions that require research.

4. *Smart instrumentation and sensors*

   Includes data loggers, remote instrumentation sensors, and analytical instruments. Devices themselves could have noncompliant chips as well as logic problems in the software used to program the devices.

5. *Human-machine interface*

   This device is used to display and input data. Interfaces should be checked for compliance along with all PC components.

6. *Motion controllers*

   Includes various type of drives, servo systems, and single-axis controllers.

7. *Computer Numerical Controls (CNC)*

   These components include motion controls that define geometry and machine motion. Fault logging, PLC type programming languages, and interfaces typify functions that should be examined within these systems.

8. *Paint, steel, and other material mixing equipment*

   Could have interfaces to numerous other systems.

9. *Weld controller*

   Includes components related to welding, welding timers, welding controllers, and stud welders.

10. *Information coprocessors*

    Includes CPU, basic, ASCII, real-time clock, and communications modules that could be embedded in a PLC or other systems.

11. *Plant process (data scan, log, and alarm) controllers and routers*

    Could pick up errant data from low-level controllers.

12. *Safety parameter display*

    These systems may contain logic that is not century compliant and requires correction.

13. *Bottling equipment*

    Specialty equipment could contain obsolete chips that must be replaced.

14. *Simulators*

    Simulators that have date logging functions should be checked out.

15. *Test equipment*

    Any test equipment should be checked out along with all production systems.

16. *Multiloop control and monitoring*

    These include SCADA and telemetry systems.

17. *Panel mounted devices—control, display, recording, and operations*

    These systems require research into the PC unit and other embedded functions.

18. *Analytical / laboratory systems*

    These systems may have problems that are similar to some of the biomedical devices discussed in an earlier section.

19. *Electrical supply*

    These systems typically manage and measure electrical supply and have built-in protection capabilities.

20. *CAD CAM and engineering systems*

    These systems may be running on obsolete hardware or have programming or interface problems.

21. *Field-based devices*

    These devices provide measurement and actuation in field situations.

4.4.3.9 Transportation

Transport systems generally fall into the high-risk category. If a plane or ship at sea has a massive computer failure, the results could be catastrophic in terms of human life. General considerations that analysts should research in this area include smart instrumentation, date/time stamping, self-checking, alarms, event logging, calculations, interfaces to ground systems, and trend analysis.

1. *Airplanes*

Current research suggests that on-board systems on newer planes are either compliant or have no date sensitivity. Old planes, such as the DC3, have no computerized instrumentation. It does seem likely, however, that some older models built since the 1960s might have noncompliant technology, but it is also clear that avionics manufacturers are aggressively certifying these systems as compliant.

2. *Trains*

While little has been written regarding the compliance of on-board computer systems for trains, it seems that these systems may also be immune to the Year 2000 problem. However, routing systems, automated switching systems, railroad yard controllers, the impact of GPS, and diagnostic systems could be a problem.

3. *Marine craft*

Marine craft, particularly large ships, have a huge array of computer systems controlling or monitoring navigation, automatic pilot, weather conditions, shipping traffic, radar, vibration, heat usage, weight distribution, and fuel management. Little information is currently available regarding these systems, but hopefully this lack of data does not reflect the level of research being performed on these systems.

4. *Cars, trucks, buses, other internal combustion vehicles*

Exposures include maintenance tracking, event logging, and failure to start. Manufacturers are claiming that these systems are or will be compliant and independent tests have shown that most vehicles should not have any Year 2000 problems. Still, there are those who believe that at least some of these systems could cause problems in internal combustion vehicles.[10]

5. *Vehicle diagnostic devices*

Diagnostic systems have been shown to contain date-sensitive functions and should be reviewed carefully by manufacturers and buyers of this equipment.

6. *Air traffic control systems*

One does not have to look far to find problems with the FAA computers. FAA systems are old and replacement projects have proved unsuccessful. A recent incident demonstrates the fragility of these systems. A problem arose when FAA systems could not recognize dates and times that fell after 14:49 Greenwich Mean Time on November 2, 1997. An initial patch did not fix the problem and an additional 100 people were required to change 150,000 lines of code, or ten percent of a 1.5-million-line system.[15] Ten percent date sensitivity is high by any measure (industry averages two to four percent) and spells trouble for teams chartered with fixing the Year 2000 problem. Exposure includes dealing with complex backup systems, interfaces, communications, signaling, security, power backup, aging hardware, radar, radios, runway management, and overrides. No data is available for non-U.S. air traffic systems, but we suspect that there will be similar problems.

7. *Signaling and radar systems*

These systems should be reviewed for the standard date/time stamping, event logging, and other considerations suggested at the beginning of this section.

4.4.4 Embedded Systems Project Strategies

The principals of investigating and correcting Year 2000 problems within embedded systems are similar to those used in an IT environment. We wanted to highlight some of the unique requirements found in an embedded systems Year 2000 initiative, although we encourage readers to consider the principals that we advocated in our last Year 2000 book,[7] particularly in the assessment phase.

4.4.4.1 Embedded Systems Assessment Process

The embedded systems assessment phase is a key step because this is where analysts track down systems and determine their level of exposure to the Year 2000 problem. Analysts performing this assessment should consider the following objectives as they go about their task.

1. *Inventory microprocessors, controllers and other embedded technologies within IT and non-IT environments.*

2. *Determine whether or not these systems contain any date-sensitive features, functions, or interfaces.*

3. *Evaluate the impact of a date-related failure in that system and when that failure is first likely to occur (defines event horizon).*

4. *Evaluate the impact of a system failure on all related systems (defined by interfaces to those systems).*

5. *Establish a plan of action for each impact system or component.*

Due to significantly reduced time frames, analysts must combine the inventory and assessment process and, in some cases, take immediate action in the remediation area. We recommend using a formal checklist (refer to Figure 4.6) to categorize systems and track date-related impacts on those systems. Assessment analysts should consider the following guidelines in researching Year 2000 embedded system issues.

1. *Inventory embedded systems*

   - Verify that skilled personnel, including engineers, are available to perform this analysis

   - Identify all plants, operational facilities, remote sensors, pipelines, offshore rigs, data tracking points, or other physical locations where systems may exist

   - Visit each site or remote location as needed to find and log each device, piece of equipment, or environment

   - Inventory microprocessors, controllers, and other embedded technologies within IT and non-IT environments

   - For each system identified, document all interfaces and high-level applications that feed or receive data to or from this system

   - For each device, perform date-sensitivity analysis as described in the next step

2. *Perform date-sensitivity analysis*

- Establish a list of date-sensitive devices or components as a guide to performing this analysis:
  - check with purchasing to obtain vendor list
  - perform preliminary vendor survey to create a baseline of vendor compliance information
  - review availability of databases that may contain vendor compliance data
- Review and/or RTC to determine if century rolls over properly
- Review and/or test BIOS to determine if century rolls over properly
- Contact hardware vendor and/or perform tests to assess date impact on device or component
- Contact operating system vendor and/or perform tests to assess date sensitivity on device or component
- Review specifications as required to assess hardware and operating systems' date sensitivity
- Interview maintenance team, engineers, or system users to assess other issues

3. *Assess date failure impact on operating environment*

- Determine if calculations might be thrown off by date problems
- Examine potential shutdown during a maintenance cycle
- Assess if timed events and alarm problems could occur
- Examine impact on reports or display screens
- Check for potential date/time stamping or event logging errors that may occur
- Review smart instrumentation to assess date-related impacts
- Document impact on interface systems based on previously identified interfaces
- Determine if trend analysis errors could occur due to date calculation errors
- Examine all calculations of averages, rates, or trends impacted by date logic
- Pay special attention to the processing of data received at specific dates or times

- Determine when failure is first likely to occur (defines event horizon) based on future, current, or historic use of date data

- Tag the system with sticker that is (a) red if the system is not compliant and (b) green if the system is deemed compliant or not impacted

- Augment this process as required to indicate compliance for BIOS, RTC, operating system, platform, and/or application

- Evaluate the impact of a system failure on all related systems (defined by interfaces to those systems)

4. *Develop remediation and testing plans*

- Establish a plan of action for each impacted system or component

- Consider triaging as many systems as possible

- Consider turning off a continuously functioning system before midnight December 31, 1999, and restarting it later if this fixes the problem (testing can determine this)

- Prioritize based on risk (see Chapter 2) to the business and to business partners

- Prioritize based on human safety factors if required

- Incorporate the remediation and testing strategies discussed in the following sections

4.4.4.2 Embedded Systems Remediation Process

The objective of the remediation phase of the project is to modify, replace, or triage these systems, as required by the assessment, prior to the point where they could fail. With time running out and large inventories of complex embedded systems looming, analysts will have to integrate at least some remediation work into the assessment phase of the project. This integration process revolves around triaging systems that are not longer valid or in use.

With this requirement in mind, the goal is to replace or modify the smallest component within a device, rather than the device itself, and to replace individual devices within a machine or environment, rather than replacing the entire machine or environment. This set of objectives recognizes that an entire device or machine may require overhauling or replacement. The following general strategies should be considered when one determines that a system or part of a system must be replaced or updated.

1. *Obsolete hardware must be upgraded or replaced by the vendor (or an alternative vendor if possible).*

2. *Manufacturer-supplied system software should be updated by the supplier and reinstalled as is to avoid warranty problems.*

3. *Third-party application software should be updated by the supplier and reinstalled as is to avoid warranty problems (although modifications to applications are common and could make this impossible).*

4. *Microcode or application software developed in-house must be corrected by in-house technicians using*

   - Procedural workarounds (windowing) where expedient and where a four-digit year is not essential

   - Expansion to support sorting, key fields, and other circumstances that require a four-digit year field for interface or business reasons

5. *Notification of interface changes to those responsible for interfacing systems should be managed by a central Project Office working with individual project teams.*

   Analysts should consider the following issues as they undertake this effort.

1. *Ensure that Year 2000 upgrades do not affect the functionality of the system.*

2. *Where possible, obtain a statement of compliance from suppliers of off-the-shelf products.*

3. *Remember that, in some cases, avoidance is the least expensive and most judicious policy—consider*

   - if a system can be shut down for a period of time and restarted to work around the problem

   - if obsolete, unused systems can be triaged

   - if problems related to displays, reports, or noncritical functions even need to be fixed

   - that replacement may be more expedient that rebuilding or reworking an existing system (not typically the case with highly integrated IT based systems)

4. *Work off a project plan, particularly where scarce resources are spread across geographic regions.*

5. *Keep a paper trail of all work completed, vendor correspondence, and certification statements.*

4.4.4.3 Embedded Systems Testing Process

Testing, in an embedded systems scenario, may be the only way to assess a system's compliance status. Unfortunately, this type of testing could be time consuming. We recommend performing a test to assess compliance only on systems that management has determined mission-critical. Again, time is of the essence and prioritizing the testing process is the only way to get through this. (Refer to Chapters 7 and 8 for more information on Year 2000 testing and priority setting.)

Testing embedded systems presents some interesting challenges. Occasionally, a system can be certified compliant (or not) using a static check (system is not running). This process tests the software while it is not running, utilizing tools that scan software and components using simulation techniques. Most of the time, a dynamic test (system is running) is required to determine if a system is compliant. Dynamic testing is complicated when a system is large, complex and cannot be brought off-line for any period of time. This situation exists at the FAA to a degree and in the airport security example discussed earlier. Dynamic testing may require total replication of the environment being tested, taking care to utilize the same microcode, operating environment, and application software to ensure that the test is valid. In other cases, a system can be brought off-line long enough so that analysts can perform a test.

General embedded system testing requirements are listed below.

1. *Ensure that subject matter experts are available to provide input to test plan and review results.*

2. *Test will need to be performed simulating a window of time that begins in late 1999 and takes the system into 2001.*

3. *Ensure that date rollover and boot up process provide proper date values.*

4. *Compare date and day of week to ensure that they are correct.*

5. *Ensure that the following key dates are tested on the system:*

   - January 1, 2000
   - February 28, 2000
   - February 29, 2000

- March 1, 2000
- December 30, 2000
- December 31, 2000
- January 1, 2001
- Selected invalid dates and key business dates (fiscal year end, quarter end, etc.)

6. *Verify that all calculations that involve a leap year window are correct.*

7. *Test all windowing solutions to ensure that comparison and calculation logic is correct.*

8. *Test all expanded data to ensure that interfaces to other systems work properly.*

9. *Check calculations that cross the 1999–2000 window.*

10. *Ensure that files have been migrated properly where applicable.*

11. *Check all audit trail reports and logs for accuracy.*

12. *Verify that all file purging works correctly.*

13. *Check all display dates and report dates to ensure that they are set properly.*

14. *Attempt to feed incorrect dates into the system to make sure that they are rejected.*

15. *Remember to test any vendor-supplied software, using the testing guidelines, specifications, and results provided by that vendor.*

4.4.5 Embedded Systems: The Bottom Line

When compared to Year 2000 problems found in IT systems, the embedded systems challenge takes on a very different face. Estimates vary, but one report claimed that of all the embedded microchips in the world, two to four percent (roughly 2 million devices) are said to have Year 2000 compliance problems.[16] This estimate may be totally inaccurate (we have encountered situations before where "experts" were way off), but these devices could still impact tens of millions of people—depending on where and how they are being used at the time of failure. Pundits claiming that we should not worry about the Year 2000 because the impact will be minimal should temper their opinions with this thought. It could be one of your friends or family members on the plane, in the hospital, or on the ship that experiences a disastrous failure due to one of these devices.

Unfortunately, little time is left to address this problem. We suggest that companies take a posture of monitoring progress carefully on all embedded systems research. The documentation alone will provide companies with an accounting of embedded systems assets that range from mission critical to totally useless. Triaging those systems falling into the useless spectrum is likely to turn into a money saver long term. Post-1999 processing will uncover a fair share of situations that teams missed during the assessment, remediation, and testing processes. These systems should, therefore, be checked and rechecked well into 2000 and possibly beyond where trend analysis is an issue.

Contingency planning, which defines what to do if a critical system fails, is discussed at length in Chapter 9. All mission-critical systems should have a contingency plan and this is especially true for embedded systems. We encourage all of those systems professionals who are engaged in identifying and correcting embedded systems for an organization to get help wherever possible from skilled resources. The appendix lists vendors that specialize in this area. In addition to this, the endnotes for this chapter highlight several sources of information that can be found on the Internet, including a date specification document.[17] Heading off operational failure, or worse, that could result from an embedded systems failure is a huge task that must be completed quickly.

Endnotes

1. "Production Turbulence Hits Boeing," by David Field, published in *USA Today*, October 9, 1997, p. 1B.

2. "Bomb Ticking for Voice, Data Nets," by Matt Hamblen, published in *Computer-World*, October 27, 1997, p. 2.

3. U.S. Nuclear Regulatory Commission in Appendix B to SECY-97-213 on 24 September 1997 at http://www.nrc.gov/NRC/Y2K/S97213B.html. Additional information is available from the Computer Information Center at http://www.compinfo.co.uk/index.htm.

4. "Utilities Pose Terrible Disaster Potential Worldwide," published in *Year/2000 Journal* (original story source *Daily Oklahoman*," November/December 1997, p. 8.)

5. "Has Y2K Steam Rolled Your Pet Projects?" by John H. Mayer, published in *Software Magazine*, December 1997, pp. 56–62.

6. "US Bank Calls for a Year 2000 Time-out," by David Bicknell, published in *Computer Weekly*, October 22, 1997.

7. *The Year 2000 Software Crisis: Challenge of the Century*, by William M. Ulrich and Ian S. Hayes, Prentice Hall, 1997.

8. IEEE Millennium Embedded Systems Working Group developed in Embedded Systems and Year 2000 Guide accessible at http://www.ieee.org.uk/2000risk/year2k08.htm#e9e2.

9. Presentation by Melvin Scott, Boeing Information Services, at ABT Y2000 Survival Course, in Atlanta, GA, April 7–9, 1997.

10. "Embedded Systems: Surprising Exposures to the Year 2000 Problem," by Stephen Greif, published in *Year/2000 Journal*, November/December 1997.

11. "Real Life Examples of Date Related Problems for Electric Utilities," by Rick Cowles, published on www.accsyst.com, October 1997.

12. "Embedded Logic and Controls," by John Catterall, published on www.accsyst.com, December 2, 1997.

13. "2000 and Embedded Systems," by Jon Huntress, published in *Computer Bits*, December 1997.

14. "How Lethal Is the Millennium Bug?" by Julia Vowler, published in *Computer Weekly*, June 11, 1997.

15. "Computer Wake-up Call FAA Glitch Highlights Serious Problems to Come," published in *Kansas City Star*, December 18, 1997.

16. "Move to the Millennium," by Jerry Dean, published in *News-Sentinel* (Knoxville, TN), September 21, 1997.

17. BSI EN 28601: 1992 Specification for representation of dates and times in information exchange [equivalent to ISO 8601:1988 Data elements and interchange formats—Information interchange—Representation of dates and times].

Chapter 5

Getting Help: Factories, Outsourcing, and Services

Procrastination, longer than anticipated project preparation, competition from other priorities, and other delays have placed many companies in a precarious position considering the volume of remediation and testing that will have to be completed within a very short period of time. The volume of effort that must be handled in parallel increases rapidly as the time to the century deadline diminishes. Companies must already attain high levels of productivity if they are to meet their compliance objectives. Each additional delay mandates even greater productivity and strains the ability of the organization to provide the resources needed to complete the project. While corporate executives may understand this predicament at an intellectual level, it has yet to spur sufficient action in many companies.

Examining a few compelling numbers demonstrates that remediation efforts already demand unprecedented rates of productivity and that further delays will make full compliance an impossibility. Figure 5.1 shows the level of productivity needed to complete remediation for three scenarios. To be fully prepared to support system testing, these productivity numbers must include detailed analysis to find impacted dates,

Organizational Productivity Requirements

Scenario 1: Beginning 9/1/1997, Complete by 12/31/1998

Portfolio Size	Lines of Code per Week	Lines of Code per Work Day *	Lines of Code per Day
5 million LOC	72,464	17,065	10,309
25 million LOC	362,319	85,324	51,546
100 million LOC	1,449,275	341,297	206,186

Scenario 2: Beginning 6/1/1998, Complete by 12/31/1998

Portfolio Size	Lines of Code per Week	Lines of Code per Work Day *	Lines of Code per Day
5 million LOC	166,667	39,370	23,697
25 million LOC	833,333	196,850	118,483
100 million LOC	3,333,333	787,402	473,934

Scenario 3: Beginning 6/1/1998, Complete by 6/1/1999

Portfolio Size	Lines of Code per Week	Lines of Code per Work Day *	Lines of Code per Day
5 million LOC	96,154	22,727	13,699
25 million LOC	480,769	113,636	68,493
100 million LOC	1,923,077	454,545	273,973

* assumes 220 work days per year

**Volume of code that must be processed per unit of time
to complete the project by the specified end date**

Figure 5.1   Organizational Productivity Requirements.

remediation of those dates, and unit testing the correctness of the changes. The first two scenarios assume a December 31, 1998 deadline to allow a full year for compliance testing and certification. The third scenario shifts the testing date to mid-1999. Note that this shift is accomplished by reducing test time by half, thereby increasing parallel testing effort and greatly increasing project risk.

As large as these figures appear, an IT organization's ability to attain them is determined by the productivity of its staff and/or consultants and the number of resources available. For example, if a programmer can fully analyze, remediate, and unit test one program per day,[1] a team of ten full-time programmers could complete a five-million line portfolio over 15 months. Unfortunately, many pilot projects to date have encountered lower than expected productivity due to tool limitations and the overhead of finding and packaging the correct source code version for each application. Since a deadline extension is out of the question, companies have only a few choices:

- Increase the productivity of existing resources

- Reduce the size of the project to remain within resource constraints

- Obtain additional resources

While increasing the productivity of existing resources appears to be the preferable option, it is unlikely that this approach alone will be successful for any but the smallest companies. Automation, highly refined processes, and training are the keys to high productivity. While tool efficiency has steadily increased over the past several years, these improvements are not enough to overcome the effects of procrastination. Further, it is unrealistic for an IT organization that is currently lagging in its Year 2000 efforts to suddenly develop the expertise and processes needed to obtain peak efficiency.

Almost all companies are attempting to reduce the size of their projects wherever possible by discarding applications, implementing minimal solutions, or instituting delaying actions. One large company managed to reduce the size of its portfolio by two-thirds by eliminating all but the most critical applications. Many of the newer tools on the market focus on minimal fixes, reducing the number of modifications and theoretically reducing testing effort. To ensure their ability to reach compliance in a timely manner, all companies should reduce project size as much as possible. It is essential to understand, however, that many reductions only delay work until after the century transition, and that "magic" tool solutions often have major side effects.

The third option to meet the century deadline is to obtain additional resources to supplement existing staff and hardware until sufficient capacity is available to handle the expected workload. Some resources may be obtained by reallocating internal resources to Year 2000 efforts; however, most organizations will be forced to obtain outside assistance to meet their full requirements. There are many sources of capacity, and these will be discussed in this chapter. When outside resources are used, this option can provide far more than just capacity. The best consulting firms bring considerable expertise in project management, effective use of tools, and best practices. This knowledge can provide a significant boost in overall productivity. Unfortunately, external resources are not a panacea. They are costly, in short supply, and can be easily misused.

Reality dictates that prudent companies adopt a combination of all three approaches. They must reduce their projects to the minimum reasonable size needed to ensure organizational operation through the century transition while applying a sufficient level of productive resources to guarantee that the projects can be completed in time. Since outside resources are central to this combination, it is crucial that companies select the right type of assistance for each project and that they do everything possible to ensure the success of those resources. This topic is the focus of this chapter.

The first section of this chapter focuses on lessons learned to date about the use of third-party services. In many cases, initial experiences with these services have been less than ideal for both the client and the vendor. This section discusses the reasons that these relationships have been less successful than desired as a means for correcting the underlying issues.

The second section describes a series of parameters that can be used to select the optimal type of assistance for a given project. It is followed by a section on enabling the success of vendor-assisted projects. This section discusses the basic practices that must be put into place to ensure that vendor work products meet expectations and that the vendor can operate at peak performance. It is followed by three sections that discuss specific issues related to software factories, consultants, and offshore vendors.

The final section of the chapter briefly examines the current state of the market for outside resources and some interesting new options for obtaining help.

5.1 Third-Party Services—Lessons Learned to Date

The need for additional assistance from consulting firms and tool vendors will reach its peak during the final two years of the Year 2000 effort when most companies are deep in the throes of full-scale remediation and testing. Companies that are behind in their efforts will need even greater numbers of consultants if they are going to have any hope of achieving compliance. While this need is good news for the hundreds of providers of tools, consulting, and factory services, time pressures, unrealistic expectations, and false hopes will create significant problems in the relationships between vendors and clients. Given the importance of maintaining good vendor relationships to ensure effective project execution, it is troubling to find that many companies are not happy with the performance of their vendors to date. Vendor bashing is a common theme at user meetings and industry conferences. Vendors are commonly taken to task at these meetings and in trade press articles as greedy opportunists or berated for not meeting productivity expectations. Especially telling was the audience response at a Year 2000 conference in San Francisco in October 1997. When a large audience was asked if they were satisfied with their primary vendors, only two hands went up. Not surprisingly, the market is seeing a lot of vendor switching as companies dissatisfied with early progress try another solution. Some companies have already switched vendors several times and remain unsatisfied.

5.1.1 The Roots of the Dilemma

How did this state of affairs evolve? Depending on the perspective of the reader, the problem is either vendors who will say anything to get a sale but are unable to deliver to their commitments or it is Year 2000 project teams that ask for the wrong things, expect too much, and do not want to do any work themselves. As usual, the truth lies somewhere between these two extremes. To be sure, the dollars being spent on Year 2000 fixes have inspired many dubious products and services and the market does not lack for frauds and incompetents. However, there are also many reputable and hardworking vendors who are truly doing everything possible to make their clients successful. In many cases, the root of the problem is miscommunication of expectations between both parties.

Year 2000 projects are especially prone to misset expectations. Most IT organizations still desperately desire a magic solution that requires minimal disruption of their normal activities. Trade press and vendor hype encourages unrealistic expectations about the level of productivity and "hands off" automation that is possible. Sales personnel are reluctant to dispel these expectations for fear of being eliminated from evaluations. As a result, the vendor selected for the project is often already set up for failure in the eyes of the client.

Figure 5.2 illustrates the missed communications and incorrect expectations throughout the sales and delivery process. Although this is a humorous example, there are important lessons that can be learned from it. The buyer begins by wanting the ultimate solution. Although emotionally attractive, this solution is clearly too costly and impractical. The buyer asks for something more reasonable but remains susceptible to someone offering something closer to their desired solution. The vendor, aware of the market hype and not having the requested solution, talks the buyer

The Roots of the Dilemma

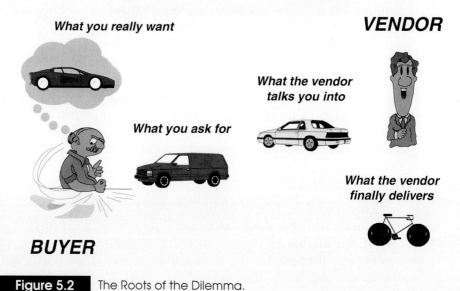

Figure 5.2 The Roots of the Dilemma.

into a compromise. This compromise has enough performance features to meet the buyer's unstated expectations. Finally, the real solution is delivered. It goes from point A to point B as promised, but with less speed and automation than expected!

5.1.2 Identifying the Most Common Mistakes

Neither party intended to arrive at the situation described above. The buyer really wants assistance on his Year 2000 project and the vendor really wants a satisfied client. Few vendors can remain in business without successful customers. Despite the temptation to blame vendors, more often than not, when a relationship becomes troubled, the buyer bears as much or more of the responsibility for the problem. Typical mistakes include the following.

- **Selecting the wrong vendor**

  Even reputable vendors have different strengths and weaknesses and may be a mismatch for the needs of a given project. For example, hiring a supplemental staffing firm to manage an enterprise-level Year 2000 project is as wrong a choice as selecting a top-tier management consulting firm to provide COBOL staff.

- **Picking the wrong solution**

  This mistake occurs when the company picks an unworkable short-cut solution and imposes it on a vendor. The project is doomed to failure from the start and the vendor takes the blame.

- **Failing to provide a complete statement of work**

  Finger pointing, dropped deliverables, cost overruns, and other disappointments are inevitable when a project lacks clearly defined roles, responsibilities, and standards.

- **Providing inadequate infrastructure support**

  Underlying infrastructure issues create insurmountable barriers to a successful project. For example, weaknesses in IT organization configuration management practices are the greatest inhibitor to the use of factories. Complaints about the amount of effort required to package and ship a complete and correct version of an application upgrade unit are an IT problem not a vendor issue.

- **Having unrealistic expectations about vendor performance**

  Many IT organizations are sorely disappointed to find that hiring a prime vendor for their Year 2000 project does not offload the entire effort to that party. They are shocked at the level of effort and expertise they are required to contribute to the project and its impact on other IT efforts. But how could the largest project in the history of IT be any different?

- **Believing unrealistic vendor promises**

  Vendors are not blameless. Salespeople overpromise and let the product or consultants underdeliver. Rather than totally understanding the company's needs and walking away if their solution doesn't match those needs, some salespeople will push their products and services regardless of fit (and likelihood of success). Bait-and-switch tactics are common, especially for Year 2000 project leaders and technical specialists. Companies expect seasoned professionals only to receive newly trained college students. The only defense is to check and recheck all claims and references before buying anything from any vendor without a long and pristine track record for performance.

5.1.3 Ground Rules for Successful Vendor Relationships

Like it or not, IT organizations have to take much of the responsibility for making sure that their vendor relationships are successful. Since the time remaining until the end of the century is limited and growing shorter by the day, the opportunity to switch vendors is rapidly fading. Avoiding the mistakes described above will go a long way toward building productive vendor relationships, which in turn lead to successful projects. Seeking methods to assist vendors wherever possible enables those vendors to do the best possible job for the company. Specific enablement suggestions will follow in subsequent sections of this chapter. Some general ground rules are

- **Match expectations with reality**

  Don't expect miracles. If a vendor or a press article offers something that sounds like the perfect solution, it is probably hype and has a fatal flaw that won't be discovered until too late. The best way to ensure success is to accept that the project will require a lot of hard work from both the vendor and IT staff.

- **Select vendors carefully**

  Be sure to pick vendors that truly fit company needs. Understand the type(s) of solutions needed to handle the company portfolio and select vendors that are skilled in those solutions. Never impose another vendor's solution on the selected vendor. More detailed criteria for vendor selection can be found later in this chapter.

- **Make the vendor successful**

  The common goal is to make the company compliant. Help the vendor by implementing necessary infrastructure improvements. Get them the information they need. Help them avoid company politics and other internal roadblocks.

- **Actively manage all vendor relationships**

  Surface and handle issues early, before they become major obstacles.

5.2 Selecting the Right Strategy

The two most critical factors for a successful vendor-assisted project are selecting the right strategies and selecting the right partner(s) to implement those strategies. As many IT organizations have discovered, these decisions are not as simple as they first seem. Year 2000 program managers face a bewildering array of strategies and assistance options. Many of these options, while intriguing, may not be suitable for a given portfolio. Other options are simply not credible when carefully evaluated. Only the smallest and most standardized IT organizations will be able to rely on a single strategy and a single vendor for their entire Year 2000 effort. In most cases, the IT organization will have to use a mixture of approaches, picking one for each major technology grouping. For example, COBOL code may be handled in-house using an internal factory, while the last, isolated MarkIV application is sent away to specialists.

This section attempts to clarify the decision process by offering a group of basic parameters for selecting the best implementation strategy for a particular technology grouping. Using these parameters, an IT organization can decide if it is best to process that technology themselves, bring in consultants, ship the code to a factory, or rely on offshore resources. The first part of the section defines the parameters; the second part of the section shows how they are used to select the right strategy; and the final part offers some criteria for selecting the right vendor to implement the strategy.

5.2.1 Strategy Selection Parameters

Given the wide array of implementation options on the market, identifying the right approach for a portfolio of applications using a given technology can be very difficult. To simplify this process, a basic set of parameters can be applied to eliminate clearly inappropriate options. This process winnows the number of choices to a reasonable number. Factors such as the technology value or volume of code affect the viability of a potential approach. For example, a heavy investment in tools and training is justified for a 25-million line-of-code (LOC) portfolio using a strategic technology but is inappropriate for a small number of obsolete applications using an ancient 4GL. Many factors can be considered in the selection process, however, the list below covers the most important ones. If desired, the decision process can be further refined by assigning different weights to each of these factors. These parameters will be used in the next part of this section to describe the ideal characteristics for each major implementation strategy category. Figure 5.3 shows the relationship of the four top strategy selection parameters: code volume, skills availability, technology value, and control needs. The fifth parameter, setup time and investment, is a secondary parameter. It is an important modifier of a selected strategy and becomes increasingly important as the century deadline approaches. Each parameter is rated using a high, medium, and low scale. Common ranges for each rating are described as follows.

The Strategy Selection Parameters

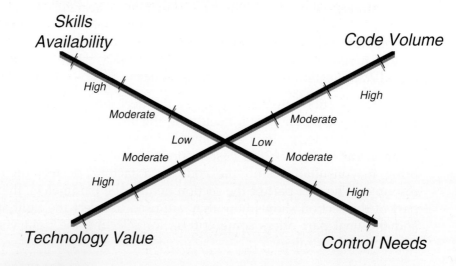

Figure 5.3 The Strategy Selection Parameters.

- **Volume of code**

  The volume of code that has to be processed using a given approach is one of the most important selection factors. Some methods, such as manual remediation, are not suitable for very large volumes of code, while others, such as internal factories cannot be justified for small volumes. Each approach has an optimum capacity which should be compared against the volume of code to be processed. If a large volume of code needs to be processed, it is essential to ensure that the selected approach facilitates very high productivity without requiring an excessive number of scarce resources. A high volume of code for a technology is over 10-million LOC; low is less than 1-million LOC.

- **Skills availability**

  The availability of appropriately trained programmers is another major consideration when evaluating options for a particular technology in the portfolio. "Do it yourself" approaches are only available to organizations with adequate internal resources. In many cases, the sheer volume of code will overwhelm the organization's internal resources, requiring it to pursue consulting-based approaches. Further, almost all IT organizations have pockets of "orphan" technologies that fall outside their core competencies. Lack of adequate skills and tools to support these technologies requires the organization to seek specialized consulting assistance. Skills availability is also a critical criterion when selecting a consulting partner. It is essential to match skill requirements against the core competencies of the potential consulting partner. A high skills rating means that there is a sufficient level of skilled resources to handle anticipated needs. A medium rating is given when skilled resources are available, but they are not sufficient to handle the entire demand. A low rating means few if any resources are available.

- **Strategic value of the portfolio's technology**

  IT organizations typically employ a number of different technologies in their application portfolios. These technologies vary widely in strategic value to the organization. Less strategic technologies may be in the process of being phased out, while major investments are being made in the strategic technologies of the future. From an implementation strategy perspective, it makes little sense to invest heavily in tools and training to handle internal remediation of a technology in the final phases of its life cycle. Conversely, the same investments are more than justified for strategic technologies. Since technologies such as COBOL will be supported well into the next century, an approach that transfers tools and knowledge to internal staff provides long-term increases in productivity. Finally, there is little tool support for less common technologies. These technologies require time-consuming and costly manual processing, making them ideal candidates for approaches that use low-cost labor. High strategic value means that a given technology is part of the organization's strategic architecture and that applications continue to be built using that technology. A medium rating implies that the technology remains in active use in production, but it is no longer used for major development efforts. A low rating means that the technology is being phased out.

- **Control and security issues**

  The need to maintain control over application source code strongly affects available solution options. There are two primary factors to consider. First, is the code highly strategic and proprietary or is it relatively generic? Off-site solutions and, in particular, offshore solutions, are often not attractive for highly confidential applications.

Conversely, generic applications, such as accounting functions, have little proprietary value and can be sent for off-site remediation with little risk. The second control issue is application volatility. If an application is modified frequently, internal remediation approaches allow better control of simultaneous changes. A highly stable application can use either an internal or external approach. Highly volatile and/or proprietary technologies receive a high rating. Very stable or generic applications receive a low rating.

- **Setup time and investment**

    The investment in time and money to set up a given approach must be factored into the selection decision. As the century deadline looms closer, IT organizations can no longer select approaches that require a long lead time to achieve full productivity. Financing is also a consideration. Some approaches, such as internal factories, require a considerable investment in tools and processes before they can productively process large volumes of code. Unless large volumes of code are to be processed, the time and cost of this investment will exceed its benefits. A high rating implies that a solution requires a considerable investment in funds, tools, training and time to be successful, such as a setting up a software factory. A manual approach for a small number of programs would receive a low rating, since it requires little, if any, setup.

5.2.2 Using the Parameters to Select a Strategy

This section illustrates how the parameters described above are used to select the optimum strategy for a given Year 2000 project. As stated in the introduction to this section, most IT organizations will need to select a number of different strategies to fully cover their application portfolio. Resist the temptation to force all technologies in the portfolio to use the strategy selected to handle the most common technology. While each additional strategy increases the effort needed for management and vendor coordination, these costs are more than compensated for by the increased quality and efficiency of processing each technology with its optimal approach.

The approaches described below have been simplified to fit within the confines of this book. The intent is to provide a framework from which the reader can extrapolate to fit their specific requirements. The examples below concentrate on the most common categories of choices: "do it yourself," supplemental staff, project consultants, factories, and offshore consulting. It is important to remember that there are vendors that are exceptions to the rules in each category. The descriptions below are meant to describe the optimum characteristics for the category rather than the parameters for an individual vendor within the category. Use common sense whenever applying general rules.

To use the parameters to select among these options, follow this simple methodology:

1. *Select a technology which needs an implementation approach.*

2. *Copy Figure 5.3 as a guide.*

3. *Rate the technology in each category using a low, medium, and high rating.*

4. *Compare the ratings against those shown for the categories below.*

5. *If desired, the ratings can be converted into a diagram, as shown in Figure 5.4. This diagram is useful for displaying and comparing requirements in presentations and reports.*

- **"Do It Yourself" (DIY)**

  The DIY approach relies exclusively on internal resources to implement the Year 2000 effort. While it is not a consulting approach, it is included here as an alternative to the use of outside resources. Figure 5.4 shows the parameters for the three most common strategies within the DIY category: manual fix, tool-assisted, and in-house factory. A detailed explanation of these approaches is found in Chapter 6.

  - **Volume of code:** The manual approach, given its inefficiency, is only viable for small volumes of code. Given its training and tool investment requirements, the tool-assisted approach is best suited for medium to high code volumes. Internal factories are justified only for high to very high code volumes.

  - **Skill availability:** The IT organization must have sufficient numbers of trained individuals to fully staff these approaches.

  - **Strategic value of the portfolio's technology:** In theory, DIY approaches can be used to handle any value technology. In practice, most organizations have not retained the skills needed to support their low value technologies.

  - **Control and security issues:** Since DIY approaches are conducted on-site, they can handle any control or security need.

  - **Setup time and investment:** Very low for manual. Moderate for tool-assisted and high for internal factories.

The "DIY" Diagram

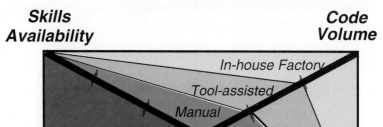

Figure 5.4 The "DIY" Diagram.

- **Supplemental Staff**

  This approach uses contract programmers to fill in gaps in internal staffing. Supplemental staffing organizations can provide a wide variety of trained resources, but the IT organization is responsible for providing the tools, methodologies, and management to operate the project. Since the supplemental staffing firm does not assume any project responsibility, the cost of their resources is usually lower on an hourly basis. Resources are provided on-site as needed. Supplemental staff resources are typically applied as if they were internal staff. As a result, the three approaches described above for DIY apply to this category. An IT organization should first select which of these three approaches it is going to use and then supplement its internal staff with consultants as needed.

  - **Volume of code:** Supplemental staffing approaches can be applied to any volume of code.

  - **Skill availability:** While supplemental staff can fill in any staffing gap, they are best mixed with internal staff. As a result, supplemental staffing is most suited for moderate skills availability.

- **Strategic value of the portfolio's technology:** This approach can be used for any value technology. Supplemental staff is especially attractive as a means of gaining expertise in unsupported technologies.

- **Control and security issues:** Since this approach is conducted on-site, it can handle almost any control or security need.

- **Setup time and investment:** Although supplemental staff members tend to be more expensive than their internal counterparts, for strategy selection purposes they are interchangeable. Follow the guidelines under DIY.

- **Project Consultants**

  Unlike supplemental consulting resources, project consultants assume all responsibility for an entire project. The project may range in scope from a single upgrade unit to an enterprise Year 2000 program. The consulting firm typically provides its own project management, staff, tools, and methodology. Project consultants rely on training, common processes, and automation where possible to offer cost-effective services. Successful project consulting firms have a strong reputation for project management and well-defined relationships with tool vendors and specialized service providers. These characteristics enable project consultants to provide their clients with higher productivity than is usually possible using internal staff or supplemental consultants. Project consulting can be performed on-site or off-site depending on the needs of the client. Off-site projects appear very similar to factories from the client's view, while on-site projects may follow one of the forms described under DIY. Some off-site consulting facilities are willing and able to handle less common technologies. Due to lack of software vendor tools, these facilities rely primarily on the expertise of their consultants backed by internally created tools. These types of facilities are an excellent option for the less common technologies in an IT portfolio. Their cost is easily justified by the IT organization's ability to avoid investing in the tools and training required for internal remediation.

  - **Volume of code:** Project consulting can handle any volume of code but is typically used for moderate to high volumes.

  - **Skill availability:** Project consulting is most valuable for low to moderate skills availability. Unlike the supplemental staffing approach, project consultants can operate without the availability of client staff.

- **Strategic value of the portfolio's technology:** Given the range and variety of firms in the market, most technologies can be covered. However, since project consulting firms usually specialize in a few key categories of technology, a combination of several firms may be required to handle a very diverse portfolio.

- **Control and security issues:** If performed on-site, this approach can handle almost any volatility or security requirement. If performed off-site, this approach is best suited for moderate to low control requirements.

- **Setup time and investment:** Project consultants are usually more costly than internal or supplemental staffing approaches. Since they bring all necessary skills, management, and tools, they require a very short startup period.

- **(Software) Factories**

    Software factories rely on a combination of tool automation, formalized processes, and dedicated staff working in an assembly line environment to achieve the maximum productivity for code analysis, remediation, and unit testing. These factories can guarantee high throughput and consistent quality for their services, and often offer a lower cost per line of code than the previous consulting options. To achieve these efficiencies, factories trade off a degree of flexibility and concentrate on the most common languages and programming styles. The input to a factory is a freestanding application or group of related applications called an upgrade unit. Internal staff assumes the responsibility for effective Quality Assurance (QA) practices before shipping the upgrade unit to the factory and upon receiving the compliant version of that unit from the vendor.

    - **Volume of code:** Factories can handle any volume of code but tend to be most cost effective for moderate to very large volumes of common technology.

    - **Skill availability:** Factories are the most attractive when skills availability is low to moderate.

    - **Strategic value of the portfolio's technology:** Factories can handle any level of technology but tend to specialize in the most common languages and platforms. When available, factory processing is especially attractive for older, nonstrategic technologies where little long-term value would be gained from reusing remediation tools or knowledge.

- **Control and security issues:** Offsite-approaches are less suitable for highly confidential or proprietary applications where security is an issue. Highly volatile applications are not suitable unless they are supported by an excellent configuration environment.

- **Setup time and investment:** Low to moderate. The cost of factory setup is distributed across all users of that factory. Some internal investment is required to implement effective processes and controls to support the factory process.

- **Offshore Services**

  Offshore firms are consulting companies with fully staffed facilities in countries with low-cost labor. They offer either factory or off-site consulting services. They rely on their low labor costs to offer similar services as local consulting firms for lower prices. These firms differ considerably in their reliance on automation versus low-cost labor to accomplish remediation. Higher-end firms processing common technologies use the same tools as their domestic counterparts, while smaller firms rely mostly on manual methods. Low labor costs make these firms particularly attractive for uncommon technologies that have to be processed manually. The use of offshore firms is limited for some applications by the risks and potential legal liability of sending confidential technology abroad. Further, time zone differences and cultural issues introduce additional complexity into working relationships.

  - **Volume of code:** Offshore vendors can handle any volume of code but are most appropriate for moderate to large volumes.

  - **Skill availability:** Offshore is most appropriate for technologies with low skills availability.

  - **Strategic value of the portfolio's technology:** While this approach can handle any value technology, it is especially attractive for technologies that must be processed manually.

  - **Control and security issues:** Offshore approaches are not suitable for highly confidential or proprietary applications where control or security are an issue. Highly volatile applications are not suitable unless they are supported by excellent configuration environment.

- **Setup time and investment:** Moderate. Requires a greater investment in processes and initial setup than factory approaches. These costs can be recouped due to lower staffing costs.

5.2.3 Selecting the Right Partner

Once the optimum strategy has been selected to remediate a given application, the next step is to select the best available partner to assist in the implementation of the strategy. At the time of this writing, many of the top-tier consulting firms are already at, or near, their capacity for Year 2000 assignments and are no longer an option for most companies. This reality forces companies seeking assistance to rely on lessor known and less experienced firms. There is no shortage of consulting firms in the Year 2000 market, but clearly not all of them are equal. The following selection criteria have been summarized from our first book.[2] It is offered as a starting point for the vendor selection process. Readers seeking a more detailed discussion of this topic should refer to the first book.

While cost considerations are a factor for most IT organizations, price should not be the primary consideration when picking a vendor. High-quality skills and services cost money; skimping on cost will usually result in lower quality support. Further, inexperienced vendors will underprice a project and then fail in its execution. The combined cost of failure and restarting with another vendor will invariably cost more than picking a more credible and expensive vendor at the onset of the project.

The selection criteria described below are based on common sense and can be applied to almost any type of consulting situation. Although originally developed to evaluate consulting firms for project work or outsourcing, these criteria remain important when seeking other forms of assistance. Any consulting firm can claim to handle century-date compliance projects, but their ability to deliver those projects is based on their reputation, project management capabilities, and expertise.

- **Fit within strategy**

    Every consulting vendor has particular areas of expertise. Select vendors that specialize in providing services that match the chosen strategies. A supplemental staffing firm is the wrong choice for managing an enterprise-level Year 2000 program and a management consulting firm is the wrong choice for coding expertise in obscure languages. If a given project is a stretch for a vendor, select another vendor.

- **Project management capabilities**

  Year 2000 projects require world-class project management. Avoid vendors without demonstrable track records in project management. Be skeptical of any vendor that must recruit project managers for their projects since the tightness of the market makes high-quality project managers extremely scarce.

- **Reputation**

  The best method for judging a consulting firm is by their track record. Given the importance and risk of a century-date compliance project, it is essential to select a vendor with the experience and track record for delivering complex projects on time and within budget. While there are no infallible criteria for evaluating the potential success of a given project, the following criteria provide a good indication of the vendor's track record.

- **Length of time in market**

  Evaluate both the length of time the vendor has been providing IT consulting services and the length of time they have been in the Year 2000 market. The best vendors have a long history in the IT market as shown by steady growth and consistent profitability.

- **Number of century-compliance projects underway**

  Clearly, winning and successfully completing a large number of projects is an important indicator of success. Don't rely strictly on the number of previous projects. Ask how many customers have used the vendor for follow-on projects as they have progressed through the phases of the project. Some early Year 2000 vendors have an impressive number of initial project wins, but extremely low rates of renewal.

- **Customer base and references**

  Checking references is a must. Do not restrict reference checks to customer names provided by the vendor. Network at tradeshows and in professional organizations to find other customers of the vendor.

- **Long-term strategy**

  Will the vendor be around when the applications it has fixed go into the next century? Pick vendors that are looking for a business relationship well past Year 2000 to ensure that they have the incentive to produce high-quality work.

- **Expertise**

  Year 2000 projects require a great deal of expertise and a large number of resources to execute. Be sure that any selected consulting firm has sufficient quantities of both to support the types of consulting it is offering. While a firm's marketing literature may be impressive, its actual practices are more telling. Strong staff training programs, availability of a formal Year 2000 methodology, and solid relationships with tool vendors demonstrate the firm's experience and commitment to the Year 2000 market. Consulting firms without these characteristics should not be considered for project assignments.

5.3 Enabling Success

The previous sections described how to select a strategy, and partners, to meet an IT organization's Year 2000 goals. To implement a chosen strategy and vendor relationship in the most productive way possible, an IT organization must have the proper techniques and infrastructure in place. To achieve a successful relationship with any kind of third-party vendor, an IT organization has to accept responsibility for, and perform, a number of tasks. These tasks are the basic criteria by which the IT organization and the vendor can measure and ensure the progress and ultimate success of the project. Unfortunately, as discussed in Section 5.1, too many IT organizations convince themselves that once they've selected and handed off a project to an outside firm they won't have any further involvement with, or responsibility for, the project. In fact, the opposite is true. While an outside vendor can perform many of the tasks necessary to bring the project to completion, the IT organization will remain responsible, both within the company and legally, for the success of the project.

While there are many factors that can influence the success or failure of a project, following are some of the most critical, common tools to ensure success.

- **Airtight Statement of Work**

  A Statement of Work (SOW) very clearly sets the expectations of all parties involved in a project. It minimally describes the goal of the project, the boundaries of the project, who is involved with the project, the tasks each party is responsible for performing, the timing and quality of deliverables, and the acceptance criteria for those deliverables. An airtight SOW aligns expectations and ensures that all parties proceed in the same direction and stay on track until completion of the project.

- **Compliance definition**

  Briefly, a compliance definition states the criteria by which an application or upgrade unit will be deemed century-compliant. The definition has many components which describe the strategy for achieving compliance, how particular date logic and fields are to be remediated, how interfaces should look, and so on. Without a definition to establish the criteria for compliance, a vendor and IT organization could conceivably differ as to whether a given application has achieved compliance. For a vendor, the compliance definition should be viewed as the specification for how all Year 2000 work is to be performed. For the IT organization, the compliance definition serves as a guide in the performance of all supporting tasks, such as test data and test script generation, that it performs while the application is under remediation with the vendor. Finally, the compliance definition will be used by the IT organization as its acceptance criteria when a remediated application is returned by the vendor.

- **Strong configuration management**

  An IT organization must have strong configuration management capabilities to support all of the activities and tasks associated with vendor remediation. Figure 5.5 illustrates these activities.

  Without these configuration management capabilities, a project is doomed to failure. The most important capabilities are

- **Ability to package a remediation release for the vendor**

  To save valuable time, IT organizations must be able to package a full, correct release of an application, with all of its components, to deliver to the vendor. Countless, frustrating hours are wasted when an IT organization fails to deliver all components, or delivers incorrect versions of components to a vendor. A vendor cannot be

Configuration Management

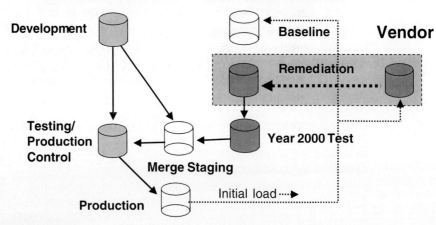

| Figure 5.5 | Configuration Management.

expected to perform its work unless it is given the appropriate application code to work on. It is not the vendor's responsibility to discover and locate missing source code. An IT organization has to be able to guarantee that it has delivered all components, in their correct versions, to the vendor.

- **Ability to maintain integrity of the release during remediation**

  Once a complete remediation package has been delivered to the vendor, the IT organization has to ensure that the release will be kept intact. Without adequate controls, critical changes may be omitted or overlaid when combining releases, or noncompliant code may be added to an otherwise compliant release. The greatest care is required when maintenance and enhancement activities are conducted in parallel with vendor remediation. Further, an IT organization will need to keep a clean copy of the original version of the release on hand to establish a baseline for bug fixing, testing, and QA purposes. If a release is packaged for the vendor, and the integrity of the release is not maintained at the IT site, then it may be extremely difficult, if not impossible, to re-create the release, when the need arises.

- **Ability to safely reintegrate the release**

  When a vendor returns the remediated release, the IT organization must have a way of reintegrating that release into its environment without overlaying or damaging the baseline, development, or production releases. The reintegrated release will generally serve as the baseline source code for testing, although it is possible that interim maintenance changes will be applied to this release. IT must maintain the integrity of this remediated release for eventual migration to production, or, if bugs are discovered, for return to the vendor for correction.

- **Ability to quickly cycle corrections**

  In a project of this size, it is inevitable that bugs will be discovered either during the QA process or testing. When an error is identified, the IT organization must be able to quickly locate and return the affected code to the vendor for rework and must be able to quickly assimilate the fixed code upon return. Lengthy cycle times or laborious check-in and check-out procedures will impede the code correction effort.

- **Ability to handle shared code**

  Every IT organization will have pieces of code or modules that are shared by several applications. If these shared pieces of code are not identified and packaged for remediation in a single pass, the result will be multiple iterations of remediation, and overlays of previously remediated code. In the best case, this redundant work will be a waste of effort. In the worst case, previously remediated versions may be overlaid, thereby compromising the compliance of previously remediated applications. The best way to account for these shared modules and ensure that they are remediated only once is to maintain the modules in a central place, designate the particular release in which the code will be remediated and refer to this central repository in all IT processes and procedures.

- **Ability to integrate maintenance changes**

  In general, non-Year 2000 maintenance changes should be strenuously avoided during the remediation process. As mentioned in the testing chapters (Chapters 7 and 8), extraneous maintenance changes complicate, or nullify, regression testing because there will be functional differences in test results that will prevent automated comparisons of results. Nevertheless, there will be circumstances where maintenance changes must be made to code that is under remediation. Extreme care has to be taken to preserve versions of maintained or "development" code so that the constituent changes can be isolated and applied to the remediated release upon its return from the vendor. Once the maintenance changes have been applied, this modified release must be retained and subject to subsequent QA and testing.

- **Well-defined processes for performing work**

  The SOW defined who was responsible for performing which tasks. To guide staff members in performing their tasks, IT organizations should explicitly define the processes used to perform those tasks. For instance, how is a release to be identified, packaged, and sent to the vendor? What happens when the vendor delivers remediated code to the IT organization? What happens if a bug is discovered during testing? There should be an explanation of how to perform these typical, common processes so that there is little or no learning curve to master and peak efficiencies can be gained. Vendors will adopt their own processes to cover the performance of their tasks.

- **Intensive QA**

  QA is a critical function that should be performed throughout the remediation process. QA ensures that compliance definitions are correct and workable, that remediation releases are packaged properly, that returned components conform to the contents of the baseline release, and that remediation has been performed according to the compliance definition. Every error discovered at this point in time by the QA process, rather than during the testing process, saves invaluable resources and money. QA, including testing, are also the final steps in ensuring that compliance is achieved, that the expectations set in the SOW are met and that the remediated release is ready for production.

- **Active involvement in the project**

  Each IT organization has to remain actively involved in its Year 2000 project, regardless of whether a vendor has been selected to work on some or all of the effort. The IT organization must ensure that the vendor receives the support, either in the form of properly packaged releases or access to subject matter experts, that the vendor needs to perform its job and must manage the vendor's performance to expectations. If problems arise in the future, it will be IT, and not the vendor, that will be accountable to the rest of the company. Further, IT management has legal responsibility and may be subject to liability for any failures, even if a vendor contributed to the problem. See Chapter 3 for a discussion of legal risks.

5.4 Enabling Factories

If a factory approach has been selected by an IT organization, there is a series of techniques available to maximize the benefits of the factory. Every IT organization using a factory should implement these techniques and ensure that they are used throughout the factory project.

A factory is a group of programmers, generally supported by tools, residing in a separate physical or logical location, that concentrates strictly on processing code for Year 2000. The goal of a factory is to use assembly-line principles in its operations to gain efficiencies. These principles ensure that the repetitive work performed by the factory is done quickly, consistently, and with the same level of quality each time. Because efficiency is the hallmark of a well-run factory, factories must concentrate on the 80/20 rule. Factories can process only the standard type of code for which they are set up, which usually means that only the most common languages, in the most common forms, will be processed. Special cases, atypical code, and uncommon platforms cannot be handled by a factory without losing the efficiencies of the assembly-line process.

At the time of writing, it appears that external factories are not being used as successfully as they might be. There are a number of possible reasons for this lack of success. First, IT organizations often have unrealistic expectations concerning the factory. They believe that once a factory has been selected, they have no more work to do, only to discover that they must be actively involved for the process to succeed. Second, packaging application or upgrade unit source code releases for factory processing can take a great deal of time and, if done incorrectly, can lead to a huge amount of wasted time in repacking and resending releases. Third, most IT organizations have made slow progress in their Year 2000 projects and are not yet at the stage of processing large volumes of code—the point where factories can provide the greatest benefit. As the end of the century approaches, and ever larger volumes of code must be processed as efficiently as possible, factories will become a much more attractive, and necessary, alternative.

There are two types of factories—external and internal. External factories are operated by vendors while internal factories are operated and staffed by members of the IT organization. Internal factories follow the same principles mentioned above, but in a less formal manner. In contrast to external factories, the use of internal factories has become more prevalent in those IT organizations that have progressed to the point of high volume remediation and testing.

Within external factories, there are three categories: factory software vendors, consulting firms, and offshore firms. Factory software vendors use their own software to locate, remediate and test century-date changes. They vary by technology supported, degree of automation, and reliability. Most factory vendors support COBOL and a few other common languages. Consulting firms offer a wide range of off-site Year 2000 services. Some sublicense technology from software vendors to automate their approach, others use manual approaches, and some use both. Consultants rely on training, common processes and automation where possible to offer cost-effective services. Offshore firms are a variation of off-site consulting firms and are located in countries with low labor rates. They typically offer the same services as consulting companies but for lower prices. Some offshore firms use automation to lower their prices, others do so using low-cost, manual labor. Higher-end firms use similar technology as their domestic counterparts.

The remainder of this section discusses the basic factory process, things that an IT organization should do before using a factory, the contents of a factory package, how to perform appropriate QA before and after the factory package is sent and returned, and the differences between internal and external factories.

5.4.1 The Basic Factory Process

The basic factory process consists of the steps needed to identify and correct century-date issues in applications. The initial step is to locate non-compliant application code and the final step is to submit a remediated, unit-tested and integration-tested application for system testing. Figure 5.6 shows the four steps involved in the basic factory process.

The four steps are

- **Step 1: Package the application or upgrade unit release**

  Performed by the IT organization, this step packages compatible versions of the "physical" components of the application or upgrade unit into a release that will undergo remediation. See Section 5.4.3 for a more detailed discussion of the contents of a factory package.

Basic Factory Process

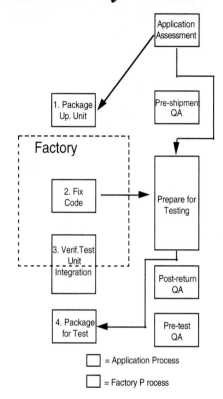

Figure 5.6   Basic Factory Process.

- **Step 2: Fix the code**

  In this step the factory makes all necessary modifications to the source code. The types of changes made during this step depend on the upgrade unit's compliance definition and implementation strategy and may involve the use of automated tools, manual methods, or a combination of both.

- **Step 3: Verification testing**

  Verification testing consists of unit and integration testing. Unit testing is traditionally performed by the programmer who implemented the code changes, which means that it should be performed by factory personnel. Integration testing will be performed partially at the factory, which will perform integration testing using those components of the upgrade unit that it has access to, and at the IT organization, which must ensure that it has access to all components, in their correct versions.

- **Step 4: Package the application or upgrade unit release for system testing**

  This final step in the process, performed by the IT organization, serves as the QA checkpoint before testing begins. Given the expense and resource requirements of system testing, it is essential to eliminate as many problems as possible before testing. The QA process is discussed in more detail in Section 5.4.4.

In addition to the basic factory process, there are a number of supporting processes that should be performed by the IT organization. These include

- **Application assessment and strategy development**

  These steps are performed by an IT organization at the beginning of its Year 2000 project and yield information concerning what components to include in an upgrade unit and what needs to be changed in those components. This information is used to develop the implementation strategy for the upgrade unit and to guide the testing process. Ultimately, all of this information will be conveyed to the factory to help it perform its work.

- **QA**

  The QA process is meant to detect problems at the earliest possible stage, before they can lead to wasted expense and resources. QA steps occur before packages are sent to the factory and upon receipt of the remediated code. Section 5.4.4 discusses the QA process in more detail.

- **Test preparation**

  While the upgrade unit is at the factory for remediation, the IT staff must prepare for the tests to be performed upon its return. These tasks include test data and test script generation and preparation of the test environment. See Chapter 8 for a discussion of these activities.

5.4.2 Before Using a Factory

Before using a factory, an IT organization should understand the processes used by the factory. The types of processes used by the factory will indicate the reliability of the factory's work and likely error rates during testing which in turn will influence what tasks the IT organization needs to perform itself. Familiarity with the factory process enables the IT to understand the division of responsibility between the factory and IT organization (as reflected in the SOW), the true input requirements of the factory (to give the factory exactly what they need to do the best job), the factory's approaches for remediation (automated, manual, or combination), when those approaches are used, and the level and methods of QA undertaken by the factory.

Similarly, the IT organization must define its own processes for implementing the factory approach before it actually begins using the factory. These processes include how to identify and assemble the contents of a factory package, how to create and perform QA on the factory package, how to perform parallel tasks, and how to handle the return of remediated code, including cycling of corrections between IT and the factory.

5.4.3 The Factory Package

As discussed in Section 5.3, each application or upgrade unit will be packaged into a release to be sent to the factory for remediation. Each factory package should include the following pieces.

- **Bill of materials**

  The bill of materials lists precisely the contents of the factory package, including names of source code modules, copy members, version numbers, and so on. This list not only identifies to the factory what they should receive in the package, it also allows the IT organization to track what was sent and to reconcile what is ultimately received from the factory.

- **Compliance definition**

  The compliance definition for the upgrade unit states the criteria by which the application will be deemed to be compliant. It includes instructions on the technical implementation strategy for the upgrade unit which are the equivalent of specifications for the remediation work.

- **Complete source code**

   The package should contain the correct versions of all components (copy members, subroutines, source code modules, etc.) comprising the upgrade unit or application. Source code packaging is one of the weakest links in the process, usually due to inadequate configuration management at the IT site.

- **Results of analysis**

   By providing the results of IT's original assessment, the factory will know which dates IT expects to be corrected. Although the factory may perform its own impact analysis, the IT information provides "seed" data for those efforts.

- **Test data/scripts**

   If the factory is to perform any testing, the IT organization should also include available test data and test scripts. In many cases, the available data will be insufficient and IT will have to separately ship the test data once it has been generated.

5.4.4 The Factory QA Process

To ensure the success of the factory process, the IT organization must perform certain QA tasks at various points in the process. The goal of QA is to detect errors early in the process before they lead to reworks at a later, and more expensive, stage. Figure 5.7 depicts the factory QA process from the initial stage, where the components of the factory package are reviewed for completeness and correctness, through the final stage of executing certification tests.

There are three major groupings of QA functions.

- **QA walk-through before shipping factory package**

   To ensure that the factory receives exactly what it needs to perform its remediation in one complete pass, IT staff must review the contents of the factory package in detail. This review focuses on the completeness of the source code and the correctness of the versions comprising the release.

- **QA walk-through after code is returned from the factory**

   When the factory returns the remediated code, the QA group must review the contents of the returned package against the bill of materials to ensure that all components have been returned. In addition,

Factory QA Process

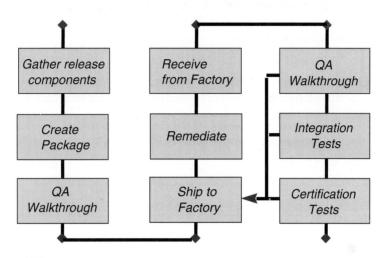

Figure 5.7   Factory QA Process.

there should be a QA review of the remediation performed to ensure that it conforms to the compliance definition for the upgrade unit or application. Further, the actual changes should be reconciled against the results of the internal assessment to determine if actual changes matched expectations. While it is likely that actual changes will differ from the initial assessment due to elimination of false positives and incorporation of false negatives, the QA group should understand the differences. Lastly, the review should determine whether the factory followed its own processes; any divergence is an indicator that the QA group may need to adjust its own review to account for these unexpected changes.

- **Testing**

The final QA review is performed during testing. The level of testing that needs to be performed by the IT organization hinges on the amount of testing done by the factory and the reliability of those tests. In most cases, the factory will do a unit test and minimal integration test of the remediated application. IT will need to perform its own integration testing to detect version mismatches and all of the tests required to certify compliance. The less confidence that IT has in the factory's level and quality of testing, the more testing it should perform. At a minimum, the application team may want to consider unit testing randomly selected programs as a double-check of the factory's effort.

5.4.5 Internal Factories

Internal factories staffed with IT resources perform the same functions as external factories although their processes may be less formal. The benefits of using an internal factory over an external factory include the ability

- to retain control over the entire process

- to resolve more quickly any hand off issues because everyone is on-site, using the same computer and resources

- to perform the work for less cost, but only if large volumes of code are being processed

If an internal factory is expected to process only a low volume of code, the startup costs associated with the factory make it an unappealing choice. Startup costs include expenses of training staff, purchasing tools and hardware, and developing processes and methodologies. Where low code volumes are expected, external factories are the inexpensive, appropriate alternative. The high startup costs associated with establishing a factory are amortized by the external factory across the larger number of clients served, and the number of applications processed. By spreading out costs in this way, no client bears a disproportionate amount of the total costs. In addition, external factories are already operating at peak efficiencies and can process code quickly without the ramp-up time that an internal factory would require.

To be successful, an internal factory must copy the processes used by an external factory and must enforce them. The factory process described above in Section 5.4.1 must be put into place and followed with discipline. Automated tools should be identified and purchased or developed in-house, training should be conducted, and tool usage should be enforced. Again, internal factories should concentrate on the 80/20 rule and should reject any nonconforming or nonstandard code or platforms to preserve the efficiencies of their processes.

An internal factory faces several obstacles. At the outset, the internal staff does not have the factory knowledge and experience to develop and hone the required processes. This limitation means that time will be wasted making mistakes that others have already made. Further, the

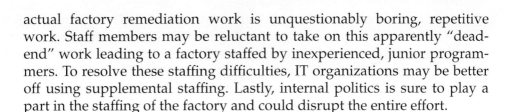

actual factory remediation work is unquestionably boring, repetitive work. Staff members may be reluctant to take on this apparently "dead-end" work leading to a factory staffed by inexperienced, junior programmers. To resolve these staffing difficulties, IT organizations may be better off using supplemental staffing. Lastly, internal politics is sure to play a part in the staffing of the factory and could disrupt the entire effort.

5.5 Enabling Consultants

If an IT organization selects consultants to assist in its Year 2000 project, there are a number of things that should be done to enable the consultants to perform their job successfully. From the enablement perspective, there are three categories of consultants: off-site project consultants, on-site project consultants, and supplemental staff. This section discusses how to deal with each of these three categories.

The general rules to enable success, set forth in Section 5.3, apply to all categories of consultants. An SOW must be drafted to delineate responsibilities of the IT organization and consultant and to set expectations accordingly. Compliance definitions must be created to detail how applications or upgrade units are to be certified compliant. IT functional experts must be identified and accessible to the consultants throughout the process. Finally, for on-site consultants, separate libraries and work areas must be established to insulate the consultants' and IT organization's work.

Off-site project consultants will reside at a separate physical location. Given this characteristic, the factory process described in Section 5.4 for external factories is ideal for managing off-site project consultants. The IT organization and consultants should follow those guidelines in the development and execution of their processes.

Supplemental staffing differs from off-site or on-site project consulting in that the consultants work alongside IT staff members using the same tools and processes and should be managed like internal staff. In this way, supplemental staffers are very similar to temporary employees. Their productivity is influenced by, and limited by, the IT environment, including the availability of tools, processes, training, and methodologies. Often, supplemental staffing is chosen to supply expertise that is missing in the current organization. IT project managers will set performance goals for the individual consultants and will manage their performance toward those goals.

In contrast to supplemental staffers, on-site project consultants manage themselves and the details of their project, generally bringing in their own tools and processes to perform their work. These consultants typically include a project manager responsible for managing and monitoring the performance of the project and the consultants. In this scenario, IT management's role is to support the on-site consultants so that they can do the best job possible and to manage their overall performance to the SOW and compliance definitions. To ensure the success of an on-site project consulting effort, an IT organization should

- **Set clear boundaries of responsibility**

  The SOW establishes areas of responsibility between the consultants and IT. IT management has to ensure that things do not fall between the cracks: that all tasks are assigned and responsibility is understood. This effort prevents fingerpointing if any problems arise down the line.

- **Balance management style**

  On-site project consultants have their own project manager overseeing the performance of the project. The general rule for IT management is to stay out of the consultants' way wherever possible. It is important not to micromanage the project but use the SOW, compliance definitions, and regular project reviews as tools to monitor and manage the consultant's performance at a high level. At the same time, to ensure the overall success of the project, internal staff must stay involved in the process, offering functional assistance and expertise and removing internal roadblocks that the consultants, as outsiders, are ill-suited to handle.

- **Understand tools and processes**

  Just as with external factories, the IT organization should familiarize itself with the tools and processes used by the on-site project consultants but should avoid dictating the tools and processes to be used. If the tools and processes used by a consulting firm are not acceptable, then select another firm. Consulting firms should be allowed to use their own tools and processes. They are already trained and experienced in the use of these tools, and if the firm is a good one, it will have selected the best tools available. Consulting firms have serviced a variety of clients and have identified "industry best practices." Why not let them bring those best practices to your organization? Similarly, if there is a conflict between internal processes and consultant processes, consider using the consultants' processes—they may be the best available in the industry. Both IT and the project consultants should establish processes, similar to those used with external factories, to handle interactions between the consultants and internal staff.

• **Perform regular QA reviews**

QA functions should be performed on a regular basis through meetings between internal staff and consultants and through reviews of project progress and deliverable quality. By having regular meetings and review, some of the formality present in the factory process (such as a bill of materials, etc.) can be eliminated.

5.6 Offshore Resources

If an IT organization chooses to contract directly with an offshore vendor for Year 2000 project services, a number of things must be done to ensure the success of the project. In general, offshore vendors should be treated the same as external factories. The processes and techniques described in Section 5.4 apply equally to offshore vendors, with some variations as described below.

At the time of writing, direct contracting between IT organizations and offshore vendors has not caught on as expected. There are a number of explanations for this situation:

• An inability to comfortably assess the expertise and quality of the company due to the lack of a track record

• Fear of the unknown and, in some cases, prejudice against foreigners

• Security concerns relating to access control, copyright protection, and other legal protections in foreign countries, many of which are not as sophisticated or strong as their U.S. counterparts.

• Inability to take corrective action, including legal action, in case of project failures

• Logistical problems due to time zone differences

• Cultural issues, typically stemming from language barriers

• Quality concerns often due to a lack of training, inexperience, or failure to understand the code

• Higher than anticipated costs

As the domestic labor market becomes more constrained, offshore resources may become a more attractive alternative. However, the long lead times required to develop relationships between offshore providers and IT organizations may inhibit many companies from considering the offshore alternative.

Despite the preceding issues, the better offshore firms are doing well. Many of these firms have established successful partnering relationships with major U.S.-based firms. In addition, several firms have sought to bolster their credibility by pursuing objective industry certifications, such as ISO 9000.

For large-volume, manually-intensive remediation projects, offshore resources may be the best choice since they can provide sufficient labor to perform the work at relatively lower costs. This alternative is attractive, however, only if the offshore firm passes on these savings to its clients.

Ultimately, the key to successful use of an offshore firm involves picking the right project.

Once an IT organization has decided to use an offshore vendor, it should do the following.

- **Choose the vendor carefully**

  As with any service provider, there are reputable companies and there are shams. Due to the lack of an established track record for many offshore vendors, it can be difficult to gauge the vendor's expertise and project success.

- **Understand tools, processes, and security measures**

  As with any vendor, the IT organization should familiarize itself with the approaches used by the offshore vendor to perform its work (automated versus manual), the tools used (are they "best in class"?), the processes followed (is there sufficient QA?) and security measures (is access to code limited?). It takes knowledge and experience to select and implement, in an assembly-line fashion, the processes needed to achieve peak efficiencies. Does the vendor have this experience?

- **Follow basic factory processes**

  The factory process steps described in Section 5.4 should be adopted for use with offshore vendors. Of particular importance are the QA processes, especially if the offshore vendor's processes show any weaknesses.

- **Establish excellent interface processes**

  First-class interface processes are needed to ensure that the logistical and cultural issues mentioned above are surmounted, and that turn-around times for code corrections or reworks are minimized. Extra time should be spent to ensure that the logistics and timing of hand-offs and communications are smooth. Direct links should be considered if security concerns need to be addressed.

- **Consider a vendor that uses "split" teams**

  Some of the more savvy offshore vendors, in an attempt to address the problems cited above, assign a small project team to work on-site with the client and to interface with the offshore team. This team handles any cultural and communications issues that may arise. They also provide the IT staff with a level of comfort, since they are visible and available during regular work hours.

5.7 Market Update

This section discusses some of the outside resources available to IT organizations for Year 2000 conversion work. The market for these resources is a dynamic one. Following is a snapshot of the state of the market at the time of writing.

North American consulting firms and service providers continue to win contracts for Year 2000 conversion work. The largest and most reputable of these vendors have been swamped with Year 2000 business and do not foresee an end to the deluge. The *Year 2000 Outlook*, a publication of the Information Technology Association of America, has consistently reported on a weekly basis the award of additional contracts to consulting firms and software vendors. Expectations are that this trend will accelerate in the next two years. During the last quarter of 1997 alone, the *Boston Globe* reported that Boston-based Keane, Inc. expected to increase its Year 2000 staff by 4,000 employees or 45 percent of its total staff and also expected Year 2000 work to account for over 50 percent of its revenue in 1998. Other large service providers, such as Electronic Data Systems Corp. (EDS), are offering intensive but short, multiweek IT/Year 2000 training courses to non-IT professionals so they can meet their staffing needs on Year 2000 projects.

Another indicator of a healthy market for consulting firms is the programming staff turnover rate. Because the market is so hot, and because higher salaries are constantly being offered to experienced Year

2000 workers, consulting firms and IT organizations are experiencing high turnover rates. For consulting firms, the turnover rate is said to be close to 30 percent. The better trained the consultants, the more their skills are in demand and the greater the likelihood that they will be enticed by larger salaries offered by competing firms and companies. When selecting a consulting firm, look for a well-established recruiting function as an indicator that the firm is doing well. This characteristic will be especially important if the Gartner Group prediction, that the Year 2000 resource market will reach 75 percent capacity during 1998, turns out to be true.

During mid-1997, some of the consulting services vendors had reported softer than anticipated demand for their Year 2000 consulting services. At the time of writing, it appears that these reports were exaggerated, or perhaps were cleverly designed marketing ploys aimed at letting the market know where available capacity could be found. While there is no doubt that some of the smaller, or less reputable, entrants into the services market have not been successful in competing for Year 2000 business, the larger providers are being inundated with work.

Unlike their North American counterparts, many offshore consulting services and conversion factories have still not drawn a large following. While some offshore capacity is being used, it appears that most IT organizations are not contracting directly with these offshore providers for Year 2000 work. Rather, the more successful offshore firms are partnering with leading U.S.-based service providers who are subcontracting conversion projects to these offshore firms. Other offshore firms that had a strong U.S. presence prior to the glut of Year 2000 work have had a somewhat easier entry into the Year 2000 market.

To meet the challenge in providing experienced personnel for Year 2000 projects, a group called "Senior Staff 2000" (www.srstaff.com) is promoting and administering a nationwide recruiting program for what they call "legacy professionals." These targeted professionals are retired, semi-retired, and part-time individuals who have worked in the past in the types of IT organizations now seeking to staff Year 2000 projects. The Senior Staff group estimates that there are approximately 600,000 of these legacy professionals across the country. While some of these people would consider relocating for Year 2000 work, the majority would prefer to telecommute from home or work locally. With the help of local schools and universities, Senior Staff is also involved in developing refresher training courses designed to update the experience of legacy professionals, particularly with those skills used in Year 2000 projects. Whether this recruiting effort will be successful remains to be seen. The Senior Staff notes that many factors need to be overcome to lead to widespread acceptance of using these "old pros." IT organizations are often reluctant to permit tele-commuting, to release source code off-site, and to use innovative hiring and staffing techniques to solve resource problems.

Endnotes

1. This calculation assumes an average program size of 1,902 LOC. See "Improving Quality with Software Metrics," by Ian S. Hayes, published in *The Handbook of IS Management*, Fifth Edition, Auerbach, 1997, pp. 669–690.

2. *The Year 2000 Software Crisis: Challenge of the Century*, by William M. Ulrich and Ian S. Hayes, Prentice Hall, 1997.

Chapter 6

Standards, Tools, and Techniques Update

Those of us working in the rapidly evolving Year 2000 field are fully aware that standards, tools, and techniques are undergoing continuous change as the market lunges forward and new companies join the battle. We therefore felt it necessary to provide an update on standards, tools, and techniques currently being deployed in the Year 2000 market. This chapter discusses current trends in Year 2000 tools and techniques, and some of the benefits and dangers associated with these trends. We also identify optimization strategies for selecting and implementing these approaches and update readers on the use of repository technology in Year 2000 projects.

6.1 Standards Update

Standards, as they apply to dates and the accommodation thereof in the Year 2000 field, continue to be missing from many mainstream project definitions. Regardless of the progress made at most of the client sites we visit, we continue to find an absence of well-defined compliance criteria for a given organization. This absence is likely due to the lack of leadership by traditional standards committees and to the abhorrence of the concept of standards in the IT field. We have provided a brief progress update in the area of standards and third-party certification, standardization of data interchange within various market sectors, and the development of a Year 2000 "firewall."

6.1.1 Date Format Standards

Traditional standard setting bodies, including the Institute of Electrical and Electronics Engineers (IEEE), the American National Standards Institute (ANSI), International Standards Organization (ISO), and the Electronic Data Interchange (EDI) standards setting groups, have moved slowly to articulate date standards that can be applied by industry. Disagreement among members (ANSI changes require that 90 percent of members concur on a given issue) and a lack of understanding over what the internal impacts would be (proposed EDI date changes were held up because members thought that internal systems would have to use an eight-character date format) are among the chief culprits here. These committees, in general, mull a topic xcover for several years before coming to a conclusion—a prospect that is clearly not conducive to helping an industry with a life span of only four or five years.

Having said this, many of the groups have now come to preliminary conclusions regarding date standards. The ANSI Accredited Standards Committee (ASC), for example, has been working through two different committees. The first is X12C and the second is ANSI ASC group X3L8. Two other excellent sources of century-compliance criteria were developed by GTE and the state of Minnesota. Their Web sites, along with the ANSI X3L8 standard and several other compliance criteria sources, are listed in Figure 6.1. The Project Office compliance coordinator should review available standards and customize this information to meet the needs of their environment. The sample shown in Figure 6.2 depicts century compliance standards for nonstrategic software systems used at one company. Without compliance standards, project managers will have difficulty setting objectives, remediation teams will argue over approaches, and testing teams will not have guidelines required to manage the quality assurance process.

6.1.2 Certification Programs

Year 2000 compliance certification programs have received some attention in the vendor market recently. The main program that comes to

---

Century Compliance Reference Sources

- Draft ANSI Standard for Representation of Date for Information Interchange X3L8/96-050, ASC NCITS L8, 12/9/96

- State of Minnesota IRM Standard 14, 3/25/97
  www.state.mn.us/ebranch/admin/ipo/hb/document/std14-2.html

- GTE Government Systems Corp., A Proposed Criteria for Century Compliance, PA96014, Waltham, MA, 1996
  www.mitre.org/research/cots/COMPLIANCE_INFO.html

- ISO 8601: 1988-06-14 and Technical Corrigendum 1 1991-05-01, Data Elements and Interchange Formats, ANSI, New York, 1988, pp.14

- Markus Kuhn, A Summary of the International Standard Date and Time Notation, 3/25/97
  www.ft.uni-erlangen.de/~mskuhn/iso-time.html#zone.

Figure 6.1 Century compliance contact information.

Implementation Approach:
- * Interpret century using a cut-off year rather than expanding fields. (Process-based approach)
- * Use 45 as the cut-off year (00-45 is 2000-2045, 46-99 is 1946-1999)
- * Leave all internal fields in two-digit year format
- * Except Birth-Year fields:
  - * Retain in two-digit format in files
  - * Interpret using cut-off year for calculations
  - * Expand for display in reports and CICS panels
- * Update all code logic performing date operations (comparisons, calculations, sorts)
- * Expand date-fields used in indices and sort fields from six-digits to eight-digits

Interfaces (Files shared with external applications)
- * Do not expand any file dates unless used as an index or within a sort key
- * Accept expanded dates when required by other applications, but continue to use two-digit year formats internally

Data Displays
- * CICS screens - Leave all years in two-digit format
  Except Birth-years which should be expanded to four-digits
- * Reports - Leave all years in two-digit format
  Except Birth-years which should be expanded to four-digits

Figure 6.2 Sample compliance definition for nonstrategic software systems.

mind is the Information Technology Association of America (ITAA) compliance certification program for software vendors. The ITAA, a vendor association, offers a program that reviews product development processes for various vendors and certifies that these products were developed using a Year 2000-compliant development process. The caveats and legal disclaimers in this program, and others, say enough about whether you would want to rely on them as a legal defense. However, the ITAA has made an effort to take third parties a step or two closer to Year 2000 compliance.

6.1.3 External Data Interchange

A number of industries either have or are attempting to set standards around date formats as they pertain to data exchanged between various organizations. Incompatibilities in date handling approaches could cause widespread havoc in cross-industry operations. In general, these efforts are being spearheaded by industry associations or ad hoc groups that have been called together to deal with this problem before it happens.

The Securities Industry Association (SIA) is focusing on data interchange integrity in its "street-wide testing" initiative. The objective is to ensure the ongoing integrity of data being shared among exchanges, depositories, utilities, clearing houses, and other entities through a process called street-wide testing. Street-wide testing is being pursued in order to verify that the trading of securities remains uninterrupted as the Year 2000 arrives. The credit card industry is pursuing similar goals in the area of data interchange as is the automotive industry through the Automotive Industry Action Group (AIAG).

The biggest challenge, of course, is getting all parties to agree on an expanded date format. In many cases, this agreement has yet to occur. Short of reaching concurrence on a four-character date format, the best that organizations can do is to assure each other that two-character year field formats have been checked for compliance and to test critical interfaces to ensure that this is the case. If an organization has a handful of strategic data interchange partners, we suggest synchronizing windowing strategies for those interfaces.

One pleasant surprise was discovered at the state and federal government levels. In October 1997, U.S. state and federal government officials gathered at a Year 2000 Summit in Pittsburgh, Pennsylvania, to outline a series of steps aimed at lowering the Year 2000 risks connected to conducting interagency governmental business. Attendees agreed to create a four-digit year field date standard to be applied across all points of state and federal data interchange. This effort established standards for more than 60 government entities across the United States, which is important because numerous transactions among state and federal government agencies rely on electronic data interchange as a means of communication.

The Pittsburgh Summit focused on creating an inventory of external interfaces and discussed compliance issues, testing, and the creation of electronic bridges. John Saunders, Year 2000 Program Manager in the state of Washington, said that having an agreement on a four-digit date standard is a step forward. Participants at this event, which was sponsored by the Commonwealth of Pennsylvania, agreed that standards should apply to interfaces and commonly shared business applications. In order to define compliance, they set a contiguous, four digit year field standard for new development and recommended a four-position field for remediation projects. Electronic bridges must be developed to facilitate data interchange between compliant and noncompliant partners. Accuracy, they said, is the responsibility of the transmitter and compliance must be announced by January 1, 1998, or as soon as legislative requirements allow.

6.1.4 Year 2000 Firewall Strategies

The concept of building a firewall has grown in popularity as organizations realize that the companies and government institutions that they do business with may not have all of their Year 2000 problems fixed in time. The firewall concept stems from the processes companies have set up to prevent Internet-borne viruses from infecting their computing environments. In this case, the goal is to prevent noncompliant data from entering an organization via electronic means. The process involves creating smart routines that intercept all external data and interrogate that data by cross-checking date values to determine compliance. For example, knowledge of the transmitted data could allow a company to check that a birth date does not exceed an employee start date. If a problem is found, the routine would interrupt data transmission and print an audit trail report summarizing its findings.

Companies and government agencies are examining the firewall concept, but the task of creating a foolproof process to screen errant data is virtually impossible. The dates required to cross-check the validity of other dates or data received from a third party may not actually accompany the information being sent by that third party. A mail-order house may receive name and address information for a certain age group, but the creator of that data may not have included birth date in the data. In this case, one could not differentiate between a 1-year-old and a 101-year-old.

The goal of a firewall is still valuable, however, and should be pursued to screen the bulk of the information being received from outsiders. Again, coordinating data interface compliance strategies between organizations that share large volumes of data will help prevent errant data from being created in the first place.

6.2 Upgrade Unit Packaging Strategies

An upgrade unit, as defined in our last book, is a subsystem, system, or group of related systems that can be treated as a single unit of work (project). While the approximate boundaries of an upgrade unit should be defined during initial assessment phases, this step gathers the correct version of each source code component to be associated with a given upgrade unit. In addition to the source code, the package contains a copy of the application's compliance definition, the results of earlier analysis efforts, and any other information that will be used in the remediation effort. Note that for projects that apply a 100 percent procedural workaround (windowing) solution, upgrade unit packaging is as important from a testing and quality assurance standpoint as it is from a remediation standpoint. If any data is being expanded within an upgrade unit, component packaging becomes even more critical to reduce bridging and additional testing requirements.

The IT industry is struggling with the upgrade unit packaging concept for several key reasons. The first, and most easily overcome challenge, is that maintenance personnel have never been asked to fix a system in its entirety before and may not know how to research and package the system. Help from skilled consultants and the Project Office can remedy this situation quickly if the people who own the code are willing to work with project packaging experts.

If IT has a poorly defined configuration management environment, the upgrade unit packaging process can be very time consuming. Missing or incorrect modules compromise the integrity of the upgrade unit and introduce difficulties throughout remediation and testing. This mix-up has been a major obstacle in Year 2000 projects. Every conversion factory vendor that we have spoken with claims that it takes five to six attempts to get the right components bundled and shipped out for off-site remediation. Of course, the clients are blaming the conversion factory vendor for the resulting time delays in the project.

Another factor complicating the upgrade unit packaging process is that most conversion factory vendors have their own view of how much code should be shipped in a given upgrade unit. One vendor requires that an upgrade unit be between 750,000 to 1.5 million lines of MVS mainframe COBOL code. Another factory director continues to push his sales team for bigger and bigger chunks of code. This practice is all well and good for the vendors—although it could help explain why more than a couple of factories are running well below peak capacity at this point. It does, however, put a tremendous strain on the in-house project team because it lengthens code-freeze windows.

Part of the packaging process involves developing a code-freeze strategy to keep the upgrade unit synchronized with the production version of the source code while the application is undergoing remediation and testing. An adequate freeze strategy is essential to prevent wasted time and effort finding and correcting code overlays. Testing 750,000 to 1.5 million lines of code will likely take several weeks in the best of circumstances, even with functional equivalence testing separated from future date testing. This time delay will likely keep these upgrade units out of production for several months—a luxury that few IT organizations can afford.

Again, the problem on the surface is that packaging teams have been unable to mobilize to the point where they are packaging and shipping the required 12 to 15 projects per month to off-site factories. This problem is only a symptom of what is probably going on behind the scenes on these Year 2000 projects. If conversion teams cannot package code for the vendors, how well can they possibly be doing on the in-house projects that are rarely exposed to public scrutiny? Time will tell.

6.3 Remediation Procedures Update

If the IT team can actually package all the code for a given system into a single upgrade unit, remediation can proceed. We next take a look at where organizations are with their Year 2000 remediation projects and provide an update based on best, and worst, industry practices. In order to maximize the effectiveness of the remediation process, it is important for project teams to clearly define available remediation options, provide criteria for selecting the right option(s), and understand the means for increasing the efficiency of those options.

6.3.1 High-volume Productivity Targets

Considering the volume of remediation and testing that has to be completed in a very short period of time, any delay in starting large-scale conversion work could be fatal to many companies. Companies must reach and sustain high productivity levels to meet their Year 2000 objectives. Additional delays will place further demands on productivity levels and reduce the number of viable compliance options. This predicament may be understood at an intellectual level but has not resulted, at a practical level, in increased conversion levels. Year 2000 projects already demand incredible rates of productivity; further delays make full compliance an unattainable dream.

In reality, it is doubtful that IT organizations will achieve necessary productivity rates to achieve full compliance by the century transition. In pilot projects conducted to date, productivity rates have been negatively impacted by tool limitations and the difficulty of finding and packaging all components, in their correct version, for upgrade units. To roughly assess required productivity rates, IT organizations can apply the productivity rates attained during pilot projects to the size of their portfolio, using the number of available resources. Compounding these required productivity rates is the elapsed time necessary to set up environments and infrastructures and to ramp up to peak production levels.

6.3.1.1 Improving Productivity

It is difficult to select the right approach or approaches to perform maximally productive, high-volume conversion projects, especially when faced with the diversity of solutions offered on the market. Vendor claims, rather than clarifying a company's choices, can increase confusion. As the Year 2000 deadline approaches and panic sets in, companies will also be susceptible to claims of "silver bullet" solutions. Companies must avoid wasting time by experimenting with, and later discarding, inappropriate solutions. To help clarify the selection process, companies should focus on four things.

- **Choose the right approach and implement it**

  There is not enough time left to review yet another solution. A final decision must be made. Choose and implement a solution now, and stop worrying about whether a slightly better solution will be available in the future. Start by eliminating solutions that obviously don't match the needs of the company. As an example, a small IT organization with a low volume of code to process should not set up an internal factory, as the overhead of doing so would be prohibitive. This option is best left for large organizations, with large volumes of code to process, that will easily recoup their investment through efficiencies of scale.

- **Focus on cost/benefit**

    A selected solution should offer the greatest overall benefit for the project. An organization cannot ignore the productivity ramifications of selecting a particular solution. Short-term gains often have high costs in terms of later productivity losses. A blatant mistake is to seek productivity increases in the remediation portion of the project while sacrificing productivity in the testing phase. Because the testing phase of a Year 2000 project is expected to account for more than 50 percent of total time, while code changes are expected to take as little as 15 percent, an increase in productivity rates during remediation that causes a decrease in productivity rates during testing is a net loss.

- **Determine the complete process for fixing the problem**

    To apply the two previous points, an organization must have a handle on the complete process required for a particular solution. By understanding the process, companies will be able to compare the various solutions and corresponding tradeoffs in productivity. For instance, companies must understand the overhead required to set up an internal factory, or the effort involved in packaging upgrade units for off-site remediation, to evaluate which approach is right for them.

- **Save and reuse all results**

    During the assessment phase of a Year 2000 project, many organizations gather valuable data about their applications and systems. Once collected and examined, this data is often discarded. By saving and referring to this initial data throughout the project, invaluable time is saved. For example, QA efforts can use this information to compare actual remediation against expected remediation to determine if date changes were missed, if extra changes were erroneously applied, if false positives were discovered, and if false negatives were rectified.

6.3.2 Field Expansion Update

Date field expansion is, by recent surveys, being used in less than 20 percent of planned Year 2000 projects. Comprehensive field expansion works in every situation and for any range of year data. As with any solution, it is not meant to fix latent date bugs—but has the added benefit of exposing those bugs during remediation and testing. The chief disadvantages of expansion are increased remediation effort, the need to change the structure of an application's data, and increased bridging requirements. Since many applications share the same files and databases, changing file structures requires significant coordination. Moreover, expansion can require a greater number of coding changes than windowing. If all fields are expanded, year fields on screens and reports typically also require reformatting. This disadvantage can be avoided by limiting expansion to only file data and internal variables.

Much of the testing effort for the expansion strategy is concentrated at the unit and integration testing levels. Testing could also increase based on the number of bridges and Application Programming Interfaces (APIs) added to the system. APIs, as defined in our first book, are simply dynamic bridges invoked from the program during an execution cycle. Bridges on the other hand, are separate batch routines. For the sake of simplicity, we will use the term bridges to mean both APIs and batch bridges.

Because dates are passed in expanded formats, errors and omissions cause mismatch errors during integration testing. This exposure reduces the number of potential errors that have to be uncovered in system testing. One added benefit is that expansion reduces complexities in future maintenance because it avoids the need for any "tricky" coding when handling date-related logic. One last point is that the level of errors introduced during the remediation of a highly date-dependent system could dramatically increase testing time frames and complexities.

6.3.3 Windowing Update

Windowing, based on recent surveys, is being used in roughly 80 percent of planned Year 2000 projects. The windowing strategy leaves date variables in their original two-digit formats and the century is determined through the use of a cutoff year. For example, if a cutoff year of "50" is used, "68" is treated as "1968" and "35" is treated as "2035." The major benefit of this strategy is avoiding the need to modify legacy data files—and expanding complicated date formats in highly date-intensive systems. Windowing also decreases the need for coordination between separate upgrade unit projects and usually saves remediation effort.

The windowing strategy has several important disadvantages. It will not work for year ranges greater than 100, it cannot be used for variables that sort and index, and it is significantly less straightforward for future maintenance projects. Moreover, the selection of a cutoff year must be coordinated to avoid mismatches across business units and external entities. For example, if one application uses "50" as its cutoff while another uses "20," the first application will interpret "31" as "2031" while the second application interprets it as "1931." This problem, by the way, is as prevalent in PC spreadsheet applications as it is in mainframe systems.

Windowing also affects testing. The correctness of a program can be verified during unit testing but the consistency of cutoff years within a system cannot be verified until system testing. Because date formats are not modified, integration testing will not expose errors and omissions. To expose these errors, incremental system tests are required for the years surrounding the cutoff year. For example, a system with a cutoff year of "50" must be tested using the years "49," "50," and "51." Depending on whether an upgrade unit uses multiple cutoff years, these incremental tests can become quite complex.

6.3.4 Expansion Using Bridges

This strategy uses both an expansion and windowing approach. Bridging routines are used to conduct data conversions between expanded and unexpanded date variables. Within the programs comprising the upgrade unit, date variables are expanded to include century information while file data is left in its original format. Linked directly to these programs are bridging routines that will convert all data using a windowing approach. This strategy has several important advantages—program modifications are straightforward, resulting in the long-term maintenance advantages of the expansion approach, and files can remain unexpanded, or may be expanded in the future when all applications accessing the file data have been converted themselves.

Because this approach involves windowing within the bridging routines, it shares the same limitations as the windowing strategy for year ranges over 100 and with sorting data. With regard to the level of required testing, this approach falls between expansion and windowing. Since the bridging routine handles all data conversion, rather than the application program, an advantage of bridging is that it requires fewer tests than application windowing to ensure its correctness.

6.3.5 Useful Notions and Worst Practices

Many Year 2000 solutions seem attractive at face value but quickly lose their appeal upon more detailed examination. Nevertheless, some IT organizations, particularly those that have procrastinated too long to implement a correct solution, will seek these solutions. If one of these solutions must be used, it should be treated as a temporary fix that will be promptly removed and properly corrected as soon as feasible.

6.3.5.1 The 19T0 Solution

The Lappen brothers recently applied for a patent that would allow hardware vendors to insert a windowing solution into their compilers. Having reviewed the state of several legacy COBOL compilers at one vendor site (some of these products are 20 years old), it seems idealistic to believe that many vendors could actually insert this solution in time to matter. This problem aside, it is likely that any proposed solution would deal only with the most simplistic conditional tests and take almost as long to implement and debug as windowing. Finally, this solution, unlike windowing and expansion, is likely to confuse maintenance programmers unclear on the use or nonuse of this approach.

6.3.5.2 Timeboxing

As the Year 2000 deadline looms, programmers are turning to new, creative methods to handle century dates. Most of these approaches rely on tricky techniques to accomplish their goals rather than changing actual program source code. The goal of these techniques is to decrease remediation effort by whatever means possible. One such approach is called "timeboxing" or "wrapping." This approach places code around a program to subtract "28" from two-digit year data before program execution and to add "28" back to the same data after program execution. The number 28 is chosen because it produces new, "virtual" dates that fall on the same day of the week as the current date. For instance, when executing in the year 2000, a program will use virtual data that appears to be from 1972, thereby avoiding any problem in processing century data.

This solution impacts business processing in a number of ways. It cannot be used when data is shared with other areas that are not using the same approach due to incompatibilities in data interpretation. Furthermore, if a program indexes a table through year values or if the program contains hard-coded year tests, processing errors are very likely to result. Many programs contain hard-coded dates that were or are meant to trigger a given event at a given point in time. Once this point in time passes, the code is left in the program assuming that it will never be invoked again—until the timeboxing solution has been implemented. Timeboxing also requires thorough testing, as do other options, but provides no information about program internals to support proper test input development.

Other concerns surrounding the timeboxing approach involve applications that have date-dependent data and logic such as insurance actuarial tables, interest rate calculations, inflation tables, and other date-dependent logic. In addition to these immediate concerns, the short- and long-term effects of this approach are questionable. The results of running a system in a timebox mode are not always predictable and are definitely hard to audit. Finally, timeboxing will ultimately serve to confuse future maintenance programmers because they will have no idea why the system was not modified using traditional techniques to make it Year 2000 compliant.

6.3.5.3 Object Code Patching

Another proposed solution (patent pending as of this writing) makes changes to machine-readable object code to handle century dates and leaves the source code untouched. This approach would increase the risk of future difficulty in maintenance by creating a situation where the program's source code does not match the program's executable functionality. This approach is not only difficult to maintain, but it also reflects an idealistic view of the problem. The inventor of this approach, by the way, claims that no testing is required. This claim, of course, is a misleading and ultimately dangerous proposition.

6.4 An Array of Implementation Choices

There are an enormous number of tools, approaches and options available to an IT organization for each phase of its Year 2000 project. In Section 6.3.1, we admonished companies to select and implement approaches quickly to jump-start and maintain necessary productivity levels. To do so, companies have to narrow the myriad of available options to choose those that fit their needs and that are credible. In many cases, IT organizations will find that no one approach fits their portfolio's needs; rather, multiple approaches will have to be selected. One easy way to subdivide these approaches is by major technology groupings.

Chapter 5 discussed implementation approaches using third-party vendors and resources and when these approaches make sense. Many IT organizations will find that, even if they do seek outside assistance, they need to apply their own resources to remediation and testing work to meet the century deadline. The next section provides an update on some of the internal approaches used by IT organizations to perform their Year 2000 work.

6.4.1 "Do It Yourself" (DIY) Update

There are three primary approaches for performing Year 2000 work using internal resources: manual fix, tool-assisted, and internal factory. The manual fix approach treats Year 2000 remediation as a typical maintenance change. While it follows the basic remediation process described in our last book, the steps tend to be applied informally. It uses standard programming techniques for impact analysis, code modification, and unit testing. This approach is typically implemented using the programmers who normally support the application. This approach relies on the software tools already available in-house, but these tools may be supplemented to fill in gaps. The greatest advantage of this approach is its minimal overhead and short setup time. Its disadvantage is its low efficiency. It offers no opportunity for efficiency of scale or standardization through common processes. As a result, this option is best suited for IT organizations with very small portfolios or for small portfolios of less common technologies in a large IT organization.

The tool-assisted approach differs from the manual approach by treating Year 2000 remediation as a formal project that justifies investment in Year 2000-specific tools and standardized processes. Each application upgrade unit is its own project and is handled by its own team which follows scripts or a Year 2000 methodology to assure consistency in its delivery. To gain the maximum level of efficiency, this approach relies on using tools to automate as many of the impact analysis, code changing, and testing tasks as possible. This approach's investment in tools and processes provides a significant increase in productivity and consistency over the manual approach. It is appropriate for moderate-size IT organizations that want the control of on-site remediation.

Internal factories, set up within an IT organization using IT staff, represent the highest level of formalized processes and tool automation. These factories adopt the same types of assembly-line principles used by manufacturing organizations to lower the cost of production. Factory staff members are specialists that are dedicated full time to the factory. Application teams send their applications as upgrade units to the factory for analysis, remediation, and unit testing. A fully operational and efficient internal factory is the cheapest of all alternatives on a per line of code basis. However, reaching this efficiency requires considerable investment in staffing, training, tools, and procedure development. As a result, internal factories require 10 to 20 million lines of code to justify the investment. For this reason, internal factories are most attractive to very large IT organizations with large quantities of code developed in a few common technologies.

6.5 Optimizing the DIY Approach

To achieve the high rates of productivity required to reach full century compliance, it is not enough to simply select and implement one or more of the approaches described in the previous section or in Chapter 5. True productivity is gained only if all members of the project operate with maximum effectiveness. If the project has any weak points, these will result in bottlenecks that will rob the project processes of their efficiency. For example, if an application team cannot package and deliver complete upgrade units on a timely basis, this failure may prevent an internal factory from reaching capacity.

To ensure that the entire remediation process works as smoothly and effectively as possible, IT must look at each of the steps in their selected approaches and determine whether they are operating as effectively as possible. In particular, IT should look for ways to automate support tasks, hone QA activities, and to improve staff effectiveness through training and documented processes.

To optimize the effectiveness of any approach, the IT organization should resist mixing routine maintenance changes with their Year 2000 changes. By mixing changes in this way, IT increases its testing effort and elevates its risk because it cannot automatically compare test results of the compliant and noncompliant versions of applications. Further, strong version control and powerful configuration managers are required to permit maintenance to be performed separately from, and eventually reintegrated with, Year 2000 changes.

The next sections explore ways to improve the effectiveness of the DIY approaches discussed in Section 6.4.1.

6.5.1 Optimizing the Manual Fix Approach

The manual fix approach, although it does not rely on automated change tools to perform century changes, does require some tool support. An IT organization may possess a variety of tools to support its maintenance processes which can also be used to support remediation and testing activities. These tools include configuration managers, debuggers, capture/playback tools, compare utilities, and documenters. Some of these tools may be in frequent use; others may be "shelfware." The Year 2000 project provides an opportunity for leveraging the capabilities of these tools.

Other tools that can assist the manual fix approach may not be found in the IT organization's current tool arsenal. Impact analyzers, which are vital tools to find affected date fields and to understand the ramifications of a given change, are not commonly used by IT groups. In certain cases, these tools can greatly improve productivity rates and reliability of results over manual approaches, easily justifying their acquisition. These tools also have value beyond the Year 2000 project for future development and maintenance. The highest quality impact analysis tools will be available only for the most common languages and platforms.

Year 2000 requirements make some specialized tools an absolute necessity. Chapters 7 and 8 discuss the tools required to support full-blown environment and system tests. These tools include date simulators to allow future date testing, bridging utilities to handle date format differences between expanded and nonexpanded files, and intelligent compare utilities to compare test results while accounting for date format differences. Further, if an automated code change tool exists for the applicable technology and the volume of code to be processed is large enough to justify the cost of the tool, an IT organization should seriously consider switching to the tool-assisted approach.

6.5.2 Optimizing the Tool-Assisted Approach

To successfully implement this approach, an IT organization first has to select appropriate tools and processes and then has to effectively sponsor their rollout and future support. Simply purchasing and installing tools is not enough. When left to their own discretion, many programmers will fail to use new tools. Tools must be well integrated into the work environment and must be backed with training and defined processes. Only if implemented in this way will tools enable maximum productivity and consistent quality of deliverables.

As mentioned above, to optimize this approach, IT organizations must first select the right tools. While separate tools for each step in the project may exist and may work fine, tools that are able to interact and share and reuse data will provide the greatest productivity gains. Data sharing is an especially important characteristic since it avoids the need to re-collect data previously gathered and permits the consistency and integrity of changes to be checked across multiple programs. It also helps to prevent many types of errors including strategy mismatches from windowing the same date field using different cutoff years in different programs.

To integrate tools and foster data sharing, an organization can implement a shared data repository. In some cases, this repository may be a vendor-supplied, proprietary tracking facility that underlies their product suite. In this situation, it is best to apply the entire tool suite that utilizes this facility to the analysis, remediation, and testing processes. In cases where multiple vendor products are being deployed, analysts should attempt to keep as much macrolevel data, gleaned from tools at each step of the process, current in a repository facility that has been customized to support a Year 2000 project. One last recommendation is to look for impact and remediation tools that can share data via an internal repository facility so that impact analysis information can be reused as needed during the code remediation stage of a project.

Many IT organizations will use a combination of technical strategies to perform their conversion work. It is best to choose tools that can support a variety of remediation strategies, such as windowing or date field expansion, so that only a single tool must be acquired, implemented and rolled out. No matter the strategy, the tool should automate as much of the conversion work as possible. Focus on accuracy of results rather than sheer speed when considering which tool to purchase. In addition, because Year 2000 projects involve so much parallel activity, be sure to select tools that can support teams of programmers working on the same upgrade unit. A repository can facilitate this type of teamwork by tracking the conversion status of components and producing audit reports of changes made and strategies selected.

Following tool selection, IT must define and document the processes required to use the tools. The documentation must explain the steps in the process, how to perform each of them (including which tools to use and how to use them), what deliverables are produced, and how the quality of those deliverables will be assured. The process should also describe when and how data will be shared with other staff members at the various QA checkpoints in the process and at test time. Someone must train each team member in the proper use of the tools and processes. Further, the use of the processes must be enforced. By incorporating the processes in an automated process manager, or at selective interface points, training effort is reduced and proper usage is encouraged.

6.5.3 Optimizing the Internal Factory Approach

To optimize an internal factory, two things need to be done. The first is to optimize the factory itself. The second is to optimize the activities of the application teams that will provide the input, or upgrade units, to the factory. The internal factory will be unable to operate at peak capacities if the application teams are unable to supply upgrade units on a timely, and complete, basis.

The internal factory is typically charged with finding and fixing code and unit testing those changes while achieving high levels of throughput and quality. Application teams must package the upgrade unit, select the compliance strategy, perform all QA activities and generate test data for the testing phase. The latter activities are more detailed and focused, offering little opportunity for economies of scale; they maximize quality at the expense of efficiency. Factory processes are consistently performed within a controlled environment. Application team processes vary by team and occur in diverse environments. To eliminate mismatched expectations and to ensure smooth handoffs of deliverables, the boundaries of the factory/application team relationship must be clearly defined.

In general, the level and quality of factory performance depend on its tools, the size and skill set of its staff, and the strength of its processes. Rudimentary tool performance can be measured by raw throughput—the number of lines of code processed by each staff member each week. More important are the tools' level of automation, reject rate, and error rate. High raw throughput is meaningless if much of an application has to be processed manually or if errors are introduced only to be detected during testing. A factory should select its tools using the same guidance as in the previous section. Because the factory staff will be well-versed in tool usage, high tool performance may be more desirable than slick integration of tools into program managers or interfaces. Again, a repository for sharing data and a strong configuration manager are essential tools.

To optimize application team performance, use a combination of well-defined and documented processes and training. It is highly unlikely that application team members will have experience in performing one-time tasks such as packaging an upgrade unit. To avoid repeating the mistakes of others, application teams should have access to a guidebook or methodology describing how to perform these tasks, especially the QA activities. Application teams, along with the internal factory, should also have access to any repository of shared data to enable audit reporting and preparation of test data. A strong configuration management tool should be available to retain and control the various upgrade unit version produced during the compliance project. To maximize QA activities, the application team should save all reports produced during the assessment phase to reconcile the results produced by the factory.

6.6 Rules of Engagement—Start Now

If your company continues to evaluate options for its Year 2000 work, stop the practice now. At this stage in the game, it is more prudent to choose an approach quickly and to select those vendors that will help you to implement the approach. Remember that the vendors selected should fit the company's approach rather than forcing the company to fit their approach. Any technical strategy chosen should be flexible. Most companies will have to implement a combination of strategies; few companies will be able to implement only windowing or only expansion.

As is true in most scenarios, it is better to do things right in the first place. If time is running out and you cannot implement the optimal solution, make sure that the right things are done first. Why build a high-capacity factory if it cannot operate at capacity due to other constraints that the company failed to alleviate? Why improve remediation productivity if it has a negative effect on testing efficiency?

When choosing a solution, don't base your choice on a few flashy components. It is crucial that all parts of the solution work together to achieve the necessary productivity gains. Optimize the selected approaches to provide the maximum benefit to your company. Understand the entire remediation process so that resources and capital can be invested where they will provide the greatest benefit.

Wherever possible, reuse work products to aid quality assurance and testing efforts. When evaluating vendor solutions, consider whether existing, valuable work products can be reused or whether they must be recreated by the vendor. Of special value are those work products that support IT activities beyond the Year 2000 crisis.

6.7 Year 2000 Tool Utilization Update

We want to update readers on the latest progress and thinking surrounding software tools that support the remediation, testing, change control, and project management aspects of a Year 2000 project. The first thing that Project Office technology analysts should remember is that there is a world of difference between an off-the-shelf software product and a consulting/conversion factory tool. The first category is characterized by a release plan, solid user documentation, automated installation capabilities, and a product name and requires little or no consulting support. The second category lacks most of these capabilities. Project startup estimates must be longer for in-house utilization of a consulting/conversion factory tool than they would be for an off-the-shelf product. For this reason, consulting/conversion factory tools are typically used by trained consultants in the isolation of an off-site factory. Testing tools must, by definition, be off-the-shelf products. Having said this, the following sections discuss the current thinking regarding various Year 2000 tool categories.

6.7.1 Automated Remediation Tools

In our last Year 2000 book, we predicted that remediation tools would improve; and we were correct. There are more tools, with broader and better capabilities, being offered for more software and hardware computing environments than one could have imagined. Some of these tools are just scanners—but there are a number of parsers now available for almost every version of COBOL, IBM Assembler, PL/I, Natural, C, C++, Visual Basic, and even FORTRAN. In addition to this, numerous vendors offer tools that integrate the impact analysis and automated (or semi-automated as the case may be) remediation process.

The debate regarding how much automation is better continues to confuse project teams. There are three levels of automation: automated assistance, automated remediation with an interim step identifying what will and will not be modified by the tool, and automation where no interim review point is considered. In addition, some tools allow users to customize the knowledge base underlying the tool to streamline the process better. A fully automated approach or a semi-automated approach that does not apply human review and intervention techniques, tends to cause the following two potential problems:

- Fixing date and date-related logic incorrectly.

- Not identifying and not fixing problems that need to be fixed.

The first problem involves a case where an error was introduced by the change itself or where a latent bug was not corrected during the remediation process. In the case of an automated fix, the problem of leaving a latent bug untouched is more common. For example, a business function may wish to process information from a prior year, using a Julian date, by subtracting 01000 from 99365 (December 31, 1999) so that it is looking at 98365 (December 31, 1998). Date field expansion changes the logic to subtract 01000 from 1999365—which in our example would now yield 1998365—which is still correct. Now assume that the application logic did not accommodate the fact that 2000 is a leap year. Subtracting 01000 from 2000366 would result in 1999366—a nonexistent date. This bug would not show up until the end of the Year 2000.[1]

The second problem is a common occurrence when analysts assume that a tool has found and fixed everything. The simple statement "subtract 1 from year," where year is defined as a two-digit integer, works until we subtract 1 from 00, which would yield a –1 or an absolute 1. Adding 1 back to this value (this is an actual example), yields a 2, which is not even close to the program's intentions. A windowing solution would likely fix the conditional logic but miss this statement—unless analysts reviewed the interim date usage and corrected the problem or unless the remediation tool used data flow analysis. It is also quite likely that testing teams would miss this error during validation efforts.

Our recommendation, particularly when time is short, is to apply automation to common languages and platforms, but to check date usage carefully based on the results of the impact analysis and other manual reviews. This technique allows one to achieve the best of both worlds: automation on the one hand and the intelligence of the remediation and application specialists on the other.

6.7.2 Date Routines—Revisited

In our last book we discussed the concept of replacing noncompliant date routines with a single, standardized date routine. Older date routines are typically written in Assembler, hard to modify, may have missing source code, and may be so numerous that fixing all of them in a reliable way was unlikely. We now believe that failed date routines are going to be a major source of frustration for application personnel who thought they had fixed and tested their systems, only to see that system crash in production. The debugging process, which will tie up time and resources, will ultimately be traced back to these routines—which, by the way, have the ability to bring down dozens of applications concurrently. We are still, however, recommending the use of date routine standardization, even if the implementation process runs into the next century.

6.7.3 Bridging Routines

Since we first identified Year 2000 tool categories, bridging routines were introduced into the market as a way of reducing physical data expansion requirements while still obtaining the benefits of date field expansion at the source program level. The process upon which this technology is based was described in more detail in Section 6.3.4. There are a growing number of bridging tool options now available. Readers should reference the appendix for more specifics on tool vendors.

6.7.4 Testing Update

The recommended Year 2000 testing tools and the importance that we have placed on their uses have not changed dramatically since we documented testing tools in our last Year 2000 book. The one exception to this observation is in the area of data aging, where several new products have emerged. Data aging tools, particularly when integrated with capture/ playback products, allow analysts to create test data that covers the 1999/ 2000 transition time frame more efficiently. This concept is expanded further in Chapters 7 and 8, which discuss testing at great length. These products can streamline the creation of future test data and should be included when assessing testing tools.

One positive sign is the commitment by vendors to package and bundle testing tools into a comprehensive solution that typically includes a testing process. Vendors offering integrated testing solutions are more appealing than those with point tools. While remediation can be done off-site to a great degree, testing is carried out most efficiently when the data, the subject matter experts, and the production environment are close at hand. For this reason, we still believe that testing tools are an essential part of every Year 2000 remediation project. The appendix provides an expanded list of tool vendors that support the testing process.

6.7.5 PC and Distributed Systems Tools

More vendors are venturing into the PC and distributed systems markets. A number of PC tools can scan a PC, determine if the BIOS is compliant, correct the BIOS (in some cases), and compare various versions of PC software for compliance against a master database. These tools are essential for widely distributed desktop environments or any business that relies heavily on PCs. Other tools have also emerged to analyze and correct C, C++, Visual Basic, and PC COBOL dialects. Another category of tool supports scanning LAN/WAN environments to determine which client connections should be further investigated. This type of scanning is important as a means of documenting distributed system utilization. The fact that these tools are emerging is useful because it was previously thought that many of these systems were compliant when, in fact, they are not.

6.7.6 Risk Simulation Tools

Risk simulation tools, as they apply to the Year 2000, are a recent addition to the market. These tools allow management to associate business function, systems, and third-party dependencies to assess the impact of the Year 2000 on the bottom line. While these tools have just been introduced to the market, executives should consider that this information is exactly what your business partners, regulators, legal counsel, and auditors want to see when they ask for a business risk assessment summary. These tools facilitate visualization of the problem and its impacts and allow executives to simulate "what if" scenarios for purposes of planning and funding. We urge executives to evaluate risk simulation tools soon.

6.8 Tracking Risks and Progress: Repository Utilization

In order to establish a vehicle for managing systems portfolio evolution, interface planning, deployment, Year 2000 project status, and related project activities, organizations should create a Year 2000 tracking repository. This repository helps track relationships among systems and system components to ensure the success of all Year 2000 planning and implementation efforts. This repository additionally establishes a basis for project status tracking during the multiyear implementation phase of the project.

This repository is recommended for Year 2000 projects at large, complex, or highly distributed IT organizations, regardless of the types of systems, languages, or hardware used within those environments. In addition, organizations with a complex set of external relationships, including suppliers, business partners, and data interfaces, require a sophisticated vehicle for tracking this information. Experience suggests that information captured during the Year 2000 inventory process needs to be consolidated and updated on an ongoing basis for ease of analysis by management teams. This task includes the tracking of Year 2000 remediation and testing projects. The repository concepts discussed below address this requirement.

6.8.1 Establishing Year 2000 Tracking Repository

The Year 2000 Project Office should establish a project tracking repository in order to consolidate and report on Year 2000 activities across multiple geographic regions and computer systems. The platform used to store this information should incorporate knowledge already available in other corporate repositories. One view of implementing this repository strategy is depicted in Figure 6.3. Successful implementation of the Year 2000 tracking repository requires the following components.

- Basic definition of the information that is to be captured and stored in this repository.

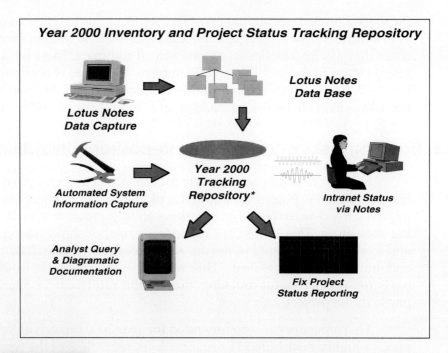

Figure 6.3 Interfaces into and out of the tracking repository must be established and maintained by project office.

- An underlying metamodel depicting the relationships of the information being stored.

- Optionally, depending on the ability of the physical repository to store enterprisewide information, an enterprise-level summary repository.

- Physical repository definition to support ease of loading, updating and access.

- A vehicle for capturing and loading information into the repository.

- A means of optionally extracting physical systems information captured by automated tools.

- Definitions of ad hoc and canned reporting and query requirements for the repository.

6.8.2 Information Requirements

The information to be loaded into the tracking repository is contained on various Year 2000 project survey forms. Infrastructure survey data, coupled with additional system software and hardware data, further augments the information required to inventory and track Year 2000 project progress for the life of the initiative.

Most IT environments share significant commonality when it comes to representing these environments in a repository information metamodel. A repository metamodel template derived from these commonalities should be flexible enough to support unique categorization schemes and query requirements within a given business unit. This flexibility is particularly critical when one attempts to meet reporting and query requirements for a Year 2000 project.

Figure 6.4 depicts a metamodel that represents major system components and relationships across an IT environment. This model can be expanded or modified to reflect unique system requirements within a given business unit. Additional entities that may be added to the model include division, region, or other organizational categories. As a rule, manager name or position should be defined as an attribute, not as an entity, due to the volatility of personnel positions within a business hierarchy.

Metamodel requirements are established to support query and reporting needs. For example, a single query should be able to identify all systems in all regions that utilize a Sybase database so that each of those systems can be updated to the proper release. A second example might require the identification of all systems written using Assembler code so that the owners of those systems may be notified regarding the availability of tools to analyze or fix the Year 2000 problem. Many other examples exist of situations where reports required from the repository are dependent on the way the underlying metadata is organized. Storing each of these entity types in a "flat" table definition, one alternative to this metamodel, could seriously hamper ad hoc query and reporting capabilities.

If a metamodel stores language, platform, or similar information as an attribute of a system, for example, it may not support these types of ad hoc or canned queries. In these cases, a search procedure may have to read every system entity to determine which systems use a given language type or run on a certain platform. This overhead could seriously impact response time given that there will easily be more than a thousand applications stored within this repository.

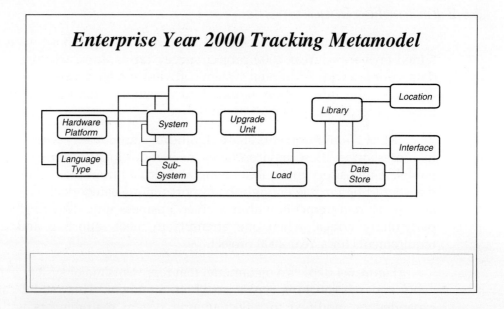

Figure 6.4   Enterprise metamodel supports tracking interfaces and migration progress at an enterprisewide level.

6.8.3 Enterprisewide Metamodel

A large organization may find that storing all of this metadata for all of its applications and systems cannot be facilitated in a single physical repository. The metamodel in Figure 6.4 stores a level of detail that includes shared data store, source program, record, interface, and other physical components across 17 business units. Once loaded, the sheer volume of information in the repository may turn the updating, query, and reporting process into a time-consuming task. One way to avert this problem is through the use of a tiered repository structure.

Creating tiered repository structures requires establishing a single repository for each business unit as shown in Figure 6.5. This information can then be uploaded into a central, enterprisewide repository that stores a subset of this information for tracking and reporting purposes like the metamodel depicted in Figure 6.4. Organizations should not attempt to omit the process of collecting basic metadata because this information is required to track project progress and component status within a given business unit.

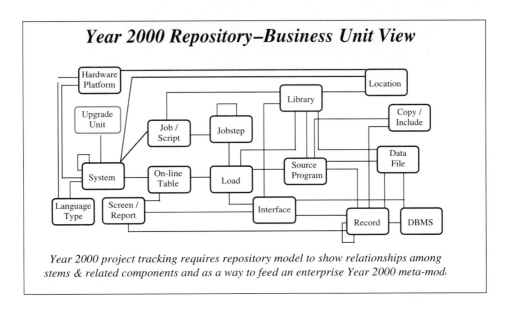

Year 2000 project tracking requires repository model to show relationships among stems & related components and as a way to feed an enterprise Year 2000 meta-mod

Figure 6.5 Detailed repository model required to track components within and across a given business unit.

6.8.4 Physical Repository Requirements

The tracking repository may be a commercially available repository or may be a relational database. It should not, however, be the native data storage capability embedded in many of the tools used to capture inventory data during a Year 2000 assessment process. This admonition is based on the fact that inventory tools use relatively fixed data structures to store physical information extracted from a software portfolio and are not capable of representing the numerous variations of organizational or project-related data required for a Year 2000 project. Most inventory tools also cannot reflect inventory data for systems that they do not directly analyze. In other words, a separate repository is needed to fully represent the status of a systems inventory over the life of a Year 2000 project.

Formal repositories and relational database structures both have the ability to represent relationships among systems, data stores, interfaces, upgrade units, management structures, and related components. Repositories additionally offer powerful loading and reporting capabilities and, in select cases, the ability to import information directly from inventory tool data structures. An enterprise-level tracking repository is the minimum level of information that is required for the Year 2000 project office. The basic repository and, if applicable, the enterprise-level repository are to be maintained centrally and under the control of the Year 2000 program office. All updating of this information and reporting should be similarly centralized.

6.8.5 Information Capture and Loading Requirements

One requirement for implementing the Year 2000 tracking repository is to be able to populate the repository with information. Many organizations capture survey information manually and/or through an online facility such as Lotus Notes. Information placed into a Lotus Notes database can be captured and loaded into the repository using automated extraction programs that can be developed in-house. Manual loading of this information can be accomplished through front-end menus that can be developed by in-house programming staff.

Physical information about a system's environment, such as program name, link between a program and a screen, program size, and other attributes can automatically be captured using various inventory and analysis tools. Other products support this requirement as well. This approach streamlines the initial metadata capture and updating process dramatically and can save hundreds of hours of effort over the life of the project in update time. The following questions regarding the use of these vendor tools should be explored.

- Do parsers scan all required physical components in a given environment?

- Do parsers run on the host or workstation?

- Do the loaders recognize and update only modified components to avoid a complete reload when updating is required?

- Do the tools have a "robust" interface to load and update the repository or database being used?

Finally, physical inventory data, such as program statistics, system scoping metrics, component relationships, and related items, should periodically be refreshed to keep information current. Analysts must also update logical data, including compliance status, interface utilization, management changes, new systems, and other information. Logical metadata must be entered by a tracking repository coordinator, typically found in the central Year 2000 office. The update process should impact only delta changes and not require the re-creation of the entire repository.

6.8.6 Inquiry and Reporting Requirements

While information in this repository should be readily accessible to relevant parties, central control of the data and the reports produced from that data should remain in the hands of the project office status tracking and project reporting coordinator. Initial inventory summaries are a required deliverable from the enterprise assessment and are readily produced from the tracking repository. In some cases, this may require a special reporting tool that extracts data from relational databases. Reporting of inventory updates and project status should become a recurring deliverable from the Year 2000 project office. Reports that should be generated from the repository for tracking purposes include the following information:

- All compliant applications.

- All compliant applications within a region.

- All compliant applications within a business unit.

- Compliant versus noncompliant applications within a business unit.

- Compliant status for IBM mainframe applications.

- All applications using a given database type, operating system, or platform.

- Owners of all noncompliant applications.

- All programs within a given application.

- Current project status within region or business unit.

- Many other queries or reports based on ongoing project requirements.

Charts and diagrams that depict relationships among systems and system components could be generated from the repository once it is loaded. Applications personnel have a tendency to create numerous system architecture charts that depict a system at a point in time and these charts quickly become out of date. Using the central repository to perform this function over the long term eliminates the tedious hours that would have to be dedicated to this activity.

Endnotes

1. Derived from "Field Expansion, Procedural Workarounds and Bridging," and "Field Expansion, Procedural Workarounds and Bridging II," by Michael D. Lips, published in *Year/2000 Journal*, July/August 1997, and September/October 1997, respectively.

Chapter 7

Year 2000
Testing Basics

Is thorough Year 2000 testing truly a necessity? It seems to be an outrageously expensive exercise that adds no value to a project that is already very costly and resource constrained. Given the size of typical Year 2000 budgets, cutting back on testing effort may appear to save millions of dollars. Studies by the Gartner Group and others estimate that testing will account for 50 percent or more of overall Year 2000 spending. Early reports from leading-edge companies exceed this percentage. Is this effort really necessary? After all, many IT organizations perform very limited testing of their normal changes. Is the Year 2000 effort any different?

The answer to these questions is a resounding yes. Although testing may be viewed primarily as an insurance policy, failure to pay its premiums will be exceptionally costly and damaging to corporate operations and may increase legal liability for any disruptions. Even if absolutely all affected software, hardware, and data are correctly and consistently checked and remediated to handle century-date processing, the cost of testing buys peace of mind and a measure of legal protection. Since no company will achieve this standard of perfection, full-scale testing is an essential phase of all Year 2000 efforts. Thorough testing provides the following benefits.

- **Serves as a safety net**

  Given the complexity and range of Year 2000 issues, it is virtually impossible for any analysis or remediation approach to guarantee that all potential exposures have been identified and corrected. Testing becomes the last line of defense for preventing those exposures from impacting operations.

- **Reduces the risk of failures**

  Each error trapped and corrected during testing eliminates one failure that would otherwise have occurred. While many Year 2000-related failures may be relatively inconsequential or short-lived, others will have a significant effect on operations. Also, the cumulative effect of many small errors may cause disruptions far in excess of the errors themselves.

- **Reduces the cost and impact of failures**

  Reducing the number of errors that reach production operations decreases the time and effort required to return to normal operations and associated operational cost and impact of the failures. A great challenge of the Year 2000 crisis is that most century-date errors will occur simultaneously within a narrow window of time. Unless these errors can be reduced to a manageable number, IT organizations will be unable to respond adequately, leading to long outages of critical functions. The cost and impact of failures can be further reduced by targeting testing efforts to the most critical components of the corporate portfolio. Assuring the integrity of these components significantly reduces the likelihood of costly errors.

- **Demonstrates reasonable care**

  Testing to assure compliance provides a level of confidence for the people dependent on the correct operation of a given system. Managers need to know that they can rely on the results of the system. Even nontechnical juries can understand the need to test a system to see if its actually works after fixing it. This makes testing a favorite topic for trial lawyers. If an application that was assumed to be compliant without testing fails during the century transition, the responsible managers will be severely hampered in their ability to defend their actions.

- **Creates an audit trail**

  Testing activities create many paper trails. They describe which tests were performed, how those tests were performed, and document the results of those tests. They also provide a checklist showing that affected components were actually tested. This information is crucial to satisfy the compliance certification requirements of internal and external auditors, government regulators, and even critical customers.

The need for adequate testing extends beyond organizational boundaries. Companies share critical data. Components come from many software vendors, hardware manufacturers, and service providers. From a business perspective, the level of compliance testing performed by a critical customer or supplier may have even greater impact on the organization than the performance of some of its internal systems. Companies that are highly dependent on the uninterrupted flow of information between them must take steps to ensure that their systems continue to work together.

Given its importance, this book splits the topic of testing into two chapters. This chapter discusses the basics of Year 2000 testing and describes the types of tests needed to assure compliance. The second chapter covers the implementation of a testing program. These chapters are meant as a detailed introduction to Year 2000 testing issues. A thorough discussion of all aspects of a Year 2000 program would fill several volumes and are clearly beyond the scope of this book. The authors encourage interested readers to obtain one of the many excellent general textbooks on testing. Also, several vendors have Year 2000-specific testing methodologies that they share with their customers.

This chapter contains five sections. The first section explores the differences between Year 2000 testing and standard IT testing efforts. The second section describes the compliance requirements that must be addressed during testing. These sections are followed by a discussion of the types and levels of tests used to meet those requirements. The fourth section examines how much testing is enough to meet organizational requirements. The final section covers a risk-based approach for targeting limited testing resources toward the functions that will provide the greatest organizational risk reductions.

7.1 Year 2000 Testing Differences

Year 2000 testing differs from typical software development life-cycle testing in several fundamental ways. Although Year 2000 projects use many of the same standard testing techniques available for software development projects, the scope, focus, and infrastructure of Year 2000 testing are unlike those of any other project. Year 2000 project managers must have a handle on these differences throughout the project, since decisions made at any stage prior to, or during, testing could reduce the effectiveness of the testing effort or waste resources. For instance, a Year 2000 test effort will usually require additional hardware resources whose installation must be planned well in advance. Likewise, planning for extensive end-user testing, which would be a normal part of a traditional test plan, is generally ineffective and unnecessary in the Year 2000 context as explained below.

This section is divided into three subsections that examine the differences in scope, focus, and infrastructures of Year 2000 testing efforts. The discussion of scope explains why Year 2000 testing is an enormous undertaking. While most organizations understand that a great volume of effort is involved in the project, it is the nuances of the project that magnify this effort to monumental proportions. These nuances must be understood before attempting to develop testing plans. Similarly, the focus of a Year 2000 testing project varies considerably from routine testing. Attempting to apply traditional testing techniques when testing century-date compliance will waste significant time and effort while failing to achieve the intended results. Finally, Year 2000 testing will strain the capacity and capabilities of the current test infrastructures in most IT organizations. To be successful, these infrastructures must provide the tools, test data, and hardware capacity needed to support the repetitive, voluminous, and methodical testing of all date-related logic.

7.1.1 Scope of Year 2000 Testing

The amount of resources and effort required to successfully implement Year 2000 testing dwarf other historical IT projects. Within a short, and decreasing, time frame, almost every application, package, operating environment, and platform must be tested for century-date compliance. The factors listed below, all of which apply to a Year 2000 project, illustrate the magnitude of the effort. While one or more of these characteristics may apply to any project, only Year 2000 projects confront all these issues.

- **Volume of effort**

  Year 2000 issues are so pervasive that virtually every application, operating system, platform, package, and environment will need to be tested, to some extent, to determine whether it is compliant and, if remediated, functionally equivalent and century validated. Many IT organizations have estimated that they will need at least one full year, or 40 percent to 60 percent of the total Year 2000 project time, to accomplish all testing. Most organizations are targeting calendar year 1999 to test their remediated applications and systems. During the testing period, hundreds of applications and other software components will vie for the same human and machine resources at the same time. The effort required to support this level of parallel activity will strain the IT organization's staff and infrastructure. Operational or environmental weaknesses or failures, such as insufficient disk space or CPU capacity, will disrupt the expected peak volumes of testing. Delays in achieving operating environment compliance or application conversions will further stress available resources and will force IT organizations to curtail or prematurely terminate their testing efforts as the close of the century approaches.

- **Effect on other efforts**

  Despite their best intentions, IT organizations cannot afford to devote all of their resources to Year 2000 projects. Year 2000 efforts will compete for personnel and hardware resources with ongoing development and maintenance projects, as well as concurrent compliance efforts. Moreover, everyday production operations will continue to require their share of resources and must be insulated from the resource crunch imposed by large-scale compliance testing. Compliance testing must be well timed and well implemented in order to not disrupt other testing and production efforts. These concerns mandate that robust test environments, with sufficient disk space and CPU capacity, be established to support the testing effort while isolating the production environment.

- **Technical diversity**

  Most IT organizations support a surprisingly diverse collection of operating systems, languages, platforms, databases, and other tools and utilities in their portfolios. This diversity increases the difficulty of year 2000 testing efforts at several levels. First, each component in this collection must be tested for compliance before the applications that use them can be certified. If any component is found to be non-compliant, the IT organization must often migrate to the latest version of the component to achieve compliance. Each migration requires its own level of testing in addition to century-date compliance testing. Each step of the testing effort may be complicated by a lack of tools and support. While common languages and platforms, such as COBOL and MVS, have widespread support in the market, organizations using uncommon technologies are often left to their own devices. Adding to this challenge are technologies that are obsolete or no longer strategic but are still used to support valuable business functions. IT organizations may find they no longer have the skills needed to properly test these environments and may have difficulty in obtaining these skills in the consulting market.

- **Future date testing**

One of the trickiest aspects of Year 2000 compliance certification is future date testing. This type of testing feeds a variety of data containing future dates in the next century to an application whose operating environment is itself set to future dates. Without this type of test, an application cannot be certified as truly compliant. The challenge in this type of testing lies in creating a test environment that can safely be set to simulate a variety of future date scenarios. The test environment must be separate from the production environment so as not to impact production data and to enable simulating future dates. Date simulators can be used to facilitate the setup of a test environment, however, Year 2000 project teams must take care to remember that the operating environment itself must be able to handle century dates and must be certified as compliant.

- **Interface testing**

Testing interfaces between both internal and external applications is a complex mixture of scheduling, coordination, and execution. Through these interfaces, applications share files, databases, and other forms of data containing dates. Any mistakes in date formats or windowing approaches between interfacing applications can lead to application failures, even in otherwise compliant applications. Thoroughly testing the interfaces between applications is the only means to avoid these errors. The testing process becomes more complicated as the level of data sharing between applications increases. In addition, when applications have interfaces to outside organizations, the testing effort is made even more difficult since the scheduling, coordination, and execution now involve multiple entities with multiple agendas. Testing a single transaction may require the execution of several different applications, running at different physical sites within different test environments. Further, until these complex interfaces are tested and found compliant, an IT organization cannot certify its own constituent applications as compliant. An IT organization could find itself "held hostage" by an outside organization whose interfacing applications remain noncompliant.

7.1.2 Focus of Year 2000 Testing

Unlike most traditional software development projects, Year 2000 projects have a highly focused goal—to ensure that applications and their operating environments will correctly process dates occurring in the next century. This tightly targeted objective streamlines the testing process by eliminating inapplicable steps found in a standard life-cycle testing process. Similarly, acceptance criteria are simplified—an application will either handle century dates correctly or it won't. At the conclusion of Year 2000 testing, the project team should know, for each application and its operating environment, that all century-date issues were found and fixed with all modifications working properly; that there are no adverse side effects on existing application functionality due to Year 2000 fixes; and that the operating environment will perform correctly in the next century.

When compared to standard life-cycle testing, the focus of Year 2000 testing differs in several important respects.

- **Existing applications**

  Since the focus of Year 2000 projects is on applications currently operating in the production environment, Year 2000 teams must view their target applications as fully functional and operational in their current state. For their purposes, they must ignore bugs and other functional problems that are not concerned with century-date processing. Two implications arise from having this perspective. First, the Year 2000 team can remain focused on its primary objective and will not be sidetracked into implementing additional functionality, fixing bugs, or waste time verifying the functional correctness of test results. Second, Year 2000 testing will not have to include those tests that are typically included in new development testing, such as stress, performance, and disaster recovery.

- **Identical functionality**

  Since Year 2000 teams are focused on identifying and remediating century-date issues, they do not add or change functionality in the remediated applications. With the exception of the ability to process century dates, this means that the compliant and noncompliant version of an application are functionally identical. Given this characteristic, end-users do not have to perform the type of detailed acceptance testing that they would normally execute when an application is modified or extended. Year 2000 test teams do not have to design and execute the types of exhaustive regression tests typically performed when the functionality of an application is modified or extended. Further, because functionality should be identical between compliant and noncompliant versions, comparing output results from regression tests, and verifying their correctness, is a straightforward exercise and can be automated by the use of tools. To obtain the foregoing benefits, Year 2000 projects should strongly resist incorporating noncentury-date functional changes into applications

- **Limited acceptance testing**

  The highly focused objective of Year 2000 testing means that traditional acceptance testing, in which end-users sign off on the functional implementation of an application, is unnecessary. As mentioned above, other than differences related to century-date processing, compliant and noncompliant versions of an application should be functionally identical. Because the remediated and unremediated applications are functionally identical, there is no new, modified, or extended functionality for end-users to test as they typically would if an application had undergone the usual type of application maintenance or enhancement. Often, a century-compliant application will have no "visible" differences for end-users to see; date representations on screens or in reports may look exactly the same prior to and after remediation. When this is the case, only Year 2000 testers within the IT organization will be able to validate and verify the remediation changes. In a Year 2000 context, end-user involvement should be sought in the design and scope of the application testing process; they can sign off on the adequacy of these testing process rather than signing off on test results.

- **Adoption of risk-based methods**

  As the close of the century approaches, many IT organizations will find that they do not have enough time or resources to design and execute a thorough test plan for all of their remediated applications. These constraints will call for IT organizations to intelligently reduce the scope of their testing effort without excessively increasing the risk that applications will fail due to undetected defects. To reduce and focus testing efforts in this "risk-based" approach, Year 2000 test teams must have access to a risk profile for each application. This risk profile reflects the priority of the application to the organization, the cost of any failure in the application, and the likelihood that failures will occur. These risk profiles will be used to determine the priority and timing of application testing and the types and levels of tests to be performed.

7.1.3 Infrastructure for Year 2000 Testing

As described in the preceding sections, Year 2000 testing demands an unprecedented amount of human and machine resources to simultaneously process a large volume of applications, platforms, languages, and operating environments in a short period of time. Meeting these overwhelming demands will strain the capabilities of most current testing infrastructures. To prepare for the testing onslaught, Year 2000 project managers should begin to examine their test infrastructures and establish their testing plans at the outset of the Year 2000 project. The testing strategy hinges on the initial data that is collected by the enterprise assessment which should include a high-level review of test environments across applications and platforms. The quality of test environments can be determined by interviews with programmers and end-users and should evaluate the sufficiency of test data, testing processes, and testing tools. This initial information should guide the Year 2000 project managers on the resources and tools that will need to be acquired or augmented to create a robust test environment on the test data that will have to be created, and on the test scripts and processes that will have to be implemented prior to actual testing.

Any time or effort invested in improving the test infrastructure for a Year 2000 project will provide future benefits to the IT organization. The improved test environment can be used in future application maintenance projects if the test data, scripts, and processes are saved, adjusted, and continually augmented with each project. Most, if not all, of the tools acquired to support Year 2000 testing are appropriate for use in other types of testing situations. Lastly, once formally versed in testing methodologies, programming staff will approach future testing with a level of knowledge and productivity certain to streamline the testing process.

To meet Year 2000 testing demands, a test infrastructure should have the characteristics listed below.

- **Centralized test management**

  To ensure that all Year 2000 testing activities and processes are leveraged to obtain the greatest possible benefit, test management should be centralized. Typically, test management, or oversight, is performed by application team members, if it is performed at all. Year 2000 test management is required at both the enterprise and application levels. At the enterprise level, test management ensures that all testing projects and activities across the enterprise occur according to an enterprise-level test plan. Enterprise test management functions reside in the Year 2000 project office and ensure that test projects, including certification testing and infrastructure improvements, occur as scheduled. Enterprise test managers resolve any conflicts between competing testing projects and monitor the relative priorities of testing projects on an ongoing basis. At the application level, test management ensures that all application testing occurs according to the application test plan. Application test management functions are vested in the application team's project manager who must ensure that testing occurs as scheduled, with the proper types and levels of tests, with appropriate test data, and that test results are verified.

- **Targeted test data**

  Thorough Year 2000 testing will require a level of test path coverage that is unlikely to be supported by current test data. Generally, these test beds are deficient for two reasons. First, most test data is extracted from production data and exercise only a small percentage of the execution paths in an application. This level of coverage will be inadequate for Year 2000 testing in which all execution paths, or minimally those that manipulate or use dates, must be tested. Second, test data must contain a variety of future dates in order to determine whether an application will operate correctly in the next century. Since production data will not contain these types of date scenarios, testers must thoughtfully manipulate the data, often using specialized tools, to ensure that future dates and boundary conditions are exercised. Third, given the impending time and resource constraints, testers cannot afford to waste precious time creating and executing redundant or useless tests.

- **Reliance on different test scripts and processes**

  Because Year 2000 testing is focused on certifying that applications can process century dates, and not on exercising other types of functional changes, the test scripts used to guide testing will differ from traditional test scripts. Year 2000 test scripts will address the "aging" of test data, the simulation of future-dated environments, the use of alternate infrastructures, tools and platforms—steps that are not normally found in typical life-cycle testing. Moreover, in the Year 2000 context, the need for test scripts is even more pressing. First, test scripts save testers valuable time since they do not have to re-create test scripts for each type and level of test to be executed. Second, test scripts ensure that tests will be executed consistently, a characteristic which is essential in validating the correctness of test results. Third, the test environment may include new tools that are unfamiliar to the testing staff. To maximize the use of these tools, test scripts should guide testers in when and how to use the tools as part of the testing process.

- **Increased reliance on tools**

  The sheer volume of testing to be accomplished in a tight window makes automated tools a necessity. Manually intensive testing approaches are time consuming and more error prone since human beings are spectacularly unable to perform repetitive, detailed testing tasks. Automated tools can ensure that tests are performed consistently and reliably across applications and during iterations of testing on a single application. To make savvy tool acquisitions, the Year 2000 project office must know what type of testing is required for their Year 2000 projects and must have a thorough knowledge of existing tools, including their strengths and weaknesses.

- **Formal test practices**

  To achieve the maximum level of efficiency, the Year 2000 project manager has to ensure that testing is conducted in a logical, formal manner and not in a haphazard, informal manner. Setting up a basic test infrastructure, certifying compliance, creating future and boundary data, and assessing test coverage are all skills that are not commonly found in IT organizations. Very few programmers have the type of formal training in testing practices to meet these goals.

Managing the testing process, tracking the status of testing, examining test results, and invoking additional testing are all crucial to the success of the testing effort and cannot be accomplished without formal practices and techniques. In addition, because multiple testing projects will occur simultaneously, many more individual testers will have to possess these skills since supply won't keep up with demand.

7.2 What Needs to Be Tested

The primary rule of Year 2000 testing is, "If it has not been tested, it is not compliant!" Countless IT organizations have been shocked to discover that programs or hardware that they assumed to be compliant failed during testing. Even applications designed to be compliant may contain errors that are exposed only during testing. A single date error in a large system is enough to make the system noncompliant and may cause the system to fail or produce erroneous results. Similarly, equipment containing embedded systems may contain dates in surprising locations. Since much of this equipment is customized, two seemingly identical pieces of equipment may differ in their century-date impact. The only method for ensuring uninterrupted operations is to check each piece of at-risk equipment.

7.2.1 Compliance Requirement for Business Software

There are many nuances for determining if a piece of software is truly century-date compliant. One criterion is that the software meet the specifications contained within its compliance definition. This document describes the precise methods that will be used to correct each type of date encountered within the system. Compliance definitions become a quality assurance screen for determining when an application is ready for full-scale testing. These documents are essential for coordinating the efforts between applications sharing data interfaces. For example, if one application creates dates using a windowing approach with a cutoff year of 50, the second application will not work correctly if it processes that data using a window cutoff of 20.

The method used to achieve compliance also has an impact on testing efforts. For instance, if a windowing approach is used, test data covering dates around the cutoff year are required to prove correctness. An application using a window cutoff of 50 must also test 49, 50, and 51 to ensure that all dates are correctly windowed. Different types of tests are needed for other compliance methods.

The requirements for application compliance can be defined using four critical categories of tests. All applications, regardless of supposed compliance status, must pass the fourth category before being considered truly compliant. The first three categories are restricted to applications that must undergo remediation to achieve compliance.

1. *Functional equivalence.*

   The goal of a Year 2000 effort is to ensure that a given application functions in exactly the same manner before and after remediation. The only difference in application functionality is the ability to handle century dates. It is crucial to ensure that existing functionality was not unintentionally broken as part of the compliance fix. To fulfill this requirement, application testing teams must conduct parallel tests using the compliant and noncompliant versions of the application. All application functionality should be reviewed regardless of its date impact to guard against unexpected programming mistakes.

2. *All instances of date-impacted code were found and changed.*

   The remediation effort must be complete. The application will fail or produce erroneous results if any date-impacted code is forgotten. Obscure coding techniques, variable reuse, and poor naming standards can result in "false negatives," which are variables that are incorrectly determined not to be dates. False negatives may appear anywhere in an application including modules which otherwise may not have any date impact. For this reason, it is critical to test all major components of an application even if they haven't been changed. Testing is the final defense for preventing problems caused by false negatives. This requirement is primarily fulfilled at the system testing level using forward-dated test environments to trigger date impacts. The degree of risk reduction is highly dependent on the level of test coverage achieved during these tests.

3. *All changes are correct.*

   All coding changes made during the remediation process must be correct. Whether code is changed manually or with automated tools, a number of different problems may be introduced through coding mistakes, module overlays, and other programming errors. In an unpublished study performed by one of the authors, programmers performing software reengineering tasks were found to average three mistakes for every hundred manual changes. This number was remarkably consistent from project to project and regardless of differences in programming skills.

Assuming that approximately 3 percent of the code in an average application is affected by century-date considerations, a million LOC application would require 30,000 changes. Applying the typical error rate, one can expect approximately 900 coding errors that must be found during QA reviews or trapped in the testing process. Many coding change errors can be identified and removed during peer reviews in the QA process or during the unit testing process. Some coding errors, however, will not be discovered until system testing.

4. *Dates are handled correctly regardless of century.*

The final, and most important, criterion is that the application will operate correctly in all circumstances regardless of its date of execution or the presence of century-impacted dates in its data. To achieve compliance for this requirement, the application must handle dates in the next century, the century transition itself, and operate correctly across a variety of date-related boundary conditions and special cases. Of special concern are common problems, such as the ability to handle the leap year (February 29, 2000), transactions that span both centuries, and circumstances where year variables may have used "99" or other numbers to flag special conditions. To meet this requirement, each application must be exercised using a variety of future dates in a future dated environment. Test data must be created to cover all of the date-related functions of the application and this data must be manipulated to simulate application execution using a series of future dates. This testing can be limited to system- level tests for applications already thought to be compliant, but applications undergoing remediation should conduct future date tests at all levels of the testing process.

Many of the tests required to prove compliance using the above criteria are application specific. Common conditions do exist, but those conditions must be modified to match the actual operation of the application. For example, if an application will definitely not be operating between December 31, 1999, and January 1, 2000, it will not have to handle user input occurring at exactly twelve midnight. Circumstances that cannot happen need not be included in test requirements. However, it is better to err on the side of caution for circumstances that have even a remote possibility of occurring. The table in Figure 7.1 shows some example date scenarios that may be used as a starting point for compliance testing. More complete lists of test criteria are available from other sources.

Test Dates		Purpose
Two-digit (for Windowing)	**Four-Digit (for Date Expansion)**	
Current-date (ex. 9/23/98)	Current-date (ex 9/23/1998)	Regression test
Year + 28 (ex. 9/23/26)	Year + 28 (ex. 9/23/2026)	"28" year rule, simple test to trap hard-coded "19s" and other century-specific errors
9/9/99	9/9/1999	Test for use of 99 as a processing flag
12/31/99	12/31/1999	Century transition
1/1/00	1/1/2000	Century transition
1/4/00	1/4/2000	First business day
2/29/00	2/29/2000	Leap y ear processing
For a window cutoff of 50		
9/23/49	should be 9/23/2049	Test for: 1. Missing windows
9/23/50	should be 9/23/1950	2. Incorrect window cutoffs
9/23/51	should be 9/23/1951	3. Mismatches between modules/application use of windows

Figure 7.1   Table of Common Date Scenarios.

To meet the requirements of category three, part of the application test planning process must include tests and quality assurance checkpoints for errors occurring during the application analysis and remediation process. The number of possible errors is endless, but the list below covers the most common situations.

- **Missing a required fix**

  At a coding level, this situation is described above in category 2. However, it can occur at many other levels. A component may be forgotten during the remediation process or may fall between the responsibility of two areas and be unintentionally omitted. Even small applications may be forgotten in the remediation process. Maintaining and frequently checking a complete inventory of year 2000 applications and components is essential to ensure complete coverage.

- **Fixing something that shouldn't be fixed**

  Applications contain many examples of fields that falsely appear to be dates ("false positives"). A classic example is YEAR-TO-DATE-TOTALS. Although related to date processing, this variable is neither a year nor a date. Accidental fixes of false positives are more commonly associated with automated approaches, but they can also be introduced manually. Quality assurance reviews of change lists are one important method for identifying potential false positive errors. Errors missed by the review must be caught by the functional equivalence tests.

- **Incorrectly implementing a fix**

  Since dates are frequently used in complex calculations and comparisons, date processing logic can be very convoluted and prone to error when changed. This is particularly true for complex Boolean expressions within IF logic. Other coding errors may be as simple as typographical errors. These errors may affect existing functionality in addition to century-date compliance. As discussed above, these errors are generally caught during QA reviews or through unit testing.

- **Incompatible fixes**

  If full date expansion were the only solution used for century-date compliance, all application interfaces would be compatible by definition. Since there are many different methods of achieving compliance, it is essential that programs and applications sharing data use compatible methods. This is true for programs within an application, applications internal to the enterprise, and for data shared with external entities. Some incompatibility problems are obvious without testing, such as one application expanding its shared data when its partner expects windowed data. More subtle errors occur when different window cutoff years are used by separate applications. Since the data itself is not modified, these errors are very difficult to identify. Published compliance definitions are one method for ensuring that all applications are fully aware of the compliance methods used by their partners. Interface testing across strings of applications is the system-level method for testing compatibility. These types of tests are logistically difficult to set up and can be very far reaching. The securities industry through the Security Industry Association is planning large-scale "street testing" involving dozens of organizations to ensure the interoperability of its remediation efforts.

- **Unexpected interactions between components**

  Modern applications are built from many components and rely on highly complex operating environments. Upgrading one component may cause unexpected impacts on other components. For example, upgrading to COBOL/370 from COBOL 74 can introduce a host of non-Year 2000 changes and problems into application code. PC environments are especially complicated in this regard. Upgrading one PC operating component may require moving to later releases of many other components ranging from network software to desktop applications. These upgrades often encounter their own range of problems and incompatibilities that must be incorporated into any test plans.

- **Encountering errors introduced after a fix**

  Even after they have passed the certification requirements listed above, applications can still have century-date failures if they are corrupted by subsequent programming changes. One IT organization discovered 18 century-date errors had been introduced into compliant applications during routine maintenance. Organizations must implement production control procedures to prevent the introduction of noncompliant changes into compliant applications. If these procedures are not "failsafe," the Year 2000 project team should continually monitor and retest mission-critical applications that have undergone significant changes since compliance certification. Typical errors include

  - Programmers coding or copying noncompliant date variable formats, calculations, or comparisons into a compliant program

  - Including a noncompliant copy member or macro

  - Adding a CALL to a noncompliant subroutine

  - Overlaying a compliant module with an older noncompliant version

End-user workstations are particularly susceptible to recorruption as nontechnical users frequently exchange data, spreadsheets, database information, and specialized programs. Unless the workstation users are well trained in Year 2000 issues, they may accept and reincorporate the noncompliant versions into their desktops.

7.2.2 End-User Systems

The complexity of end-user systems is primarily caused by the large number of unique components. These components include hardware and software that come from multiple vendors and exist in a mixture of compliant and noncompliant versions. End-user system testing can be divided into three distinct categories: hardware, purchased software, and user-developed software. The basic criteria for compliance remain the same for each category, but the methods and responsibility for testing vary by category.

- **Hardware**

  Many PCs encounter century-date issues in their processor and/or BIOS. While many of these problems are not severe and can be corrected with simple measures, each PC must be tested for compliance. Even identical PC models may differ in their level of compliance since different chips may have been installed during manufacturing. PC checking software is available from a number of different sources. Network and server hardware must also be tested. Several network vendors have reported that some of their older equipment is not compliant and must be upgraded.

- **PC Packaged Software**

  End-users depend heavily on purchased software such as word processors, spreadsheets, and databases. The first challenge is to create an inventory of this software along with the currently installed version on each PC. These versions must be compared against lists of known compliant versions provided by the manufacturers. All noncompliant versions must be upgraded to compliant versions. This presents a number of testing challenges.

  - Testing must be performed in separate test environments to avoid unintended damage to production PC applications.

  - The compliance of packaged software may need to be verified by the Year 2000 team. While the most reputable vendors are honest in their statements of compliance, some vendors will fail to provide compliance information or may provide incorrect data.

  - Upgrades may affect user-developed applications such as spreadsheets and databases that use the upgraded package. These must be corrected and retested to assure functional equivalence. It is important to remember that even if the package is compliant, the user-developed applications using the package may not be compliant. Some software requires user applications to be rewritten in a nontypical manner to achieve compliance.

  - Software packages interact with each other and may suffer from incompatibilities necessitating additional upgrades. For example, migrating from Windows 3.1 to Windows 95 requires upgrading a number of software packages to Windows 95 versions. Once the final environment has been developed, a full test should be conducted to ensure all software packages operate together and that their methods of handling century-date compliance are compatible.

- **End-User Applications**

  These are the spreadsheets, BASIC applications, databases, and other user-created software that reside on the PC. This software must be treated just like any other internally created software for the sake of analysis, remediation, and testing. The criteria described for business applications apply equally to these applications, although the organizational risk of noncompliance may be less. Although similar types of tests are needed to prove compliance, PC testing methods vary, and nontechnical users will require assistance to assure adequate testing.

7.2.3 Compliance Requirement for Embedded Technology

Assuring the compliance of embedded technology is one of the most difficult tasks facing Year 2000 project teams. Date processing failures in embedded systems may take many forms including incorrect reports, inability to set dates beyond 1999, endless loops due to zero-divide conditions, shutdown due to inspection date requirements, and incorrect performance of date-based functions. The first difficulty faced by the Year 2000 project team is finding these systems. They may occur virtually anywhere. While most systems are not concerned with dates and are therefore not subject to failure, a number contain date processing logic in surprising places. Given their variety, it is not possible to define a universal testing method for embedded technology. Each device has its own unique characteristics, and in many cases, it is not possible to perform adequate user testing of these systems for compliance. Where possible, the Year 2000 project team should rely on compliance and testing information provided by the manufacturer of the equipment. While not exhaustive, the list below provides some basic test requirements for embedded technology.

- Ability to transition between December 31, 1999, and January 1, 2000.

- Ability to handle February 29, 2000.

- No usage of Year fields "99" or "00" as special conditions.

- Ability to set dates correctly after December 31, 1999.

- Ability to return to the correct date after failure. (Some devices work properly through the transition but reset back to this century if a failure occurs.)

- Correct functioning of all date-based functions. This feature is especially important for security systems and other equipment that understand and vary performance for holidays and weekends.

7.3 Types and Levels of Testing

Most readers are familiar with the standard types and levels of testing used in application maintenance and development. These levels proceed from the detailed, unit testing level which verifies modules at the code level, through system testing which validates functionality across an entire application. All these levels of testing apply to Year 2000 efforts. The concept of test types, however, is unique to Year 2000 projects. Year 2000 projects must test for a variety of current date, boundary date, and future date scenarios. Each of these scenarios requires its own type of test environment and specialized test data. For the purposes of this book, these scenarios are referred to as types of tests. As shown in Figure 7.2, each type of test is executed at each level of testing. For example, current date (regression) testing is performed at the unit, integration, and system testing levels. The following subsections discuss the types and levels of tests applicable to Year 2000 testing and develop a baseline terminology for use throughout this and the next chapter.

Test Type	Test Level		
	Unit	Integration	System
Compliance Assessment			X
Current Date Regression	X	X	X
Future Date Regression	X	X	X
Boundary Date	X		X
External Interface			X
Fault Tolerance Tests	X		X

Figure 7.2   Types and Levels of Tests.

7.3.1 Types of Tests

There are many kinds or types of tests that are executed at the various test levels discussed in Section 7.3.2. For example, one type of test—a regression test—is performed to verify that existing application functionality has not inadvertently been affected by century-date changes. Regression tests can be performed at all levels of the testing cycle from unit tests to system tests. There are basically six different types of Year 2000 tests, including compliance assessment tests, regression tests, future date tests, boundary tests, external interface tests, and fault tolerance tests.

- **Compliance Assessment Tests**

    Compliance assessment tests are quick tests run to screen applications for century-date compliance. Screening for compliance requires a subset of future date and boundary testing. These tests enable quick, targeted execution of code areas most susceptible to failure, such as date boundaries, date-intensive calculations, and date-based decisions. If an organization definitely knows that an application is noncompliant, then compliance assessment testing can obviously be skipped. Compliance assessment tests are meant for those applications that could be compliant, but nobody really knows for sure. Failing a compliance test proves that an application is noncompliant; however, passing a compliance test cannot guarantee that an application is compliant. False negatives are possible due to the limited nature of the compliance tests. To avoid false negatives, compliance assessments tests should be used only to supplement more detailed code analysis.

- **Current Date Regression Tests**

    Standard, or current date, regression tests ensure that existing application functionality is not adversely affected or damaged by Year 2000 remediation. Theoretically, Year 2000 remediation should not affect existing application functionality other than enabling the application to process century dates. To run a regression test, use current test data with current dates. Validate test results by comparing parallel executions of compliant and noncompliant versions of the application, adjusting for any anticipated date variances. Accounting for any date adjustments, the results should be identical. If any other functional changes were introduced into the compliant version of the application, then simple regression tests would be unreliable as test results might differ in areas other than dates.

- **Future Date Regression Tests**

    Future date regression tests ensure that an application processes data correctly after the change of century. Functionally, these tests are the same as standard regression tests. In practice, they are performed in an environment that has been set to a future date. For this reason, future date testing can only be done with the compliant version of an application since the noncompliant version will likely fail in a future dated environment. Future date tests are executed by taking standard regression data and forward-dating it by some increment (usually by 28 years) and then incrementing the run date or system date of the test environment by the same amount. Validating future date test results is a little trickier than validating the results of simple regression tests. Validation can be accomplished by comparing parallel runs of the compliant and noncompliant versions of the application, but with the following caveats. First, the future test data used with the compliant application must start with the identical regression data used for the noncompliant application and then must be forward dated. Second, before comparing the results of the parallel runs, the results of the future test must be modified or rolled back to the current date or an intelligent date-compare utility must be used to ignore the differences in the years. Third, no other functional changes may be incorporated into the compliant application or else the results of the tests will be unreliable.

- **Boundary Date Tests**

  Boundary tests are invaluable to check special case conditions and unique events that will be encountered during and after century transition. To exercise these conditions and events, specialized test data will have to be created. For instance, a boundary test case may involve a transaction that straddles the century change, or that occurs precisely at midnight on December 31, 1999, or that occurs on February 29 of the first leap year in the next century. As with future date tests, noncompliant applications cannot be subject to boundary testing since they will not handle future dates. Boundary tests are useful because they stress an application in ways not typically thought of in normal testing. This characteristic means that boundary tests will exercise those areas of an application that aren't usually executed and often contain bugs.

- **External Interface Tests**

  External interface tests exercise the connections between applications. Applications are connected through data stores, such as files, or other methods of communications. When applications interface with other applications, they must all be tested together to ensure that the interfaces between them work properly and consistently and follow the same remediation strategy. These tests are used to check the bridging mechanisms that are used between compliant and noncompliant applications during the remediation phase. If incompatible remediation approaches were taken by different application teams, external interface tests would expose these problems.

- **Fault Tolerance Tests**

  Fault tolerance tests typically test an application's error processing, that is, the ability to handle bad data passed from another application. In addition to ordinary remediation changes, mission-critical applications may need augmented error handling to protect them against bad data introduced by external sources. At a minimum, every application should be able to recover, or die gracefully, after encountering bad data. Fault tolerance tests use specially created test data that anticipate the kinds of errors, or bad data, that may occur. These types of tests are not necessary for all applications but should be performed for those applications with a high level of external data interchange.

7.3.2 Levels of Tests

The typical testing life cycle involves a sequential progression through a series of different test levels, beginning with unit tests and completing with user acceptance. Testing levels vary by the portion of an application tested, the tools used, and the parties responsible for executing the test. For instance, an environment test focuses on hardware platforms, operating software, and tools. At the most rudimentary level are unit tests. At a higher level are system and environment tests.

There are two major categories of testing levels used with applications. One category, called "verification tests," is technically focused. It concentrates on testing individual changes in code. The second category is called "validation tests." These tests focus on testing application functionality. Figure 7.3 illustrates the relationship between these categories of tests. Each of these test levels has different nuances in the Year 2000 context. For instance, as mentioned in Section 7.1, traditional acceptance testing is limited in the Year 2000 context.

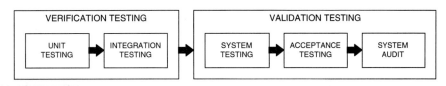

Figure 7.3   The Testing Life Cycle.

- **Verification Testing: Unit and Integration Tests**

  Verification testing includes unit- and integration-level tests. These tests focus on verifying that coding changes are correct. Verification tests are conducted at the component level. They ensure that separate components—a program, JCL, control statements, files, databases, and so on—were properly modified and operate correctly on their own and when combined into larger modules.

  The basic techniques for executing Year 2000 verification tests are the same as those used for regular application testing, however, the test data are extended to include forward-dated test cases in addition to the standard current-date regression test data. The programmer running the tests will generally review and verify the test results manually.

  Unit tests verify that Year 2000 program or module changes are correct. Any program, module, or other low-level component changed during the remediation effort must be subject to unit testing. Unit test cases are designed to prove that internal program processing functions correctly, and that each module produces expected valid outputs. Typically, the programmer who performed the modifications performs the unit tests. The tools used to perform unit tests consist of debuggers, execution simulators, and interactive testing tools. Small test data files are created for debuggers, or selective decision points are set for execution simulators. The programmer performing the test will also manually validate the test results.

  Integration tests exercise the interfaces between low-level sets of modules. Unlike system tests where an entire application is tested as a whole, integration tests bundle groups of lower-level modules. For instance, an integration test might consist of linking related functional modules into a single executable module or might focus on combining modules to produce an executable subsystem. See Figure 7.4 for some examples of integration tests. The purpose of integration tests is to expose mismatched module versions or incorrect module interfaces rather than to thoroughly exercise the module's functions. Checking for mismatched interfaces is especially important when the date-expansion strategy is used for remediation. Many, if not most, of the coding errors made in a date-expansion approach are exposed at the integration test level. Integration tests use many of the same tools and techniques as unit testing, and, if the module groupings are larger, system-level tools and techniques may be used. For century-compliance efforts, checking interfaces is especially important since dates are usually passed through interfaces.

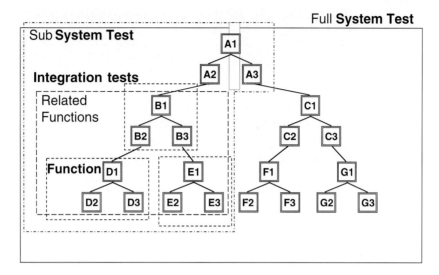

Figure 7.4   Layering Integration Tests.

- **Validation Testing: System Tests, Acceptance Tests, and System Audits**

  Validation tests are performed at the application level and focus on the correctness of application functionality. Unlike verification tests, validation tests are often performed by a separate testing or quality assurance group. System tests, acceptance tests, and system audits concentrate on "validating" that the entire application, including interfaces and environments, work correctly within business requirements. These tests ensure that

  - The application as a whole handles century dates correctly.

  - Existing application functionality was not unintentionally modified or damaged by Year 2000 remediation.

  - Business transactions distributed across several applications complete properly.

  - External data exchange files are handled correctly and follow standard date formats.

  - Application and processing environments recover correctly in the event of some disaster such as a hardware or software failure.

In the Year 2000 project, existing application functionality has not been changed. This characteristic permits test results to be validated automatically by comparing parallel runs of compliant and non-compliant versions of an application, saving an enormous quantity of effort, and enhancing the confidence of test results.

System testing is comprised of test cases designed to ensure that an application, along with its supporting hardware and software components, properly processes business data and transactions. Regression test techniques are used to validate that functions meet defined business requirements. All facets of application functionality are tested, mimicking the application's production operation. These tests may be run using either current or future dates. System-level tests are essential when using windowing techniques for remediation. If incompatible windows are used in two separate modules, the errors will not be exposed until system testing. Each module will test correctly at the unit and integration levels but will produce incorrect results when properly system tested.

Acceptance testing (or user acceptance testing) typically means that an end-user performs final application testing before it is released to production. End-users get to "sign off" on whether an application meets their requirements and produces correct results. As discussed in Section 7.1, traditional end-user acceptance testing has little value as often there will be no visible, external differences between compliant and noncompliant versions of an application. Moreover, functional equivalence and the ability to process century dates are validated during system testing. Accordingly, acceptance testing functions mainly as a review and sign-off of the testing process and its results.

System audits are used to ensure that an application continues to function correctly after its release to production. Daily results of operations are reviewed to ensure that application functionality has not been adversely affected. Before an application reaches its Year 2000 compliance window, a final audit should be done to validate that no noncompliant changes have been introduced.

- **Environment Tests**

Distinct from verification and validation tests, but equally important, are environment tests. Even if an application is compliant, it is unusable if its operating environment cannot function properly through the century transition and beyond. An environment test includes hardware platforms, operating systems, system utilities, databases, file management software, telecommunications software, network software, and other infrastructure software. Although it is possible to test an application using current date data in a noncompliant environment, system-level future date testing and final application validation must be performed in a compliant environment. To make the environment compliant, technical upgrades may be necessary. If these upgrades require changes to application code, or if they may adversely affect application functionality, a separate series of tests should be performed after the upgrade. Technical upgrade testing must not be combined with standard Year 2000 testing. Environment tests are likely to be performed by systems programmers (for mainframe and minicomputers) or by technical support specialists (for workstations and networks).

7.4 How Much Testing Is Enough?

Given an infinite amount of time and resources, software could be tested to achieve a zero percent error rate in production. Even under the best of circumstances, it is extremely difficult, if not impossible, to reach this level of risk reduction. Each organization must define the optimal amount of testing for each application in its portfolio. To make this determination, the risk tolerance of the organization and the affected business areas must be balanced against the amount of time and resources to test. Keeping in mind the law of diminishing returns, it is possible to achieve an acceptable level of reduction in risk for an acceptable amount of time and resources. When the time crunch arrives, and it surely will, the best that organizations can do will be to ensure that the most costly and the most likely failure points have been tested. These points are best determined through risk analysis.

Understanding risks from a business, technical, and project level is a critical first step in developing a testing plan. Chapter 2 contains a through discussion of risk analysis. The next step is to balance the consequences of a given failure against the likelihood of that failure occurring. It makes little sense to spend considerable cost and effort protecting against an error that is either inconsequential or highly unlikely to occur. Developing a test plan based on this balance is the underlying principle behind the "risk-based" testing approach described in the next section. It is up to each organization to make sure that they manage their testing process wisely and according to the risk analysis. This testing approach will help to demonstrate that an organization took the most prudent course toward minimizing the most risky failures.

The ultimate goal of Year 2000 testing is to reduce the risk, and cost, of failures from the century transition. The thorny issue in Year 2000 testing efforts is the amount of testing necessary to ensure that an application is century-date compliant. A range of options is available to IT organizations to help them reduce the risks and costs of failures. At one end of the spectrum is bearing the cost and resources to attain "failsafe" status. At the other end are a set of options that, while inexpensive, minimally reduce risk. Somewhere in this range lies an optimal balance for each IT organization Before discussing risk-based testing, it is important to understand the actions necessary to conduct "failsafe" testing and to compare those actions against the minimal methods used for routine application testing.

7.4.1 "Failsafe" Testing

To achieve this failsafe level of testing, every test path in every module must be tested whether or not they contain century-date affected code and all contingencies must be covered. Achieving this level of testing guarantees that all internal software is compliant, but an organization may still be impacted by failures in external organizations.

Failsafe levels of testing are costly. Creating the test cases necessary to ensure 100 percent coverage and a test environment capable of mimicking the total variety of date situations required is prohibitively expensive to develop and maintain. Since modern business applications and their operating environments are quite complex, this level of reliability may not be achievable at all.

To achieve failsafe levels of testing and ensure that all corporate software is compliant, the following conditions must be met.

- **Test all execution paths**

   Within an application, all processing paths must be tested to ensure that they produce results that are functionally equivalent to the original version and can process dates in the next century including any boundary conditions. In particular, all error handling routines must be exercised, since they are often triggered by date-related conditions.

- **Test all interfaces**

   In addition to exercising all execution paths within an application, all interfaces between applications that share data must be exercised to ensure that compliant applications will work as a group. This includes interfaces between internal applications and those in other organizations.

- **Test all hardware and software**

  The operating environment must itself be certified as compliant. This certification involves testing all hardware and software comprising the operating environment, including the operating systems, languages, and utilities, for century compliance. As with applications, tests must ensure that dates during and after the century transition are handled correctly.

- **Incorporate and test error handling for invalid dates**

  Because so many applications share data, whether with an internal or external application, it is crucial to ensure that error handling routines are robust enough to detect and reject noncompliant data before production data is corrupted and propagated among many applications. This is especially important with applications that accept data from external sources since the risk of corrupt data is out of the control of the IT organization.

7.4.2 Typical Application Testing

Year 2000 teams that do not spend enough time understanding the nuances of century-date testing may be tempted to rely on the same level of testing as typically used by application teams for routine maintenance and enhancements. The most common approach is to perform unit testing on only the modules that have been modified and to use a subset of production data for system-level regression testing. While this approach is better than no testing at all, it falls short for a number of important reasons.

- **Poor test coverage**

  Production data rarely cover more than 10 percent of the possible execution paths in an application. The remaining paths involve error handling routines or uncommon situations that simply do not appear in routine production data. While using a subset of production helps to ensure the compliance of basic processing, the greatest risk of failure exists in the remaining, less common paths.

- **Excessive test data**

  For the reasons described above, a test library derived from production data usually contains many test cases that cover the same paths. This test data duplication increases the cost and effort to execute the tests and validate their results without providing an equivalent decrease in overall risk.

- **Lack of Year 2000-specific data**

  Future-date scenarios and other year 2000-specific testing require-ments need data that cannot appear within production data regard-less of the completeness of its coverage. These scenarios can only be tested through custom-created test data.

7.5 Risk-Based Targeting

Where testing time and resources are constrained—a highly likely scenario in most IT organizations—risk-based approaches to prioritizing and tailoring testing may relieve those pressures. Risk-based methods attempt to achieve the optimal balance of risk reduction and testing effort to keep the risk and cost of failure within acceptable business tolerances and acceptable cost guidelines. Risk-based techniques allow resources to be shifted from less risky testing efforts to those that provide the maxi-mum level of reduction to the corporation. The basic principle behind risk-based testing is to stack-rank all testing activities by their ability to reduce overall business risk. Using this method, testing starts with the most important functions and works its way down the list until an acceptable level of risk tolerance is reached. It is important to understand that unlike failsafe testing, risk-based testing accepts something less than perfection. For a noncritical application, the difference in coverage may be significant, resulting in greater risk of failure, but freeing resources for other tasks.

Risk-based testing attempts to strike the optimal balance between reducing the risk of application failures and expending the testing effort to achieve those reductions. The relationship between these two elements is illustrated in Figure 7.5. The level of testing effort required to reduce the risk of Year 2000 failures is the amount of time and resources to test an application, including building the necessary infrastructure, managing the testing process, creating test data, scripts, and processes, executing the tests, and verifying the results.

As depicted, the risk curve starts out very high, and the effort curve starts out very low, assuming that no testing has been done to ensure com-pliance of corporate software. As testing effort is expended, the risk of noncompliance, and therefore failures, is reduced until it is eliminated. To eliminate all risk, a prohibitively large amount of testing effort must be expended. Just as certain risks may be intolerable for a business, spending

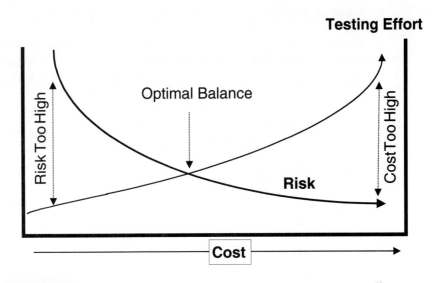

Figure 7.5 Risks versus Costs.

money on testing efforts beyond certain levels is also intolerable and draws resources that could be used more productively elsewhere. The optimal balance for a given application exists somewhere between the two extremes. It is the job of each application team to work with their business area coordinators and the Year 2000 team to determine the optimal point for their application.

7.5.1 Elements of Risk-Based Analysis

Many risks exist in a Year 2000 project, ranging from the risk of misprinting a report heading to immobilizing an entire business operation. Ultimately, the most costly risks are those measured by loss of production, loss of customers, loss of goodwill, and loss of stock value. These risks should be captured and quantified using the methods described in Chapter 2. These risks are captured at the business level and must be tied back to specific applications, functions, and even test paths. Year 2000 remediation teams provide the technical aspects of the risk equation by listing the modules and lines of code that were changed as part of the remediation process. In combination, these inputs are used to determine the two primary elements of risk planning—the cost of failure and the likelihood of failure.

- **Cost of failure**

  Failures arising from century noncompliance have different costs. Some failures, while annoying, have little cost or few ramifications. Misprinting a report heading on an internal report is an example of such a failure. Other failures can destroy a business, threaten human safety, or result in substantial costs or litigation. These failures can have catastrophic consequences and should be avoided no matter what the cost. To quantify the cost of failure in the Year 2000 context, add the costs of software effort to find and fix errors; operational effort to find and fix corrupted data and reschedule and rerun jobs; and consequential damages resulting from loss of business, lawsuits, and so forth.

- **Likelihood of failure**

  The cost of a given failure must be balanced against the likelihood of that failure's occurring. With time and resource constraints, it is more critical to address a $70,000 error that has a 90 percent chance of occurring than a $250,000 error that has a minute chance (for example, less than one in ten million) of occurring. To determine the likelihood of failure, consider two types of malfunctions: those based on circumstances and those based on the correctness of the remediation effort. Circumstantial malfunctions involve the occurrence of multiple circumstances before an event will occur. For example, a circumstantial error could occur if a data entry operator keyed in an invalid social security number which happened to match a deceased customer who died during a two-month period in 1971 in which rebates were in effect, thereby triggering the software application to invoke an obsolete subroutine to cut a refund check to the customer's beneficiary. If each of these circumstances is unlikely to happen, the probability of a failure occurring is very small. In contrast, the likelihood of a failure due to an error within the remediation effort can be related to factors such as the number of changes made, the techniques used, and the technical quality of the application code. For example, if an application had minimal changes and those changes were identical to ones recently and successfully tested in a very similar application, then the likelihood of a technical failure is probably low. Conversely, if an inexperienced programmer made substantial and unique changes to a complex, poorly structured, and undocumented application, the likelihood of failure can be expected to be much higher than in other situations.

Test planners assess these risk elements by interviewing IT staff and business area personnel. IT staff can estimate the cost of testing and, to a certain extent, the likelihood of failure and cost of failure (based on their knowledge of the software and the cost of software and operational error correction). The business area personnel must supply the cost of consequential failures and risk tolerance data.

7.5.2 Components Affected by Risk-Based Testing Strategies

The application risk data gathered through interviews with the business areas and technical personnel can be used to tailor testing plans in an attempt to achieve the optimal balance between risk reduction and testing effort discussed earlier in this section. To reduce risk and decrease testing effort, the risk data is used to select and prioritize applications, functions within applications, and test paths within functions. This ranking ensures that critical components are addressed first and can also be used to reduce the scope of and number of tests in the testing effort. The savings achieved in testing effort are offset somewhat by an increase in the level of overall risk as portions of an application will go untested. However, if the prioritization process is applied correctly, the increased risks will be low and within the risk tolerance of the organization. Further, if the Year 2000 effort must be halted prematurely, overall organizational risk will be far lower than possible without risk-based planning.

Before applying risk-based testing strategies, it is important to understand the components that are covered in Year 2000 testing: applications, functions, and paths.

- **Applications**

  Applications are the highest-level, and most important, component in a risk-based testing plan. Assuming that every application will be retained after the year 2000, it is likely that every application will undergo some level of testing. An application's priority to the organization will determine the timing and order in which it is tested. In addition, the types and levels of testing to be conducted can be reduced based on an application's priority to the organization. In crisis situations, if triage strategies are invoked, testing may be bypassed for noncritical applications. As a general rule, application risk information should be used to prioritize testing tasks and to reduce levels of testing within a given application to reach an acceptable level of resource investment rather than to eliminate that application from testing altogether.

- **Functions**

  Each application is comprised of several functions. In the testing context, functions are units of code that correspond to specific business
  requirements. These units may consist of a piece of a program, an
  entire program, or a group of related programs. For instance, a function may involve cutting checks for vendor invoices. Like applications,
  functions are given a business priority based on their risk data. Functions can be prioritized within an application so that the more critical
  functions are tested first, followed by less critical functions. The level
  of functional testing can be reduced by eliminating those functions
  that are entirely unaffected by century-date changes, although this
  approach will not detect the failure to make necessary changes.

- **Paths**

  Within a given function, many test paths exist. These paths represent the control flow of a particular piece of code. Ideally, there is a
  one-to-one correspondence between test cases and test paths for
  each function. Tools exist that can count test paths and determine
  the extent of test coverage associated with a given test suite.
  Although a function may have a high degree of century-date
  changes, it is likely that a large number of paths will be unaffected
  by the remediation. Levels of testing can be reduced by eliminating
  those paths that are unaffected by century-date changes. These
  reductions directly decrease the number of test cases that must be
  generated and executed.

The relationship between these components is shown in Figure 7.6.

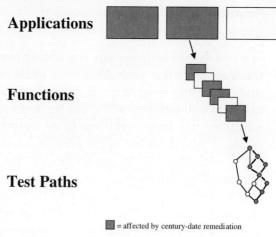

= affected by century-date remediation

Figure 7.6 Relationship of Components.

7.5.3 *Applying Risk-Based Testing Strategies*

To customize their own risk-based strategies, organizations should follow a few basic strategies that use the risk data mentioned above. First, risk data influences when a particular component is scheduled for testing. Components that enter the testing phase concurrently will need to be ordered in some logical way to ensure that the most critical ones are tested first. Second, risk data can also be used to develop strategies that decrease testing effort in two ways: by reducing what is tested and by reducing the types and categories of tests to be performed. By eliminating certain components from testing altogether, and by reducing the types of tests performed, overall risk will increase. However, this risk does not increase linearly because certain components, such as date routines, bear a higher level of risk than, for example, a report routine.

- **Scheduling by priority**

  As discussed at the beginning of this chapter, one of the goals of Year 2000 testing is to reduce the risk curve as steeply and quickly as possible. By prioritizing the components to be tested and by executing the tests according to their relative priority, the risk curve will drop quickly and precipitously. If multiple applications are ready to be tested at the same time and the infrastructure for testing each of them is in place, then the most critical applications should be tested before the less critical ones. The same principle is true for functions within applications and test paths within functions. Applications are prioritized within the enterprise-level test plan and functions and test paths are prioritized within the individual application test plans. All tests are then executed in the order of priority. By adhering to a priority-based schedule, the IT organization can gauge the ramifications and risks should testing be terminated early.

- **Reducing what is tested**

  Testing effort can be decreased by reducing what is tested. This decrease results from eliminating paths, functions, and applications from test plans after careful assessment of the risk data. Depending on the risk tolerance of the organization, these reductions can be severe, eliminating entire components from any level of testing whatsoever, or moderate, eliminating only certain test paths and functions from testing while retaining applications.

  The first method of reducing the number of components designated for testing is based on the risk that any of them will malfunction due to century-date changes. This risk is captured in the "likelihood of failure" risk element. The level of change to a component is an indicator of the level of risk that is involved. Clearly, components that were not remediated have a lower risk of failure than those that were. Test plans may call for unremediated components to forgo testing. However, even unmodified components are at risk because it is possible that necessary changes were forgotten or overlaid. Therefore, any test plan purely based upon whether a component was modified will still contain some risk.

The second method of reducing testing effort eliminates components based on their business value and/or business risk. This risk is captured in the "cost of failure" risk element. Even though a component may have Year 2000 changes, it may not be critical to the business. These components may be subject to little or no testing because they can easily be remedied, with little cost, if they fail later in production or they may be covered by an acceptable contingency plan. If it turns out that the component performs correctly in production, then the savings from bypassing testing will be realized.

Both of these reduction methods can be applied simultaneously to produce an optimal risk-based strategy for a particular component as illustrated by Figure 7.7. This graph contains two axes depicting the two risk elements: "cost of failure" (indicating the business value of the component) and "likelihood of failure" (indicating the level of remediation to the component). The upper level of the graph indicates those components that are most critical to the business as determined by the consequences of failure. The right-hand side of the graph indicates those components that have been most heavily remediated.

Components can be prioritized by their position within the graph. Components having the highest priority are located in block (1). These components are critical to the business and have the highest likelihood of failure since they have incurred the most remediation. Components with the lowest priority are found in block (6) and consist of those which have low business value and no modifications. The components found in block (3), critical components with no modifications, are stack-ranked ahead of those found in block (4), low-value components with modifications. Ranking unmodified, critical components ahead of modified, low-value components reflects the risk that required data changes were not identified and remediated and that unintended side effects were triggered by other

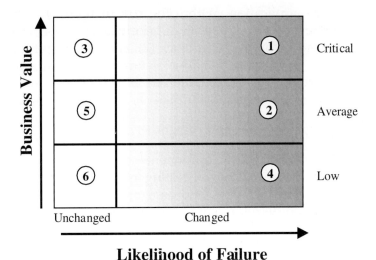

= relative priority

Figure 7.7 Risk-Based Priority Ranking.

century-date changes. The probability that either of these risks will occur may be low; however, in critical components, the cost of failure is likely to be higher than in low-value components.

While the graph captures two of the most important risk elements in a Year 2000 project, there are other elements that can be added to this oversimplified picture. For instance, the time-to-failure of a given component should be taken into account when scheduling remediation and testing efforts to ensure that short time horizons are dealt with first. The presence or absence of a contingency plan for a given component may influence its relative priority in the remediation and testing scheme. Similarly, the time needed to recover from a failure if it does occur can also influence the priority.

Using the rankings derived from the graph, an organization can choose its reduction strategy. For example, applications having the highest business value will have all of their functions, residing in blocks (1) through (6), tested. A moderately important application may have functions residing in blocks (1) through (4) tested. Low-value applications may have functions residing only in blocks (1) and (2) tested. Using these rules, a test plan should be created for each application. Within the test plan, the functions to be tested should be listed in order of priority. Functions in block (1) should be tested before those in block (2), and so forth. If the application test plan is executed in order of priority, then if testing is terminated early for some reason, the Year 2000 project team can be assured that the most important components were tested first.

- **Reducing types and categories of tests**

  After prioritizing components and windowing those components which will be tested, testing effort can further be decreased by reducing the types and categories of tests. See Section 7.3 for a detailed discussion of types and categories of tests.

  This method relies on logic and common sense to eliminate categories of tests when most, if not all, of their functions are handled by subsequent tests or if resources are so constrained that only the most valuable test can be executed.

  One example of this approach is skipping unit testing in favor of complete system testing for applications thought to be compliant or for applications that require very few modifications. In this case, the testing team relies on the coverage of the system test to catch the errors that would normally have been trapped using lower-level tests. This approach is successful and saves resources if the system test data is complete and there are very few errors. If the system test data is not complete, errors that would otherwise have been trapped will reach production. If a large number of errors are encountered, the savings of skipping unit testing are quickly lost to the increased cost of repeating system testing.

  At the other end of the spectrum, a testing team may rely on very thorough unit testing to avoid most of the subsequent system-level tests. This is a high-risk practice that should not be attempted on critical applications. Nor should this approach be used in conjunction with windowing techniques, since cutoff year incompatibilities cannot be found without system testing. If all modules can be thoroughly tested at the unit level for all necessary current and future-date scenarios and if all interfaces between modules are carefully coded to a common compliance definition, the odds of the application being compliant are high. Accidental mismatches in interfaces or unanticipated integration problems may still cause failures if system testing is omitted, however, this approach to testing is still likely to produce better results than standard application testing techniques.

The most practical use of this approach, however, is to perform limited cutbacks of specific tests. For example, the testing team may unit test only those modules that have undergone remediation, relying on higher- level tests to handle unanticipated errors in unmodified modules. In any case, the principles of risk-based testing should be used to weigh the increase in risk caused by the decrease in testing against the resources that will be saved.

7.6 Applying Testing

This final section in this chapter uses a simple case study to illustrate the concepts contained in the previous sections. A failsafe testing approach would require testing all parts of the example application. Instead, risk-based techniques are used to significantly reduce the quantity of tests without incurring an unacceptable level of risk.

An organization that produced lighting fixtures identified as mission-critical its Central Order Processing System (COPS). If the COPS application malfunctioned, the chief information officer and chief financial officer estimated that orders could not be taken or filled, products could not be shipped, and customers would turn to other light fixture providers. Fortunately, only 4 of the 12 functions comprising the application were modified to support the change of century. Of those modified functions, two produced internally used quarterly reports and were lightly modified. The remaining two modified functions—order entry and inventory matching—were both critical to the operation of COPS. The order entry function was heavily modified but the code was in good shape—well structured and well documented. The programmer who had changed this function was very confident that the changes would all operate as planned. The last function, the inventory matching function, was also heavily modified. The code for this function was poorly structured and undocumented. Further, due to the resignation of the senior programmer, a very junior programmer had made the changes and was very unsure as to whether the modified version would perform as expected.

The risk graph for the COPS application, created after interviews with IT staff and business area personnel, is depicted in Figure 7.8. The quarterly report functions appear in block (4), indicating that they have a low likelihood of failure due to the light amount of century-date changes, and that they are not critical to the performance of the application. The

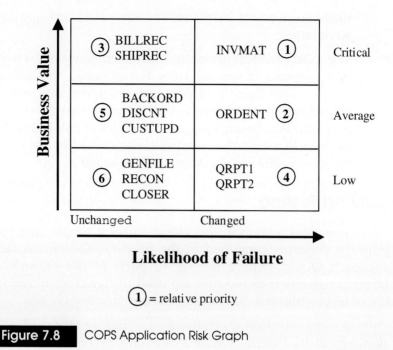

= relative priority

| Figure 7.8 | COPS Application Risk Graph |

order entry system function appears in block (2), indicating an average likelihood of failure due to the extensive century-date changes tempered by the fact that the code was in good shape and well documented. In addition, this function, while critical to the application, was not indispensable, as a disaster recovery plan indicated that there was a way to take paper orders for a short period of time until any malfunctions were cured. The inventory matching function appears in block (1), indicating a high likelihood of failure because of the extensive remediation, poor code quality, and inexperience of the programmer making the changes. In addition, this function is critical to the application since business area managers interviewed had stated that any malfunction affecting inventory control could literally put the company out of business.

Of the remaining functions, two were identified as critical with little likelihood of failure because there were no Year 2000 changes made. Three functions were moderately critical with no Year 2000 changes. The remaining three functions were not critical and unremediated.

The application manager developed an application test plan for the COPS application as follows. In his first iteration, the plan specified the following functional tests in order of priority:

1.   *Inventory matching function (INVMAT)*

2.   *Order entry function (ORDENT)*

3.   *Critical functions without changes (BILLREC and SHIPREC)*

4.   *Quarterly report functions (QRPT1 and QRPT2)*

Next, the application manager began to detail the types and categories of tests to be performed. The four modified functions from blocks (1), (2), and (4) were to undergo unit testing and integration testing to verify the correctness of the Year 2000 changes. A system test was planned for the COPS application to ensure that it operated without errors and with all pre-existing functionality intact. Regression tests were planned for the inventory matching function [block (1)] and the additional, critical functions from block (3) (BILLREC and SHIPREC). Block (3) functions were selected in order to detect any latent errors introduced by the remediation effort.

Chapter 8

Implementing a Year 2000 Test Program

Year 2000 project managers are well aware by now that they will face significant time and resource constraints as they attempt to test all of the applications, components, and environments within their organization. In the face of these constraints, organizations have to be careful not to indiscriminately reduce, curtail, or rush testing, especially given the specter of future litigation as discussed in Chapter 3. Through advance planning and by following some common approaches, a meaningful test program can be implemented. To implement a successful program, roles and responsibilities of members of the project office and individual application teams must be delineated and understood, plans must be developed and adhered to, and numerous testing tasks must proceed in parallel to ensure timely completion. As with most test programs, the effort spent upfront in assessing the current environment and in defining and implementing test plans, at both the enterprise and application levels, greatly enhances the effectiveness of the effort and avoids pandemonium in the months preceding the century change. For enterprise project managers, having a firm grasp of where and when testing tasks and activities occur within the enterprise time line enables effective test planning and management. For application managers, creating and implementing detailed application test plans not only enables them to effectively manage their own application tests, but also to advise the project office project manager of the application's testing needs and timetable.

This chapter focuses on the test planning and test management aspects of Year 2000 certification. It discusses infrastructure assessment, planning, management, and execution tasks at both the enterprise and application levels. It consists of seven sections. The first three are devoted to enterprise test management issues and the remaining sections are devoted to application issues.

Section 8.1 discusses the setup of an enterprise Year 2000 testing function within the project office and lists the roles and responsibilities of that function. Section 8.2 discusses the assessment and improvement of the enterprise-level test infrastructure. This infrastructure must be assessed and improved early in the project to ensure that the IT organization will have time to complete required upgrades or changes and to augment weak or deficient areas. Some activities, such as acquiring additional hardware resources or arranging for off-site testing, have long lead times and must be started early to ensure that they will be fully functional and available when needed. Section 8.3 describes the creation of the master test plan for the enterprise. This test plan sets the policies for, and coordinates the efforts of, all testing efforts within the enterprise.

Section 8.4 discusses the roles and responsibilities of the application testing teams and describes the phases of the application testing process. This process begins with an application infrastructure assessment and concludes with the sign-off and acceptance of certification following results validation. Section 8.5 describes the contents and nuances of a basic application test plan. Each application in the portfolio needs its own plan in order to manage and ensure the quality of its testing process. Section 8.6 covers the creation of an application test plan for a software package and Section 8.7 covers the same topic for applications that have undergone off-site remediation.

8.1 Managing the Enterprise-Level Testing Effort

Year 2000 testing is far too complex and fraught with dependencies to be accomplished by application teams as a series of independent projects. While application teams remain responsible for verifying the compliance of their own applications, an enterprise view of testing is required to ensure that Year 2000 testing will operate as smoothly as possible across the entire organization. An enterprise view of testing is more than just a perspective—it includes activities, tasks, and techniques for managing the overall testing process across the enterprise. This type of centralized control and management is necessary to

- Effectively manage testing project resources and time to ensure that resources are distributed in a manner that provides the greatest benefit to the enterprise.

- Improve the productivity and efficiency of individual application projects by promoting sharing of test infrastructures, tools, and resources.

- Ensure that the supporting infrastructure components are in place when needed.

- Establish priorities for individual application projects based upon relative risk assessments and contingency plans.

- Resolve conflicts between individual application projects competing for the same resources at the same time.

- Monitor and adjust testing schedules when individual application projects experience delays to avoid adverse impact on other projects.

- Coordinate the myriad of activities spawned by all application projects.

This section discusses the setup and roles of an enterprise testing function. This function is responsible for preparing the enterprise testing infrastructure to support certification requirements and for the creation and monitoring of an enterprise-level master test plan. Section 8.2 discusses enterprise testing infrastructure issues and Section 8.3 discusses the creation of the master test plan.

8.1.1 The Testing Function of the Project Office

Given their size, complexity, and resource requirements, Year 2000 testing activities merit their own project management structures. To meet this requirement, a separate testing function should be established within the Year 2000 project office. This function reports to the Year 2000 project director and is charged with performing and overseeing all enterprise-level test management tasks. It is responsible for accomplishing all of the objectives described above. Enterprise-level test management activities include tracking and monitoring project schedules to the master time line, resolving conflicts that arise during the execution of the test plan, scheduling major tests, and ensuring that auditors and users sign off on test results. In effect, these activities embody traditional project management techniques applied to large-scale testing efforts.

The initial activity of the testing function is to create a plan for enterprise test infrastructure improvements and a master plan for the overall testing effort. To create this plan, project office test managers will be responsible for gathering test readiness and risk information for the enterprise. To gather this information, the project office will require business areas, application areas, and other groups to perform their own discrete assessments of the applications and components under their control and to report the results back to the Project Office. Figure 8.1 shows how the plans and testing activities are derived from assessment results.

The role of the testing function is not limited to software applications. Project office test managers will have to work with responsible organizational areas to assess non-IT applications, such as embedded systems found in manufacturing and telephony equipment, to determine how to test these systems for compliance and the risk to the enterprise that would

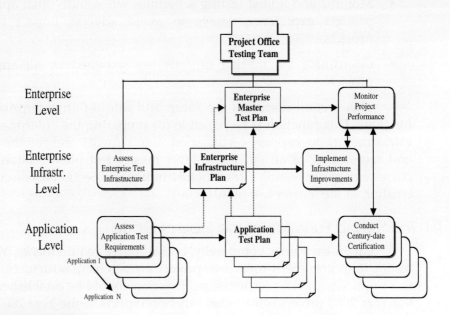

Figure 8.1   Relationship between Enterprise and Application Testing Activities.

arise from failures of these non-IT systems. To accomplish this type of non-IT assessment, test managers will rely heavily on the business area personnel who regularly use those systems who will in turn rely on the vendors of the equipment to provide compliance status and testing guidance. For more information on embedded systems, please refer to Chapter 4.

Once the various plans are in place, the testing function has the responsibility for coordinating and overseeing their execution. It must constantly monitor and adjust the plans and resolve conflicts as they arise. This function continues throughout the life of the Year 2000 effort, completing only after the final applications are certified as stable and operating correctly in production some time after the turn of the century.

8.1.2 Roles and Responsibilities

To centralize the control and management of an enterprisewide test program, responsibility must be vested in one or more dedicated individuals within the project office. These individuals should be empowered by senior management to enforce testing standards and be able to draw resources from other departments as needed to perform their tasks effectively. Without backing by executive management, the testing team members will lack the clout to ensure cooperation among these various interest groups.

To an extent not found in other typical testing efforts, testing team members must remain constantly attuned to the business risk factors governing the testing process. Since the administration of the enterprise test plan is a dynamic task, and since the individual testing projects themselves can be expected to diverge from the time line at various points, testing team members must always apply the "risk filter" to any adjustments that they make. The testing team members must constantly keep in mind that one of their primary objectives is to minimize business risks for the most critical corporate functions. Although adjustments can, and will need to be, made, they should not impact, or exacerbate, risk levels set by the organization.

The exact size and composition of the project office testing team will vary by the overall size of the project and the testing philosophy chosen by the company. For example, a smaller central testing team is required if application teams are responsible for certifying their applications than if final certification is the responsibility of the central team. Generally, the central function is best organized as a small management and consulting group supported by implementation resources from other areas. Key roles within the testing function are listed below.

- **Testing Manager**

  The testing manager should be a senior individual with strong QA and testing experience. He or she must be skilled in management and highly regarded within the IT organization. The testing manager reports directly to the Year 2000 program director and is empowered to draw on the necessary resources to perform the assessment, planning, improvement, and management tasks necessary to successfully accomplish Year 2000 testing.

- **Testing/QA Specialists**

  These specialists are responsible for developing quality assurance and certification standards, supporting training and knowledge transfer activities, and assisting application teams on a consulting basis. These individuals must be skilled in standard QA and testing techniques and must be familiar with the tools chosen by the IT organization. They may be drawn from internal staff or hired from a consulting organization.

- **Systems Support/System Programmers**

  These individuals are responsible for the enterprise testing infrastructures including the installation and support of testing tools, acquisition and implementation of testing environments, and support of testing processes. These individuals may be drawn from existing technology support functions.

- **Auditors**

  Internal IT auditors can monitor the efforts of individual applications teams as they conduct their testing efforts. They check to see if teams are conforming to standards and completing all necessary steps.

8.2 Enterprise-Level Test Infrastructures

Although all IT organizations perform testing as part of their routine application support activities, few organizations are prepared to handle the concentrated level of testing needed to support an enterprisewide Year 2000 project. IT test infrastructures must be upgraded to provide needed capabilities, such as future date simulation environments, and sufficient capacity to handle large volumes of simultaneous testing activities. The volume of Year 2000 testing will strain even experienced organizations as they discover unexpected procedural limitations and hardware capacity constraints that limit their ability to test at desired levels. Preplanning enables organizations to identify and correct potential problems before they impact testing efforts. Since most infrastructure improvements require long lead times to implement, it is essential to assess the current infrastructure, identify necessary improvements, and begin upgrade projects as quickly as possible. Fortunately, these upgrade projects can proceed in parallel with other Year 2000 activities. It is the responsibility of the testing team in the Year 2000 project office to ensure that these upgrades are completed in time to support project testing requirements.

Infrastructure improvements may be needed at both the enterprise and application levels. This section deals with enterprise-level issues such as tools, shared processes, and hardware capacity. Application-level infrastructure improvements focus on issues such as test data availability and test script creation and are discussed later in this chapter. This section breaks enterprise infrastructure improvements into three subtopics: assessing enterprise infrastructures, determining infrastructure improvements, and implementing infrastructure improvements.

8.2.1 Assessing Enterprise Test Infrastructures

Enterprise test assessment activities have two goals: understanding organizational requirements for Year 2000 testing and evaluating the readiness of the enterprise to handle those requirements. A key component of this understanding is the risk assessment process described in detail in Chapter 2. Since few companies will be able to implement all desired improvements, it is essential that they focus their efforts on those improvements that provide the greatest level of risk reduction to the enterprise as a whole.

The assessment process has several critical steps. The first step is evaluating and understanding the current state of the test environment. In parallel, application team members should perform their own assessment of their application-specific test infrastructures. Although many application-level improvements will be the responsibility of the application teams themselves, requirements for tools and shared testing capacity must be rolled up into enterprise improvement requirements. The next step is to supplement the general test infrastructure improvement requirements with the additional requirements for century-date certification testing. Certification testing requires special tools, such as date simulators and intelligent comparison utilities, special testing procedures, and special audit procedures to ensure that compliance is maintained after release to production. The final step of the process is to create an enterprise test infrastructure improvement plan for execution under the direction of the Year 2000 project office.

The evaluation process will include interviews with or surveys of key personnel, subject matter experts, end-users, system support staff, and IT managers. It should yield information concerning current test hardware, tools, scripts, processes, volume, scheduling, and the myriad of other details involved with regular testing. The project office should understand the minimum level of test environment required to support certification testing. The project office must compare these century-date certification requirements to the baseline test environment to determine where the environment is deficient and what kinds of improvements are required. Additional, more specific testing requirements will be communicated to the project office by the individual application test teams and business areas upon the conclusion of their own assessment activities.

Assessing the test requirements of embedded systems presents another series of challenges. Few of these systems will be supported by adequate test environments or even have instructions on how to conduct tests. Further, the diversity of these systems precludes common approaches to their testing. Where there is no baseline test environment for these embedded systems, organizations should contact equipment and system vendors to determine compliance status and, if possible, how to test the equipment or system. Once the organization knows what is required to test the system, they can assess whether there are any setup or improvement activities that will have to be performed prior to test execution.

Upon completion of the enterprise test readiness assessment, the project office should have the following information:

- A thorough and accurate depiction of the current test environment and its capabilities

- An enterprise-level test infrastructure improvement plan showing

    - Current status of the test environment

    - Required upgrades or acquisitions to support Year 2000 testing, along with why and when each upgrade/acquisition is needed

    - Implementation plan for the upgrades/acquisitions

8.2.2 Determining Enterprise Infrastructure Improvements

During the assessment phase, the current state of the test environment is examined and specific infrastructure improvements are identified. Test infrastructure activities and tasks are targeted to implement those improvements and set up the test environments. Test environments are composed of testing tools, platforms, and procedures. Different types of environments, at different levels of maturity, are required to support the various phases of a Year 2000 project. To support verification testing (unit and integration tests), basic test environments must be established prior to the remediation phase of the Year 2000 project. To support certification tests, test environments must accommodate future dating or simulate future dating. Stand-alone or dedicated test environments may be required to support large-scale system tests.

Infrastructure improvement activities may include upgrades to existing, or acquisitions of, new capacity (equipment/hardware), test tools, and test and/or audit procedures.

8.2.2.1 Determining Capacity Requirements

Determining the appropriate level of hardware capacity for Year 2000 testing is a difficult task. There are no global "rules of thumb" that can be applied to all organizations. Capacity requirements will vary by application depending on the number and type of tests required and the overhead needed to support those tests. Further, capacity must be sufficient to support peak demand. Any project slippage during remediation decreases the time available for testing, requiring additional capacity to support more parallel activities.

There may be many constraints affecting test capacity. Listed below are a few of the more common constraints.

- **Processors**

    Processor constraints revolve around CPU horsepower, channel speed, memory, and other processor components and will vary depending on platform. Mainframes tend to have more memory available while workstations may face memory constraints. Testing tools often require significant CPU and I/O resources over normal processing demands. Voluminous testing will challenge I/O channels which are the most typically constrained components in production operating environments.

- **Disk Storage**

  Voluminous Year 2000 test data and test results will require a major increase in disk storage capacity. Duplicate production data may be created as a baseline for test data and to support bridging between compliant and noncompliant applications.

- **Scheduling**

  Typically, an organization has its processors operating at capacity during the day and schedules testing at night or on weekends when excess capacity is available. Certification tests that require forward dating of processors must be scheduled to avoid any impact on production schedules or other non-Year 2000 testing efforts. As the turn of the century approaches, test scheduling will become even more constrained.

- **"Wall Clock"**

  "Wall clock," or elapsed time, is a measure of how long it takes an application to complete a full execution cycle. In a normal environment, application testing is often tightly scheduled so as not to conflict with production runs. In the Year 2000 context, the voluminous and I/O-intensive testing requirements will exacerbate wall clock constraints. This problem is not limited to mainframe applications. For some PC applications, a full regression test may take hours and may need to be scheduled over a weekend. Separate testing platforms will eliminate many of these constraints but may not be feasible due to cost or setup time.

The only method of estimating test capacity that assures any degree of accuracy is a "bottom-up" approach that captures the requirements for each individual application and then rolls those requirements up to the enterprise level. This method enables application requirements to be scheduled, and where possible, allows projects to be shifted to smooth peaks in demand. This approach is applied at two levels:

- **Level 1: Estimate Application Capacity Requirements**

  These steps are performed for each application that will undergo Year 2000 testing. Note that virtually all applications must estimate their capacity requirements before the enterprise estimates can be created. Omitting a major application may cause a significant capacity shortfall.

1. *Establish resources used to support the current level of testing.*

    The current test environment supports at least the current level of testing. Understanding the number of tests that are typically performed and the quantity of resources used by those tests provides a baseline to extrapolate Year 2000 testing requirements.

2. *Estimate the level of Year 2000 testing as a function of existing testing.*

    For each capacity constraint, develop a ratio between current levels of testing and the quantity of testing anticipated for Year 2000. For example, normal maintenance requires testing only 15 percent of the modules in the application while Year 2000 will affect 90 percent of the modules.

3. *Extrapolate Year 2000 resource requirements using these ratios.*

    For example, if normal maintenance tests 15 percent of the modules in the application while Year 2000 requires testing 90 percent of the modules, unit testing will require six times the current level of resources used for testing.

4. *Add additional capacity for bridging, increased file sizes, data duplication, and other Year 2000-specific activities.*

5. *Use a project management tool to chart the dates and duration that each testing resource is required.*

    This information is vital to facilitate the sharing of scarce resources across multiple teams and to enable the smoothing of peak demands.

- **Level 2: Estimate Enterprise Capacity Requirements**

  Once testing requirements have been estimated for each application, those requirements are rolled up to the enterprise level. This plan merges the individual requirements and seeks opportunities for resource sharing and schedule shifted to balance requirements against resource availability.

  1. *Roll up application schedules and requirements into an enterprise-level project plan.*

2. *Identify peak capacity demands.*

Undoubtedly, every application team will want the same one-month period for testing. Shifting team schedules frees critical capacity by moving peak loads into lower demand time slots.

3. *Perform gap analysis of difference between adjusted demand and current capacity to identify additional capacity requirements.*

8.2.2.2 Determining Testing Tool Requirements

Year 2000 testing will rely heavily on automated testing tools as manually intensive approaches will be too time consuming and error prone due to the large volume of effort. Most IT organizations will already have a number of decent testing tools, although given the diversity of applications, languages, and environments that must be tested, it is unlikely that their current tool set is sufficient to handle all Year 2000 requirements. Existing tools should be reused wherever possible since IT staffers are already familiar with their operation. New tools should be considered to supplement gaps in coverage, handle less-common platforms, or provide Year 2000-specific functionality. Testing tool coverage for uncommon platforms will be limited by the lack of commercially available solutions. Year 2000 project teams should budget significant additional people resources for applications without testing tool support.

To determine testing tool requirements, begin by examining the tools in the current portfolio. Contact the vendor for each tool that is not currently at the latest release to see if any Year 2000-specific enhancements are available in a more recent release. Categorize these tools using the list below and note the languages and platform types covered by each tool. Entering this information in a spreadsheet format is an easy means for identifying gaps in coverage. Obtain new tools to close these gaps if there is a large volume of testing to be performed for that technology or if the consequences of failure are severe.

The list below identifies the most important testing tool categories for century-date certification efforts.

- **Test Coverage Analyzers**

  Test data is typically created by either duplicating or selecting a subset of production data. This data may or may not be sufficient to test an application adequately. For those risky, mission-critical applications, it is important that test coverage be high enough to ensure a good degree of comfort in the test results. Test coverage analyzers can determine the number of paths exercised in an application using a given set of test data, thereby exposing inadequately tested areas.

- **Tools to Create and Manipulate Test Data**

  Where existing test data are insufficient, application teams will have to create new test data. In addition, to certify that an application is truly compliant, the application test data will have to be set to a variety of future dates. When creating or changing test data, care has to be taken to preserve dependencies and other relationships between data fields. This process can be tricky and time consuming. To save time, automated tools that permit the creation of new data, or that permit easy access to and manipulation of existing test data, are invaluable.

- **Interactive Testing Tools**

  Interactive testing tools allow a programmer to execute an application under their full control. They enable the programmer to observe execution flow and query and set application variables during execution. This capability is especially useful for unit testing, where a programmer tends to heavily exercise portions of changed code, using a variety of limited, targeted test data. Debuggers, execution simulators, and online capture/playback tools offer these types of interactive capabilities.

- **Comparison Tools**

  During regression testing, outputs from compliant and noncompliant versions of applications must be compared to determine whether Year 2000 changes caused inadvertent side effects. While some differences in outputs may be expected, particularly with date fields, in general the outputs should be identical. Without automated comparison tools, this evaluation would be too time consuming and costly to effect manually. While most IT organizations already own comparison tools, the recent development of intelligent comparison tools merits consideration. These tools are able to understand and ignore differences in date formats when performing their comparisons. This feature significantly reduces results validation efforts and allows the tools to be used with field expansion solutions.

- **Date Simulation Tools**

  Date simulation tools are an essential requirement for all Year 2000 projects. Certification testing requires that a remediated application be tested for compliance in an environment that is forward dated. Instead of actually setting the test environment to a future date, date simulation tools emulate the future date for the applications and systems that execute within the environment. This feature simplifies test scheduling and reduces impact on production operations. It is the only option for IT organizations without dedicated test environments.

- **Test Management Tools**

  To perform the test management activities necessary to oversee the enterprise test plan, the project office should have a repository or other database in which to store plans, documents, and other important information. A formal project tracking and scheduling tool should also be available to create and manage the enterprise test plan. In addition, an issue tracking system should be established to track the status of testing, error resolution, and associated testing activities. To offer the company protection in the event of future litigation, these tools should facilitate the storage of multiple versions of plans and documents to ensure that changes can be tracked and justified. Additional tools that are vital not only to the testing effort but also the remediation effort are library management and configuration management systems capable of controlling access to and packaging source code.

8.2.2.3 Determining Test Procedure Requirements

Improving the test infrastructure and implementing new testing tools will yield few benefits if people do not understand how to use the new environment and tools effectively. A variety of procedures and standards will need to be in place to permit the orderly and efficient execution of all the tests to be performed by the application test teams. These procedures may include configuration management procedures, scheduling procedures, problem tracking procedures, and production release procedures. While these procedures are already in place in most IT organizations, they must be evaluated to ensure their ability to support Year 2000 workloads and handle Year 2000-specific requirements.

The goal of proper testing procedures is to establish an efficient, reliable, and repeatable way of performing Year 2000 testing by all application teams. These procedures may be provided in a variety of forms including:

- Written instructions, guidelines, or methodologies

- EXECs or PROCs to use new configuration managers, libraries, and environments

- Routines to upload and download information to and from mainframes and PCs

- Process manager access to new testing tools

Associated training materials or documentation will be required to show people how to use the procedures and the underlying infrastructure components and tools.

In addition to standard testing and support processes, additional audit procedures will be required to ensure that completed applications remain compliant after they have been moved into production. It is always possible that a compliant application may be corrupted by future maintenance, especially if incorrect versions of modules, copy members, or routines are accidentally linked into an application. Audit procedures focus on prevention and periodic reviews. Prevention is accomplished through standards for maintenance and enhancement efforts, technical reviews of changes, and enhanced configuration management controls. Periodic reviews may require application test teams or quality assurance groups to recertify previously compliant applications after they undergo significant modifications. To recertify applications as compliant, testing should include the same regression tests originally used as part of the certification testing.

8.2.3 Implementing Enterprise Infrastructure Improvements

The primary deliverable of the enterprise test infrastructure assessment is an infrastructure improvement plan. The timing of tasks within this improvement plan must reflect the needs of the overall enterprise testing effort. Some infrastructure improvements, such as hardware and tool acquisitions and installations, have long lead times and must occur early in the enterprise project time line. As most infrastructure improvements require interaction with outside vendors, contract departments and legal counsel will be involved in the acquisition process, further lengthening lead times. Other infrastructure improvements, especially those that are not widely shared but are used by one or a few applications, may be slated for implementation at later points in the time line. In general, if the costs can be supported, it is better to make infrastructure upgrades as early as possible in the process so that if an individual testing project comes in ahead of schedule, it is not delayed in its testing effort.

Although the project office, as part of its management activities, will oversee the implementation of infrastructure improvements, the actual details and responsibility for the implementation will often be delegated to the system programming group. Specialized improvements may require skills and experience levels that do not currently exist in the organization, necessitating hiring additional staff. In addition, before making infrastructure improvements generally available for individual testing projects, the system programming group will have to subject the new infrastructure to exhaustive testing. In particular, the systems programming group must ensure that the test environment, with all infrastructure upgrades, mimics the production environment as closely as possible so that certification tests are reliable.

Many infrastructure improvements will be ongoing efforts throughout the enterprise time line. Although implementation may be a one-time event, ongoing training in tool and environment usage may be required. Hardware resources may need to be continually monitored, adjusted and brought online and off-line to accommodate testing schedules. To minimize costs, organizations should monitor usage and free costly resources as soon as the testing schedule permits.

8.3 Enterprise-Level Master Test Plan

The goal of enterprise planning activities is to develop a master, enterprise-level test plan. The enterprise test plan will contain an abundance of useful information, most important of which is a master time line for the entire Year 2000 testing effort. This master time line contains scheduling information for all of the individual certification projects and for any necessary infrastructure improvements. Project office managers will manage Year 2000 testing against the master time line. Because so many certification tests will occur in parallel, it is essential that a master time line is created and maintained to achieve necessary efficiencies and to control and coordinate the entire testing process.

The enterprise test plan is not mere window dressing. In a Year 2000 project, there are just too many tasks, dependencies, and resources to manage without the complete and thorough list embodied by the test plan. The dependencies of the testing effort are especially critical.

Without an organizational view of the testing process, infrastructure upgrades and individual application testing efforts could be delayed, thereby impacting other testing efforts and compromising the organization's century compliance. The project office has to monitor, coordinate, and resolve conflicts to ensure that the certification process occurs efficiently and as scheduled.

The accuracy and thoroughness of the enterprise test plan depends, in part, on the quality of the individual application test plans that are submitted to the project office. Creation of application test plans must proceed in parallel with enterprise-level activities to ensure they are available to the project office for planning purposes. Delays in creating application test plans will delay the generation of the enterprise test plan.

When the enterprise planning activities are complete, and a test plan created, the project office should know

- How it will manage the enterprise test plan and its constituent activities to achieve corporate goals and risk levels

- How it will handle the competing resource demands, synergies, and dependencies between individual application projects

- How it will manage the necessary infrastructure improvements, including tool acquisition and implementation, capacity upgrades, and other test environment component upgrades

Developing an enterprise-level master plan is a time-consuming and involved process. Rather than attempting to describe every step in the process, this section discusses the six major components of a completed plan. While enterprise test plans vary from organization to organization, they share these common requirements. The fundamental components of the plan serve as the building blocks for a more elaborate enterprise test plan.

Few IT organizations have experience in designing a test plan of the magnitude required for Year 2000 certification efforts. Consequently, many organizations may find it advantageous to seek outside assistance from experts as they construct their master plans.

8.3.1 High-Level Summary

The master test plan should contain a summary of its contents to enable corporate managers and Year 2000 team members to quickly understand the goals of the effort. This summary typically starts with a discussion of the scope of the plan. Given the size of a Year 2000 plan, setting the scope of the effort is critical so that the testing team understands their test objectives and focuses on meeting those objectives. Will end-user applications be tested? If so, by whom? How will non-IT systems be tested? Are all business units at all company locations covered? How will the testing team know when it is done?

The summary should also give an overview of the plan and its components, including testing strategy, corporate goals, expected schedule, resource requirements, risk management goals, and other significant factors affecting the plan. Consider attaching any backup materials, corporate statements, or other risk or strategy plans that served as input to the test plan.

8.3.2 Testing Strategy

While individual applications will have their own testing strategies, the enterprise must articulate an overall testing strategy for the organization. This enterprise test strategy must be disseminated to each application team before they can develop their own test plans. The enterprise test strategy establishes certain basic requirements. Each application test plan must then live within this overall strategy. For instance, if the enterprise strategy is to conduct application testing during the last six months of 1998, an application testing strategy cannot assume that there will be nine months of testing available starting January 1, 1999. This is not to say that the enterprise test strategy is insulated from the needs of its applications. On the contrary, the enterprise test strategy must take into account the needs of the individual applications. It does an organization little good to establish an enterprise test plan that is unrealistic for one or more of its critical applications.

The enterprise test strategy may advocate risk-based testing techniques. At the enterprise level, this would mean establishing an organizational risk summary and using this information to determine relative application priority, test schedule, and resource allocation. The more critical applications will be scheduled for earlier testing and will be allocated more resources. The enterprise test strategy will establish the criteria for certifying application compliance and the procedures used to validate compliance. It will also establish contingency plans and triage strategies in the event of project failures or delays. To summarize these components:

- **Organizational Risk Summary**

    Using the risk data gathered during the assessment phase, a summary is created describing the organization's preference for dealing with risk and the ranking of applications and projects to reflect this risk. From a senior management perspective, this summary may describe and rank risks—from the intolerable to the tolerable—and the dollar amount that the company is willing to spend to mitigate these risks. Risks will be ranked by their cost to the enterprise and their likelihood of occurrence.

It is up to the enterprise test team to understand and reflect organizational risks in the enterprise test plan. The team will relate these risks to the application projects comprising the plan. The applications will be ranked by risk, and these rankings will be reflected in the allocation of resources to the application throughout the testing process.

- **Certification Standards**

  The enterprise must articulate standards for certifying application compliance. The compliance definition should establish guidelines for when a date field expansion versus windowing approach is permissible. An application will be deemed to be compliant only if it meets the enterprise-level certification criteria. While the enterprise compliance definition may establish the organization's ideal level of compliance, it should also provide exceptions to the rule. For instance, the compliance definition may be less strict for applications that are slated for replacement in early 2000 or that will cause slight inconvenience if noncompliant.

- **Test Processes**

  The enterprise test strategy should recommend certain standard testing processes to be used to certify applications as compliant, including levels and types of tests. For instance, boundary testing using certain dates such as December 31, 1999, February 29, 2000, and May 18, 2026 (28-year rule) may be required. Depending on individual application needs, these processes may be varied.

- **Test Execution Strategies**

  The enterprise test strategy should provide overall recommendations for test execution. These recommendations may include workstation testing, off-hours testing, use of consultants or factories, preferred or available platforms, use of tools, and so on. Applications will pursue those recommendations that make sense given their particular circumstances.

- **Contingency Strategies**

  Contingency plans, as discussed in more detail in Chapter 9, specify how an organization should respond when an application fails to be compliant in time, or when an application's remediation is so delayed that failure is inevitable. At the enterprise level, contingency plans could include triage strategies (i.e., no testing), reduced testing, reallocation of testing resources, or augmenting testing resources. These enterprise-level contingency plans may also recommend preferred application-level contingency plans such as dropping less risky functions from test plans.

- **Disaster Recovery Strategies**

  Most IT organizations have a disaster recovery plan in place for their routine operations to deal with hardware/power failures, destruction, and malfunctions. This plan must be updated to take the Year 2000 effort into consideration. For example, what would happen if a natural disaster occurred in the middle of 1999? How would the Year 2000 testing environment be restored? Would the bridging and scaffolding code for partially completed production applications be properly restored? To support the Year 2000 effort, existing plans and backup procedures must evolve to match the current state of the production environment and must include critical test data and environments as part of the restoration process.

8.3.3 Application Consolidation

Each application has its own test plan and requirements that must be rolled up and consolidated at the enterprise level. As individual application test plans are created or changed, the enterprise-level plan must reflect those changes. Within the enterprise test plan, two levels of summaries should be maintained. One level should summarize the requirements of all applications as a group, listing the total resources required to execute the test plan and related infrastructure requirements and improvements. The second level should summarize each application briefly, listing its test readiness, certification strategy, risk-based testing strategy, and resource requirements.

8.3.4 Infrastructure Requirements

This section is a summary of the enterprise infrastructure improvement plan. It is included within the master test plan to ensure that its milestones and dependencies are integrated with those of the individual testing projects. It consolidates the infrastructure needs of each application with the enterprise infrastructure improvement needs. The summary should include the tools, platforms, test procedures, resources, and skills currently available (as determined during the enterprise assessment phase) and should indicate required upgrades or improvements to support the objectives outlined by the individual application test plans.

8.3.5 Test Projects List

A list of all test projects comprising the enterprise test plan should be created. A test project may correspond to one or multiple applications. This list will be constantly updated to reflect additional projects or changes. The list need not be overly detailed but should minimally include the following for each project:

- Summary of the application(s) or other systems to be tested, or the infrastructure improvement to be made

- Relative priority (per risk analysis)

- Responsible manager

- Staff requirements

- Special infrastructure requirements

- Estimated scope and duration of the project

- Current status and significant milestones and deliverables

8.3.6 Master Project Time Line

The master project time line is a high-level project plan incorporating the most significant tasks and deliverables of the enterprise testing effort. Tasks correspond to individual testing efforts (which may be application certification testing, infrastructure improvements, or non-IT systems testing) which are mapped to specific dates on the master time line. The time line also includes checkpoints to determine project progress. In creating the time line, dependencies between projects must be noted, and any resource or other conflicts must be resolved. The project office testing function will manage all Year 2000 testing against this master time line. Ideally, the master time line should be generated and managed using a commercially available project tracking tool.

The master timeline should include:

- **Tasks**

  The major tasks appearing in the time line correspond to the individual testing projects appearing in the test project list mentioned above. Detailed, application-level tasks are left to the individual application test plans. Tasks appear in the time line according to their relative priority and risk within the organization.

- **Estimates**

  The scope and duration estimates from the test project list are used as input to the master time line. If appropriate, multiple estimates can be created based on risk data to indicate critical, necessary, and optional tasks. In this way, if the project faces a severe testing shortage, the most essential tasks can be performed first to assure minimum safety levels.

- **Milestones**

  Interim milestones and deliverables should be specified to track project progress. In the master time line, milestones equate to major milestones in the individual projects. For instance, milestones may consist of the start of a testing project, the point that a future-dated test environment is required, and the date for production release.

- **Schedule**

  The heart of the enterprise time line is the schedule—a calendar view of the project. The schedule indicates the dates on which certain tasks begin and end, when deliverables are produced, and when resource assignments and allocations need to be made. The schedule pulls together all the information in the project time line.

- **Resource Allocations**

  To balance competing resource demands and to avoid conflicts, the master time line will track the people and hardware resources required by the individual projects. This resource allocation will be at a very gross level, defined by category, as the individual allocations and assignments will be made at the subproject level.

8.4 Managing Application-Level Testing Efforts

While the enterprise-level efforts of the Year 2000 Project Office provide guidance, coordination, management, resources, and assistance to application teams, the bulk of Year 2000 testing effort is performed at the application level. Each application team must undertake its own test planning and preparation measures. The team also must assess the test readiness of the application and develop a detailed plan for certifying the compliance of that application. These activities will proceed in parallel with their enterprise-level counterparts. Where an application team must provide information to the enterprise team for rollup into the enterprise test plan, the application teams must complete their work before the enterprise team can finish. In some cases, this timing constraint will mean that an application has to provide the enterprise team with educated estimates which will need to be refined later. Further, the application team must create the necessary test data and scripts, execute the tests, and validate the results of those tests to certify the application as compliant.

Figure 8.2 depicts the process flow that will be used by an application team to conduct its certification efforts. While many of these processes are the same as those used for routine application testing, the demands of a Year 2000 effort require a greater level of thoroughness than most teams are accustomed to performing.

This section discusses the personnel required to launch and manage application test activities and describes the activities shown in Figure 8.2 in greater detail. Following this process discussion, Section 8.5 describes how to create a basic application test plan. Section 8.6 covers plans for software packages and Section 8.7 covers plans for off-site remediation.

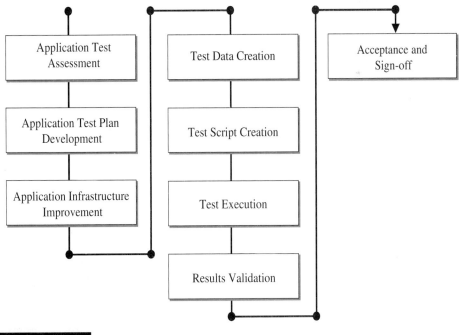

Figure 8.2 Application Testing Process Flow.

8.4.1 Roles and Responsibilities

Ultimately, the responsibility for application certification resides with the application team members who ordinarily maintain and test the application. If the application encounters any Year 2000 problems, it is these team members who are held accountable for their correction. Therefore, application team members must be directly involved in the testing effort even if some of the testing resources are drawn from other organizations.

In general, IT organizations should follow their existing organizational practices when preparing for Year 2000 certification. If the existing approach requires application teams to perform all of their own testing, this practice should continue for Year 2000 certification. Likewise, if a separate quality assurance organization is normally responsible for final testing activities, this practice can continue provided that the organization is properly staffed to handle the additional work volume. Organizations that normally rely on application teams for testing should not attempt to build a separate QA organization to execute Year 2000 certification tests. The cultural change involved in the use of a separate QA team is too extensive to be successfully implemented in the time remaining before the year 2000. Depending on the requirements of the application, certain team members may be dedicated to the Year 2000 project or all team members may be required to participate.

Application teams need higher-level sponsorship in the same way that the project office does. For the application teams, however, the project office functions as the sponsor. If properly empowered by senior management, the project office can serve as a shield and as a sword for the application teams that it oversees. It can assist application teams in adjusting priorities with their business users, obtaining people and hardware resources, and gaining internal or external consulting expertise. To make this relationship run smoothly, application teams must be highly responsive to requests from the project office. A renegade application team that is unresponsive, or consistently late, could jeopardize the success of the entire Year 2000 testing effort.

Each application team must have a test manager responsible for creating the application test plan and for overseeing the various testing activities comprising the plan. The application test manager will manage all testing according to the application plan. Application-level test management activities include tracking and monitoring the execution of all test cases, managing the test data, test scripts, and test libraries, ensuring that results have been verified, tracking the resolution of any problems exposed during testing, obtaining sign-off of test results, and monitoring the production release of the compliant application.

To effectively manage the testing process, the application test manager must apply sound project management techniques within a highly constrained environment. In addition, the application test manager must constantly communicate the status of the application testing effort to the enterprise team so that timely adjustments can be made to the enterprise test plan, if required.

8.4.2 Application Test Assessment Activities

Application test assessment activities have two goals: to evaluate the test readiness of a particular application and to conduct a project risk assessment of the application based on its test readiness. Risk information will be forwarded to the project office testing team for inclusion in its final risk assessment of the application. The application project risk assessment differs from the business risk assessment conducted by the business or risk management areas. It focuses on technical and resource risks that can affect the success of the project. For example, applications that have grossly inadequate test environments are deemed to be more at risk than applications having a state-of-the-art test infrastructure. Risk assessments are discussed in more detail in Chapter 2.

Application test readiness determines whether the necessary infrastructure is in place to support the types and levels of tests that must be performed to certify an application as compliant. This analysis evaluates the quality and quantity of test data, the availability of test scripts and testing tools, and provides a rough estimate of required hardware capacity.

There are really two tiers of application test assessments that must be performed. The first tier encompasses the activities described above with the goal of providing an initial assessment to the enterprise team for their planning efforts. Because of time constraints, this first-tier examination is necessarily cursory. The second tier builds upon the information gathered in the first tier. The extra detail gathered during the second-tier examination is needed by the application team to hone its own test plan. If the more detailed assessment information diverges significantly from the initial information provided to the enterprise team, then the enterprise-level information must be correspondingly adjusted.

A detailed assessment of an application's infrastructure is required to determine the specific improvements that must be made before the application can be tested. The application testing teams will have to examine capacity, platform, and tool needs and will have to inform the project office of any required upgrades or additions. Other activities performed during the assessment include a review of test data and test scripts. The enterprise team will implement shared infrastructure components but the bulk of the application's infrastructure will be improved by the application team itself and will focus on creating test data and scripts.

Upon completing an application test readiness assessment, the application team should have the following information:

- A thorough and accurate depiction of the current application test environment and its capabilities

- An application-level test infrastructure improvement plan showing:

  — Current status of the application test environment

  — Required upgrades or acquisitions to support application testing, along with why and when each upgrade/acquisition is needed

  — Implementation plan for the upgrades/acquisitions

8.4.3 Determining Application Infrastructure Improvements

Each application team will assess the current state of its test environment and come up with a plan to upgrade their test infrastructure to support the required certification testing. As described above, the enterprise infrastructure team will be responsible for shared upgrades, while application teams are responsible for implementing improvements unique to their applications. These improvements may include upgrades to existing, or creation of new test data and test scripts.

8.4.3.1 Test Data

The quality and quantity of test data are crucial components of the application test environment. A single application may extract test data from multiple files and databases. These test files and databases are usually populated by extracting a subset of production data. As discussed in Chapter 7, subsets of production data are rarely sufficient for validating century compliance. Ideally, all test paths in an application should be exercised to ensure that an application is truly century compliant. Production data seldom covers more than a small percentage of these paths. In reality, very few applications will be subject to this type of exhaustive testing because of the time and resource constraints placed on the test environment. Therefore, the challenge for application teams is to ensure that the test data is robust enough to reliably certify the compliance of the application within the risk tolerances of the organization.

To assess the current test data, and determine specific improvements, application teams should examine

- **Availability and quality of existing test data**

  To determine whether existing test data can serve as the basis for Year 2000 test data, the application team must know who owns and uses the test data and how and when it was created. If multiple application teams have created and use the test data, then these teams will need to coordinate any upgrades to the data. If the test data was created when the application was first developed and has not been maintained or updated in the interim, then it may no longer be valid. If the quality of the test data cannot be determined easily, then the application team may need to create new test data from scratch.

- **Test data creation techniques**

  The application team must determine if it has the tools and techniques needed to create, improve the quality of, and manipulate its test data. Test data will have to be manipulated to create boundary test cases and future date regression test cases. Can this be done manually? Is a data aging tool required and available? What types of files and databases are involved? Are there specific tools available for manipulating these types of data stores?

- **Test coverage**

  Application teams need to be able to determine whether their existing or upgraded test data is sufficient to adequately test and certify the application. To accomplish this goal, application teams should use a test coverage analyzer. These analyzers measure the level of coverage achieved by a given set of test data and assist the application teams in determining when to add new or remove redundant test cases. Assessing test coverage is an ongoing task that occurs throughout the test data creation process. As additional test data is created, application testing teams should reanalyze coverage to determine if they are reaching their coverage goals.

8.4.3.2 Test Scripts

Test scripts either launch and perform a particular test or series of tests, or contain instructions on how to perform those tests. It is unlikely that existing test scripts are complete enough to meet the needs of a Year 2000 project. Additional scripts will be required to handle the setup and future dating of a test environment, support regression testing, and save test results for validation. Application teams should review and assess existing test scripts to see if they can serve as baselines for more extended scripts. For instance, the batch JCL steps required to execute an application can most likely be adapted to support the execution of a Year 2000 test. Similarly, batch compile and link steps should be able to be modified to point to appropriate test libraries and, if needed, upgraded compilers. A good representative sample of test scripts performing these baseline functions should be identified for later Year 2000-specific modification.

8.4.4 Creating an Application Test Plan

Every application requires its own test plan. This plan enables the test manager to reliably certify the application as century compliant. Without a test plan, it is extremely difficult to ensure that adequate test data was prepared, that the proper tests were conducted, that the results were verified, and that the proper sign-offs were obtained. Due to the possibility of future litigation, organizations need to be careful to create a suitable paper trail that can be used to justify the reasonableness of their testing effort.

The test plan describes the processes, tools, and data that will be used to ensure that the application meets the requirements specified in its compliance definition. The test plan also contains the time line with activities and milestones for conducting the testing and certification of the application. This time line is essential for scheduling people and hardware resources and managing subproject dependencies. It is rolled up to the enterprise master plan to be merged with the time lines of other applications. All testing subprojects are managed against a combination of their own time line and the master time line.

The goal of application planning activities is to develop the test plan. This plan is typically created by the application project leader or by its testing manager. Depending on the kinds of applications found in an organization, and the testing strategy for each application, different varieties of test plans will be required. In-house-developed applications will use one type of standard test plan, software package applications will use another type of test plan which may be created with the assistance of the package vendor. Applications whose test strategy calls for them to be packaged and sent to an off-site factory for testing will require yet another version of a test plan. All these types of plans share some basic components but will vary in other respects as noted later in this subsection. Section 8.5 describes how to create a basic application test plan. Section 8.6 covers plans for software packages and Section 8.7 covers plans for off-site remediation.

When the application planning activities are complete and a test plan created, the application test manager should know

- How to manage the application test plan and its constituent activities to certify century compliance within the risk tolerances established by the organization

- How to schedule the infrastructure and testing activities comprising the test plan

8.4.5 Test Data Creation

The primary goal for an application's Year 2000 testing effort is to create a high-quality test bed of regression test data to serve as a base for all testing activities. The data within this test bed is aged and manipulated as needed to provide Year 2000-specific test cases. Spending time and effort in establishing a thorough regression test bed is a far more valuable exercise for the Year 2000 effort and beyond than spending time building custom data to test three or five different random years in the twenty-first century.

A good Year 2000 regression test bed will minimally exercise every path in an application that is affected by century remediation. A better regression test bed will exercise other, nondate-related code to ensure that the remediation effort did not result in unintended side effects. Surprisingly, it does not take a great amount of test data to exercise a large portion of the test paths in an application. More often, test data contains redundant test cases that repeatedly exercise the same piece of code. This situation is especially common when a subset of production data is used for testing. When creating a regression test bed, a test coverage analyzer should be used to ensure that adequate test coverage is achieved and that redundant test data is removed to lower the cost of test execution and validation.

There are four basic ways to create test data.

- **From production data**

  Extracting a subset of data from production data is one of the most common ways to create a test bed. Since production data provides limited coverage, this data will need to be extended using other techniques. Data can be extracted using utility programs or custom-written code. The more sophisticated the extraction technique, the higher the quality of the test data. Again, the coverage of this data will have to be measured using a test analyzer and the content of the data will have to be manipulated for future date regression tests and boundary tests.

- **From scratch**

  If the quality or quantity of existing test data is deficient, testing teams will have to create test data from scratch. For some tests, such as boundary tests, this method will be the only alternative available. Building test data from scratch is a very labor-intensive proposition. It can be done manually or using tools such as test data generators and capture/playback facilities. Test data generators require a great amount of initial specification to generate test cases. Capture/playback tools collect data entered into an online, interactive application so that this data can be reused for future tests. Manual editing of test data involves using an editor or similar utility to create test cases.

- **From regression test beds**

  If the application assessment indicates that an adequate regression test bed currently exists, this test bed can be extended by adding century-specific test cases. If the test coverage of the initial test bed is sufficient, it will not be necessary to subject later iterations of test cases to test coverage analysis.

- **From other applications**

  Test output produced by one application can be used as input test data to a downstream application. The higher quality the test bed run through the initial application, the higher the quality of the output data. In addition, subsequent applications may need to have the test data augmented to exercise certain unique conditions, especially error handling. The timing of this approach has to be carefully coordinated. If downstream applications are ready for testing before upstream applications, this approach may impose too much of a delay.

Once a robust regression test bed has been created, this data will have to be extended to handle future date regression tests, boundary tests, and, if necessary, special interface tests. The easiest way to extend the data is to manipulate the current regression test bed to modify date fields as required using tools, such as 4GLs or file utilities, or with custom programs. The way in which the test data is manipulated will depend, in part, on the compliance definition for the application. Applications that use a data expansion approach will need test data containing original, two-digit year fields and expanded, four-digit year fields. Applications that use a data windowing approach will not need to have expanded data but should test the cutoff, and surrounding, year values. For future date regression tests, the manipulation process means incrementing the dates by some consistent amount of time so that there will be a variety of dates occurring in the next century. When manipulating the data, care will have to be taken to preserve dependencies between sets of dates. For instance, a birth date should still be less than a date of death. Moreover, certain applications will be sensitive to the day of the week on which a date falls. To handle this situation, incrementing year fields by 28 years will yield a date in the future that falls on the same day of the week. Again, for some applications, dates cannot be incremented by 28 years since the application is not expecting, or cannot handle dates that far into the future. A variety of boundary test cases should also be created to stress certain uncommon conditions—transactions spanning both centuries, the last day of the nineteenth century, the first day of the twentieth century, February 29, 2000 (the first leap year), and so on. Certain special interface tests may also have to be created to stress error handling detection and recovery.

All test data created for Year 2000 testing needs to be cataloged and maintained. The usual practice of discarding test data after use is very ineffective in a Year 2000 project where the same tests may be executed many times. Test cases created by programmers for unit testing and interface testing should be recorded as test cases so that they can become part of the regression test suite for later system testing. In addition, if an application fails any tests and undergoes additional remediation, the testing team has to be able to rerun exactly the same test to ensure that any problems have been rectified. Testing teams will only be able to perform these reruns if the test data has been retained in the same form between runs.

Once created, test suites need to be managed in the same way that software is managed using configuration tools. Applications will typically have multiple versions of test data corresponding to different types of tests and these versions will need to be cataloged and kept current. In addition, testers will need to be able to quickly locate and access the test data they need for a particular test. Ideally, a repository will be established that can store and catalog the myriad test suites that will be developed for the entire Year 2000 project.

8.4.6 Test Script Creation

Test scripts contain instructions for executing a particular test. These instructions walk either a person or computer through the steps required to set up and run a test. For online, interactive applications, a test script will tell an end-user how to bring up the test application, enter a variety of data, and terminate a session. For batch applications, test scripts contain JCL statements and other system directives to prepare the test environment, point to the appropriate test libraries and test data, launch a particular test, compare the output results, and either terminate the test environment or proceed to a subsequent step. Test scripts can also contain documentation that explains the contents and objective of the script and any other requirements that have to be met prior to performing the script. Although an application may have some existing test scripts, these will have to be modified to handle the particular requirements for Year 2000 testing such as the setup of an insulated, forward-dated test environment, external bridging utilities, comparison of regression outputs, and so on.

8.4.7 Test Execution

Testing teams can begin executing their test plans once the application has been remediated, the test data and test scripts have been prepared, the test environment is operational, and any additional infrastructure improvements in terms of capacity and tools have been implemented. The programmers who perform the remediation typically execute unit and integration tests for the modules that they have remediated. System-level tests are usually a team effort. At each level, testers will execute the planned Year 2000 tests for the application, including all regression, forward-date, and boundary condition tests. Given adequate test scripts, test data, and test plans, the application testing team should be able to cycle through the test execution in an expeditious, assembly-line fashion.

The order in which tests are executed should correspond to the risk profile for the application. The most critical functions should be tested first and low-risk functions deferred until the end. In addition, tests can be progressively layered, with each layer attaining a higher level of coverage and safety, until they reach the desired balance between risk and testing effort.

For instance, the risk profile of a mission-critical application may indicate that it is to be subject to the full range of testing. For more information on risk-based testing methods, please refer to Chapter 7.

Application testers must periodically monitor the level of test coverage achieved during testing to ensure that adequate coverage has been reached. They must also collect information about bugs or application failures. In general, the testing team should attempt to complete as many tests as possible before waiting for an updated correction release. Problem information is captured and passed to the application teams for correction throughout the process. The application team creates a new release when all critical bugs have been corrected. The goal of this approach is to reduce the number of costly and time-consuming cycles between testing and correction. The testing team is responsible for noting all bugs in the issue tracking system or repository and in verifying that all bugs have been fixed upon subsequent retesting.

Upon completion of their tests, the test executors should ensure that all test outputs are retained for subsequent results validation. Although the test scripts should ensure that all output files, databases, and reports are retained, the test executors should provide a final check. Given the volume of testing to be accomplished, testing teams cannot afford to rerun tests due to the loss of test results.

8.4.8 Results Validation

Results validation occurs after test execution and uses the test results produced by the execution phase to certify the century compliance of an application. Its goal is to ensure that the application produced correct results in all of its tests. In addition, a final quality assurance checkpoint is conducted to ensure that the validated application conforms to the view of the application initially set forth in the assessment and planning phases. Results validation ensures that all components requiring modification were modified, that those modifications are correct, and that other application functionality was not inadvertently changed or impaired.

Validation is highly repetitive work composed of tedious, detailed tasks. For example, regression tests require that all test results for the remediated and unremediated applications be compared to ensure that the outputs are identical, after accounting for any date differences. Huge volumes of test results are produced and errors are often buried within the depth of these results. For this reason, manual validation is extremely costly, time consuming, and fraught with errors. Given the volume of data, it is easy for humans to miss important discrepancies. Results can, and should, be compared using automated tools whenever possible. Because output date fields may be different between the remediated and unremediated applications, an intelligent comparison tool is required to ignore differences in date field formats.

If application functionality was changed beyond what was required to achieve century-date compliance, then the validation process will be seriously impaired. Functional changes cause differences in test results precluding the use of automated comparisons for parallel tests. Having to manually compare outputs and verify the correctness of functional changes compromises the entire Year 2000 testing process by adding a layer of risk, time, and resource overhead that cannot be supported.

When conducting current date regression testing, outputs should be identical except that, when a data expansion technique was used, the remediated application will produce output date fields with a different format. When conducting a future date regression test, the unremediated application cannot be executed using the future dates because it cannot handle future dates. Therefore, only the remediated application can be subject to future date testing. To validate the results of the future date test, the output date fields will either have to be "rolled back" to current dates or else the comparison utility will have to be able to convert or ignore the date fields.

Like future-date regression tests, boundary tests can be conducted only on the remediated application; hence there is no boundary test output from the unremediated application to use as a baseline. All boundary test results will have to be manually validated.

As part of the validation process, the testing team will be responsible for collecting and documenting any bugs discovered during the output review. These bugs should be logged and forwarded to the application remediation teams for correction. After correction, and upon subsequent retests, the validation team should ensure that all outstanding bugs have been addressed.

During the output validation process, a quality assurance review of the remediated application should be completed. This review ensures that the remediated application conforms to the view of the application produced during the assessment and planning phases. The quality assurance team will reconcile the application components—their versions, the code changes, the data definitions, the output files, and so on—to the information contained in the original inventory list, compliance definition, and test plan. Unfortunately, it is not at all uncommon for an application to successfully pass all of its tests only to find that the remediation technique is incompatible with that of another application, or find that a code change was slipped in after testing that causes a new bug.

If the validation and quality assurance teams are satisfied with the results of their reviews, they will forward the application for acceptance and sign-off.

8.4.9 Acceptance and Sign-Off

As mentioned in Chapter 7, due to the focused nature of Year 2000 remediation, traditional end-user acceptance and sign-off procedures are not applicable. Rather, end-users will review and sign off on the compliance definition and the testing process for a given application when those definitions and processes are formulated. At the end of the validation process, the application team should establish, to the end-users' satisfaction, that the agreed-upon test procedures were executed. This step can be accomplished by showing end-users high-level or summary information from the validation phase demonstrating that the procedures were executed and compliance definitions met. For those applications that were remediated and perhaps tested at an off-site factory, this sign-off step is crucial to ensure that end-users have some level of oversight over the factory process.

Once the end-users have accepted the results of the validation phase and signed off on the remediated application, the application testing team will turn over the application for production release.

8.5 Creating Application Test Plans

This section is meant to be a guide for developing a standard application test plan. Rather than attempting to describe every step in the process, this section discusses the five major components of a completed plan. This plan is used for applications that have been developed, and will be tested, in-house. Although each organization will create its own version of a "standard" test plan, these can be expected to share some common components. These common components can serve as building blocks for a variety of test plans. The level of detail found in each component will vary depending on the type of application. For example, a mission-critical system with a high-risk profile will contain more test cases and will be subject to more exhaustive testing than a relatively low-value single-user PC application.

Very few application maintenance or support teams have experience in designing a test plan with the level of detail required to certify century compliance. In contrast, most new development projects have highly refined test plans. Application support teams may find that they need additional training or reference materials to assist them in creating their Year 2000 test plans and should look to new development teams or outside specialists for pointers.

A solid application test plan contains five basic components. These components and their common elements are discussed below.

8.5.1 High-Level Summary

Each application test plan should contain summary information about the application including a brief description of the application itself, its users, the support team, and the application's relative priority to the organization and within the Year 2000 enterprise test plan. The summary should also indicate the level of testing to be performed for the application. Information about the application's current test environment and test history should be outlined and any special or unique requirements should be noted. Application teams should also consider attaching any backup materials, corporate statements, or other risk or strategy plans that served as input to the test plan.

8.5.2 Testing Strategy

Each application team develops a specific testing strategy to certify the compliance of its application. This strategy defines the acceptance criteria for certification, the types of tests to be used, the depth of testing to be performed, and the methods for executing and validating those tests. The application testing strategy must fit within the overall strategy developed by the project office testing team. For instance, if the enterprise test strategy states that all testing must be performed using IT staff, an application's test strategy cannot assume that outside consultants will be engaged to conduct testing. However, within the confines of these basic requirements, each application must articulate its own testing strategy.

One of the most important determinants of an application's test strategy is its risk profile. As discussed in Chapter 7, the risk profile of an application will influence the types and levels of tests that will be conducted. Further, testing resource requirements, balanced against time and resource constraints, may also influence the test strategy. For example, these constraints may require that additional hardware or testing tools be acquired to jump-start testing.

The test strategy should be articulated in the test plan and any subsequent decision to change the test plan should be examined against the strategy. Changes in strategy should be cleared with the Year 2000 project office. The test strategy should establish the criteria for certifying application compliance and the procedures that will be used to validate compliance. The following components should comprise the test strategy.

- **Application Risk Summary**

  Using the risk data gathered during the enterprise and application assessment phases, the application team, in conjunction with the Year 2000 project office, will develop a risk profile for the application. This risk profile describes the application's priority to the business, the potential cost of the failure of the application, and the likelihood that a failure will occur. Depending on the application, each functional component of the application may also have its own risk profile, indicating the relative priority of each function within the application. Certain functions, such as a daily transaction update, may be more important than other functions, such as a yearly summary report.

- **Certification Standards**

  As part of the remediation process, each application has a compliance definition specifying how the application is to be modified to achieve century compliance and how the application team will know when compliance is achieved. This definition is included in the test plan as the application's certification standards.

  An application will be deemed to be compliant only if it meets the certification standards specified in the compliance definition. In some ways, these certification standards are akin to the functional requirements that are typically specified and tested in new development projects. If an application's certification standards require it to use a windowing technique based on a cutoff year of "30," the application will not be deemed compliant if it windows using a cutoff year of "50."

- **Test Types and Levels**

  The test strategy should specify the types and levels of tests to be performed on the application. For example, a noncritical application may only undergo current and future-date system-level regression tests, while a critical application will undergo the full suite of tests. As discussed in Chapter 7, the types and levels of tests to be performed will depend, in part, on the risk profile for the application. Higher-priority applications will undergo more types and levels of tests, while lesser-priority applications may skip certain types of tests.

The compliance definition for the application will also influence the types and levels of tests to be performed. For example, an application using windowing techniques will need additional system-level tests to verify the correctness of its interpretation and handling of the cutoff year. In addition, the characteristics of an application will influence the levels of tests to be conducted. An application that has multiple interfaces will have a proportionately greater number of interface tests and an application that has external interfaces will have tests scheduled with outside entities.

- **Functional Decomposition**

  Where lower-level verification tests focus their efforts on application code and technical architecture, system-level validation tests concentrate on functionality. To support validation testing, each application must be broken down into its constituent functions and specific tests must be created to ensure that these functions operate correctly. This decomposition should be reflected in charts, grids, maps, or cross-reference listings that summarize the functions, their relative priority, the actual source code modules for the functions, and the tests to be executed to certify compliance for each function. Figure 8.3 shows how application functions relate to the application test plan, test cases, test scripts, and test data.

  Providing a functional decomposition as part of the test plan enables testers to focus their efforts based on the needs of each function. The risk profile for a particular function (based on its importance to the business and its level of date impact) will determine its priority in the testing cycle and determine the depth of testing that must be performed. This information is an extremely useful aid in further refining and reducing the amount of testing to be performed on an application.

- **Test Execution Strategy**

  The application test strategy should describe how the tests described in the previous sections will be executed. This description includes where the tests will be executed (workstation, mainframe, etc.), who will perform the tests (IT staff, consultants, etc.), what tools will be used, and how results will be validated. Any depen-

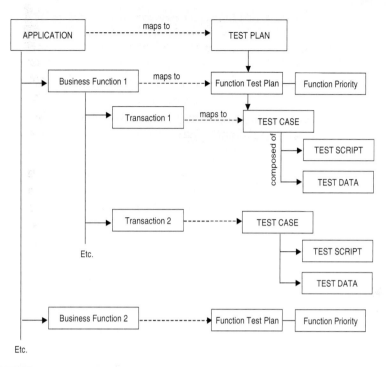

Figure 8.3 Functional Breakdown within a Test Plan.

dence on resources other than the application team should be noted here and the roles and responsibilities of those outside resources should be clearly delineated.

8.5.3 Test Environment

This section of the application test plan describes the test environment required to certify the application as compliant. This description should cover the tools, platforms, hardware, test scripts, resources, and skills that must be in place to support application testing. Many of these components have long lead times and will correspond to infrastructure improvement tasks in the enterprise and application time line. In particular, this section of the test plan should cover

- **Capacity/Platform**

  The specific platform and capacity requirements for application testing, as determined during the assessment phase, should be outlined. It should be indicated if certain platforms or hardware resources are needed only for certain types or levels of tests, such as a dedicated test platform for future-date regression testing.

- **Tools**

  Any tools required to support certification testing and test management activities should be listed along with the locations of available documentation and training materials. If particular tool capabilities are needed, but the application team has not found a tool possessing those capabilities, the capabilities should be described as requirements for the enterprise test infrastructure improvement project. The project office, as part of its review and consolidation of application test plans, may be able to identify and acquire tools that have the requested capabilities.

- **Test Scripts**

  Each application test will have certain prescribed steps that must be taken to accomplish the test. Often, these steps are not memorialized in any type of document, script, EXEC, PROC, or other guide but are performed by memory by the application team members. Because Year 2000 testing is different from typical testing in that it has different goals, types of tests, and test environment requirements, it is crucial that scripts be put in place so that tests can be run easily, efficiently, and reliably. These scripts have to be in place before the commencement of application testing. The creation of these scripts will have to be scheduled as tasks in the application time line.

- **People Resources**

  Application team members that will be involved in the testing process should be identified and their associated assignments listed. If specific personnel, test skills, or application knowledge are required to implement the test plan, these resources should be identified and plans should be made to obtain and release these resources when needed. If any of these individuals require training to carry out test activities, the training requirements should be noted here.

8.5.4 Detailed Test Descriptions

This section expands upon the information found in the "Test Types and Levels" subsection of Section 8.5.2. Detailed descriptions of each test are provided, indicating their category (current-date regression, future-date regression, etc.), their priority, associated test scripts and procedures, and any other information relevant to executing the test. A balance must be struck between providing enough information to enable application members to easily execute each test without inundating them with mundane details. Some important pieces of information include input and output data requirements, tools, environments, validation criteria, and scripts.

8.5.5 Application Project Time Line

The application project time line is a high-level project plan incorporating the most significant tasks and deliverables of the application testing effort. Tasks correspond to individual testing activities (which may be test data creation, test execution, or production release) and are mapped to specific dates on the time line. The time line also includes checkpoints to determine project progress. In creating the time line, dependencies between subprojects must be noted. The application test manager will manage all application testing against this time line. Ideally, the application time line should be generated and managed using a commercially available project tracking tool.

The application time line should include

- **Tasks**

  The major tasks appearing in the time line correspond to the individual testing activities such as test data or test script generation, environment setup, test execution, or production release. Each task will have associated resource assignments, deliverables, and effort/duration estimates. Tasks appear in the time line according to their relative priority so that if contingency plans must be invoked, the highest-priority tasks have a chance of being completed.

- **Estimates**

  The estimates for each of the tasks appearing in the time line are combined to produce a single estimate for the application testing effort. If appropriate, multiple estimates can be created, based on the risk profile of the application, to indicate critical, necessary, and optional tasks. For instance, one estimate may reflect the execution of all functional tests while another estimate may reflect the execution of all high- and medium-priority functions within the application.

- **Milestones**

  Interim milestones and deliverables should be specified to track testing progress. In a risk-based testing context, milestones are critical measures as they allow the application team, and the project office, to confirm that the highest-risk components have been tested.

- **Schedule**

  The heart of the application time line is the schedule—a calendar view of the testing project. The schedule indicates the dates on which certain tasks begin and end, when deliverables are produced, and when resource assignments and allocations need to be made. The schedule pulls together all of the information in the project time line.

- **Resource Allocations**

  Each task in the time line will have associated resource assignments and allocations. By the time the application test plan is complete, assignments should be made by name, and each individual should be aware of those tasks for which he or she is responsible.

8.6 Creating an Application Test Plan for Packaged Software

Most companies use software packages created by third parties as part of their normal business processing. The vendors of these packages typically provide maintenance or periodic updates to the software under the terms of a maintenance agreement between the vendor and the organization. At a technical level, packaged software has the same types of Year 2000 issues as in-house developed software. From a strategy and testing perspective, packaged software poses a number of additional challenges. First, the vendor may decide to go out of business rather than spend costly effort to provide updated software. Depending on whether the IT organization has access to the source code for the package, it may have to fix the package itself or purchase and install a replacement package. Second, even if a vendor will provide compliant software, the organization may not have a current maintenance agreement entitling it to the upgrade, may not be using the current version of the software, or may have previously modified the package. Finally, the compliant version of the software provided by a vendor may not be truly compliant, or it may not have been adequately tested.

The discussion that follows focuses on those factors that will influence testing and approaches to modifying the standard plan for software package testing found in Section 8.5.

8.6.1 Factors Affecting Software Package Testing

Software packages are similar to internal applications on a technical level but present numerous challenges in how they are maintained and upgraded as follows.

- **Back-level releases**

  It is not uncommon for an organization to be using an older version of the software package than is currently offered and supported by the vendor. Software vendors will usually provide updates only to the most current version of the package. To install a Year 2000-compliant package release, the IT organization will have to migrate to the latest release of the package. New releases are apt to have major functional changes, which means that the package will have to undergo significant functional testing. As discussed in Chapter 7, functional changes preclude the use of automated tools to validate test results, significantly increasing the cost and risk of testing.

- **Internal modifications**

  Many IT organizations customize software packages to support their own unique processing requirements. These modifications mean that the installation of a new release is not a straightforward process, since the customization will have to be applied to the new version of the software. Finding the necessary modifications and applying them to new software, which has most likely been significantly changed, will be a difficult and error-prone process. Additional testing effort is required to ensure the compliance of the internal changes and to catch errors introduced during their implementation.

- **Responsibility for upgrades**

  The contract between the vendor and the IT organization will determine who is responsible for making compliance upgrades. Typically, a vendor will be responsible for making upgrades under the terms of a maintenance agreement. If an IT organization has let maintenance lapse, purchasing it now can be costly since many vendors will require that the IT organization become current on all prior maintenance fees. Even if the software vendor is responsible for, and does provide, compliance upgrades, how responsive can or will the vendor be if bugs are uncovered during testing at the IT organization?

- **Timing issues**

  The vendor will control the timing of the release of its Year 2000-compliant package. Depending on the schedule of the release, an IT organization may find itself strapped for time to install, customize, and test the release before the production application will fail. Packages, more than internal applications, will require detailed contingency plans in the event that a vendor's release date does not permit the IT organization to implement and properly test the new package in time.

- **Remediation approaches**

  It is very likely that the vendor will select its own remediation approach without consulting the IT organization. For example, one major vendor uses flag bytes to indicate century rather than using an industry-standard approach such as field expansion or windowing. IT organizations will have to thoroughly understand the vendor's remediation approach and its implications on the testing process. Testing teams may have to adjust their own strategies if the vendor's approach differs from theirs.

8.6.2 Approaches to Testing Packaged Software

Most compliance upgrades to software packages will come in the form of updated releases of the software. In general, the IT organization should approach the testing of this new release as it would traditionally approach the testing of any new software release but add some Year 2000 concepts to the testing process. For instance, most new releases will have functional changes requiring a level of functional testing and traditional end-user sign-off not found in Year 2000 testing. Any modifications or customizations that are applied on top of the new release will also have to undergo testing. Finally, the package must be certified as century compliant. Because functional changes were made to the software package, automated validation of test results between the old and new packages will be impossible. Results will have to be manually validated, which will increase the duration of the testing cycle, and require more resources.

Risk-based testing methods can also be applied to packaged software but additional factors should be considered. The internal risk assessment, based upon cost of failure and likelihood of failure, must also weigh the vendor's competence and industry reputation, differences between the vendor's test environment and that of the IT organization, and the level of change to the package as factors influencing the likelihood of failure for the application. To understand how to weigh these factors, IT organizations should inform themselves of the vendor's remediation approach, test environment, certification processes, and test results. If possible, the IT organization should ask the vendor for a review of its testing process for the package release. This review should examine the test plan and the results of test execution and validation. If a vendor is unwilling or unable to provide this information, it is an important warning flag indicating that stepped-up testing and contingency planning are required. Finally, if the IT organization had to apply internal modifications on top of the new release, these additional changes will increase the difficulty of testing and the likelihood of failure for the application.

8.6.3 Developing a Test Plan for Packaged Software

Incorporating the approaches to testing described above, an IT organization can develop a test plan specifically for a software package. Starting with the standard application test plan as a base, the following changes can be made.

- **Testing Strategy**

  The testing strategy for a new release is impacted by the amount of functional change included in the package. Because of the high level of functional change, which increases the likelihood of application failure, the application, and its constituent components, will have a heightened risk profile. In addition, functional changes mean that traditional acceptance testing and end-user sign-off procedures will have to be included. If internal modifications were applied to the new release, then these modifications will have to be tested too.

- **Scheduling**

  The most obvious difference in a test schedule for a software package versus an internal application is that testing cannot proceed until the vendor delivers the new release. Despite this fact, IT organizations must determine the date that the production application package will fail and then attempt to back into the date when they need to have the new release installed for testing. With this date in hand, IT organizations may need to negotiate earlier deliveries with their vendors, reduce their testing effort, or may have to invoke contingency plans. Even if the vendor delivers the new release on time, the IT organization must have contingency plans in place in case the testing process reveals serious shortcomings with the release. See Chapter 9 for a discussion of contingency plans in the context of third-party software.

8.7 Creating an Application Test Plan for Factory Remediation

Off-site resources or "factories" provide a cost-effective means for remediating software applications, and are part of the Year 2000 strategy for many IT organizations. These factories typically use a combination of people resources and automated tools to process large volumes of code. The selection and use of factories is discussed in Chapter 5. While factories are highly efficient at remediating code, they impose additional quality assurance and testing steps on the application testers. While testing factory-remediated applications is similar to testing in-house remediated applications, application testers must take greater care to ensure that all components, and the correct versions of components, were remediated and that the remediation efforts complied with the compliance definition for the application. In addition, if the factory used proper testing and quality assurance techniques in its process, the application testers may be able to reduce their efforts accordingly. Conversely, if factory testing efforts are inadequate or suspect, application teams will need to step up their efforts.

8.7.1 Factors Affecting Testing of Factory-Remediated Software

When using off-site resources to remediate application software, two basic issues arise. The first issue is that the work is performed off-site with potentially less control and oversight than found in internal remediation efforts. The second issue is the lack of application-specific knowledge within the factory team. These two issues lead to the following points.

- **Conversion strategy**

  Factories may use manual methods, automated methods, or a combination of both to perform the remediation. Each method has its own risk profile and requires the testing approach to be modified to catch its most likely errors. To ascertain the competence of the factory personnel and to increase the level of comfort in their work, an IT organization should know what methods (manual or automated) the factory uses and when, the tools used, and any methodologies applied.

- **Reliability of analysis and remediation effort**

  Factory personnel will not have the same detailed level of knowledge about an application as the internal IT staff. Generally, this level of knowledge is not required to make the obvious types of modifications called for by the compliance definition for the application. However, this level of knowledge is crucial in understanding those obscure or tricky areas of an application that may be impacted by, or require, date-related code changes. Without this knowledge, factory personnel are likely to miss application-specific nuances during analysis, remediation, and testing. Knowing this, IT organizations should devote additional effort to testing factory-remediated applications for unremediated date definitions, references, and processing.

- **Application or upgrade unit packaging**

  IT organizations often underestimate the level of effort required to locate and package an entire application or upgrade unit, with all of its components, for factory remediation. The factory may have no way of knowing if the IT staff forgets a component, or includes an incorrect version of a component. Including a wrong version of a component can lead to bizarre errors during testing, and costly reworks as application code must be sent back to the factory for additional remediation. The IT organization must also have strong controls in place to ensure that concurrent internal modifications of application components during the factory remediation process are properly merged with factory-provided changes.

8.7.2 Approaches to Testing Factory-Remediated Software

Many factories will perform some level of testing on the applications that they remediate. This testing, along with the fact that many factories guarantee the correctness of their conversion work, can lull IT organizations into a false sense of security, believing that they can safely reinstall the application after only minimal testing. IT managers must realize that in the event of future litigation, they will be ultimately responsible for any defects or failures in the software and must therefore take reasonable steps to guard against them. Accepting factory remediated code without performing an adequate level of testing may be totally irresponsible and unreasonable, if simple certification tests could have been designed and executed by the IT organization.

Legal reasons aside, there are important technical reasons for performing an adequate level of internal tests. No factory is immune from human or tool errors during its operations. Further, the factory testing environment is unlikely to be identical to the environment in the IT organization. These faults and differences lead to software errors that need to be exposed by certification testing. Unless the factory is provided with adequate application test data, it cannot conduct thorough testing of all application functions. The issues involved in running off-site system tests lead most factories to limit their efforts to unit testing. The IT organization remains responsible for integration and all system-level testing. Even if unit testing is performed adequately, it cannot catch interface errors between modules or uncover module version mismatches.

Just as with packaged software, the risk assessment of the factory-remediated application must incorporate additional factors. The internal risk assessment, based upon cost of failure and likelihood of failure, must also weigh the factory's competence and industry reputation, differences between the factory's test environment and that of the IT organization, and the level of change as factors influencing the likelihood of failure for the application. To understand how to weigh these factors, IT organizations should inform themselves of the factory's remediation approach, test environment, certification processes, and test results. Similarly, by understanding the remediation approaches used by the factory—manual and automated—the IT organization can determine the expected level of change to the application and adjust its risk profile accordingly.

The test strategy for factory-remediated software will be very different from that used for internal systems. A sample quality assurance process for factories is illustrated in Chapter 5. This strategy begins with the quality assurance process implemented to ensure that all components of an application or upgrade unit are properly located and packaged for remediation. Configuration management routines will also have to be put in place to either permit or prohibit software from being changed internally while it is at the factory for remediation. During the factory remediation process, the application team is responsible for preparing the test data, test scripts, and test environment needed to certify the remediated application. The application team must also prepare a process for handling remediated code that is returned from the factory. This process should include a review of the components of the returned application, matching these against what was delivered to the factory, a review of the actual changes made against the application's compliance definition, and a review of any test results produced by the factory. In addition, if any software was changed by the IT staff during the factory remediation process, these internal changes will have to be merged with the remediated software. Finally, depending on the types and levels of tests executed by the factory and the risk profile of the application, certification testing should be performed.

8.7.3 Developing a Test Plan for Factory-Remediated Software

Incorporating the approaches to testing described above, an IT organization can develop a test plan specifically for factory-remediated software. Starting with the standard application test plan as a base, the following changes can be made.

- **Testing Strategy**

  The testing strategy section of the application test plan should firmly delineate which tests the factory performs and which tests are performed internally. It must be extended to include the quality assurance activities described in Chapter 5 and refer to the approaches and activities identified in Section 8.7.2.

- **Application Project Time Line**

  The time line will have to include tasks, estimates, milestones, and deliverables for the preparatory activities involved in packaging the upgrade units and for the acceptance activities involved in handling the returned software.

- **Detailed Test Descriptions**

  Depending on the types of tests performed by the factory and the integrity of the factory testing process, the IT organization may be able to eliminate tests from its test suites that would duplicate those tests run by the factory. If the factory process is highly manual and its level of testing is suspect, additional verification and validation tests will be required.

Chapter 9

Contingency Planning: When Time Runs Out

What happens to an organization if mission-critical systems are not century-date compliant in time for the new millennium? Could the loss of an order entry system, a production assembly system, a trading system, a claims system, a patient admitting system, or a key supplier bring a company to its knees? As organizations around the world struggle to meet the impending Year 2000 deadline, business executives must search for answers to this increasingly realistic possibility. If management does not plan for contingencies in various functional and technical environments, the survival of the company, or even a given industry, could be at stake. This chapter addresses contingency planning and contingency invocation.

Creating contingency plans is one thing. Knowing when and how to invoke those plans is quite another. This chapter walks the reader through the process of identifying contingency requirements as well as the process of building plans to address contingencies in a variety of situations. We also outline sample contingency plans for a number of different industries, including the public sector. Contingency invocation is discussed with a focus on time criticality which includes pre-2000 plan invocation and post-1999 plan invocation. We also introduce the concept of contingency management which refocuses executive attention on creating and monitoring fallback situations for mission-critical functions as an integrated part of information asset management. Finally, we felt obliged to comment on personal contingency planning as a means of protecting oneself when the new millennium arrives.

This chapter attempts to get the reader comfortable with the concept of contingency planning through logical discussions that cover issues in a number of industries. There is no magic answer to this process—it involves planning, thoughtfulness, and foresight. The reader should note that although this chapter falls into the latter section of this book, this does not imply that contingency planning is not an upfront Year 2000 planning activity. It does reflect that contingency invocation typically occurs during the later stages of a Year 2000 project.

9.1 What Is Contingency Planning?

Contingency planning, by definition, establishes alternative Year 2000 resolution options when an initial action plan fails or falls short of its goal. Contingency planning requires that management be ready to take action when things do not go as originally planned, when unforeseen problems arise, or when original delivery time frames are exceeded. If everything always went the way we originally planned, there would be no need to consider alternatives. But Murphy's law states that "what can go wrong, will go wrong." Even if all goes according to plan, unforeseen problems or bugs will arise during the late-1999 and early-2000 transition window. Exceeding project deadlines is an area where IT has typically not created fallback positions, an unacceptable option in a Year 2000 project.

These three challenges form the root cause for contingency planning and are a backdrop for the remainder of this chapter. This section discusses contingency requirements, differences between business and technical contingency planning, internally versus externally driven requirements, and who should participate in contingency planning.

9.1.1 Why Plan for Contingencies

There is an unjustified sense of optimism surrounding the Year 2000 problem. A 1997 International Data Corporation (IDC) study found that only 2.8 percent of CIOs surveyed believe that they will miss their Year 2000 deadline. Furthermore, the survey found that 73 percent of chief executive officers and 71 percent of chief financial officers claimed that they have a strategy in place to address the problem. This response is not unexpected given that these individuals are responsible for the financial success of publicly traded companies. Misplaced optimism spawns complacency and complacency, coupled with the overwhelming challenge ahead, dictates that contingency planning will become an increasingly critical requirement for businesses during the next two years.

Contingency plans should be generated as a fallback position for key business functions, although the mere existence of a business function, a system, or an external entity does not necessarily generate a need for a contingency plan. Organizations will not have time to create a plan for every last item in an enterprise, which means that the building of contingency plans must be prioritized in the same manner as remediation projects and test plans. The risk assessment, developed in Chapter 2, provides the key to this prioritization process and is a basic prerequisite for the development of a contingency plan. Plan for contingencies only in situations which involve key business functions.

9.1.1.1 Not Every System Will Be Fixed

One should assume at this point that not every system can be fixed—nor should every system be fixed. Systems ranked as low priority by the risk assessment, technologically obsolete systems, certain end-user-based systems, and systems being retired due to a de-emphasis of one or more business functions may not be scheduled for remediation. The fact that no remediation work is scheduled in support of one or more business functions means that contingency plans may need to be developed for those areas. For example, a leasing system may be retired because the leasing business was sold to another company. There may need to be a contingency plan, however, to build a facility to migrate the customer database for use by other systems.

In other situations, systems which were supposed to be corrected may be left off the remediation schedule due to the fact that remediation and testing teams ran out of time. If these systems support key functions, a contingency plan must be deployed to ensure that these functions are not impaired because of a systems failure. Every system may not be fixed, but this does not mean that business operations should suffer as a result.

9.1.1.2 Not Every External Entity Will Reach Compliance

The numerous business partners, suppliers, agents, brokers, and other external entities upon which your organization relies on may not be ready to support your requirements as their systems begin to encounter individual failure dates. These same organizations may run into problems with their suppliers or business partners. The risks inherent in these complex interdependencies demand that executives build contingency plans for each business function that, in whole or in part, relies on a third party.

Whom can you trust? Third parties that are likely to survive the Year 2000 problem have multiple remediation projects underway, a plan stating that key systems will be stabilized in time, reliable status reporting, and a management team that is ready to admit that ultimately, not every system will be fixed. Some executive teams, which have none of these pieces in place, may still feel quite comfortable with their progress and believe that every system will be fixed and tested by late 1998. The second organizational category includes many companies that are lulling themselves into a false sense of security. Contingency efforts must initially focus on the evaluation of third-party compliance.

9.1.1.3 Corrected Systems Will Have Bugs

As an example, a clearing house for monetary instruments got an early jump on their Year 2000 project and completed the bulk of their conversion work by 1997. Upon inspection of some of the remediated code, they discovered 14 noncompliant code changes had been made to the system since it had been fixed. These changes would have caused problems in the Year 2000 that would have required a defect correction and, possibly, invocation of one or more contingency options. In other cases, systems that were fixed incorrectly, had Year 2000 problems that were missed by the remediation process, or were tested inadequately will likely cause problems well into the next century. Technical and business-driven contingency options should be created to handle these circumstances when they arise.

9.1.2 *Technical versus Business-Driven Contingency Plans*

In many situations, planning teams will need to concurrently create a business contingency option and a technical contingency option to deal with problems arising from a given Year 2000 failure. For example, a failure in an accounting system during the first few days of January 2000 may require technical teams to scramble to fix the problem (the technical contingency option) while accounting clerks cut checks manually for a week or two (the business contingency option). Other examples may require triaging a system (letting it fail and/or shutting it off), modifying business processes in the functional area that the system supports, and implementing an off-the-shelf package.

In other cases, there may be no technical alternative to a Year 2000 dilemma. For example, a remediation project may be so complex, time consuming, and expensive that management cannot justify pursuing it. In these cases, management may decide to sell off the business unit as a contingency alternative. A business partner or supplier failure is another example where business teams are solely responsible for correcting the problem. Another example, failure of a chip that is embedded in a product you sold to a customer, could require monetary compensation as the only way out of the problem. Situations where the business-driven contingency plan is the only option require longer lead times, demand more senior executive review, and have farther reaching effects than cases where there is a technical alternative.

Certain circumstances may arise where no business-driven contingency plan can be created to fix the situation. This situation is typically true when a piece of system software fails and shuts down every application system that relies on that system software. In these cases, systems personnel may just have to dig in and fix the problem as quickly as possible. It is important for planning teams to view every situation where a contingency option may apply from a business and a technical perspective. This perspective will allow joint planning teams to create fallback positions to accommodate the technical and business issues that may arise.

9.1.3 Internally versus Externally Driven Requirements

Internally driven contingency requirements arise from failures within application software, system software, end-user-based systems, embedded technology, and other in-house technologies. When planning for problems in these areas, management needs to have a high degree of control over the decisions made at each step of the process. This management control means that a decision to reduce testing for a system can be coupled with focusing on contingency planning for that system. Internally driven requirements, which are more clearly defined than externally driven requirements, lend themselves to a defined planning horizon and should, therefore, be accommodated more readily if and when a problem occurs.

Externally driven contingency requirements stem from potential problems with external data interchange, business partners, regulators, suppliers, government agencies, patients, constituents, or customers. Issues may also arise when a software or hardware supplier fails to live up to a delivery date or other commitment. When building contingency plans for externally driven issues, longer planning lead times are necessary. Management must, therefore, consider factors which it typically has no control over as a top planning priority during risk assessment and contingency planning.

9.1.4 Contingency Planning Participants

When it comes down to building a contingency plan, who will do the work? With IT personnel working frenetically on fixing and testing noncompliant systems and business analysts caught up in other day-to-day activities, little focus is likely to be put on key contingency planning tasks. The Year 2000 Project Office must, therefore, work with business sponsors to ensure that every business unit, division, or department takes responsibility for building and monitoring a contingency plan.

The personnel required to perform contingency planning depends on the type of business that one is in, the systems one supports, and the third parties involved. Jointly defined and staffed contingency planning teams ensure that each business function has technical and business contingencies built into the plan and schedule. The emphasis and lead times for building contingency plans also have an impact on when various personnel must perform this work. A long lead time is required for business analysts to invoke a business selloff strategy, while a shorter lead time is required to invoke an emergency system upgrade plan. The team leader for contingency planning should be the business unit sponsor for a given business area. Distributed team organization across multiple business units is depicted in Figure 9.1.

Success requires that the Project Office assist in developing a contingency support infrastructure that interfaces with senior executives, application teams, business analysts, and external entities as needed. Planning teams should keep in mind that while centralized support for contingency planning is essential, the analysis and decisions must be made within the business units impacted by those decisions.

Contingency Planning Teams – Securities Trading Firm, Inc.

International Funds Transfer - J. Smith/Sponsor - C. Jones/IT rep - H. Mudd/Bus. rep	**Trading Sector** - J. Hardy/Sponsor - S. Snead/IT rep - T. Maxx/Bus. rep	**Private Investing** - J. Hardy/Sponsor - S. Snead/IT rep - T. Maxx/Bus. rep
Commercial - Roberts/Sponsor - P. Wendt/IT rep - W. Smith/Bus. rep	**Funds Processing** - M. Ward/Sponsor - S. Toms/IT rep - N. Hays/Bus. rep	**Clearing** - M. Day/Sponsor - I. Terr/IT rep - J. Brink/Bus. rep

---

Figure 9.1 Each business area requires a contingency planning and monitoring team with the business sponsor for that area serving as team leader.

9.2 Identifying Contingency Requirements

Management should develop contingency plans for all mission-critical functions, the automated systems and external entities that support those functions, and other areas that might possibly be affected. Identifying these requirements in advance may require extensive research and relies heavily on the risk assessment work discussed in Chapter 2. This section discusses contingency planning requirements for hardware and infrastructure issues, system and application software, and business specific areas.

9.2.1 Hardware and Infrastructure-Driven Requirements

The technical infrastructure, in the context of this discussion, includes all forms of in-house computer technology, telecommunications equipment, facilities and office equipment, embedded technology used in the course of doing business, and products sold to end customers. This information may form an extensive checklist of technology depending on a company's industry and level of automation. Organizations should prioritize efforts to establish contingency options for each area based on the relative downside of a failure in a given category. Clearly the best source for this information is the vendor of the hardware or the equipment itself.

9.2.1.1 Mainframes to Micros

Up-to-date mainframe computers have, for the most part, been tested to ensure that they are Year 2000 compliant. IBM, for example, can provide customers with detailed test results for various mainframe and peripheral equipment that minimize the need for creating contingency plans for the hardware component of these systems. Older IBM devices, equipment from manufacturers that have not declared compliance or provided detailed test results, older minicomputers, and noncompliant PC and workstation platforms should require contingency plans based on their impact on the business. Controllers, storage devices, and other gear should also be tested as required to determine compliance prior to the century rollover.

Planning for contingencies in the hardware area is difficult due to the long lead times required to deactivate old hardware, procure and activate new hardware, and migrate existing systems to the new environment. Contingency planning in the mainframe or centralized minicomputer area is a matter of testing these systems to ensure that they work. If hardware malfunctions, standard disaster recovery options should be invoked. In the PC, workstation, or peripheral area, however, the creation of backup plans to stave off isolated failures is absolutely warranted. Any backup plan should be closely coordinated with the applications and functional areas that these systems support. In these cases, contingency coordination between various project teams is essential—you would not want one contingency plan eliminating the platform upon which a second contingency plan relies.

9.2.1.2 Telecommunications Equipment

Functions that rely on telecommunications equipment, whether owned outright, leased from a third-party, or linked to the shared telecommunications infrastructure of a service provider, require the creation of a contingency plan. The failure of internal or external telecommunications equipment is likely to have catastrophic results in most companies or government agencies. The creation of backup plans in this area might involve establishing alternate service or leasing agreements with secondary telecommunication providers or creating a parallel backup system that utilizes newer equipment. This process should begin quickly because contingency planning involving complex communication infrastructures requires extensive planning and setup work.

Reality dictates that the rapid deployment of a backup communications infrastructure is highly unlikely at organizations of any size or complexity. Contingency planning in these situations may need to include shifting broad business strategies. For example, a help-desk facility can be shifted to another division or outsourced as a fallback plan. Management should coordinate this effort across business units within larger enterprises.

9.2.1.3 Facilities and Office Equipment

Some organizations have already researched in-house security systems, elevators, HVAC systems, environmental controls, automated mail delivery systems, and other computerized controls. Many have not. If you own a building site, you are responsible for testing computerized mechanisms within that facility—regardless of vendor compliance claims. A contingency plan for a broken elevator may include opening all stairwells to public traffic. A backup plan to a security system failure may require staffing excess security personnel for a period of time or identifying a secondary provider that could upgrade security systems should they fail. Any safety-based systems that have the potential of doing harm to an individual should be checked and rechecked—with contingency plans focused around shutting down these systems at the first sign of trouble.

As far as office equipment is concerned, individual stand-alone machines should be tested at the departmental level to ensure compliance. If this testing is done in advance of the century rollover, minimal contingency planning should be required. In the event that one of these systems does fail, however, there should be a backup plan, such as sharing equipment from other areas, putting a vendor on notice that you may need to make an emergency upgrade to a given type of equipment, or just going to a backup communication or workaround plan.

9.2.1.4 Embedded Technology

As discussed in Chapter 4, embedded systems exist everywhere and numerous industries rely on these systems for a wide variety of functions. In the private sector, contingency plans should be developed for manufacturing equipment, retail point-of-sale technology, power grid controllers, banking equipment, communications systems, on-board transportation and navigation systems, credit card processing hardware, research equipment, medical equipment, and any other type of risk technology that a company may use to transact business. Manual workarounds for many of these systems may be the only solution. Because many of these embedded technologies are industry specific, detailed guidelines for contingency planning are presented in Section 9.5.

Many government agencies depend on embedded technology. The defense sector is rife with command and control systems, radar systems, weapons systems, and a host of other technologies. The contingency plan for many of these systems may be to hunker down, do without the systems for a period of time and order new equipment as problems arise. A radar system failure may require falling back to older navigation options. It is likely that many defense-related Year 2000 problems will slip through the analysis and upgrade process now in place. Contingency planning and execution will be the way of life for defense agencies for quite some time.

Other federal agencies have embedded technology that helps manage air traffic control, weather forecasting, global positioning analysis, onboard space craft, lighthouse functions, fish and game tracking, and numerous other functions. Contingency planning in each of these situations could involve grave safety concerns. Grounding aircraft for a window of time, rerouting planes, delaying space missions, falling back to non-date-compliant forecasting techniques, temporarily manning lighthouses, or ignoring fish and game tracking systems could all be considered options when developing contingency plans for these systems.

At the state and local level, contingency plans for traffic lights, water distribution, irrigation, automated drawbridges and a host of other real-time systems must be established. Where a manual solution is available, ensure that resources are in place at critical failure windows including January 1, 2000, and February 29, 2000. In a worst case scenario, the potential of a nuclear reactor failure could involve upgrading failsafe mechanisms or reinforcing the core against potential meltdown problems.

9.2.1.5 Computerized Products

If you sell products that contain computerized technology, you will minimally require two sets of contingency strategies. The first involves discontinued product lines suspected or known to be noncompliant. In these cases, contingency plans may require creating replacement offerings, launching a customer communication strategy, and creating a hot line to deal with customer inquiries. One consideration involves the legal liability of a manufacturer should an obsolete product fail. If there is no such liability (check with in-house legal counsel), customer goodwill must still be maintained.

The second product contingency requirement involves mitigating risks for existing product lines still being sold to customers. Support requirements in these situations are higher to support the continued growth of revenue streams and the customer base. If another company relies on your product to make their product and that product contains noncompliant computer technology, the pressure will be on your company to correct this situation or lose the account. Contingency planning in these cases demands long lead times because you may have acquired the embedded technology from a supplier. In this case, supply chain contingency options include procuring backup parts from a second supplier. If you created the embedded technology in-house, consider creating replacement components. If the product is being considered for discontinuation, management may want to expedite this move as a business-based contingency plan.

If your company builds computerized consumer products, as is the case with PC and appliance manufacturers, consider upgrade options, public relations campaigns, and other strategies to keep customers happy. One computer manufacturer has, for example, announced that it will provide a no-cost upgrade if you buy a product made after October 1997. This announcement was made because they could not guarantee that products shipped after that date would contain BIOS technology that would function beyond 1999. This situation exemplifies how a contingency plan was invoked, in advance, to supplement inadequate inventory controls and supplier management. Time will tell if this policy will avoid souring customers' attitudes. This type of contingency plan must still be augmented to include a public relations strategy to keep customers satisfied.

9.2.2 Software-Driven Requirements

The core effort dedicated to internal Year 2000 initiatives typically includes numerous application and system software upgrades to in-house and vendor package systems. While many companies believe this process is under control, contingency plans must be developed for systems that have not been upgraded, replaced, or repaired. A given plan, as stated earlier, is based on the type of system and its business impact. This section discusses system software, in-house application systems, and application packages.

9.2.2.1 System Software

System software, which includes operating, network control, database, tape management, and a host of other utility-based systems, have a longer contingency planning lead time than their application software counterparts. As with hardware, the ripple effect of a failed system software component impacts all applications that depend on that component. This constraint requires that analysts perform early identification and upgrades of noncompliant system software. Ironically, mainframe operating environments are less likely to encounter problems due to the heavy attention being paid to those systems. Network, PC, workstation and other "new" system software components may be assumed compliant but in many cases are not. This area is where contingency planning comes into play.

For example, an IT manager at an airline was responsible for a client/server system based on C++ that contained problematic leap year routines. These problems were being diagnosed and fixed in preparation for the Year 2000 when the manager learned, to his surprise, that the HP UX Release 10.30 operating system that supported his application had Year 2000 bugs. When told that HP UX Release 11 was required to make the operating environment compliant, he decided to upgrade the UNIX system. At issue here was not whether the software would be upgraded, but would it be upgraded in time to prevent reliant applications from failing. Timing is a critical issue for contingency planning teams. In this example, a contingency plan must be established to ensure that a compliant operating environment will be in place as a backup.

Network software is another at risk area that has been ignored or assumed compliant. Novelle Network Release 4.1 has known Year 2000 problems. If this network software is not replaced prior to January 1, 2000, client/server systems relying on this software, and the functions that these systems support, will cease to function. Networking software may require the creation of a backup network that has been tested and is known to be compliant. Again, the assumed compliance of a distributed system software product could lead to a domino effect of system failures.

Questionable or unreliable database software may similarly require the creation of a backup database that has been initialized in a pre-2000 mode. This backup will be necessary depending on the date reliance of the applications using these databases, but noncompliant database environments have been known to lock up and deny users access to critical data.

PC and desktop systems, spread across a wide variety of end-user areas, demand a unique approach to contingency planning. When a PC fails due to a noncompliant piece of operating software (we can pretty much guarantee that this will occur), users will be confused and require quick access to a centralized help desk. The help desk should be equipped to deliver new versions of operating systems, databases, spreadsheets, and other software needed to ensure that end-user environments continue to function properly.

One type of system utility that applications personnel may have ignored is the date routine. Most companies continue to use dozens of nonstandard and inconsistent date handling and date conversion routines that will not function properly when they encounter dates in the next century. The "not invented here" syndrome, prevalent within many system software teams, has caused companies to shun standardization in this area. When these systems fail, applications personnel may spend days trying to debug dozens of applications when the underlying problem is in a date conversion utility with Year 2000 bugs. The contingency plan here is to either identify or procure a standard backup routine that can be used to replace these routines prior to or immediately after the point where they actually fail.

To drive home the importance of contingency planning for system software components, consider the following. A securities processing firm, having completed its Year 2000 conversion effort well ahead of actual deadlines, performed an off-site test to determine if the environment would function properly in the next century. No application problems emerged during the test. However, tape management systems, databases, and several other system software components required upgrading in order to get the entire environment functioning properly. Given that most organizations are unlikely to be this diligent during enterprise testing, we should continue to develop backup options in the system software area.

9.2.2.2 In-House Application Systems

Clearly in-house applications, whether under the control of the IT organization or end-user, are where the majority of IT resources have been focused to resolve Year 2000 problems. Application system contingency plans are driven by the business criticality of the functions that those systems ultimately support, the time to failure, and the time required to enact various contingency options. The term "ultimately" is important because it reflects the need to understand how a given system supports other systems that support a mission-critical function.

The risk models outlined in Chapter 2 are key to creating contingency plans for application systems because a single mission-critical function may rely on several IT and end-user systems. Fixing a single system, without understanding the interdependencies of other systems and functions, may not achieve risk mitigation objectives for that business area. Contingency plans are, therefore, driven by the functions that a given system or systems support. Taking this approach ensures that organizations do not spend time building extravagant contingency plans for systems that appear important on the surface but that do not actually relate to a mission-critical business function.

In the IT area, technical contingency plans are based on numerous factors that intertwine revenue and customer impacts, regulatory and legal risks, cross-industry dependencies, and strategic business plans for an organization. Contingency planning for end-user systems is based on the same complexities. Business professionals and IT analysts must, therefore, work together to build business- and technology-based fallback plans to mitigate business risks posed by noncompliant systems. One cannot successfully execute such plans without the help of the other.

For application systems that have been fixed and certified compliant, or for systems that were built to be compliant and tested to ensure that they work properly in the long-term, contingency planning focuses on quick-strike corrections if and when bugs surface. Small errors may have crept into systems after repair work was completed, errors may have been introduced during the conversion itself and missed during testing, or a date function may have been overlooked during the remediation process and missed during the test cycle. In these cases, technical contingency plans structure repair priorities (upstream systems may, for example, need to be fixed first) accordingly. Business contingency plans focus on how end-users can keep operations functioning while the system is being repaired. Figure 9.2 depicts an example of one business area's multifaceted contingency plan for this situation.

Other application system contingency planning options include triaging low-priority systems, letting systems run incorrectly for a given window of time until they self-correct, merging data and users from one redundant system into another, or bridging system data via windowing techniques (see Chapter 6 for more on this topic) until a system can be replaced. We will discuss contingency strategies for various industries, market sectors, and situations in subsequent sections within this chapter.

Business Area Contingency Plan

Function: ***Commercial Monetary Funds Transfer***

Related Systems: Worldwide Funds Processing
International Monetary Unit Conversion
Funds Transfer Reporting

Business Plan: 1. Process top 20% of revenue accounts manually
2. Hold fund processing requests for bottom 80% of accounts
3. Shift processing to a prearranged business partner
4. Communicate issue to customers, proactively head off problems

Technical Plan: 1. Correct errors in core Worldwide Funds Processing system first
2. Perform monetary unit conversion manually
3. Correct errors in International Monetary Unit Conversion next
4. Correct reporting system last
5. Deliver data to business partner for offsite processing

Figure 9.2   Contingency plans must be coordinated carefully to assess business and technical areas.

9.2.2.3 Application Package Software

Many times, the greatest exposure to an IT organization lies within situations that are beyond the control of application support personnel. Nowhere is this more true than in situations where an application is comprised, in whole or in part, of a third-party vendor software package. Chapter 2 discussed the risks inherent under a variety of vendor package upgrade scenarios. As with other application-related upgrades, contingency plans are driven by the timing and business criticality of the functions that a package supports.

If a vendor fixes the system but it is later found to be noncompliant, in-house support teams must move quickly to secure another upgrade. A contingency option would involve having analysts work around the problem by developing or modifying in-house code and, if necessary, having business users manually compensate for system shortcomings during the interim period. If a vendor is fixing the system but misses the compliance deadline, the same options apply. In this case, however, more radical business strategies may be required. A low-priority business function may, for example, drive business and IT analysts to let the function run in error for a window of time and correct problems manually during that same period.

If a vendor will not provide compliance status or refuses to fix the system at all, radical action is required by the business and IT team. For high-impact systems, options include fixing the system in-house, filing a class action lawsuit with other package users, or replacing the system with a comparable system if time allows. For medium-impact systems, analysts should work with business users to determine workaround techniques or to change the business model to reduce system dependency. For low-impact systems, analysts should examine standard triage options for the system discussed later in this chapter.

Again, application package contingency planning options must reflect the impact of the system on the business environment, vendor cooperation, time to failure, and the time needed to implement in-house corrections. Other factors are industry- and situation-dependent as discussed in subsequent sections within this chapter.

9.2.3 Development/Replacement Projects

Monitoring package replacement and in-house development projects across an enterprise is an important responsibility of the Year 2000 Project Office. For example, a new package replacement project may be slated for a November 1998 delivery date and the failure date for the superseded in-house application is January 1999. Leaving only a two-month window between project delivery and system failure is a very high risk situation. The window between time to failure and the projected time required to complete an emergency Year 2000 upgrade establishes the invocation date for launching a contingency project. Timing is discussed in more detail in Section 9.6.

The primary contingency plan, in many package replacement or in-house development projects, requires that IT analysts complete an emergency remediation project to keep the current system functioning. These types of projects take a minimalist approach that normally involves a windowing fix applied as sparingly as possible. While this emergency remediation is going on, secondary fallback plans could include dumping the replacement project and moving to an alternative package or in-house option. IT teams monitor these types of projects and report back to senior executives at the first sign of trouble. The application implementation team may tell executives not to worry about the deadline—even when all facts indicate it will be missed. The Project Office plays an oversight role in these situations to keep business operations functioning through contingency invocation.

9.2.4 Business-Driven Contingency Requirements

Many people believe that contingency planning involves responding only to inadequacies within applications, technical infrastructures, or other IT-based technologies. Risks can result from a number of other factors that range from supply chain breakdown to the collapse of the Internet. Risks stemming from business areas require that business sponsors within each business unit extend their risk assessment into the area of contingency planning. In most cases, the threat from a non-IT problem will not be noticed by IT personnel at all. The business-driven risk assessment must, therefore, include monitoring business risks well into the Year 2000 and beyond. Business managers should craft their own backup plans that may extend beyond the scope of the plans jointly crafted between the business unit and IT. Discussion of various threats and contingency-based responses are discussed in the following sections.

9.2.4.1 Erroneous Data

End-users must be wary of errant data, generated either by IT systems or by end-user systems, that is used to make business decisions. There is much discussion within the industry that much of the financial data currently generated through spreadsheets and even some IT-based systems may be wrong. This insidious error will only get worse as unnoticed problems spawn more errant data. This problem is considered an internal threat to the business, and business executives should establish a quality assurance review process that spot-checks data periodically to assess its integrity. In some cases, an end-user may not be able to tell if something is wrong. In other situations, the fact that numbers do not add up or look skewed may be readily apparent.

A contingency plan, should problems occur, involves the creation of a Quality Assurance (QA) function within a business unit, recasting data using newly created spreadsheets, working with external business partners to let them know of the potential impacts, and creating a prioritized list of corrections for IT. The QA function should remain in place for at least 9 to 12 months after the arrival of the Year 2000 in order to detect ongoing problems.

Externally developed bad data may come directly into business units that procure this information. IT personnel should be made aware of these situations, but the onus is on the business unit to create contingency plans should errant data infect an organization. One applicable contingency concept is the creation of a "firewall" to identify and highlight bad data as it comes in. Cross-checking expiration dates with initiation dates, for example, could catch errors in a business partner's windowing routines. Other contingency options involve securing this data from another source when the original is found to be in error, correcting the data internally when possible or omitting this data from your processing cycle altogether.

9.2.4.2 Product Supply Chains

The supply chain is a highly susceptible area for any business that relies on other companies to create goods used in the course of their business or in the development of their product. The potential domino effect of the supply chain was discussed in Chapter 4. Reacting to a supply chain problem is clearly a high priority—particularly when early research led management to believe that critical supply chain partners had the Year 2000 problem under control. Supply chain responses include replacing tier-one suppliers, buying a company in the supply chain that failed or, in low-impact areas, discontinuing the product or service that relies on that supply chain partner.

These options establish a fallback position that should be pursued only after the initial supply chain strategies discussed in Chapter 4 have been thoroughly explored. More supply chain examples will be highlighted in subsequent sections that discuss industry-specific contingency planning.

9.2.4.3 Business Partner Problems

Even if an organization performs a detailed analysis of a business partner's Year 2000 compliance status, failures could arise that prevent that business partner from fulfilling its obligation. As with other risk-related issues, the level of analysis and contingency planning must be commensurate with the potential downside associated with having this business partner fail. For example, if you work for a U.S.-based bank, and all the banking transactions performed in the Benelux countries rely on a third-party bank based in Brussels, management will want to work as a team to mitigate Year 2000 risks with the Brussels bank.

A contingency plan may state that you will send a Year 2000 team to Brussels at the end of 1999 to participate in the transition management for that bank. If a key system fails, you will be assured of two things. The first is that you will know what banking functions are vulnerable rather than finding out secondhand. Your bank will then be better prepared to address problems in various areas proactively. The second factor is that, with your people on-site, the likelihood of getting the problem fixed quickly increases dramatically. Again, the time and commitment dedicated to this effort must be driven by the nature of the relationship and the revenue upside.

Other business partner arrangements may not need to be so elaborate. Low-impact partners may be eliminated completely in some cases. In other situations, you may just move forward without certain service offerings until a replacement partner can be found. Having replacement partners identified in advance is, of course, a key contingency strategy for all high- and medium-impact partners.

9.2.4.4 Supplier Requirements

A supplier of a critical service may be hard to replace. If a utility company shuts power off for an extended period of time, a business could fail. Management must weigh the cost of a contingency plan against the odds of this type of problem occurring. If you work for a health care provider, for example, your hospital may have only three days of backup power in its generator. Is it worth buying the generator equipment required to generate one week's worth of backup power? The answer to this question depends, in many cases, on profit margins. In a life or death situation (two people died at a New York hospital during a power outage when backup generators failed), this is a difficult decision. One contingency option is to pool resources with other local hospitals in the case of an emergency. If the power fails, all intensive care patients could be moved to a single site with enough backup power to last two to three weeks or longer.

For product suppliers, a typical contingency plan may increase just-in-time inventory levels from 8–12 hours to two to three weeks. Other options involve finding a secondary supplier, taking over the supplier's operations, or pooling resources with competitors to create an alternative supply source. Critical service suppliers, such as utilities, telecommunication firms, and water sources, pose a more difficult challenge. Generators and secondary telecommunication lines can help an organization plan for certain contingencies in these cases. Other service suppliers may need to be replaced by others.

Working with industry associations can help reduce the magnitude of research required in a given industry by any individual company. One example involves the health care community using a not-for-profit foundation to research monitoring and diagnostic equipment for compliance. This level of cooperation should be integrated into the contingency planning process. It may be possible to create a cross-industry contingency plan that pressures a supplier into taking action, works with that supplier to ensure product or service continuity, or jointly builds an alternative supply source.

Suppliers fall across a wide planning spectrum that begins with mission-critical suppliers and ends with extraneous relationships ripe for termination. Some companies have over 50,000 first-tier suppliers and are, therefore, unlikely to create a contingency plan for each one. On the other hand, suppliers linked to the most mission-critical functions, as determined in the business risk assessment outlined in Chapter 2, must be considered in a proactive Year 2000 contingency plan. Low-priority suppliers may even be triaged at some point in the process. Figure 9.3 depicts different contingency requirements based on the relative importance of a given group of suppliers.

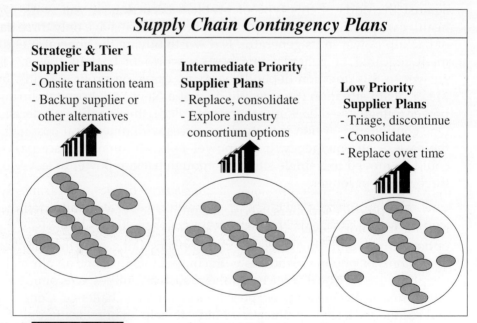

Figure 9.3   Supply chain contingency plans are based on mission criticality.

9.2.4.5 Internet Issues

The Internet is the fastest growing area of technology within and outside the IT area. Business executives, end-users, and IT management are increasingly trying to find new and innovative ways to utilize the power of the "Web." By the Year 2000, Internet and intranet dependency is likely to increase dramatically within most companies. This dependence is exemplified by the proliferation of online trading that has recently emerged within the securities industry. Traders learned first-hand of the risks inherent in the blind reliance on a technology that is beyond the control of those who depend on that technology. During peak trading windows on October 27 and 28 of 1997, the Dow Jones Industrial Average fell and rose several hundred points in the course of a 36-hour span. Online trading was at a standstill due to Internet overload which exposed some of the vulnerabilities inherent in using the Internet for critical functions.

Fast-forward to the end of 1999. Internet usage is at an all-time high. The industry has created an interminable spider web of technology that includes Internet servers, data access links, and client code that resides on the PC. Further consider that Java, C, C++, Visual Basic, and a host of other "new" tools are susceptible to the Year 2000 problem. Now couple this with the fact that UNIX operating systems, such as the HP UX release discussed earlier, are assumed Year 2000 compliant when they are not. The stage is set for server failures and system errors that affect not just one company, but a multitude of industries worldwide. The Internet is down for weeks or months, and the information superhighway is closed for the foreseeable future.

What is your contingency plan for dealing with the loss of the Internet or the loss of your intranet environment? We recommend that you begin taking action now to create backup plans for situations where a primary information access route, such as an internal intranet system or the Internet, fails. Alternate options include dedicated lines, mainframe systems, or other backup facilities. It is worth investigating and definitely worth creating contingency plans should major problems occur.

9.3 Building a Contingency Plan

Thus far, we have focused on why an organization should create a Year 2000 contingency plan. Along the way, we introduced numerous examples of what a contingency plan would address in various software, hardware, infrastructure, and business-related areas. This section is meant to provide a general framework for developing a contingency plan.

9.3.1 Planning Overview

Building a contingency plan is a distribution process performed jointly by IT and business teams. The goal is to establish a set of fallback strategies that support technical and business areas that can be invoked in a timely manner to keep business functions working uninterrupted through the Year 2000.

Risk identification, performed during the business risk assessment discussed in Chapter 2, is the basis for building a contingency plan. Obtaining a model of at-risk functions, along with the systems and external entities that support those functions, is a prerequisite for beginning the contingency planning stage. Priority rankings of external entities and various computer systems are also required to ensure that the level of contingency planning and action to be taken is commensurate with the importance of each function, system, and external entity.

9.3.1.1 Assign Consequences, Probability to Risk Factors

The first step in building a contingency plan is to examine the consequences and the probability of the risks associated with each function, system, and external entity. Analysts should consider the following steps in assessing consequences and probabilities.

1. *Determine the types of events that might adversely affect a business unit for each high-risk function.*

2. *Examine the upside and downside of various failure scenarios for each system and/or external entity linked to those functions.*

3. *Assess the damage that these events could cause as time approaches and surpasses Year 2000 failure dates.*

4. *Review these events, beginning with the most catastrophic to the least catastrophic based on the financial, legal, regulatory, or other impacts identified during the risk assessment.*

5. *Examine the odds of each high-impact event happening and rank, in order, from the most probable to the least probable scenario.*

6. *Eliminate very low probability and low-impact events from the list.*

An example of how this process would work can be found in a policy issuance function found within an insurance company. The external entities upon which this function depends include insurance brokers and agents.

The downside of a complete shutdown of broker services is a 40 percent loss in revenue. Agent failures would account for another 55 percent revenue loss. A major IT-based downside involves the loss of the policy system that issues and bills for policies. The financial risks involved in shutting down the policy system could impact up to 100 percent of revenues. Other external and internal risks should be categorized appropriately.

The odds of a policy system failure are 20 percent based on remediation work currently underway. The odds of an agent failure at the field level are 30 percent based on analysis of technical field capabilities and Internet-related risks. Broker failure is estimated to be a 10 percent risk based on the fact that the system used to input policies by brokers is relatively new and deemed compliant. Ranking the odds of failure across this business unit will help determine the level of spending and effort to be associated with contingency plans in each area.

9.3.1.2 Identify Technology-Based Risk Reduction Alternatives

If a technology-based problem occurs, analysts must determine the appropriate IT and business-based responses to mitigate risks related to that problem. In many cases, the IT contingency response to a system error is to "fix the system." The planning process should be pursued for each business area under examination as follows.

1. *For each application system in the group, list the correction priorities to be applied if the system fails:*

    • prior to the failure date: one day turnaround

    • after potential failure date: one-to-two day turnaround if pre-2000

    • after 2000: three-to-five day turnaround (due to prediction of slow post-2000 response capability)

2. *If a data file or database is contaminated:*

    • back up to an earlier version

    • isolate and stop the source of errant data

    • correct the error in the data

    • replace the source of the data

3. *For each external data interface that fails, assess options to:*

    • correct the data after receiving it

    • run the system without the data until corrected

- work with external source to correct the problem (weighed against dropping them)

- establish an alternative source for that data

- discontinue use of data based on marginal value

4. *For the hardware device supporting various application systems, identify how support areas would respond if that hardware has problems:*

- assess impact on application areas

- determine maximum allowable downtime

- seek alternative hardware or processing options (disaster recovery)

5. *For each application package supporting a system, list the sequence of responses that would be required to fix or supplement the functions of that package:*

- fix the system in-house

- work with vendor to correct problem

- drop in a quick replacement option

- use another in-house system or package

- discontinue use of system functions in business area

6. *Where potential embedded technology failures might occur, list the likely response including:*

- backup options from other business areas

- replacement or upgrade options

- alternate business options

7. *If reporting or query functions fail, consider rebuild options that could supplement the data provided by those functions.*

9.3.1.3 Identify Business-Based Risk Reduction Alternatives

The response to business-related problems that might occur due to the Year 2000 tend to differ from technology-driven responses. This category includes responses to direct threats to the business from suppliers, embedded technology, business partners, bad external data, or the Internet. Business professionals must also plan to respond to IT-related problems that may stem from system or infrastructure failures. General guidelines are listed below.

1. *If a system failure is imminent and the IT team has no way to fix it, consider:*

    - selling off a low-margin business unit or division and dramatically reducing Year 2000 upgrade efforts

    - shifting to a similar in-house application that is already servicing a different segment of the business

    - changing the underlying business model to eliminate or reduce the need for an existing system

2. *If a system failure occurs and the IT team has no way to fix it, consider:*

    - changing the underlying business model to eliminate or reduce the need for an existing system

    - shifting users to a similar in-house application that is already servicing a different segment of the business

3. *If a system is going to be down for a brief period and repairs are underway, consider:*

    - having end-users work with a paper trail (built as a contingency) to remain productive while system is fixed (works best with accounting or billing systems)

    - determining if manual processes could be applied by business analysts during an interim period while the system is fixed

    - turning system off and working around it until impact window closes (if system has forward/backward date referencing limited to 30 days or less)

4. *If a product fails that was acquired from a supplier:*

    - determine if a replacement can be obtained in time to correct the problem

    - obtain product from a backup supplier (this option should be researched and established during this planning process)

    - assess options to have business units work without the product (this is time-dependent in many cases)

5. *If a service supplier fails to continue to deliver that service:*

   - assess how long you can continue to function in the absence of this service

   - move to a backup source for that service (power generator, performing service inhouse, etc.)

   - determine if a replacement service can be obtained (establish options based on criticality and probability of failure)

6. *If a product fails that was sold to a customer:*

   - build a hot line service to accommodate customer inquiries

   - send out a replacement offering quickly (if available and monetarily feasible)

   - for discontinued product lines, determine best course of action based on input from legal team and marketing

7. *If a business partner fails:*

   - work with that partner to correct the problem as quickly as possible

   - seek out replacement partners to fulfill these requirements

   - determine if the function can be brought in-house

   - determine if another existing business partner can fulfill these service commitments

   - eliminate the function/business unit that depends on this service (this is a proactive contingency plan)

9.3.1.4 Prioritize Risk Reduction Options

As soon as various contingency options have been identified for each situation, function, system, and business area, analysts must prioritize responses to each situation that may arise. This effort is a matter of ranking each response to a given problem beginning with the most desirable to the least desirable based on the impact of that response. For example, stopping production of a product may be less desirable than selling the product at a loss for a period of time. Response ranking should be applied to both technical contingency and to business contingency options. Business unit sponsors and other executives should review and approve these plans and the applicable rankings that have been assigned to each situation/response in a given business area.

Analysts should note that executives may argue that this level of contingency analysis is unnecessary because management can make these decisions "on the spot" as they do now when other crisis situations arise. Analysts should make it clear to these executives that there may be hundreds of concurrent problems arising during the late-1999 and early-2000 transition window. Many of the decisions to be made during this time will have a ripple effect on other systems, functions, and third parties. Preparedness, based on a well-thought-through action plan, may be what differentiates Year 2000 survivors from those that panic and cannot fulfill financial, legal, and regulatory obligations

9.3.1.5 Monitor Year 2000 Progress and Checkpoints

Once basic plans are in place, management, working through the Project Office, should closely monitor checkpoints so that the "point of no return" for a replacement or a remediation project does not pass unnoticed. If the window of opportunity passes on a date field expansion project, for example, management may need to invoke an emergency fix to that system or alternatively launch a procedural workaround solution. The Project Office must also keep business sponsors and end-users informed of progress so that event horizons or other checkpoint events do not end up blindsiding the business community. The business community has a similar obligation as far as monitoring and updating management on the status of suppliers, business partners, end-user systems, and external data interfaces. When critical deadlines for a business unit come to pass, the management team for that business unit must identify and correct problems before they arise.

9.3.2 Business Model Redesign Options

Business model redesign concepts require business teams to take action to avert problems generated from IT system failures or external partner/supplier failures. While we have selected an example from a government agency, the more common application of the business model or design option is likely to occur in the private sector—particularly in small to mid-sized companies.

At the U.S. Congressional Year 2000 subcommittee hearings held in April 1996, one of the interviewees suggested that a contingency option for the Internal Revenue Service could involve converting current tax codes to a flat tax or to a national sales tax. The premise is that IT could implement a fairly simple computer system to process a single tax rate for all taxpayers in a relatively short time frame. The agency itself would have to undergo radical simplification as well—a process that many argue is long overdue. The issue of back taxes would need to be accommodated on a special handling basis. This example demonstrates how changing the business model underlying a system (changing the graduated income tax code to a more simplified tax code) can facilitate a solution to the Year 2000 problem for an organization. It is ironic that government agencies are rife with situations where contingency options are required, but where political resistance is most likely to constrain the exploration of those options.

9.3.3 Business Unit Shutdown Options

Occasionally, it may be more judicious to shut down a business unit or to stop offering a given product or service to compensate for an inability to correct the problem or to fund an expensive fix. An example from a diversified financial institution helps illustrate this point. This company performed a Year 2000 assessment and found that they could not justify the cost of upgrading their Assembler applications at a leasing division based on the marginal profits produced by that division. Because leasing was not a strategic business for this company, they opted to sell the division to another company. They profited from the sale and avoided the multimillion dollar expense of a system upgrade. The acquiring company, which was essentially looking to incorporate the customer base into their existing leasing business, prospered as well. While management had planned to sell off the leasing division anyway, the Year 2000 strategy expedited the sale.

9.3.4 Business Function Consolidation Options

Another special case situation focuses on the "crash" consolidation of IT and functional areas. A major insurance provider, through a series of acquisitions, amassed a portfolio of more than 120 million lines of source code—three times the size of their original portfolio. Under management's ten-year strategy, consolidation plans revolved around the phased integration of business functions and system architectures. Realizing that they could not make every system Year 2000 compliant during the interim period based on capacity constraints, drove management to opt for a more aggressive plan. This new plan meant eliminating redundant systems wherever possible over a one to two year period.

In one case, the Commercial Lines Division targeted two of their three claims systems for elimination after migrating customers to the remaining system. This action eliminated 18 million lines of code, which resulted in the company's saving $20 million in Year 2000 upgrade costs. The real benefit, however, was in being able to meet critical remediation deadlines that otherwise would have been missed. This approach, as with many other contingency options, has its risks. In the consolidation option some customers will experience service problems while IT enhances the remaining system to support those customers. The alternative, however, is to allow these systems to fail in production with little or no time for IT personnel to react.

9.3.5 Triage: The De Facto Contingency Plan

The value of pursuing a Year 2000 triage concept, where systems or third parties are shut down or left to fail, is based on reducing the overall level of effort while leaving important business functions intact. Unfortunately, triage is one of the most overused and misunderstood concepts in the Year 2000 field. Some people believe that triage is the only contingency option available. It is true that the concept of letting systems fail or shutting them down completely is likely to be an increasingly applied option as time runs out. However, the wealth of contingency strategies discussed thus far provide far greater benefit to an organization than does the stand-alone concept of triage—which is akin to giving up entirely on selected systems, third parties, and related business functions.

We strongly encourage management not to view contingency planning in such black and white terms. For mission-critical functions, triage is a low-ranking contingency option. In other situations, triage can be combined with many of the other contingency strategies presented thus far. Finally, triage should be viewed as a first choice only in situations where a system, and the functions supported by that system, are obsolete or being discontinued anyway. In the following sections, we have outlined different scenarios where triage may be applied as a stand-alone option or in conjunction with other contingency alternatives.

9.3.5.1 Planned Triage For Low-Impact Systems

Low-impact systems and subsystems may be intentionally shut down if they no longer provide business value. For example, an insurance company that found 97 percent of the reports produced by a reporting system were not utilized by anyone. Management found that they could triage virtually the entire subsystem. Other examples like this abound in IT organizations. Many of the systems now in production are not used by end-users. Finding this out during the initial inventory stage of a project and scheduling these systems for deactivation is the ultimate example of proactive contingency management. We highly recommend that this "low hanging fruit" be plucked early in a Year 2000 project.

9.3.5.2 Temporary Triage

Some systems have a very short window where Year 2000 problems can actually occur. It is possible to not fix a system and either shut it down or let it run in a broken state for a period of time. Take, for example, an inventory system that tracks stock levels over a two-week window. This particular system will begin failing on January 1, 2000. In response, business managers arrange to stock enough inventory to support production for a three-week period while system outputs are ignored. This situation is an example of temporary triage. The system could also be shut down for the two-week window.

This example, taken from a real-life situation, required extensive work to reconcile manually collected information and address impacts to billing and other key systems. This plan is not a simple solution but is an option that has a number of cost- and risk-related benefits over launching a remediation project for the system. As with any other Year 2000 plan, testing the impacts of this option is a critical task. Temporary triage is a realistic alternative in these types of situations.

9.3.5.3 Integrating Triage into Other Contingency Strategies

Triage can be combined with other contingency plans if a business model can be adjusted to eliminate the need for a system, or if a system can be eliminated in favor of existing systems that already perform the same functions. In either case, business executives must embrace this concept because end-users typically must commit to compensate for the elimination of a system. The functional consolidation example, discussed in Section 9.3.4, requires triaging a system, but saving the data and maintaining the business unit that used that system. This process shifts at least some of the effort to end-users who are required to learn how to use another system.

Another example involves triaging systems that support a discontinued business unit. Section 9.3.3 discussed selling a division and shutting down the systems that supported that business unit. This scenario presents a clean solution for IT because the functions that the system supported disappear entirely. The earlier consolidation example required some degree of effort by IT to incorporate functional support into one system while triaging a redundant system. These are only two examples of how IT can triage systems in support of a broader contingency plan. Analysts should look for other such opportunities during contingency planning.

9.3.5.4 Planned Triage of External Entities

The triage concept also applies to external entities and data interfaces if the business can demonstrate that they can function without these external entities. Consolidation and triage of suppliers was a major undertaking for the U.S. automotive industry over the last several years. Other industries may soon discover the benefits of working with a consolidated subset of suppliers, business partners, and providers and receivers of external data. This type of triage is primarily driven by business analysts with input from IT. The biggest constraint to completing this type of triage is that the business analysts that must make these decisions are not fully engaged in pursuing Year 2000 solutions at this time. This lack of involvement is a dangerous situation and will fuel problems when third-party failures begin to emerge late in this century.

9.3.5.5 Unplanned Triage: A Worst Case Scenario

Surprises are not a welcome prospect in a Year 2000 project. System failures must be anticipated or assumed. In the first case, bugs may arise in compliant systems because some level of errors have slipped through the remediation and testing process. A contingency plan would, in these cases, dictate the planned level of response and how end-users can cope during the interim.

In the second case, where problems are assumed to exist because the system was purposely not fixed, a triage strategy states that when the system fails, you will either shut it off or work with problematic results for a period of time. Business professionals can even plan to handle problematic results from a manual perspective. If you have no idea what status your systems are in, however, a key system could fail and management may be caught completely off guard with no plan as to how to respond. The impact of a system that supports mission-critical business functions could severely cripple a business—or a third-party business partner or supplier. Management must, therefore, have backup plans, even if they involve triaging a system or third party, to ride out the problem.

Encountering unplanned problems is much more likely to occur in two areas that fall outside the direct control of the IT department. End-user systems, particularly spreadsheet applications, are likely to have a string of errors associated with them because little attention was paid to their compliance status during the Year 2000 project. Rebuilding these systems may be the only option—which means they will be thrown out during the interim period. The second and more problematic category where unplanned triage is likely to occur involves embedded systems. Again, the reason for this is that the research into the compliance status of these systems is time consuming, requires special skills that are difficult to find, and has started way too late in many cases to be completed on time.

If core IT systems begin to encounter unplanned triage scenarios, financial and legal costs will begin to skyrocket. Meta Group, in a 1997 survey, stated that 40 percent of users will be forced to triage mission-critical systems. If this percentage is true, and we believe there is a significant chance of core system triage based on the lack of progress in various market sectors, the economic impact on these companies will affect earnings and, possibly, their viability. The bottom line is that the higher the degree of unplanned triage you experience, the more likely you will encounter failures that make it difficult for you to compete or even stay in business.

9.4 Contingency Planning by Industry

Year 2000 contingency requirements and options differ based on the internal and external business requirements of a given industry. There are, of course, common requirements which are shared across industries. Manufacturing, health care, and retail, for example, all depend on suppliers—although retail and health care supply chains are much flatter than multitiered manufacturing supply chains. The real similarities exist within certain vertical markets. Industry executives should collectively consider that, at least for now, cooperation could benefit an industry as a whole to a much greater degree than competition. The auto industry's supply chain analysis, which is being coordinated by the AIAG, is one example of this type of cooperation. Similar consortia have been formed in the health care, securities, and other industries.

To this end, we thought that it would be helpful to outline some contingency strategies for a number of different industries. The approach that we used to outline industry-specific contingency options was to list three to four Year 2000-related issues for a given vertical market. Beneath each topic, we have listed a number of ideas that could be used as input to building a contingency plan for each of these areas. Hopefully, these ideas can help business and IT analysts structure their thoughts around contingency planning for their organization—and for their industry. Note that some of these contingency options require a multiyear advance planning window to structure external agreements.

9.4.1 Financial Institutions

Our discussion of financial institutions includes banks, credit card companies, securities processing firms, clearing houses, brokerage houses, and other organizations that handle or manage large amounts of monetary instruments as their main line of business.

1. *Data interchange interruptions or errors*

    - work jointly with creators of data to correct the problem

    - switch to alternate source of data from a backup data supplier

    - attempt to correct data errors once information has been received

    - for low-impact systems, freeze processing of this data until problem is resolved

    - work with industry association to freeze trading of financial instruments for a period of time until problem is resolved (when no alternatives exist)

2. *Credit card processing failure in banking system*

    - if volume is low, work around the failure manually until system is corrected

    - determine if card supplier or another source could provide a backup processing system

    - discontinue acceptance of this type of card

    - work with credit card company to assess other alternatives

3. *Trading system failure*

  - determine if a second trading system (under your direct control) could be modified to accept these trades

  - for low-impact or nonstrategic monetary instruments, halt trading until situation is resolved

  - work with a third party to have them process trades as a service to you

4. *Clearing house processing failure*

  - work with clearing house to correct problem

  - switch to alternate clearing house if possible

  - work with SEC to determine if alternate clearing house can be used or established

9.4.2 Insurance Companies

Insurance companies, particularly in the area of electronic data interchange and claims processing, must establish contingency plans so profitable business units will remain viable beyond 2000. Insurance companies must take care not to alienate their customer base during this critical transition window.

1. *EDI data interruption halts claims processing*

  - deploy backup data interchange plan that utilizes more traditional communication exchange

  - launch Internet data exchange system

  - process claims manually until source of problem is corrected

  - work with company (depends on size and strategic position) to resolve problem

2. *Claims processing system fails*

  - process claims manually while system is corrected

  - switch processing to alternate claims processing system (determined in advance)

  - if low-margin or nonprofitable business unit, discontinue service

3. *Broker system failure*

- insurance company may discontinue use of that broker

- insurance technical support could help fix or replace broker system

- insurance company may recommend that broker obtain a system from another broker for a price

9.4.3 Health Care Providers

Thousands of hospitals rely on data interchange with insurance companies and other providers, computer-controlled monitoring, diagnostic and other types of equipment, numerous application packages, and a wealth of computer technologies. These organizations will experience problems and must put plans in place to overcome them.

1. *Failure in diagnostic equipment embedded technology*

- utilize alternative diagnostic techniques until problem is corrected

- immediately replace most critical products

- send patients to another hospital during interim period

2. *Failure in heart defibrillator*

- refer heart patients to another hospital until situation is fixed

- order new product from manufacturer

- use alternative equipment or techniques until the product is replaced

3. *Data interchange/EDI failure*

- perform data exchange with providers, doctors, and insurance companies manually until problem is corrected

- seek help from partners, insurance providers, or other sources to correct problem

4. *Major patient, billing and processing system failure*

- admit, bill, and process patients manually until system is fixed (this only works for a limited time frame)

- buy or lease an alternative system as soon as possible (requires retraining personnel)

- sell your hospital (this should be established prior to Year 2000) to another hospital that has corrected the problem—typically when profit margins prevent remediation

9.4.4 Manufacturing and Retail Industries

Manufacturing and retail are presented jointly here because of the interdependencies between these two industries. Without product to sell, retailers will go out of business. Conversely, if a manufacturer has no retail outlets in which to sell their products, they will eventually go out of business.

1. *Programmable logic controller fails, shutting down production line*

   - attempt to replace embedded technology as soon as possible (hopefully with a component that was already procured based on contingency plans)

   - ship product that may have been backlogged as a contingency plan

   - determine if an alternate product can be shipped to fulfill customer requirements

   - if possible, determine if manual processes can supplement automated production

   - determine if you can buy product elsewhere and pass it on to customers at a loss until problem is resolved

2. *Inventory control system miscalculates stock levels*

   - inventory levels should be stocked to allow a three- to four-week window, if possible, while system is being repaired

   - begin fixing system immediately

   - determine if business analysts can manage inventory levels manually for a period of time

3. *Manufacturing supply chain shuts down—you cannot obtain parts*

   - contact backup supplier identified during contingency planning process

   - work with intermediate suppliers between your company and the company that failed to come up with alternate product solutions

- buy the company that failed and move the production process in-house

- continue making products with backlogged supplies as long as you can

4. *Retail supplier shuts down*

- for strategic supplier, put a team on-site to help correct the problem

- for medium-impact supplier, consider replacing supplier with new supplier

- for low-impact supplier, consider dropping product offering

9.4.5 Service Industries

There are numerous service companies, including transportation, legal services, accounting firms, restaurants, and others, that could be impacted by the Year 2000. Some contingency issues are discussed below.

1. *Systems failure shuts down law firm*

- work around the problems manually, ideally with a paper trail that was created as a contingency strategy

- try to fix system with systems supplier

- see if a replacement system can be installed

2. *Reservations system fails at an airline*

- keep planes flying and issue guidelines to on-line reservations clerks

- tell people to come to the airport and they will be handled on a first-come/first-served basis

- continue to try to fix the system as quickly as possible

- issue customer bonuses and other perks so they will work with you during the crisis

- determine if you can lease reservation system time from another airline

3. *Restaurant point of sale system fails*

   - issue guidelines on how to handle the problem (should be issued prior to failure date as part of contingency plan)

   - work with system provider or in-house teams to correct and redeploy the system

   - have replacement system identified and ready to deploy immediately

4. *Older PCs at a radio station fail, shutting down broadcast capability*

   - triage the old system

   - replace with new system—if the budget is available

   - sell the station if the money is unavailable

9.4.6 Utilities and Telecommunications

Utility and telecommunications companies have several things in common that caused us to group them together under contingency analysis. Both are highly regulated, use a high degree of embedded technologies, and impact millions of consumers on a regular basis.

1. *Power company's power grid computer shuts off power to millions of people*

   - put a full-time team on the problem immediately

   - establish a hot line for customers communicating exactly what is happening and how they should respond

   - establish a Web site for customers (for access by people with battery-powered PCs) to find out what is happening

   - attempt to procure backup power, if applicable, from alternate sources

   - work with industry groups to correct problem more quickly

   - get to various news outlets to communicate what is happening and when it will be fixed

2. *Nuclear power plant control system will not be compliant in time*

   - create backup power sources in advance—just in case there are problems

   - build reinforcements around the plant, including under it, as a failsafe strategy

3. *Telecommunication data interchange fails and fouls up millions of billing records*

   - open a hot line and Web site to communicate what happened

   - put a team on the problem to fix it as soon as possible

   - offer discounted service for a certain period after the problem is fixed

4. *Embedded communication equipment fails*

   - put team on problem immediately

   - look for backup communication lines that could be leased from another provider

   - if problem goes on for a long time, consider selling business unit to a competitor

9.4.7 Government Strategies

Government agencies have both advantages and disadvantages when dealing with Year 2000 contingencies. Procurement, regulations, and bureaucracy all slow matters down, but then again, if you are the U.S. federal government, you can always rewrite the rules.

1. *Revenue collection and tax system fails*

   - convert graduated tax code to a flat tax or national sales tax if current system cannot be corrected in time

   - create public relations campaign to make sure the public understands the process

2. *Entitlements disbursement system crashes, checks cannot be issued*

   - fix the system if you can

   - rig system to write checks manually with equal amounts (probably resulting in overpayments) going out to all parties to avoid underpayment

   - pass a law to overhaul the system so that a new, simplified disbursements system can be implemented

   - create a hot line to communicate issues to general public

3. *Weather monitoring equipment fails*

   - attempt to fix the system as quickly as possible

   - triage outdated equipment and replace it with new equipment

4. *Real-time weapon systems fail during a post-2000 test*

   - communicate this information on a need-to-know basis only (which includes allies that are using the same equipment)

   - triage older systems in favor of newer replacement systems (could be a big money saver)

   - eliminate the system/weapons completely if defense hierarchy deems this acceptable

9.4.8 Small Company Contingency Planning

Contingency options for small companies differ in terms of awareness, available budget, and the ability to complete system and business rule modifications. Most small to mid-size companies have yet to launch a full-scale Year 2000 initiative. When they do, they are likely to be able to deliver system modifications more quickly due to their smaller size. They can also more readily modify core business rules to meet the challenge. Contingency plans may involve more radical options than a large corporation. Contingency strategies could include the following options.

1. *Replacing the entire set of application systems in favor of deploying a compliant replacement package.*

2. *Replacing all hardware and software to achieve full compliance.*

3. *Retraining end-users to accommodate radical replacement initiatives.*

4. *For manufacturing companies, shifting product development strategies to accommodate new production line technologies.*

5. *Merging with a company in the same industry that has already addressed the Year 2000 problem.*

6. *Being acquired by a company and merging operations into that company.*

Numerous factors, the most important of which is timing, come into play when planning for Year 2000 contingencies. If you are a small company and are totally unprepared for the Year 2000, you may want to start looking for suitors sooner versus later. The field of suitors may get crowded beginning in 1999 and it could become a real "buyer's" market.

9.5 Contingency Plan Invocation

Contingency planning is proactive and not reactive in nature. This characteristic means that business executives must invoke a contingency plan with enough lead time to maintain normal business operations. This option is not always possible, but a good contingency plan avoids major interruptions in mission-critical cases. A worst case contingency scenario involves a situation where a system fails, a business function crashes, and business analysts scramble to work around the problem. Invocation timing dictates the success or failure of a contingency plan. This section discusses a number of contingency invocation-related issues.

9.5.1 Time Criticality Defines Success

Contingency plans will be invoked at an increasing rate beginning now and continuing throughout the Year 2000. The invocation of contingency plans will also continue well beyond 2000. Many date problems will occur at each quarter end during 2000, around leap day, at fiscal year end, and at calendar year end. Contingency monitoring must, therefore, begin immediately and continue for at least one year beyond January 1, 2000.

Senior executives must, therefore, keep their attention focused on the Year 2000 problem for a window that leads up to and surpasses the actual century rollover. This effort may be difficult given the wealth of other issues on their agenda and the fact that many believe that the Year 2000 problem is isolated to a brief period near the end of December 1999. Committees and bureaucratic hierarchies are often unable, due to their size, to invoke plans in a timely manner. This problem is more likely to arise in government agencies and large corporations but must be neutralized.

9.5.2 Replacement Project Invocation

The Project Office must closely monitor replacement projects to ensure that contingency plans are invoked in a timely manner. Figure 9.4 depicts key checkpoints in the life of a Year 2000 project. The first checkpoint comes when the impact analysis determines a system-, interface-, or partner-related failure date. Let us assume, for argument's sake, that this checkpoint falls in the early part of 1999. Now assume that management has launched a credit card processing system replacement project that has a completion date that comes very close to overlapping with the projected Year 2000 failure date. The Project Office should, at this point, raise a yellow flag for that business area and closely monitor progress on that conversion project.

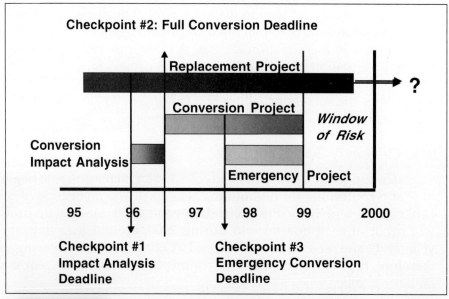

Figure 9.4 Contingency timing requires monitoring checkpoints after impact analysis and beyond points where a full or emergency conversion is still doable.

The next checkpoint, where management must decide if a Year 2000 conversion project should be launched, is determined by the event horizon defined between a required remediation project start date and the system failure date. If management decides to let this date pass without taking action, the available solution options begin to shrink. The third checkpoint comes when an emergency fix can still be applied to the existing system to keep it functioning beyond its failure date. In this example, a patch to the credit card system requires that maintenance teams hard code a "99" into the year field of the expiration date for each card issued. This action will keep the system working until the end of 1999 and allow the replacement project enough time to deliver a new, compliant system into production.

Other checkpoints can be established beyond checkpoint 3 if necessary. For example, if the replacement project is not going to be finished by the end of 1999, a windowing solution may be applied to the system during 1999 to keep it working until the replacement system is completed. Other contingency options may also be invoked during this time frame.

For example, the credit card company may decide to outsource credit processing to another financial institution until the new system is installed. This example is highly unlikely, but in other industries this option should not be dismissed too quickly.

9.5.3 Invocation Based on Package-Provider Problems

Checkpoints are particularly critical for packages where companies find themselves waiting for an upgrade that arrives too late to stop the current system from failing. The first checkpoint, in this case, is when you first suspect that something is seriously amiss with the information the vendor is providing. Management must learn how to read between the lines of vendor promises and raise the red flag early. With packages, lead times are critical. The second checkpoint is when a vendor miss its first delivery date and also the point where contingency teams must spring into action. Correcting the code yourself, replacing the package, shutting down the business unit, and other plans should be invoked accordingly—and at the proper time.

9.5.4 Internal System Failure Identification and Invocation

In-house remediation projects, embedded system upgrades, hardware replacement, and other in-house projects must be monitored by the Project Office and the application/business unit that is responsible for those systems. A pre-2000 failure date may arrive prior to the completion of a remediation project and require that a system be patched to keep it from breaking. Major crashes should be avoided if the degree of failure can be minimized. This avoidance is due to the domino effect that could occur when internal systems fail. Again, each case differs and requires common sense on the part of management.

9.5.5 External Problem Identification and Invocation

Knowing when to invoke contingency plans that involve external entities is an even more complicated process than targeting internal invocation dates. Supply chains are probably the most difficult area, where monitoring a fourth-tier supplier is difficult without total cooperation from the first-, second- and third-tier suppliers in the chain. Working closely with suppliers should help with this process.

Business partners, particularly if the relationship is a close one, should be easier to monitor and assess if a problem is going to occur. In either case, finding backup partners, working through industry associations, changing your business model and a wealth of other options require that management track progress at these external entities closely.

9.5.6 Pre-2000 and Post-2000 Contingency Invocation

Pre-2000 problems, as we alluded to earlier, may be treated differently than post-2000 problems. This difference is because there will be more resources focused on fixes prior to 2000 and more correction options, including selectively patching just the portion of the code that looks past 2000, available. While post-2000 patches are possible, the ripple effect is much less predictable. Expect contingency plan invocation prior to the end of the century to be handled more judiciously than post-2000 invocation. This difference is due to how focused people are on the problem.

After 2000 any number of different types of failures can occur. The most common problem involves finding post-1999 bugs in remediated systems. IT and business analysts must invoke contingency plans quickly to prioritize and correct bugs, while end-users keep operational functions working. Major crashes in key systems may involve more radical action—such as selling a division or business unit. Several companies are rumored to be stockpiling cash to buy failed companies. If you are one of these companies, you are likely to get a great deal after the Year 2000.

9.5.7 Who Makes Contingency Decisions?

In numerous situations, the contingency action required to avert an information systems disaster and keep business operations running smoothly must be driven by business executives and not by the IT department. In other words, contingency planning in high-impact scenarios shifts the decision for handling the Year 2000 problem from the IT department to business executives. There are numerous reasons for this shift. First, business personnel have more at stake than do IT personnel. A second reason is that business management has more knowledge of the overall situation and, therefore, have more options open to them. Finally, business executives have both the authority and the motivation to step in and take radical action to keep business operations functioning in the face of a systems failure.

9.6 Shift toward Contingency Management

Contingency planning and invocation is not a Year 2000-specific solution. Rather, IT and business management should consider that contingency-based management practices transcend the Year 2000 problem.

9.6.1 *Contingency Management Is Continuous*

Contingency management means that every project plan has a backup or alternative option that can be invoked when a project is late or not delivered at all. One would think that this would be a standard practice for an industry where projects are late, not delivered at all, or delivered with less functionality than originally intended more than 90 percent of the time. Every replacement and package implementation project requires a contingency plan. Management, however, cannot seem to accept that things will not go as planned.

9.6.2 *Contingency Options at an Industry Level*

Some industries should jointly develop contingency plans. The securities industry, for example, shares so much data that a failure at one company could ripple through hundreds of firms. Dependencies are also significant in the automotive oligopoly, the health care field, the utility industry, and the telecommunications market. Interdependencies are so complex in many of these areas, and the consequences so severe, that industry associations, with any help that may be provided by government regulatory agencies, should focus on developing industrywide contingency plans.

9.6.3 *Contingency Options at a National Level*

At the national level, the federal government should encourage or require contingency plans for industries where safety is a major concern. The utility, power, atomic energy, health care, and telecommunications industries are already monitored and regulated by various government commissions or agencies. Year 2000 planning should be incorporated into the functions of these agencies because the structure is already in place to do so. There are also disaster planning commissions in place that could encompass the Year 2000 problem based on a little education and some support from those in higher office. National contingency planning in other countries should be a major priority since many of those countries have made little progress in resolving the Year 2000 problem.

9.7 Personal Contingency Planning

Planning for contingencies at the personal level is not that difficult to do and we felt obligated to mention this fact in closing out this chapter. Check the compliance status of your bank, insurance company, broker, and employer. Suspicious answers might give you enough evidence to switch to a new company. Keep bank accounts below the FDIC insurance coverage levels. Keep a paper trail of all monetary transactions beginning in 1999 and throughout 2000. Stay off airplanes around December 31, 1999, and shortly thereafter—including February 29, 2000.

Careful investing is one area that individuals should research. If you have stock in a fund or with a broker that is not compliant, switch over. Furthermore, investing in companies that have disclosed their compliance status is another good idea. Use common sense, keep good records and think through other contingency plans you may want to employ. You certainly would not want to take any chances personally that you would never take in your official capacity on the job.

Chapter 10

Managing the Transition: Surviving the Inevitable

The salvation of the world depends only on the individuals whose world it is. At least, every individual must act as if the whole future of the world, of humanity itself, depended on him. Anything less is a shifting of the responsibility and is itself a dehumanizing force, for anything less encourages the individual to look upon himself as a mere actor in a drama written by anonymous agents, as less than a whole person, and that is the beginning of passivity and aimlessness.

Computer Power and Human Reason by Joseph Weizenbaum

While the focus of this book deals with organizational preparation, versus that of the individual, we wanted to communicate the important role that the individual must play in the century transition process. One way to do this is to ensure that technology and business professionals continue to spread the message of how to best deal with the Year 2000 crisis as they go about their daily lives. This chapter addresses this concept in section 10.8 entitled "Think Globally—Act Locally." The main goal of this chapter is to examine how the world should prepare for the century transition, which includes examining Year

2000 problems reported to date, as well as discussing what we can expect over the next several years.

Looking at how key industries are likely to be impacted under various Year 2000 scenarios helps management prepare for problems that may arise during the transition window. We outline the potential ripple effect that projected problems in key industries will have on those industries, related investment strategies, and the overall economy. In terms of managing the transition window, we outline the development of a transition management team, transition strategies, internal and external planning requirements, and contingency plan invocation. We also outline how the Year 2000 problem could change how we view IT and how IT meets long-term goals. Finally, we discuss the role we can all play in helping communities, charities, schools, and society make it through this difficult time.

10.1 Defining the "Transition Window"

The transition window is the period of time where Year 2000 problems escalate, peak, and taper off. Due to the fact that problems are already occurring, as discussed in the next section, we have, as of late 1997, already entered this transition window. Figure 10.1 shows how Year 2000 failures and resulting problems will ramp up, peak, and ramp down over a period of many years. We have divided the activities that management must plan for and deal with during these time frames into three categories; the project management window, the crisis management window, and the cleanup management window.

Project management is where most organizations are right now: taking care of the planning and conversion work required to fend off Year 2000 problems. Crisis management begins right around New Year's Eve 1999 (earlier for a handful of companies) and runs until an organization once again achieves stability. The cleanup management window could extend for many years, but it runs through 2005 in our example. By the way, Figure 10.1 is in no way meant to imply that after 2005 the problem goes away. Many problems will crop up years from now that will in some way be related to the Year 2000. Legal issues, for example, will haunt companies for decades.

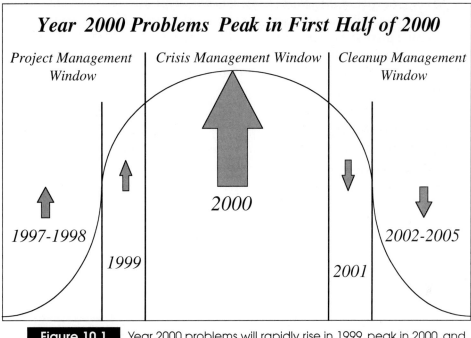

Figure 10.1 Year 2000 problems will rapidly rise in 1999, peak in 2000, and taper off in 2001–2005.

The process of preparing for and managing the crisis and cleanup windows is covered in subsequent sections of this chapter. For the record, nothing would please us more than to be proven wrong about our belief that the world has little chance of reaching 2000 without countless major and minor disruptions. Having said this, we plan to take readers through what we believe is a phased progression of how the problem will unfold, beginning now and carrying through 2005. We close off this section with a discussion of two areas that will definitely extend beyond 2005: insurance claims and legal liabilities.

10.1.1 Problems to Date

Year 2000 problems pop up every day around the world. We do not hear about them because most of them are internal to a company's systems and management strives to keep this kind of information contained. As more problems emerge, however, companies will have a hard time keeping many of these incidents quiet. We highlight a few Year 2000- or date-related problems that have already occurred below.

1. *In Orange County, North Carolina, animal control officers became alarmed when, despite their best efforts to vaccinate more animals to prevent rabies, computers showed a continually declining rate of vaccinated pets. The county's mainframe computer was recording newly vaccinated pets as having received shots in 1897 and, therefore, expired.[1]*

2. *A small fruit and vegetable market owner sued an Atlanta-based company because the cash register hardware and software could not handle post-1999 dates. The company filed a lawsuit in the state of Michigan against TEC America—maker of the equipment. A TEC spokesperson blamed the credit card company.[1]*

3. *At midnight on December 30, 1996, the Tiwai Point aluminum smelter in New Zealand malfunctioned. Each of the 660 process control computers hung up simultaneously as the date turned to December 31—the 366th day of 1996, a leap year. Most, but not all, computers had little problem with 1996 leap year processing. The Year 2000, which many programmers and engineers did not consider a leap year, will be another story.[1]*

4. *Market Day grocery store of Washington, D.C. sells specialty foods and accepts credit cards, unless your card has a "00" in the expiration date year field. Their system does not handle dates after 1999.[2]*

5. *In late 1997, a computer at a bank just outside of Chicago flagged a business loan that was to come due in 2003 as more than 90 years past due. The Year 2000 bug struck early in this case.[3]*

6. *In Kansas, a 104-year-old woman received a letter telling her to register for kindergarten.[4]*

7. *In Washington, D.C., a Pentagon supplier with a contract for delivery of goods in 2003 received a warning that it was 94 years behind schedule.[4]*

8. *Godiva Chocolatier's 150 North American retail stores cannot handle credit cards with a post-1999 date. Employees have been instructed to manually enter card information and put an expiration date of 12/99 in to "trick" the system into thinking that it is a valid card.[5]*

The credit card problem is "no big deal" according to VISA which estimates that 99 percent of the 14 million locations worldwide that accept its card can handle Year 2000 transactions without a problem.[2] That means that 140,000 locations cannot recognize post-1999 dates, a significant number of retail outlets. American Express has, for this reason, decided to continue issuing credit cards with a "99," as opposed to a "00" in the expiration date year field.[5] AT&T is also holding off on issuing cards with post-1999 expiration dates to its 13 million card holders.[5]

These isolated circumstances will increase over time and eventually flood the Internet, computer publications, and the mainstream press. As of late 1997/early 1998, however, published Year 2000 problems were still exceptions, not the rule.

10.1.2 Predictions: 1998

As more and more systems begin to encounter post-1999 dates, problems will appear at an increasing rate. Credit card rejections will become commonplace. Patient scheduling, licensing, and other systems that look one to two years into the future will begin to see problems. Sometimes they will be ignored, sometimes end-users will work around the problem, and sometimes the issue will receive heightened attention. Retail problems, or glitches, that directly reach the consumer will get the most coverage but not necessarily be the problems that have the biggest impact.

In the financial community, business professionals utilize millions of spreadsheets to recast mainframe-derived data, assess market impacts, reapportion funds, and perform countless other functions. Many of these professionals may be assuming that the data coming into or produced by these spreadsheets is correct. Analysts suspect that there are already date-related problems in many of these systems that are flying "below the radar screen" of IT professionals and internal auditors. If this is true, companies may already be writing off expensive Year 2000 problems as rounding errors.

Some predictions for 1998 include

1. *An increase in credit card rejections by more retailers;*

2. *Credit card companies, banks, and the National Retail Federation (NRF) debating "00" expiration date strategy;*

3. *Problems appearing in state and local government licensing systems;*

4. *Government systems sending out date-related notices to the wrong people;*

5. *Health care companies banding together to research embedded system problems in medical devices;*

6. *Telecommunications industry working jointly (influenced by government action) to establish information interchange formats;*

7. *Securities industry finding that street testing is even more complicated than anticipated, with concerns surrounding data interchange spilling into other industries;*

8. *Growing number of problems reported in forecasting, financial, and insurance claim systems;*

9. *Object code patching and other horrific shortcut solutions beginning to take hold within technical community;*

10. *Management beginning to pursue system and supplier triage options;*

11. *Federal government regulatory agencies stepping in to force disclosure of Year 2000 compliance status of publicly traded companies; and*

12. *Public at large remaining uninterested in the Year 2000 problem.*

In the past, when our predictions came true, they did so later than we had anticipated. Many of the above items will likely occur sooner or later. It is our hope that some of the more constructive items listed above happen before 1999—when things will begin to get really crazy.

10.1.3 Predictions: 1999

We believe that 1999 will be a year of anxiety within the IT community. People are already anxious based on the lack of solid Year 2000 status information. Previously cooperative efforts could be undermined by companies fighting for resources and survival. Predictions also include the resignation of numerous CIOs, or even directors, who do not want to own a Year 2000 disaster. In the latter half of 1999, companies will begin to execute pre-2000 contingency options. In addition, system and supplier triage will increase dramatically as the reality of what can and cannot be accomplished sets in.

Survival and transition strategies will emerge within the IT and business communities. Survival training, focusing on how business and IT professionals can handle large-scale failures, while maintaining business continuity, will become commonplace.

Predictions for 1999 include

1. *Reported Year 2000 problems beginning to escalate, including major problems that begin to impact company performance and investor strategies;*

2. *More and more of the IT and business community being pulled into the examination and correction of application and embedded systems;*

3. *Leading-edge companies beginning to focus on crisis management as they face 2000;*

4. *Federal government scrutinizing utilities and taking action to shut down power plants that cannot prove compliance;*

5. *Management demanding more detailed compliance information from suppliers;*

6. *Early claims stating that corporate Year 2000 projects are in great shape are found to be untrue—forcing the resignation of key executives and board members;*

7. *Federal government passing legislation forcing publicly traded companies to disclose compliance status;*

8. *More airlines joining KLM airline in claiming that they will not fly near the end of 1999 and the beginning of 2000;*

9. *Large manufacturers rethinking their supply chain and product strategies in light of evidence that breakdowns are inevitable;*

10. *Litigation problems beginning to emerge on a larger scale;*

11. *Mainstream press beginning to run daily millennium watch stories as problems mount; and*

12. *Local communities banding together to establish contingency plans.*

Whatever happens, people should not panic. Our projections are not meant to sound prophetic, they are merely extensions of everything that we see going on right now. However, things will get intense for IT personnel, budgets will be reallocated, systems will break, and the public, at least at some level, will be concerned.

10.1.4 January 1, 2000

Welcome to the crisis management stage of the Year 2000 project. Figure 10.2 shows how problems will hit in force in January 2000. The arrival of January 2000 will be like "death by a thousand small cuts" which could take months or years to correct, depending on the state of preparation of a given company. Another rash of problems will be triggered on February 29, 2000 (leap day) and December 31, 2000 (day 366 of a year that many systems think has only 365 days). The process of correcting these problems will need to be spread out over a much longer period of time, which could be a nightmare if a company has not made much headway when the second and third waves of problems strike. Supply chain-reliant industries will see a delayed impact, possibly peaking in the second and third quarters of 2000.

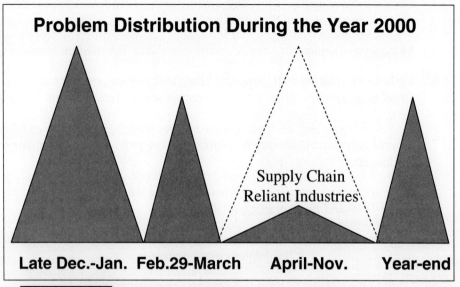

Problem Distribution During the Year 2000

Supply Chain
Reliant Industries

Late Dec.-Jan.   Feb.29-March   April-Nov.   Year-end

| Figure 10.2 | Immediate impacts will peak in January, late February, and at year end. Supply chain impacts will be drawn out over time. |

Why will January 2000 be so bad? According to Martyn Emery, who adapted the Hurricane model used to predict weather damage to the process of predicting regional Year 2000 damage,

> *even using the best approaches to software development, companies can expect 4 to 5 errors per 1000 lines of code. Files are triaged that should not be. Mistakes are made in remediation. Date-dependent logic or data is overlooked. And as time passes, code quality deteriorates. Employees come and go. Code may be shipped to unfamiliar hands off-shore for correction. Programmers enjoying the higher salaries and bonuses of Y2K projects start acting differently. The error rate per thousand lines of code doubles or triples.*

A critical systems failure may occur from time-to-time, but the more common situation will involve hundreds of inconveniences that pile up day after day. Some companies will go out of business, but most should weather the storm. We will see a dramatic increase in the need to audit the results of systems that handle financial results, revenue, regulatory reporting, and customer processing. Systems that were corrected for Year 2000 defects are likely to encounter production bugs that may not be caught until several cycles into the new year. IT personnel will be consumed for a long time fixing systems and upgrading others.

In the Year 2000, the situation is likely to evolve as follows:

1. *Programmers will keep busy for the bulk of the year fixing application system bugs;*

2. *Internal hot lines will be flooded with calls from end-users with system problems or questions;*

3. *Priority setting and decision making will be chaotic if not managed effectively;*

4. *Systems that IT had no idea even existed will fail and they will receive phone calls for help;*

5. *Mission-critical hardware, system software, and packages that were not upgraded will undergo replacement;*

6. *Embedded technologies will typically fail at one of three points—on January 1, on February 29, or on December 31, 2000 (day 366 of the leap year);*

7. *Government notices and threatening letters will be sent out to citizens on a regular basis;*

8. *Temporary personnel shortages will occur as temps are brought in to supplement or work around failed computer systems;*

9. *Hospitals that are totally unprepared for the Year 2000 and experience problems in medical devices may end up being acquired by larger, better prepared facilities;*

10. *Supply chain problems, which will likely begin hitting in the second quarter of 2000, will continue to wreak havoc for the remainder of the year;*

11. *Legal challenges and litigation will become a way of life for some vendor and many end-user companies; and*

12. *Certain companies will be sold at a real bargain when their systems fail.*

In reality, what will truly happen in the Year 2000 is difficult, if not impossible, to predict. There are too many interconnected factors to project just how hard a given industry will be hit. This situation is also true within government, the military, and on an international basis. Individual factors can be predicted with some degree of certainty and will help fill in some pieces of the puzzle over time.

10.1.5 Cleaning Up the Mess: 2001–2005

Companies that are well prepared for the Year 2000 will pass through the crisis window quickly, as long as their business partners, supply chain, and external support infrastructure remain stable. For these lucky companies, the cleanup window begins some time in 2000. For those companies that are less prepared, where a company is highly dependent on a complex supply chain or for many government agencies, the crisis period may drag beyond 2000. If this occurs in the private sector, a company could go out of business. In the public sector, citizens may just have to wait until things get fixed. For the survivors of 2000, the years between 2001 and 2005 will be cleanup time.

Between the years 2000 and 2005, IT personnel will be consumed with correcting half-baked solutions that corrupted systems en masse. Executives, frustrated with the inability of IT to deal with this problem, may turn to outsourcing as a long-term strategy. Outsourcing may contain costs and off-load the headache of systems management, but it will likely undermine efforts to leverage the power of information and information technology. On the other hand, executives who have the foresight to leverage results from the Year 2000 project into information asset transition strategies will be the real winners long term.

Beginning in early 2001, and running for several years depending on the company, companies should look at pursuing some of the following options:

1. *Removing object code patches and other quick-fix solutions or replacing those systems entirely;*

2. *Removing windowing solutions in favor of gradual migration to a four-character year field in select databases and systems;*

3. *Introducing replacement products for failed embedded system devices;*

4. *Keeping a project office in place to support customer, end-user, executive, and legal counsel questions;*

5. *Having internal audit seek out and resolve discrepancies in system processing results;*

6. *Outsourcing the entire IT environment based on senior management's dissatisfaction with the Year 2000 situation and the IT organization in general;*

7. *Increasing package acquisition and implementation activity depending on the degree that an organization wishes to adapt in-house business rules to those found in off-the-shelf packages;*

8. *Leveraging the analysis captured in the Year 2000 repository as a way of dramatically improving information asset management;*

9. *Increasing merger and acquisition activity that will ultimately result in heightened IT project activity for years to come; and*

10. *Continuing demand for technical resources needed to transition legacy systems into target architectures that more effectively support strategic business requirements.*

Management has several options that they can pursue during the post-2000 cleanup period. They can throw up their hands and outsource the IT environment, they can dig in and salvage valuable business assets utilizing systems redevelopment strategies, they can choose to utilize off-the-shelf application packages, or they can continue down the same path they are on now. The last option is obviously the least desirable.

10.1.6 Insurance Claims and Legal Action

Some executives have recently stated that they would rely on corporate insurance coverage to take care of outstanding Year 2000 problems or claims. According to insurance industry sources in the United States and the U.K., however, these companies should not count on collecting damage claims or getting reimbursed for the cost of fixing the problem any time soon. According to the Association of British Insurers, "insurance coverage is about covering the unexpected and not the inevitable. Millennium risks were never covered."[6] In the United States, insurance regulators in 25 states have approved wording for general liability policies that exclude any claim for losses related to the failure of computer systems to recognize dates during 2000 and beyond. According to David Oswald of the Insurance Services Office, "If anybody wants coverage for this, we think it is only proper that something extra be charged."[7]

A few insurance companies have put together packages for companies wishing to insure themselves from Year 2000 liability, but these packages come with stiff requirements. They typically require that the company undergo a comprehensive third-party audit before qualifying for the insurance policy. The premium for some policies may cost anywhere from 50 to 80 percent of the total value of the policy. If a company buys one of these policies, one could interpret this as already admitting failure. The one thing that many companies are truly afraid of is liability.

Because many IT, business, and legal professionals have determined that time is better spent addressing the Year 2000 problem than it would be sitting around a courtroom, most lawsuits have been postponed for now. This stance will definitely change as problems emerge that impact customers, market values drop and anger stockholders, vendors are challenged to provide no-cost Year 2000 upgrades, and constituents denied government services band together to take legal action. Chapter 3 outlined Year 2000 legal issues and strategies that can be applied to the entire transition window. As organizations move into the crisis management phase of their Year 2000 project, the following situations are likely to arise.

1. *IT and business professionals from corporations, vendor companies, and government will be called in to support the discovery and litigation process.*

2. *Extensive research into Year 2000 background at companies will disrupt crisis and cleanup management efforts for years to come.*

3. *There will be a growing demand for IT personnel to serve as expert witnesses in legal suits.*

4. *Backlog of lawsuits will clog the court systems and convince many parties to attempt to settle out of court.*

5. *Some vendors and certain corporations will end up paying major damages when all is said and done.*

6. *Litigation will drag on for many years after 2005.*

10.2 Looking Forward: Industry by Industry

Looking at certain key industries that are particularly vulnerable to the Year 2000 problem will help those who work with those industries deal more effectively with them. This discussion includes the financial, health care, manufacturing, utilities and telecommunications, transportation, and international markets.

10.2.1 Financial Industry

The financial industry will be directly impacted by Year 2000 project funding outlays and the cost of noncompliance. Other indirect impacts, including a downturn in certain market sectors, could ultimately hurt financial institutions' bottom line to an even greater degree than some of the direct impacts. Direct costs, to the financial industry for example, are significant. A survey by BT Alex. Brown, Inc. of 13 of the top 25 U.S. banks stated that, on average, banks are spending roughly $42 million in 1997 to correct the Year 2000 problem. This spending is likely to increase in 1998 and 1999 as full-scale deployment proceeds.

The cost of noncompliance is where many institutions will ultimately be hurt financially. For example, Chase Manhattan Corp. is
spending $250 million to examine 2,000 separate systems that process 2–4
million individual computer transactions. In addition, Chase's computers maintain 2,900 data links to third-party computers, many of which
could serve as an entry way for bad data to contaminate a corporate database. Problems stemming from an internal date error to a financial transaction or from data contamination could disrupt billions in transaction
dollars.[8] The cost of noncompliance typically outweighs the cost of fixing
one's systems.

One indirect impact that the financial industry may be unprepared
for can be attributed to those institutions that service high-risk Year 2000
market sectors like manufacturing, health care, or foreign markets. While
internal system compliance problems are likely to begin impacting banks
in the 1998–1999 time frame and peak in 2000, indirect impacts will ultimately hit a financial institution's bottom line in the mid- to latter part of
2000. This timeline means that the crisis window for the financial services
industry could begin in 1999 and run out past the end of 2000.

10.2.2 Health Care

Health care providers should have three major concerns: administrative systems which include scheduling and admitting, medical devices,
and Electronic Data Interchange (EDI) with insurance companies and doctors. Scheduling and admitting problems are likely to occur in late 1998
and continue into 2000. It is unlikely that any pre-2000 systems problem
would push a hospital into crisis mode. Medical devices are likely to have
problems in January 2000, around the end of February (leap day), and at
year-end 2000 (day 366 of the year). EDI problems will likely plague health
care providers for years if not handled properly. Based on these issues, a
health care provider would enter the crisis window at the end of 1999 and
could stay in a crisis state well into 2000 or beyond.

10.2.3 Manufacturing

Manufacturing sensitivity to embedded systems technology and to
supply chain problems puts this industry in a situation where problems
would peak at several points during 2000. Embedded technology, again, is
sensitive to the January 1, February 29, and December 31 dates discussed
earlier. In addition, Figure 10.2 shows that supply chain problems, which
tend to have a delayed impact due to the time it takes for inventory levels
to deplete, are likely to keep management busy well past January 2000. In

manufacturing, the crisis window is likely to begin on January 1, 2000, and run into 2001 if supply chain problems are not corrected quickly.

10.2.4 Utilities and Telecommunications

Utilities will experience problems over the early course of January 2000 if nonsafety-related computer technology fails and problems ripple across a plant site. As stated earlier, embedded technologies are vulnerable on January 1, February 29, and December 31. Of great concern is the failure of power plants or the fact that the government may order certain nuclear plants to go off-line during the winter of 1999/2000. If this situation occurs, the industry, and all those serviced by it, will truly be in a state of crisis. Plant problems could take months or years to correct. This situation occurred in the past when certain plants were taken off-line for an extended period of time after the Three Mile Island incident.

The telecommunications industry may experience data interchange, embedded system, and administrative (billing and collection) system problems that could stretch from early 2000 well into the following year. Again, embedded systems failures would hit hard and early. Data interchange problems may lag behind these failures for a few days or weeks — depending on how long it takes to realize that a problem exists. Billing and collection problems could take much longer to straighten out. The crisis window for this industry could last a few months, for those that are ready, or years, for those that are not.

10.2.5 Transportation

The foremost problem area in the transportation category is the Federal Aviation Administration (FAA). If KLM airline cancels flights in late 1999/early 2000, and other airlines follow suit, the crisis period for this industry will begin early and, possibly, end some time in January. That is the optimistic viewpoint. If FAA systems are truly as old and problematic as some people believe, or if on-board systems actually have compliance problems as KLM claims, the transportation industry may be in a state of crisis for years to come. If this happens, we can only hope that the railroads and automotive industry resolve their problems quickly so we can all still get around.

10.2.6 International Implications

According to the *New York Times*, only 5 percent of foreign banks are at least halfway finished correcting the Year 2000 problem.[8] Foreign banks, and U.S. banks that depend on foreign banks and foreign companies (who are also behind) are particularly vulnerable to the Year 2000. The impact of problems in foreign markets will be most readily felt by companies that have subsidiaries or do considerable business in those markets. The delayed impact could hit U.S. companies in the first quarter of 2000 but are more likely to stretch out over the year. The overall impact of foreign market problems is likely to hit the financial industry, and the economy in general, the hardest.

10.3 Investment and Economic Impacts

It is becoming apparent that the Year 2000 will have an impact on investment strategies in the short and long term. A second effect that is being discussed more and more is that the Year 2000 will have a negative impact on the economy in the United States and worldwide.

10.3.1 Investment Impacts

The impact of the Year 2000 on corporate spending will be greater in the 1998/2000 time frame than many people think. Future Year 2000 spending will increase in 1998/1999 because

- that is when most of the remediation and testing work will be completed;

- IT projects rarely come in on time or under budget and the Year 2000 is no exception; and

- few companies have budgeted for work to be done at the business unit level.

Further, most companies have not budgeted for crisis management during 2000 or the cleanup and litigation work required after that. In addition to these additional spending requirements, a vibrant 1996/1997 economy allowed companies to more readily absorb Year 2000 funding requirements into existing corporate budgets. Increased spending requirements, coupled with a potential downturn in the economy, means that a greater percentage of budgets will need to be applied to the Year 2000, which could depress corporate profits into 2000 and beyond.

These spending patterns could ultimately hurt corporate performance, which would in turn cause investors to sell stock. The real risks that companies and industries face, however, are from failures that become public and ultimately scare off investors and customers. Wary investors would be wise to watch the various crisis indicators listed in previous sections of this chapter to assess how a company, market sector, or entire industry is faring as time progresses. For example, the automotive sector of the manufacturing industry could see a domino effect of failures if one or two key suppliers (the auto industry has more than 50,000) fail. A secondary impact could find banks that service manufacturing-intensive regions experiencing revenue declines.

From an investment perspective, the IT industry has seen a rise in the stocks of Year 2000 tool vendors and solution providers, particularly those that offer testing tools and workstation-based remediation tools to support the mid-tier market. This group will likely see continued revenue growth in 1998. Solution providers, particularly firms having difficulty achieving projected 1998 hiring targets, could see a flattening of 1998 revenues. Hardware vendors and disk storage providers should see an increase in sales due to increased capacity requirements from 1998/1999 testing projects. Consultants and in-house technicians will need to be retained throughout the crisis management time frame, and likely well into the cleanup period.

10.3.2 Economic Impacts

Of concern in economic circles is whether the Year 2000 problem might trigger a recession in 2000. This question was put to economist Edward Yardeni, chief economist at Deutsche Morgan Grenfell. According to Yardeni, "we very well could have an OPEC-style recession. Just the way the OPEC energy crisis of 1973–1974 disrupted the global economy and produced a global recession, I think the Year 2000 problem has at least a 40 percent chance of doing the same thing."[9] As discussed in Chapter 1, Yardeni later increased his estimate of the odds of a recession to 60 percent.

What is behind this economic problem? The problems noted earlier in the various industries affected by this issue all contribute. A quick list of industry impacts is provided below.

1. *Major manufacturing market sectors, particularly automotive and aerospace, are extremely vulnerable to supply chain, embedded systems, and inventory system failures.*

2. *Financial sector manages an infinitely complex information supply chain that, should problems occur, could accidentally misappropriate millions or billions of dollars.*

3. The real estate market could experience hiccups from mortgage processing and property tax processing problems.[10]

4. The government collects and redistributes huge sums of money every day that greatly impact the economy—failure at a few key agencies could ripple through the private sector.

5. The health care market is comprised of thousands of hospitals with marginal profit margins that could falter should medical devices, EDI, or patient systems fail.

6. Major problems in the transportation industry, which is highly computer-dependent, could hurt numerous other industries (remember the UPS strike?).

7. The insurance market could get hit with numerous claims, as well as Year 2000 problems that could tie up companies in litigation for years.

8. Telecommunications and utility companies depend on technology. Should key technologies fail in these sectors, revenue streams could dry up.

9. International markets are already well behind schedule. European noncompliance, or problems in Asian markets, could also have a negative impact on worldwide economies.

Citing the potential economic impacts of the Year 2000 problem is aimed at alerting executives and government leaders to the overall and cross-industry problems so they can be prepared to address them during the Year 2000 transition window.

10.4 Building a Crisis Management Team

The Year 2000 Project Office must be able to support all three phases of the Year 2000 project including the project management window, the crisis management window, and the cleanup management window. As of today, most Project Offices are only set up to address the project management phase of the Year 2000. The critical task for these Project Office teams is to establish a crisis management team that can work through problems and make quick decisions when failures arise. The good news for most organizations is that they actually have time to establish this function and get it right.

A crisis management team is comprised of a small group of IT and business professionals, paired by business unit or area of responsibility, who can make decisions without the need for lengthy meetings or group consensus. Hundreds of decisions that could ultimately affect bottom-line profits must be made swiftly in order for operations to continue running smoothly. Most of these decisions will need to be made jointly by business unit managers and their application counterparts. Required specialty crisis management functions are shown below.

1. *Business unit coordinators*

   - Work with application unit coordinators to prioritize short-term corrections required for systems that have Year 2000 problems.

   - Brief business end-users in their area on how crisis management is to be coordinated.

   - Ultimately make the call, with input from superiors, on critical decisions.

2. *Application unit coordinators*

   - Work with business unit coordinators to prioritize short-term corrections required for systems that have Year 2000 problems.

   - Ensure that application area resources are available to correct problems on short-term notice.

   - Provide input to contingency plan invocation—particularly where a system is to be triaged in favor of an alternative decision.

3. *Hot-line interface coordinators*

   - Train standard hot line teams to support incoming Year 2000 problems.

   - Provide second-level support to hot line questions and serve as liaison to business unit and application coordinators (depending on current organizational infrastructure).

4. *Mainframe systems software and hardware coordinators*

   - Interface with vendor and operations for any problems reported in mainframe system software or hardware.

   - Work with application and business unit coordinators to ensure that system software and hardware repairs are prioritized by business criticality.

5. *Network, distributed systems software and hardware coordinators*

   - Interface with vendor and operations for any problems reported in network environment.

   - Work with application and business unit coordinators to ensure that network repairs are prioritized by business criticality.

6. *Supplier compliance managers*

   - Function as first point of contact for all reported supplier problems.

   - Work with business unit coordinators to ensure that supplier-related decisions (triage, replace, help) are prioritized by business criticality.

7. *Interface compliance managers*

   - Manage SWAT team support function to review errant data or other compliance problems detected by application or business units.

   - Work with applications and business unit coordinators to ensure that problem interface-related problems are corrected based on business criticality.

   - Provide input to invocation of contingency plans.

8. *Embedded technology compliance managers*

   - Coordinate any problems that may arise with security, elevator, or other computerized facility functions.

   - Provide input to invocation of contingency plans.

9. *Facilities compliance managers*

   - Function as first point of contact for problems that may arise with security, elevator, or other computerized facility functions.

   - Work with vendors to get problems fixed immediately.

10. *Communications managers*

    - Function as first point of contact for external queries regarding Year 2000 problem.

- Work closely with project office, communications department, and senior executives to craft stockholder, customer, and media statements regarding Year 2000.

- Manage damage control process.

11. *Third-party support coordinators*

- Handle all consultant/contractor coordination for project.

- Ensure that additional staff is available as needed to fix application or other problems.

12. *Project office director*

- Coordinates all activities of crisis management team.

- Tracks triage, contingency, and other priority-based decisions in central database.

- Provides situation analysis to senior management, legal counsel, and internal audit on a regular basis.

- Assigns additional staff as required to manage crisis smoothly.

10.5 Year 2000 Crisis Management

Transition management, particularly during the critical crisis management time frame, requires rapid situation analysis and fast decisions by small teams empowered to make decisions at the business unit level. Major decisions, including invocation of triage and high-impact contingency options, may require one or more business units to make a quick consensus decision. When these situations arise, senior executives must get involved quickly to make a call. This section outlines crisis management requirements, internal and external planning considerations, crisis plan development, call-in center requirements, contingency and triage management, and the process of shifting business strategies in crisis mode.

10.5.1 Crisis Management Requirements

As the Year 2000 Project Office shifts its operational strategy from project management to crisis management during the century transition cycle, the following issues should be addressed.

1. *Within a given business unit and related application area, multiple problems will occur simultaneously. Analysts must determine which problems will be assigned which level of resolution priority quickly so that correction teams are not overwhelmed.*

2. *How will management deal with the consequences of an unanticipated failure including*

- Plant operations halted

- Environmental or safety system compromised

- Erroneous financial data sent to a customer, supplier, or government agency

3. *When is an application problem bad enough to pull it off-line?*

- If a screen displays erroneous results, should the database be considered at risk?

- How can one quickly determine the difference between a superficial problem or a more serious problem in data integrity?

- When should an external interface be shut down?

4. *How will remote problems be handled for distributed systems and end-users that are located at off-site facilities and subsidiaries?*

Because the operating environment of a given organization dictates which issues will arise and how they are to be resolved, organizations should utilize risk management and contingency plans as input to the crisis management planning process.

10.5.2 Internal Planning Considerations

Many problems will arise due to internal failures or unanticipated situations that occur within the domain of IT or in various business units. Planning teams must consider the following internal considerations.

1. *Incoming calls from a large number of end-users, all of which expect immediate responses, about problems with IT-supported applications.*

2. *System software and hardware failures, unexpected license expirations, and other unforeseen operational problems.*

3. *Network failures in the IT environment, across business units, and at remote sites.*

4. *Calls from non-IT sites that are experiencing system failures in applications that were never included in the inventory.*

5. *Routine calls to help end-users with desktop systems that were either not compliant or are interpreting dates differently than expected.*

6. *Embedded system problems at plants, in facility systems, at corporate and other remote sites.*

10.5.3 External Impact Considerations

It is important to be prepared to manage problems related to critical dependencies that are external to or exist outside of an organization. This includes suppliers of information, goods, services, and infrastructure-related requirements.

1. *Incoming calls from customers that are directly impacted by application system failures.*

2. *Calls from government regulators who discover irregularities in information that they have received.*

3. *Delays in receiving government-provided services.*

4. *Critical infrastructure failures at*

    - Electric power utility
    - Gas company (becomes problematic based on climate)
    - Telecommunication companies
    - Internet provider
    - Water problems

5. *Delays or problems related to service suppliers including*

    - Banking or financial services
    - Transportation providers
    - External accounting, payroll, or IT processing services
    - Maintenance and landscaping
    - Legal or advisory services

6. *Delays or cancellation of shipment from suppliers including*

    - Parts and raw materials
    - Products used in the course of doing business
    - Computer-based technologies

7. *Business partner failures in performing their agreed-upon role.*

8. *Major problems with the local or national economy.*

9. *Delays in obtaining employee health care services or insurance.*

10. *Local catastrophes (nuclear plant problems, etc.).*

10.5.4 The Crisis Management Plan

The Year 2000 Project Office must have an action plan for managing through the crisis window that includes the following items.

1. *Roles and responsibilities required to manage tasks during the crisis window as defined in section 10.4.*

2. *Recovery strategies for all likely failure scenarios, including*

   - application system problems, data integrity errors, and embedded system failures

   - external supplier-, business partner-, data interface-, and infrastructure-related failures

3. *Priority listing, by business unit, indicating which systems and subsystems are to be fixed in which order.*

4. *Management escalation procedures for problems unique to a business unit and for problems that are common across multiple business units.*

5. *Plan for dealing with external supplier, partner, and related infrastructure problems.*

6. *Interface, EDI, and firewall problem identification and correction strategy, including*

   - a plan for working with third parties that have had their data corrupted

   - a plan for working with third parties whose data your company corrupted

7. *Executive strategy for having top-level management or the board work with other industry leaders to deal with community-based problems (i.e., transportation, infrastructure).*

8. *Contingency plan triggering criteria including*

   - Defining who has the authority to pull the trigger on a contingency plan

   - Establishment of planned and unplanned (as defined in Chapter 9) triage criteria

9. *Communication strategy as defined by the communications coordinator, including*

   - Customer communication issues

   - Who tells what to whom

- What are the stockholders told and when
- When does the government need to be notified of regulatory issues
- When (and how) to notify a party when bad data has been sent to them or when their operations may be interrupted

10. *Legal strategy that includes*

- Building a detailed audit trail of every correction, prioritization, contingency, and triage decision made during the crisis window
- Document tracking and management
- Responding to legal problems or challenges that may arise
- Addressing externally driven problems via legal options
- Clear understanding of when the legal department should get involved

10.5.5 Crisis Call-In Center

The hot line or "crisis call-in center" should be established as a central point for receiving incoming problem reports related to Year 2000 failures. All categories of problems discussed to this point, including general Year 2000 inquiries, should be handled by this hot line. A large, highly distributed company may want to consider multiple call-in centers that have expertise in various business unit functions. The following topics should be managed by the call-in center, which must be established and operational during the latter half of 1999 and remain in force throughout the crisis management window.

1. *End-user, business analyst, and operations inquiries:*

- Able to talk through common problems and fixes for desktop environments
- Determine if an application problem is truly a problem and assess level of severity
- Put end-user in touch with business unit or application coordinator for their area
- Report all embedded technology problems to the embedded technology coordinator

2. *Train existing customer hot line staff to be prepared for potential Year 2000 issues:*

- Standard issue/response handling
- How to identify issues

- How to assist customers with inquiries
- How to escalate to the right sources when necessary

3. *Supplier problems:*

- Can assess level of problem
- Contact supplier coordinator

4. *Facility, equipment, or infrastructure problems:*

- Assess severity of problem
- Determine if facility or other coordinators should be notified
- Address common questions before escalating

5. *Legal issues:*

- Assess if an issue is truly a legal problem
- Escalate problem to the legal coordinator

6. *General issue handling:*

- Log all calls by time, date, type, and area impacted (including systems if applicable)
- Provide daily log reports to communications coordinator and project office/crisis management director
- Provide trend analysis in problem type reporting and feeds this back into customer hot line training process and management decision-making process

10.5.6 Contingency Planning and Triage Center

The "contingency planning and triage center" is the nerve center for monitoring and triggering contingency and triage strategies. This group is made up of high-level business unit executives, key IT executives, the embedded systems coordinator, facility coordinator, supplier coordinator, legal counsel, and other team representatives as required. Their responsibilities include

1. *Reviewing problem logs, and reports from the IT and business unit coordinators on a regular basis.*

2. *Making the final call on system, third-party, and interface triage.*

3. *Making the final call on contingency options that have a major or cross-functional business impact.*

4. *Deciding when to reallocate resources from one project to another.*

5. *Escalating problems to top-level executives, legal counsel, or other areas as needed.*

10.5.7 Shifting Business Strategies in Crisis Mode

The most difficult thing that an organization must face is being forced to shift business strategies to accommodate the Year 2000 problem. These issues will have to be managed on a case-by-case basis and cleared with the contingency/triage center and senior management. The types of strategies and decisions that a company may pursue are unique to the business in which they are engaged. Some examples of proactive strategies are listed below.

1. *A publisher may decide to publish the January edition of a magazine in December so that internal problems or a transportation problem do not hold up an issue.*

2. *A manufacturing company may want to stockpile inventory of key parts or other materials in December 1999 in anticipation of supplier or transportation problems.*

3. *Retailers, in response from customer calls, may supplement similar products at a discount if inventories run low.*

4. *Manufacturers may not want to launch any new offerings in early 2000 unless they are convinced they can meet the demand based on supplier compliance capabilities.*

5. *Service companies that anticipate requirements for additional staff to handle manual credit card entry or other problems may want to keep holiday staff on into New Year 2000.*

6. *Airlines may offer deals to entice people to take vacations before year end, given that they have advance knowledge of problems that might prevent travel around January 1, 2000.*

7. *Companies may want to move up financial closing dates into December 1999.*

8. *Securities firms and exchanges might schedule days off around early 2000 to repair any problems that turn up after the turn of the century.*

10.6 Cleanup Management Window

After the crisis subsides and various organizations regain stability, the Project Office must handle the aftermath of the problem. The crisis can be considered over when

1. *Internal system Year 2000 problem reporting is reduced to normal pre-2000 reporting levels;*

2. *Critically important suppliers are stabilized;*

3. *Key business partners are compliant and functioning normally;*

4. *Infrastructure-related problems have passed;*

5. *The embedded systems coordinator has given an all-clear on problems in this area;*

6. *Facilities are all operational;*

7. *Legal issues have been brought under some level of reasonable control;*

8. *All major financial, legal, or regulatory problems that could threaten corporate viability have passed; and*

9. *The need to invoke contingency and triage decisions has subsided.*

Once an organization has moved into the cleanup management phase of the transition window, many decisions that had been put on hold will need to be addressed. This transition management phase should continue to be coordinated through the Year 2000 Project Office because they will have established the central infrastructure needed to facilitated communications among business units, application teams, IT support teams, the legal area, internal audit, and the executive team. The following cleanup tasks apply.

1. *Verify that budget is available based on a requirement to fulfill any or all of the following tasks.*

2. *Redefine roles and responsibilities, including:*

   - Retain project tracking function to provide ongoing status of Year 2000 cleanup

   - Reduce or eliminate special function roles that are no longer required (after determining they are truly no longer required)

   - Add a cleanup coordinator (which should be an existing project office team member)

   - Add a legal support contact coordinator

3. *Identify which systems had shortcut and temporary fixes applied and review for removal as follows:*

   - Schedule removal of all object code patches, -28-year tricks and other nonstandard solutions that are impossible to maintain

   - Consider removing windowing solutions for any systems that are being migrated to a new platform, are considered strategic, or will be around for three or more years

   - Fully expand partial expansion solutions where analysts determine that data stores should be more consistently defined

   - Cleanup or repair data stores that may have been compromised during the crisis window

4. *Work with business unit management teams to:*

   - Implement high-priority change requests that had been delayed

   - Reestablish priorities for project work that can accommodate the cleanup effort

   - Undo any business-based contingency plans that were only temporary strategies

   - Reestablish relationships with suppliers or business partners as required

5. *Work with application teams to undo technical contingency plans including:*

   - Fixing and reinstalling systems that were temporarily triaged

   - Repairing and reactivating external data interfaces as required

   - Cleaning up data stores that may have been compromised during the crisis period

6. *Work with the audit team to continue checking the reliability of output results, spreadsheet data, and other system interfaces as long as required.*

7. *Build up the litigation support team as required.*

8. *Continue to fulfill any regulatory requirements that may have slipped.*

9. *Shut down operations of Year 2000-specific Project Office functions (note that the Project Office will change into a general-purpose project office—see next section):*

   - Tally final costs

   - File all materials and turn over to internal audit

The cleanup period could last for years. IT and related business functions are well advised to continue this process until all Year 2000 problems have been vanquished.

10.7 Year 2000 Will Change IT Landscape

It is becoming increasingly apparent that IT, as it currently exists, will change, by default or by necessity, after the Year 2000. In our last book, we discussed the kinds of things that companies can do to evolve systems over the short and long term. All of these recommendations still apply. There are, however, some organizational issues which need to be addressed first—which is where the general-purpose project office can help. In addition, companies must revisit backlog reduction, outsourcing issues, and strategic migration options.

10.7.1 Institutionalize the Project Office

While some executives may currently believe that they can eliminate the project office in January 2000, they will discover that it must be retained through the crisis window. There will be tremendous pressure, however, to shut down the project office as the crisis window subsides. If this is done, management will lose control of the central project monitoring and reporting vehicle that they spent so much time and effort to put into place. Not only will the cleanup management process suffer, but management will also lose the benefit of having a central project office in place long term to help track and improve the work being done in the information technology area.

The project office should be institutionalized to

1. *Manage resources at the enterprise level.*

2. *Track project progress and report on risks and weaknesses in all phases of project management.*

3. *Serve as general advisors to project teams in project management skills.*

4. *Ensure that tools are used to leverage the project management function.*[11]

10.7.2 IT Must Move On

What have we learned from the Year 2000 problem? First, in the future, management is unlikely to put up with poorly managed information assets. We must learn to track the whereabouts of our systems, interfaces, and files much more carefully than we have in the past. Second, we also have learned that legacy systems are valuable, extremely hard to replace, and will be around for a long time. Third, senior executives must position the IT organization more strategically and not tell CIOs that their number-one priority is cost cutting, as was done in the early 1990s. Finally, we need to value the skills in our computer professionals (beyond knowing JAVA), especially the business knowledge that they have acquired over the years. Other lessons include

1. *Shortcuts do not pay (this lesson will continue to haunt us for years due to shortcut solutions to the Year 2000 problem).*

2. *Organizations must formally manage all systems under an integrated strategy which includes:*

   - In-house application systems and application packages

   - Hardware, system software, and utilities

   - Desktop technologies

   - Embedded systems and related applications

   - End-user systems

   - Interfaces to third parties

3. *Fix problems discovered in mission-critical systems during the analysis, remediation, and testing process—or they will come back and haunt us.*

4. *Prevent future problems, which means:*

   - Putting standards and controls in place to prevent future occurrences

   - Utilizing tools and methodologies for maintenance projects

   - Finishing the process of stabilizing testing environments that was begun on the Year 2000 project

5. *Never let test environments get out of hand again—it can cost organizational stability.*

6. *As we move forward into the world of the Internet, intranet, and distributed systems, systems are even more likely to get out of control. Manage them carefully!*

A final note is that many computer professionals who still plan to be around after 2000 tend to be concerned about their career options. If you are a COBOL programmer take heart; the future is bright. There should be a fair amount of work for you in the years after 2000. Many of these mainframe systems have incredible staying power and somebody has to clean up the post-2000 mess. Companies will also require help deciphering what these systems do so that they can be maintained, migrated to new platforms, or systematically deactivated in favor of packages, which of course will take another five to ten years.

10.7.3 IT Outsourcing: Be Careful

One message worth reiterating to management is that your existing systems are valuable business assets that contain the business rules controlling daily operations. These assets should be managed and nurtured and not treated like disposable commodities. Before you make a decision to outsource all of your IT functions, including these mission-critical assets, please consider that you may well be putting the future of your organization in the hands of people who will not treat it as if it is their own. You cannot outsource your responsibillity for your IT assests.

10.8 Think Globally—Act Locally

Our final message focuses on personal responsibility and the Year 2000. Even though many of us find ourselves consumed with Year 2000 work, we must still try to take the time to seek out and help local communities achieve greater awareness in dealing with the Year 2000 issue. We have found this work to be rewarding, and are personally asking those of you who have developed business or technical skills in dealing with this issue to step up and donate time to your community, schools, or favorite charity. You may even volunteer time at local retail outlets or a friend's home-based business.

The more we look around, the more we see things that are likely to break. Here are some areas where your time is needed.

1. *Nonprofit organizations and charities may have things under control at the national level but could use help at the local level.*

2. *Schools, particularly small ones with limited budgets, can use help ensuring that their computers have been checked out for a valid BIOS and are running the latest software.*

3. *Help with community transition management. You can help local businesses by working with your chamber of commerce to get the word out about the Year 2000.*

4. *Local governments may be working on IT projects, but we have found that non-IT departments that also utilize computer technology tend to be unaware of the problem.*

5. *Speak at your local club, schools, or church about the problem and offer a hand where you can.*

6. *Calm people down. We will get through this as long as people know what to expect.*

Authors' Note

The current Western calendar was crafted by a monk named Dionysius Exiguus (Little Dennis) in the sixth century. Because Little Dennis omitted the year zero from the calendar, the twenty-first century actually begins on January 1, 2001.[12] Every so often, readers remind us that the next millennium does not begin on January 1, 2000—although this date is certainly ground zero for computer systems. The Year 2000 is actually the last year of this millennium—certainly no cause for special celebration. These facts are unlikely to motivate people to cancel their New Year's Eve reservations on December 31, 1999, but they may provide some consolation to those transition team members working the millennium watch when the clock strikes midnight on the last day of 1999. Good luck to all of us.

Endnotes

1. "The Computer Time Bomb," by Peter Lewis, *Seattle Times*, November 2, 1997.

2. "Year 2000 Preview," by Rajiv Chandrasekaran, *Washington Post*, January 2, 1998.

3. "Millennium Bug May Already Be At Work in Financial Institutions," by Knight-Ridder, *Lubbock Avalanche-Journal*, December 4, 1997.

4. "Millennium Bug Alarms Unilever," *Sunday Times* (*U.K.*), December 21, 1997.

5. "Year 2000 Glitch Hits Credit Card/Automated Approval Stymied," *Newsday*, January 3, 1998.

6. "No Millennium Insurance," CNNfn, November 13, 1997.

7. "Insurance: US Insurers Limit Their Losses," by Christopher Adams, *Financial Times*, December 22, 1997.

8. "Foreign Banks Are Behind in Repairing 2000 Bug," by Saul Hansell, *New York Times*, November 10, 1997.

9. "Apocalypse 2000," by Eneida Guzman, Investor.msn.com, November 13, 1997.

10. "Year 2000 Bug Could Create Real Estate Woes," by Bradley Inman, *San Jose Mercury News*, December 20, 1997.

11. "The Project Office Answer," by Lois Zells, *AD Trends*, April 1997.

12. "Myths of the Millennium," by Stephen Jay Gould, *USA Weekend*, September 19–21, 1997.

Vendor Lists

The vendor list presented in this appendix is offered as a service to the readers of this book. It lists examples of vendors offering the tools and services described throughout the book. It by no means represents all of the Year 2000 vendors on the market. Inclusion of a vendor does not imply endorsement by the authors, nor does exclusion imply any negative opinions of the authors. Although the authors are thoroughly familiar with many of the tools on the market, they have not personally evaluated each offering.

This vendor list is meant as a starting point for research. The authors highly recommend that readers perform their own market survey when selecting tools or services. The Year 2000 tool market is so volatile that any vendor or tool list such as this quickly becomes obsolete. Since starting this book, the authors have seen dozens of companies enter the market and several vendors be acquired by other companies. Further, changes in vendor technology, management, or strategy can dramatically affect the viability of that vendor's solutions against its competition.

The list is divided into four subsections: consulting firms, software tool vendors, conversion services, and information about the authors' firms.

A.1 Consulting Firms

The following list represents only a small percentage of the consulting firms offering Year 2000 services.

- **ACE Technologies, Inc.**

  Web Site: www.acetek.com

  Offshore services including code analysis, discovering and fixing interdependencies, and testing.

- **AnswerThink Consulting Group**

  Web Site: www.answerthink.com

  Approach includes strategic prioritization using key metrics, early test/compliance planning, and process control.

- **BDM International, Inc.** (under agreement with TRW, Inc.)

  Web Site: www.bdm.com

  Provides full life-cycle services including configuration management, quality assurance, and testing.

- **Bellcore**

  Web Site: www.bellcore.com

  Services include establishing conversion methodologies, assisting in creating Y2K project offices, managing enterprise project plans, and designing and implementing testing methodologies.

- **BRC Holdings, Inc.**

  Web Site: www.brcp.com

  Uses the Matridigm process to achieve automated documentation, renovation, and maintenance of legacy COBOL code.

- **CACI International Inc.**

  Web Site: www.caci.com

  Divides the existing system architecture into work units enabling Year 2000 upgrades to be done in parallel with regularly scheduled system maintenance.

- **Cap Gemini America**

  Web Site: www.capgemini.com

  Through its TransMillennium© services, CAP GEMINI offers end-to-end project and outsourcing services for century-date compliance projects. CAP Gemini supports its services with its own ISO 9001 certified methodology and a full set of proprietary tools.

- **CIBER Inc.**

  Web Site: www.ciber.com

  CIBER offers project consulting services for all phases of Year 2000 initiatives. CIBER delivers its services through a combination of on-site consulting and an off-site automated conversion facility. The conversion facility uses Peritus technology.

- **Cogni-Case Inc.**

  Web Site: www.cognicase.com

  Automated conversion tool set.

- **Comdisco Inc.**

  Web Site: www.comdisco.com

  Offers controlled testing environments.

- **Computer Horizons Corporation**

  Web Site: www.chccorp.com

  Computer Horizons offers project and outsourcing capabilities for all phases of a Year 2000 initiative. Computer Horizons uses its own proprietary toolkit and methodology to support its consulting services.

- **Computer Sciences Corporation (CSC)**

  Web Site: www.csc.com

  CSC offers project and outsourcing services covering enterprise assessments, migration, testing/validation, and acceptance deployment. CSC bases its practice on its own Year 2000 methodology and Peritus technology.

- **Computer Task Group**

  Web Site: www.ctg.com

  Identifies obsolete and missing code, identifies date fields, and performs testing; includes Year 2000 information repository and project management methodology.

- **Comsys Information Technology Services**

  Web Site: www.comsysinc.com

  On-site or off-site conversion and testing services.

- **Coopers & Lybrand LLP**

  Web Site: www.colybrand.com

  Quality assurance and impact analysis methodology combined with consulting services.

- **CTA Inc.**

  Web Site: www.cta.com

  Offers services for all phases of a Year 2000 project.

- **Data General**

  Web Site: www.dg.com

  Provides impact analysis; establishes implementation plans for converting and testing COBOL application programs and data files.

- **Digital Equipment Corp.**

  Web Site: www.digital.com/year2000

  Provides systems and application inventory, code analysis, implementation strategy, acceptance criteria, and implementation project plan.

- **DMR Consulting Group, Inc.**

  Web Site: www.dmr.com

  Offers program design and implementation, project management, enterprise assessment, impact analysis, and component conversion.

- **Dun & Bradstreet Satayam Software (DBSS)**

  Web Site: www.dnbcorp.com

  DBSS is a division of Dun & Bradstreet with headquarters in Madras, India and offices in the United States. DBSS offers impact analysis, migration planning, and upgrade implementation services using its own tools and U.S. and offshore resources.

- **Edge Information Group**

  Telephone: (914) 592-3145

  Offers services for all phases of a Year 2000 project.

- **EDS**

  Web Site: www.eds.com

  EDS offers Year 2000 services for large projects and outsourcing engagements.

- **HCL James Martin**

  Web Site: www.hcl-jmi.com

  HCL James Martin provides quality systems redevelopment and Year 2000 solutions. The company provides solutions to help clients leverage their investments in existing business-critical systems while preparing them to meet current and future information technology demands.

- **IBM Worldwide Consulting Services**

  Web Site: www.software.ibm.com/year2000

  Offers services for all phases of a Year 2000 project using its own methodology.

- **IBS Conversions, Inc.**

  Web Site: www.ibs.com

  Includes scanning tools/services and conversion and repair tools/services for COBOL, PL/I, RPG II, and RPG/400.

- **Information Management Resources (IMR)**

  Web Site: www.imr.com

  IMR is a U.S.-based company with dedicated offshore facilities that uses its own proprietary methodology and reengineering tool set to perform Year 2000 work.

- **Infosys Technologies Ltd.**

  Web Site: www.inf.com

  Offshore development and maintenance methodology based on analysis, change, and testing tools.

- **Keane, Inc.**

  Web Site: www.keane.com

  Keane is a large national services firm offering project and outsourcing Year 2000 services that include enterprise assessments, planning, application migration, and testing. Keane uses its own proprietary methodology and is partnered with VIASOFT, Inc.

- **KPMG Peat Marwick LLP**

  Web Site: www.kpmg.com

  Offers a full range of century-date compliance service offerings ranging from application migration to application replacement.

- **LGS Group Inc.**

  Web Site: www.lgs.ca

  Service offering covers analysis and planning, conversion, and validation/deployment.

- **Mastech Corporation**

  Web Site: www.mastech.com

  Software services firm with three offshore development facilities in India. Mastech offers a full range of Year 2000 offerings that can be performed on-site, off-site, or offshore.

- **MCI Systemhouse**

  Web Site: www.systemhouse.mci.com

  Offers services for all phases of a Year 2000 project.

- **Millennia III**

  Web Site: www.millennia3.com

  Offers a multiphased Year 2000 process using various implementation tools.

- **Millennium Consulting, Inc.**

  Telephone: (408) 973-9608

  Year 2000 strategic consulting for planning and tool and vendor selection.

- **Millennium Solutions, Inc.**

  Web Site: www.2k-solutions.com

  Analyses COBOL systems; identifies and fixes date fields.

- **Millennium Technology Consulting Group**

  Web Site: www.mtcg.com

  Uses offshore conversion factories to provide analysis project framework, testing, and postconversion support. Specializes in C, C++, PL/I, and COBOL.

- **PKS Information Services, Inc.**

  Web Site: www.pksis.com

  Offers computer resources and consulting services. Consulting services handle evaluation, planning, migration projects, and establishing customer-specific migration environments within PKS's processing environment. PKS is partnered with VIASOFT, Inc.

- **Shell Services Company**

  Web Site: www.shellus.com

  Provides methodology, project management, system diagnostics, migration tools, and testing facility for oil and gas industries.

- **Sicor LLC**

  Web Site: www.sicor.com

  Includes methodologies and tools for impact analysis, automated conversion, testing, and integration.

- **Software AG**

  Web Site: www.softwareag.com

  Using proprietary tools, performs inventory, analysis, and remediation. Maintains an off-site conversion factory.

- **Software Productivity Research, Inc.**

  Web Site: www.spr.com

  Management consulting firm with specialty in collecting data on the economic impact of the Year 2000 problem. See "The Year 2000 Software Problem: Quantifying the Costs and Assessing the Consequences" by Capers Jones, chairman of Software Productivity Research.

- **SPR Inc.**

  Web Site: www.sprinc.com

  Methodology includes preparation, assessment, planning, and implementation phases.

- **Strategia**

  Web Site: www.strategiacorp.com

  Includes conversion and impact analysis tools and compliance-testing centers.

- **SunGard Computer Services**

  Web Site: www.sungard.com

  Provides IBM mainframe, client/server, and network support services offering separate Year 2000 logical partitions.

- **Syntel Corp.**

  Web Site: www.syntelinc.com

  Migrates applications and data, builds bridging routines, and performs unit, system, and customer tests.

- **Tata Consultancy Services**

  Web Site: www.tcs.com

  Offshore software company providing services for all phases of a Year 2000 project using its own toolkit.

- **TAVA Technologies**

  Telephone: (303) 935-1221

  Embedded systems methodology and services.

- **21st Century Systems, Inc.**

  Web Site: www.21stsystems.com

  Provides impact assessment for S/36 and AS/400 environments, compliance audits, upgrade planning, and implementation and conversions.

- **Unibol**

  Web Site: www.unibol.com

  Offers impact analysis and other life-cycle services using proprietary tool. For IBM midrange systems.

- **Unisys Corp.**

  Web Site: www.unisys.com

  Includes methodology desktop services, tools, data center facilities, factory and offshore programming.

- **Wang Federal Inc.**

  Web Site: N/A

  Offers a full range of Year 2000 services for business and scientific systems in multivendor networks.

- **Wipro Systems**

  Web Site: www.wiprosystems.com

  On-site and offshore services including impact analysis, data and source conversions, and testing.

- **Zitel Corp.**

  Web Site: www.zitel.com

  Offers project management planning, analysis, and testing; uses MatriDigm tool for code conversion; supports windowing or packed binary code renovation.

A.2 Tool Vendors

The following vendors sell software tools useful for century-date compliance projects. Some of these vendors offer solution packages that can contain consulting and training services in addition to software.

- **Accler8 Technology Corp.**

  Web Site: www.accelr8.com

  Tool offering scans and identifies date-change requirements; methodology aids in impact analysis, conversion, and acceptance testing.

- **Advanced Systems Concepts**

  Web Site: www.asc-as400.com

  Automated date-field location, impact analysis, date-field expansion, and data conversion.

- **American Software**

  Web Site: www.amsoftware.com

  Supply chain management business model.

- **Applied Business Technology Corporation (ABT)**

  Telephone: (212) 219-8945

  ABT offers project management and methodology management tools.

- **Ascent Logic Corp.**

  Web Site: www.year2000plus.com

  Business system engineering methodology and software tool suite for engineering and project management.

- **Bridging Data Technology, Inc.**

  Web Site: www.bridging.com

  Bridging software with a choice of date-change formats including file expansion, date compression, and date windowing.

- **B-Tree**

  Web Site: www.btree.com

  Embedded systems testing product.

- **CCD Online Systems Inc.**

  Web Site: www.ccdonline.com

  A conversion factory tool set that combines parsing and date impact technology for IBM mainframe or AS/400 applications.

- **Computer Associates International, Inc. (CA)**

  Web Site: www.cai.com

  CA offers a combination of products and services. CA handles MVS, VSE, and PC platforms and includes tools for configuration management, COBOL to COBOL/370 migration, change integration, dynamic coverage analyzer, impact analysis, remediation migration environments, and testing.

- **Computer Software Corp.**

  Web Site: www.dateserver.com

  Performs date comparisons and validity testing for mainframe applications without converting existing date formats.

- **Compuware Corporation**

  Web Site: www.compuware.com

  Compuware offers a combination of products and services to handle all phases of a century compliance project. Its tools operate on mainframe and PC platforms. Compuware has tools for data migration, execution simulation/debugging, metrics analysis, structuring, testing, and virtual date setting.

- **Cyrano**

  Web Site: www.cyrano2000.com

  Supports Year 2000 project work with emphasis on automated testing support.

- **Databorough Inc.**

  Web Site: www.databorough.net

  Products that analyze systems and provide reports on impact analysis and conversion costs and also identify and convert date fields.

- **Double E Computer Systems**

  Web Site: www.doublee.com

  PC century compliance diagnostic tool.

- **Gladstone Computer Services**

  Web Site: www.happyrock.com

  Software tools for data analysis, data migrations, file comparisons, and test data generation.

- **Greenwich Mean Time**

  Web Site: www.gmt-2000.com

  PC Year 2000 diagnostic tools.

- **INTERSOLV**

  Web Site: www.intersolv.com

  Offers PC-based tools for configuration management and impact analysis on the program and system levels.

- **INTO 2000 Inc. (Acquired by Unibol)**

  Web Site: www.into2000.com

  Offers tools and a methodology for RPG applications on the AS/400 platform.

- **IPT Corp.**

  Web Site: www.iptweb.com

  Source code analyzer for Fortran.

- **Isogon Corporation**

  Web Site: www.isogon.com

  Inventory tool that locates, identifies, and monitors use of all mainframe software. Also offers a virtual date utility.

- **Janus Technologies**

  Web Site: www.janus-tech.com

  Tracks costs associated with Y2K conversion efforts, monitors process, and tracks vendor and in-house software compliance.

- **Mainware, Inc.**

  Web Site: www.mainware.com

  Offers a virtual date utility.

- **McCabe & Associates**

  Web Site: www.mccabe.com

  Offers products for code slicing, metrics analysis, and test coverage analysis.

- **Mercury Interactive**

  Web Site: www.merc-int.com

  Provides integrated functional testing, test management, and test data generation.

- **Micro Focus**

  Web Site: www.microfocus.com

  Offers PC-based solutions for mainframe and PC applications. Product set covers inventory and cross reference, impact analysis, interactive analysis, date field expansion, environment simulation and testing.

- **Millennium Dynamics Inc. (Acquired by Peritus)**

  Web Site: www.dynam.com

  Provides impact analysis, planning, conversion, testing, application tool set, process model, and consulting services.

- **MS Millennium**

  Web Site: www.matlensilver.com

  Inventories system, creates repository, converts mainframe code, identifies and corrects date fields.

- **NeoMedia Technologies**

  Web Site: www.allgnt.com

  Automates impact analysis, code conversion, and data conversion. Includes date processing routine library.

- **New Art Communications**

  Web Site: www.newarttech.com

  Products for impact analysis, assessment, and COBOL and C++ code parsing.

- **One Up Corp.**

  Web Site: www.1up.com

  Tool set to assist users in analyzing and remediating desktop applications.

- **Optima Software, Inc.**

  Web Site: www.optimasoft.com

  Process-based SCM solution that tracks all component modifications and manages the version merging process.

- **Platinum Technology, Inc.**

  Web Site: www.platinum.com

  Offers a wide range of products including those formerly sold by ADPAC. Its capabilities include configuration management, inventory and cross reference, impact analysis, interactive date analysis, repository technology and testing.

- **Prince Software, Inc.**

  Web Site: www.princesoftware.com

  Offers a series of tools and migration services. Tools cover cross referencing, COBOL-version migrations, data migration, impact analysis, automated change, interface/bridge generation, and virtual date testing.

- **Princeton SOFTECH**

  Web Site: www.princetonsoftech.com

  Tool for application source code change integration that reconciles different versions of package software and merges compliant source code with other maintenance changes made during the migration process.

- **Quinitic/RCG Systems**

  Web Site: www.quintic.com

  Provides analysis, automatic remediation, testing tools, and methodologies.

- **Ravel Software Turnkey 2000**

  Web Site: www.unravel.com

  Aids in determining scope of conversion project; includes compliance editor, analysis, repair, and testing tools for many languages.

- **Reasoning, Inc.**

  Web Site: www.reasoning.com

  Automated, scalable analysis plug-in for the Reasoning5 codebase management system; converts applications; analyzes and remediates MVS COBOL code.

- **SEEC**

  Web Site: www.seec.com

  Offers PC-based tools that handle inventory and cross reference, impact analysis, and interactive analysis.

- **Segue Software**

  Web Site: www.segue.com

  Automated testing tool.

- **Serena**

  Web Site: www.serena.com

  Intellligent file comparison utility for source code and data files.

- **Software Emancipation Technology, Inc.**

  Web Site: www.setech.com

  Offers tools for code slicing, inventory and cross-referencing, and impact analysis for C and C++ applications.

- **STA America**

  Web Site: www.fieldex.com

  Identifies and converts date variables and provides project documentation for COBOL-based Y2K projects.

- **Sterling Software—Application Engineering Division**

  Web Site: www.sterling.com

  Offers a combination of software and training courses. Software tools cover audit support, data migration, impact analysis, interactive analysis, static analysis, metrics analysis, structuring, and testing.

- **Thinking Tools**

    Web Site: www.thinkingtools.com

    Offers an interactive risk management tool, with integrated documentation capabilities, to graphically assess an organization's potential business impact from the Y2K problem using a variety of project and remediation scenarios.

- **Transition Software**

    Web Site: www.transition-software.com

    Product offerings for inventory analysis, conversion planning, project management, code modification, and testing.

- **VIASOFT, Inc.**

    Web Site: www.viasoft.com

    VIASOFT offers a full range of century-compliance solutions that include products, training, and consulting services. VIASOFT's tool set covers estimation, inventory, and cross reference, impact analysis, static analysis, interactive analysis, metrics analysis, code slicing, testing, and virtual date setting.

- **Wincap Software**

    Web Site: www.wincapsoftware.com

    Provides a workbench containing repository technology and a built-in toolset. Graphically maps components, showing interrelationships, processes, and procedures (including software and hardware). Stores and maintains data in a repository that can be queried.

- **Xinotech**

    Web Site: www.xinotech.com

    Provides integrated reengineering for date problems in COBOL code.

A.3 Conversion Vendors

The vendors listed below fall in between tool vendors and consulting firms by offering a customized mixture of tools and consulting. These vendors specialize in a variety of conversion services and many have adapted existing conversion software and techniques to handle Year 2000 projects.

- **Alydaar Software Corp.**

  Web Site: www.alydaar.com

  Offers computer language translation and migration services, including Year 2000 analysis, remediation, and testing, for a variety of languages and platforms.

- **Ernst & Young**

  Web Site: www.ey.com

  Establishes program management structure including quality assurance processes, project management, assessment and planning, acceptance testing, and implementation; provides off-site conversion center.

- **MatriDigm Corp.**

  Web Site: www.matridigmusa.com

  Uses a factory process to analyze, find, modify, and test date-related fields; uses packed binary date technology.

- **Peritus Software Services, Inc.**

  Web Site: www.peritus.com

  Peritus has created a process and a set of software tools for analyzing, migrating, verifying, and generating test data for Year 2000 projects. While Peritus offers its services directly, it primarily offers its facilities through other consulting vendors.

- **The Source Recovery Company, Inc.**

  Web Site: www.source-recovery.com

  The Source Recovery Company offers services for re-creating missing source code from load modules. Their services recover COBOL, assembly language, and BMS maps.

- **Trigent Software, Inc.**

   Web Site: www.trigent.com

   Trigent has off-site and offshore facilities in Massachusetts and India for performing a full range of Y2K and outsourcing services.

- **Vector Software Inc.**

   Web Site: www.vectors.com

   Services cover Unisys Mapper.

A.4 The Authors' Firms

- **Clarity Consulting, Inc.—Ian S. Hayes**

   Telephone: (978) 468-8080

   E-mail: clarity@telcocom.com

   Clarity Consulting specializes in improving the effectiveness of Information Technology (IT) organizations. Clarity Consulting works with IT organizations, product vendors, and other consulting organizations to develop comprehensive solutions to complex IT issues such as the Year 2000 crisis. Clarity Consulting's Year 2000 offerings include strategic planning, guiding enterprise assessments, solution development and ongoing quality assurance/migration issue resolution.

- **Tactical Strategy Group, Inc.—William M. Ulrich**

   Telephone: (408) 464-5344

   Email: tsginc@cruzio.com

   TSG specializes in architecture transition planning strategies and research work in leading edge IT issues. TSG provides risk management and contingency planning services to senior executives faced with high-risk/high-payback IT projects.

- **Triaxsys Research LLC**

   Web Site: www.triaxsys.com

   Triaxsys publishes research reports on the technological, legal, and financial aspects of major IT challenges including the Year 2000. Triaxsys offers a global, interdisciplinary perspective on these challenges to IT professionals, business executives, investors, lawyers, and others to enable them to succeed in the year 2000 and beyond.

Index

and control and security issues, 193
defined, 201
enabling, 201-9
factory package, 205-6
fixing the code, 203
internal, 208-9, 233-34
packaging the application/upgrading unit
release, 202
for system testing, 204
QA process, 204, 206-8
and setup time and investment, 193
and skill availability, 192
and strategic value of portfolio technology, 192-93
test preparation, 204
verification testing, 203-4
and volume of code, 192-93
Factory package, 205-6
bill of materials, 205
complete source code, 206
compliance definition, 205
results of analysis, 206
test data/scripts, 206
Factory QA process, 204, 206-8
testing, 207-8
walk-through before shipping factory
package, 206
walk-through on code's return from factory, 206-7
Factory-remediated software
application project time line, 337
application/upgrade unit packaging, 336
conversion strategy, 334
factors affecting, 334-35
remediation effort, reliability of, 335
test descriptions, 337
testing approaches, 335-37
testing strategy, 337
test plan, 334-37
developing, 337
Failsafe testing, 274-75
False positives, 261
Fault logging, 165
Fault tolerance tests, 269
Fax machines, 155
Federal Accounting Standards Board (FASB), 102
Federal Aviation Administration (FAA), 10, 133,
168, 173, 398
Federal Communications Commission (FCC), 22
Federal government, Year 2000 status, 29-32
Federal Reserve Board, 115
compliance questionnaire, 16
Field-based devices, 157
Field expansion update, 225-26
Financial industry:
automated teller systems, 160
contingency planning for, 371-72

credit card systems, 160
and embedded technology, 160
and non-IT problems, 134-35
point-of-sale systems, 160
predictions for, 396-97
safes/vaults, 160
scanner/cash systems, 160
Fire control systems, 159
Firewall strategies, 221-22
First-party insurance policies, 112-14
Fixing the code, 203
Flow monitoring, 158
Foreign banks, 398-99
Fossil fuel plants, 155-56
Full-scale deployment, achieving, 44-46
Functional decomposition, application-level
testing, 326
Function logic, 155, 157
Future date regression tests, 267-68
Future date testing, 252

G

Gas detectors, 153
Gas metering devices, 156
General liability policies, 112-13
Generators, 158
Gladstone Computer Services, 429
Global Positioning Systems (GPSs), 20, 133, 155
Government, and non-IT problems, 135
Government agencies/legislatures, 114-18
Congress, 116-17
contingency planning for, 377-78
and embedded technology, 160-62
emergency response systems, 162
environmental monitoring equipment, 162
parking/metering systems, 161
regulatory agencies, 114-16
revenue-/customer-related risks, 66
state government, 117-18
ticketing systems/machines, 161
traffic lights, 161
water distribution, 161
water and sewage systems, 161
Government update, 29-35
federal government, 29-32
local governments, 34
school/universities, 34-35
state governments, 33-34
U.S. Department of Defense (DOD), 32-33
Greenwich Mean Time (vendor), 429

H

Hardware, 297-300
testing, 145, 263-64, 275

√ **Are you suffering from information overload about the rapidly changing world of information technology?**

√ **Have you searched through newsletters, magazines, the Internet and found nothing but fragmented information about small pieces of the puzzle?**

TRIAXSYS RESEARCH LLC

At last… Your ***single source*** of interdisciplinary research and analysis on all aspects of major information technology challenges – technical, legal, financial and more.

Triaxsys Research LLC was founded by Ian S. Hayes and William M. Ulrich along with Steven L. Hock and Marta Pierpoint with the goal of providing up-to-the minute research on the Year 2000 crisis and other critical IT issues. It offers readers of the *Year 2000 Software Crisis: The Continuing Challenge* with a means of receiving regular updates on the latest trends and techniques.

Triaxsys publishes eight research reports annually for IT professionals, executives, managers, auditors, attorneys, consultants and others who need to stay on the cutting edge of IT issues.

A wide variety of subscription options allows you to take full advantage of the research and analysis Triaxsys provides:

- Annual subscription rate of $995
- Volume discounts available for corporations, government agencies, partnerships, other legal entities and individuals for:
  - Subscriptions for internal use
  - Subscriptions for their suppliers, customers, or other third-parties
- Annual Intranet site licenses for internal use

To order by FAX, send this form to (406) 542-8811
or download a fax form from our website at www.triaxsys.com
To order by PHONE, call 1-888-320-8882

- -

Name_____Title_____

Organization_____

Address _____

_____

City_____State_____Zip_____Country_____

Telephone (___)_____Fax (___)_____

    ( ) Fee enclosed   ( ) Please bill me   ( ) Confirming earlier phone order

Please charge my: ( ) Visa ( ) Master Card ( ) American Express

Account Number_____Expiration Date_____

Signature_____